INDIVIDUALISM
AND
COLLECTIVISM

CROSS-CULTURAL RESEARCH AND METHODOLOGY SERIES

Series Editors

Walter J. Lonner, *Department of Psychology, Western Washington University (United States)*
John W. Berry, *Department of Psychology, Queen's University, Kingston, Ontario (Canada)*

Volumes in this series:

INDIVIDUALISM
AND
COLLECTIVISM

THEORY, METHOD, AND APPLICATIONS

UICHOL KIM
HARRY C. TRIANDIS
ÇIĞDEM KÂĞITÇIBAŞI
SANG-CHIN CHOI
GENE YOON
EDITORS

Published on behalf of the Korean Psychological Association

Volume 18, Cross-Cultural Research and Methodology Series

SAGE Publications
International Educational and Professional Publisher
Thousand Oaks   London   New Delhi

For information address:

SAGE Publications, Inc.
2455 Teller Road
Thousand Oaks, California 91320

SAGE Publications Ltd.
6 Bonhill Street
London EC2A 4PU
United Kingdom

SAGE Publications India Pvt. Ltd.
M-32 Market
Greater Kailash I
New Delhi 110 048 India

Printed in the United States of America

Library of Congress Cataloging-in-Publication Data

Main entry under title:

Individualism and collectivism: Theory, method, and applications /
    edited by Uichol Kim . . . [et al.].
        p.   cm.   —   (Cross-cultural research and methodology series : v. 18
    Includes bibliographical references and indexes.
    ISBN 0-8039-5762-9   —   ISBN 0-8039-5763-7 (pbk).
        1. Social values.   2. Individualism—Psychological aspects.
3. Collectivism—Psychology aspects.   I. Kim, Uichol.   II. Series.
HM216.I63   1994
302.5'4—dc20   94-15342

                    98   10   9   8   7   6   5   4   3

Sage Production Editor: Astrid Virding

CONTENTS

FOREWORD

The relationship of an author with his or her brainchildren resembles to some extent the relationship of a parent with his or her children. The nature of the latter, of course, depends on the type of society—which puts us right in the middle of our topic. In my society, at least, feelings of parents about their grown-up children are usually mixed. If a child does well, the parent feels proud and thankful; yet, having become a person in his or her own right, the same child unavoidably sometimes moves in directions that puzzle or worry the parent.

They say my 1980 book *Culture's Consequences* started the interest in individualism and collectivism (henceforth abbreviated as I/C) in cross-cultural psychology, which puts me in the position of a spiritual parent, and I do recognize the moods described above with regard to this intellectual offspring. Surprisingly, *Culture's Consequences* is not really a psychological treatise at all. It does not belong to any single social science discipline. If one tries to transgress the borderlines of national cultures, one piece of intellectual luggage that has to be left at home is the division of labor among the social sciences as it has been developed in Europe and North America in the past hundred years. I have always considered this academic division as most unfortunate anyway. Psychology, social psychology, sociology, anthropology, economics, and political science all study only facets of the same social reality. Academic inbreeding and atomization in the West have led to extensive production of irrelevant speculations. The system has become self-destructive in that it punishes rather than encourages borrowing from related disciplines.

Cross-cultural social sciences therefore cannot but be cross-disciplinary at the same time. If, for example, one moves to an East Asian environment where the concept of the person as a separate entity is debatable, one cannot stay within the limits of psychology as defined in Western universities. Part of my worries about the present use of the I/C dimension in cross-cultural psychology is that monocultural habits die hard, and that psychologists groomed in the Western style will try to domesticate cross-cultural psychology into a subdiscipline of psychology rather than into a metadiscipline beyond Western psychology.

In *Culture's Consequences* I compare survey data from matched samples of respondents from 40 countries, a number extended to 50, plus 3 multicountry regions, in later publications. I found that about one-half of the country-to-country differences could be explained by four dimensions: large versus small *power distance,* strong versus weak *uncertainty avoidance, individualism versus collectivism,* and *masculinity versus femininity.* Later research by Michael Bond, who used questionnaire items designed by Chinese scholars, led to the addition of a fifth dimension, *Confucian dynamism,* or *long-term* versus *short-term orientation.*

The dimension of I/C, empirically derived, made theoretical sense in terms of classic sociology. It resembled, for example, a distinction described by the German scholar Tönnies (1887/1957) as *gesellschaft versus gemeinschaft,* or *society versus community.*

Out of the five dimensions, I/C was the one that most directly appealed to psychologists. Other dimensions were more immediately relevant to other academic fields. Power distance and uncertainty avoidance became favorite dimensions in comparative management and organization theory; masculinity versus femininity is crucial for a number of political science and comparative religion issues; Confucian dynamism has consequences for economics. *Culture's Consequences* has been cited, approvingly or critically, in such disparate contexts as theoretical history, airline safety, sociology of law, comparative accounting, and comparative medicine. Its dimensional framework is used in many intercultural training programs.

Psychologists are attracted to I/C because the relationship between the individual and other individuals has traditionally been a central concern in Western psychology. However, as stated above, the dimension I introduced is sociological and not at all psychological. It does not compare different personalities, but different societal contexts within which children grow up and develop their personalities. It is not about individuals, but about the constraints within which, in different countries, a psychology of relatedness (to use the term proposed by Kagitçibasi, Chapter 4, this volume) should be developed.

A key issue in any type of cross-cultural social science, and therefore also in cross-cultural psychology, is the influence of the researcher's own culture on the outcomes of his or her research. It is inconsistent to study differences in psychological functioning of people in different countries or societies without including the psychologist's own functioning in one's relativism. Cultural background determines, among other things, what one considers desirable as well as one's feelings and biases in this particular area. Psychologists from less individualist societies have rightly felt a certain condescension in the way their colleagues from more individualist societies have handled collectivism.

One issue that comes up repeatedly in this volume is whether individualism and collectivism are not really two separate dimensions. The answer should depend on whether we mean the sociological dimension, distinguishing societies, or a psychological dimension developed by psychologists for distinguishing the personalities of individuals within societies. In *Cultures's Consequences* I deal exclusively with differences between societies, and I found that a single, bipolar, dimension is a useful construct (that is, conceptual tool) for subsuming a complex set of differences. Scores on this dimension, empirically derived, correlate significantly with a multitude of external measures, providing extensive validation for the bipolar construct. This does not mean, of course, that a country's Individualism Index score tells all there is to be known about the backgrounds and structures of relationship patterns in that country. It is an abstraction that should not be extended beyond its limited area of usefulness.

Culture's Consequences makes no assumption about the suitability or dimensionality of individualism and collectivism as *psychological* concepts. If one were to ask me, I would suppose that at the individual level a multidimensional model would be more useful than a unidimensional one. The latter revives too much, to my taste, the search for a "modal personality" in the anthropology of the 1930s to 1950s, which led to unwanted stereotyping. A culture does not consist of modal personalities; culture is no king-size personality. A culture is the anthropological equivalent of a "biotope" in biology: the population of animals and plants that belongs to a particular habitat. A culture is a population of different, complementary, and interdependent personalities and conditions. This is statistically reflected in the fact that correlations between variables at the culture level (based upon the mean scores of the various individuals within the culture) can be completely different from the correlations of the same variables at the individual level. Thus it is quite possible that the same set of variables produces a bipolar dimension at the culture level and two or more unipolar dimensions at the level of individuals.

An indispensable insight for cross-cultural psychologists, I think, is that concerning the distinction between *emic* and *etic* points of view. This distinction belongs to anthropology, not to psychology. It is actually borrowed from linguistics, as an analogy to the distinction between phonemics and phonetics: the study of carriers of meaning versus the study of sounds. An emic point of view is taken from within a culture, usually the author's own. An etic point of view is a "view from the bridge," comparing different cultures according to criteria supposed to apply to all of them. My approach in *Culture's Consequences* is obviously entirely etic. The emic and the etic points of view are almost by definition complementary. The ethnic psychologies that are developing within various non-Western societies are necessary emic complements to the imposed Western emic of classical Western psychology. However, in order to learn from each other we also need an etic meeting ground and a terminology with which we can explore our common concerns and our differences. Occasionally, an author from one particular country has tried to disprove the dimensional model in *Culture's Consequences* with insights from within his or her own culture. But this means applying emic reasoning to an etic problem; it is like attempting to draw a regression line through one single point.

The external measures used in *Culture's Consequences* for validating the empirically derived country Individualism Index consist of both measures taken at the country level (such as an index of press freedom or the relative frequency of traffic deaths) and measures based on surveys of other matched samples of individuals from the same countries, reported by other researchers. One of the strongest correlations found is between the Individualism Index and national wealth (per capita gross national product, as reported by the World Bank). The correlation coefficient (for 40 countries, using 1970 data) is .82, which means that $.82^2 = 67\%$ of the variance in country Individualism Index scores can be accounted for by differences in national wealth. Wealth goes hand in hand with *modernity,* and it should surprise no one if many symptoms of individualism are related to modernity. Many, but not all: A part of the unique cultural inheritance of countries with regard to individualism and collectivism survives in spite of poverty or affluence. India and Japan, based on my 1970 data, both scored about halfway on the Individualism/Collectivism Index scale, but, according to its average poverty, India could have been expected to score even more collectivist, and on the basis of its wealth, Japan could have been expected to score more individualist. There is, by the way, a persistent myth that I found Japan to score at the extreme end of the Collectivism Index scale. In fact, among 53 countries and regions, Japan came in at a shared twenty-second and twenty-third position on the individualist side. True, all affluent Western countries scored more individualist than Japan, but among the poor countries, India was the only one that did not score more collectivist than Japan, and only marginally so.

One crystal clear implication for the psychology of relatedness, of cultural differences on the I/C dimension, is the need to distinguish in-group from out-group members. Many classical experiments in Western social psychology are about "ego" and "other(s)." In culturally collectivist societies, this distinction will not do. It all depends whether the others are from ego's in-group or not. This also means that there is no relationship between cultural collectivism and altruism, as some researchers have postulated. Collectivism is not altruism, but in-group egoism. In a collectivist society, a poor relative can expect to be helped, but not necessarily a poor stranger. Whether a stranger can expect to be helped depends on the society's degree of "femininity." The Good Samaritan does not represent the collectivist society, but the feminine one.

This brings me to my last point, a caution not to take the I/C distinction as a catchall for cultural differences in general. The usefulness of the five-dimensional model based on Bond's work and my own is precisely that it discriminates among different kinds of cultural influences. Some cultural differences can be expected to relate to the I/C dimension, some to one or more of the other dimensions, and some will probably be idiosyncratic to a given country or society and not related to any known dimension at all. In particular, I believe the masculinity versus femininity dimension deserves more attention from cross-cultural psychologists than it has received so far. A conceptual framework based on the two dimensions of I/C and masculinity/femininity is a lot richer and potentially more revealing than the single pair of concepts to which this volume is devoted.

This is not meant to play down the significance of the present book. It is, of course, no accident that the initiative for the conference at which these papers were collected and the actual publication of this volume, and its companions, was taken in Korea. In my 1970 data, Korea scored strongly collectivist: at the forty-third position out of 53 countries and regions. On the other hand, many Koreans have been exposed to Western ideas and theories, and the country's affluence has increased at a rate unparalleled in human history. This situation has provided the creative tension that explains why Koreans, in particular, would support this landmark initiative. The kind but firm leadership of Uichol Kim, a Korean himself, made it all happen. He should be warmly complimented.

Geert Hofstede

SERIES EDITORS' INTRODUCTION

Every now and then, a paradigm, model, or concept comes along in an academic and research enterprise, usually confined to a specialization area within a discipline, that attracts significant attention. Like magnets, these developments draw the attention of most people who identify with particular disciplines. Such is the case with individualism and collectivism, concepts that appear to define the endpoints of a hypothesized continuum that can be used effectively to help explain sources of variability in human thought and interaction.

During the past 15 years, the individualism/collectivism continuum has been the focus of dozens of studies done in and across various cultures and societies. Indeed, as the editors of this volume point out in their introduction, the 1980s might be characterized as "the decade of I/C." It has also been the focus of numerous symposia at international meetings. Probably the most influential meeting ever held on the topic, at least from a cross-cultural psychological perspective, was a well-attended conference sponsored by the Korean Psychological Association and held in Seoul, Korea, in July 1990. Because many psychologists interested in the role played by culture in shaping human behavior were planning to attend conferences in Japan that summer (primarily the meeting of the International Association for Cross-Cultural Psychology, held in Nara, and the meeting of the International Association of Applied Psychology, which took place in Kyoto), a significant number took the opportunity to attend the unique Seoul conference. Uichol Kim, senior editor of this volume, was a key figure in the planning of the conference, along with influential Korean psychologists Sang-Chin Choi and Gene Yoon, who also are co-editors. Harry Triandis, a leading figure in the development of cross-cultural psychology and the second editor of the volume, has for about a decade been the central figure in studies of individualism/collectivism. The third editor of the volume, Çigdem Kagitçibasi, has also been very active in this area, and has written major articles and book chapters dealing with this concept. Together, the five editors formed an effective team in assembling the volume. Their job was a difficult one, for they had to choose among a large number of manuscripts that were vying for inclusion. The result is an important collection of chapters written by accomplished researchers, all of whom have made significant contributions to the ways in which individualism and collectivism might be understood, both conceptually and methodologically. A foreword by Geert Hofstede, who has made significant contributions toward the understanding of individualism/collectivism and other human dimensions, completes the package.

Although we doubt that anyone views the continuum of I/C as a paradigm shift of Kuhnian proportions, we do think that the overall idea is very compelling and well worth close scrutiny. This volume is an excellent collection of contemporary research on the topic. As such, it will help define future research in this area, and will influence many during the next decade of continued research.

For those not familiar with the nature and intent of the Sage Publications Cross-Cultural Research and Methodology Series, a few words are in order. The series was created to present comparative studies on cross-cultural topics and interdisciplinary research. Inaugurated in 1975, the series is designed to satisfy a growing and continuing need to integrate research method and theory and to dissect issues from a comparative perspective. We believe that a truly international approach to the study of behavioral, social, and cultural variables can be done only within such a methodological framework.

Each volume in the series presents substantive cross-cultural studies and considerations of the strengths, interrelationships, and weaknesses of the various methodologies, drawing upon work done in anthropology, political science, psychology, and sociology. Both individual researchers knowledgeable in more than one discipline and teams of specialists with differing disciplinary backgrounds have contributed to the series. Although each individual volume may represent the integration of only a few disciplines, the cumulative totality of the series reflects an effort to bridge gaps of methodology and conceptualization across the various disciplines and many cultures.

We welcome you to the current volume.

—Walter J. Lonner
Western Washington University
—John W. Berry
Queen's University

PREFACE

The present volume is the culmination of work that was presented at the First International Conference on Individualism and Collectivism: Psychocultural Perspectives From East and West, July 9-13, 1990. The conference was sponsored by the Korean Psychological Association and held at the scenic surrounds of the Academy of Korean Studies. Approximately 300 participants attended the conference, and 70 papers were presented on the topic of individualism and collectivism. The conference also served as a rare opportunity to invite scholars who previously would not have been able to participate: The thawing of the Cold War allowed scholars from Eastern Bloc nations (i.e., Estonia, Poland, Yugoslavia, and the former Soviet Union) to take part, and travel funds were provided for scholars from developing countries. It was a truly unique international conference devoted to a topic that has dominated cross-cultural research since the 1980s.

Although the academic seed had been planted in 1980 by Geert Hofstede and subsequently watered by Harry Triandis and his colleagues, the organizational seed of the conference was planted when the first two editors of this volume organized two symposia devoted to the topic of individualism and collectivism for the Eighth International Congress of Cross-Cultural Psychology in 1986, held in Istanbul, Turkey. Interest in this topic grew, and Yoshihisa Kashima, in cooperation with the first two editors, organized four symposia in 1988 for the Ninth International Congress of Cross-Cultural Psychology, held in Newcastle, Australia. The very success of these symposia suggested a need to develop a workshop devoted to the topic of individualism and collectivism.

In 1990, Uichol Kim planned to hold a special workshop in Seoul, Korea, prior to the Tenth International Congress of Cross-Cultural Psychology in Nara, Japan. Dr. Gene Yoon, co-organizer of the conference, suggested that the Korean Psychological Association become involved and be the official sponsor the workshop. With the full support of the Korean

Psychological Association and the Korean Ministry of Education, what was planned as a workshop blossomed into an international conference.

The conference was made possible through the support of various organizations. The Korean Psychological Association provided full support for the execution of all phases of the conference, and special appreciation is extended to that organization's Executive Council: Dr. Neung-Bin Im, president; Dr. Heung-Wha Koh, president-elect; Dr. Shin-Ho Ahn, vice president; Dr. Sung-Soo Chang, secretary-general; Dr. Jin-Hun Sohn, public relations; and Dr. Myung-Un Kim, treasurer. We also would like to thank Advisory Committee members Kwan-Yong Rhee, Chang-Ho Lee, Chang-Woo Lee, Jae-Ho Cha, and Chung-Hoon Cho; Organizing Committee members Gene Yoon, Uichol Kim, Kyung-Hwang Min, Myung-Un Kim, Kyung-Ja Oh, Jin-Hwan Lee, Jean-Kyung Chung, Geung-Ho Cho, Sang-Chin Choi, and Doug-Woong Han; and operations manager Keum-Joo Kwak. Graduate students from various Korean universities and the University of Hawaii also assisted in the execution of the conference, and we are grateful for their help.

The conference also received financial support from several organizations. The Ministry of Education, Republic of Korea, contributed major financial support, in addition to the Opening Address provided by the minister of education, Dr. Won-Shik Chung. The Academy of Korean Studies provided the facilities: meeting rooms, dormitory, and restaurants. Major funding was also provided by the Korea Institute for Socioeconomic Affairs, the Federation of Korean Industries, and Sam-Sung Company Limited. Additional funding was also obtained from the following companies: Sam Seong Publisher, Dong-A Publisher & Printing Co., Chung-Ang Chuck Sung Publishing Co., Tam-Gu-Dang Publisher, Bob Mun Sa and Sam-Sung Electronics Co. We would like extend our gratitude to all of these organizations for their support.

After the successful completion of the conference, individual presenters were asked to submit their papers for publication. An editorial board consisting of the five editors for this volume was established to review, select, and prepare the papers to be published. Each submitted paper was read by two reviewers and the editors. We would like to thank those scholars, in addition to chapter contributors, who served as reviewers: John Adamopoulos, Marc Bosche, Gui-Young Hong, Harry Hui, Lisa Ilola, Yoshihisa Kashima, Kwok Leung, Kate Partridge, Ype Poortinga, Paul Schmitz, Peter Smith, Peter Weinreich, and John Williams. The present volume represents approximately 30% of the papers submitted for publication. Significant contributors to the area of individualism and collectivism who could not participate in the conference were also invited to submit papers. We extend special thanks to Drs. Walt Lonner and John

Berry, editors of the Sage Cross-Cultural Research and Methodology Series, who guided and supported the project. The chapters in the present volume represent a truly collaborative effort on the part of the editors, the contributing authors, the reviewers, the series editors, and the Korean Psychological Association.

We would like to thank the following people for their editorial assistance: Maria Chun, Ann-Marie Horvath, Genie and Patrick Lester, Yi-Jin Lin, Kunling Lu, Lalita Suzuki, and Kozue Ueki.

The first editor would like to express his gratitude for the first institutional support provided by the Department of Psychology, University of Hawaii at Monoa and the Department of Social Psychology, The University of Tokyo.

Uichol Kim
Harry C. Triandis
Çigdem Kagitçibasi
Sang-Chin Choi
Gene Yoon

1

INTRODUCTION

UICHOL KIM
HARRY C. TRIANDIS
ÇIGDEM KAGITÇIBASI
SANG-CHIN CHOI
GENE YOON

The topic of individualism and collectivism (I/C) has been the focus of a great deal of research interest in cross-cultural psychology, so much so that Çigdem Kagitçibasi, in Chapter 4 of this volume, labels the 1980s "the decade of I/C." This interest culminated in the Korean Psychological Association's sponsorship of the First International Conference on Individualism and Collectivism: Psychocultural Perspectives From East and West, which was held July 9-13, 1990, in Seoul, Korea. The conference attempted to integrate and consolidate an ever-proliferating area of research. The occasion also marked the tenth anniversary of the publication of Geert Hofstede's (1980) classic contribution to this area, *Culture's Consequences: International Differences in Work-Related Values.*

Hofstede (1980, 1983b), in a study of more than 117,000 IBM employees in 66 countries, found four dimensions of cultural variation: power distance, uncertainty avoidance, individualism, and masculinity. The dimension of individualism captured the interest of cross-cultural psychologists. It is considered by many to be a bipolar dimension, with individualism on one end and collectivism on the other. The United States, Canada, and Western European countries were found to be high on the individualist end of this dimension. Asian, Latin American, and African nations were found to be high on the collectivist side.

The I/C constructs provided structure for the rather fuzzy construct of culture. They allowed the linkage of psychological phenomena to a cultural dimension (see Bond, Chapter 5, this volume). They revitalized cross-cultural psychology by providing a theoretical framework for a field that had been unable to operationalize the concept of culture (Rohner, 1984) and that was largely defined by its comparative methodologies rather than by its coherence of content (Triandis, 1980a). I/C proved to be a more concise, coherent, integrated, and empirically testable dimension of cultural variation (see, in this volume, Triandis, Chapter 3, and Bond, Chapter 5). These constructs also allowed fruitful integration of knowledge within the discipline of psychology (such as cognitive, developmental, social, organizational, and clinical psychology) and across disciplines (such as anthropology, sociology, economics, and management), and suggested convergence across different methodologies (such as ethnographies, surveys, and experiments).

DEFINITION OF I/C

Hofstede (1991) defines individualism and collectivism as follows:

> *Individualism* pertains to societies in which the ties between individuals are loose: everyone is expected to look after himself or herself and his or her immediate family. *Collectivism* as its opposite pertains to societies in which people from birth onwards are integrated into strong, cohesive ingroups, which throughout people's lifetime continue to protect them in exchange for unquestioning loyalty. (p. 51)

According to Hofstede (1980), individualist societies emphasize "I" consciousness, autonomy, emotional independence, individual initiative, right to privacy, pleasure seeking, financial security, need for specific friendship, and universalism. Collectivist societies, on the other hand, stress "we" consciousness, collective identity, emotional dependence, group solidarity, sharing, duties and obligations, need for stable and predetermined friendship, group decision, and particularism. Similar definitions are given by Hui and Triandis (1986) and Sinha and Verma (1987).

At the psychological level, Triandis, Leung, Villareal, and Clark (1985) propose the personality dimensions of *idiocentrism* and *allocentrism* to parallel I/C at the cultural level. Markus and Kitayama (1991) similarly propose the *independent view* and *interdependent view* of the self. They describe individuals who uphold the independent view as being "egocentric, separate, autonomous, idiocentric, and self-contained" (p. 226). Interdependent individuals are "sociocentric, holistic, collective, allocentric, ensembled, constitutive, contextualist, and relational" (p. 227). These bipolar categorizations, although useful, are broad approximations. They need to be refined and elaborated further.

THEORETICAL AND CONCEPTUAL ISSUES

In this section we examine critical issues salient to I/C: theoretical assumptions, levels of analysis, dimensionality, interactionism, conceptual integration, and research strategies.

Theoretical Assumptions

In 1852, Comte asked, "How can the individual be at once cause and consequence of society?" (cited in G. W. Allport, 1968, p. 8). This dilemma is at the heart of the current debate about I/C. It touches on issues of the philosophy of science (O'Neill, 1976), such as whether the individual or the group should be the basic unit of analysis in the social sciences. Psychology has adopted the individual as the basic unit of analysis (Hogan, 1975; Pepitone, 1976; Sampson, 1977; Spence, 1985), following Floyd Allport (1924), who rejected the cultural level of analysis. Social psychology has been defined by his brother, Gordon Allport (1968), as "an attempt to understand and explain how the thought, feeling, and behavior of individuals are influenced by the actual, imagined, or implied presence of others" (p. 3), showing that the group and cultural levels of analysis were not considered. As a result, these levels of analysis were neglected (Pepitone, 1976, 1981; Sampson, 1977).

In sociology, Popper (1976) also assumes that individuals constitute the basic unit of analysis. This methodological individualism (O'Neill, 1976) provides a limited view of how social phenomena should be explained: Group and cultural phenomena have to be explained in terms of individual behaviors. A contrasting position emphasizes that the collective determines and explains the psychological makeup of individuals (Brodbeck, 1976; Hsu, 1972).

Both the strict micro approach (focusing on individuals) and the macro approach (focusing on culture, society) are too narrow and reductionist. In the present formulation, these two approaches are considered as two different levels that interact with one another. Multidimensional and multifaceted models have been articulated to capture these features (e.g., see, in this volume, Kim, Chapter 2; Triandis, Chapter 3; Schwartz, Chapter 7; Sinha & Tripathi, Chapter 8; Ho & Chiu, Chapter 9).

Levels of Analysis

Individuals and cultures need to be considered as two different units of analysis reflecting two different levels of analysis (Hofstede, 1980; see also, in this volume, Hofstede's foreword; Kim, Chapter 2; Triandis, Chapter 3; Schwartz, Chapter 7). Collective entities such as group, society, culture, history, and language need to be recognized as more than the mere sums of individual characteristics or contributions. Collective entities need to be understood in their own right. They emerge from the interactions of individuals and constitute phenomena not reducible to the actions of individuals.

According to Hofstede (1980), when data are based on culture-level measurements (e.g., GNP, epidemiological rates), cross-cultural comparisons are valid. When data are based on individual-level measurements (e.g., attitude, values, behaviors), researchers should limit their interpretations to within-culture analysis. An *ecological fallacy* is committed when a researcher uses a culture-level correlation to interpret individual behavior. Hofstede (1980) and Leung (1989) document that patterns observed at the cultural or "ecological" level can be different from patterns observed at the individual level.

A *reverse ecological fallacy* is committed when researchers construct cultural or ecological indices based upon individual-level measurements. Hofstede (1980) points out that cultures should not be treated as individuals: "They are wholes, and their internal logic cannot be understood in the terms used for the personality dynamics of individuals" (p. 31). Both the ecological fallacy and the reverse ecological fallacy point to the need to separate the levels of analysis and to interpret results at appropriate levels.

The discrepancy between the cultural level and the individual level can arise when there is no one-to-one correspondence between a culture-level phenomenon and an individual-level phenomenon. For example, Hofstede (1980) empirically derived the I/C dimension at the cultural level, but he did not find any comparable dimension at the individual level. This does not, however, preclude the existence of some correspondence, in some domains, as demonstrated by Bond (Chapter 5) and Schwartz (Chapter 7) in this volume. Moreover, these two levels interact through intermediate structures (such as institutions, norms, and beliefs). We will explore the relationship between the two levels further in the following section.

Dimensionality

Hofstede (1980) empirically derived *individualism* as a unidimensional construct at the cultural level. Much of the criticism of Hofstede's work questions the unidimensionality of the construct at the individual level. This construct, however, was not conceived by Hofstede to describe or explain phenomena at the individual level. Hofstede speculates that at the individual level, it may be more appropriate to develop multidimensional models to describe and explain I/C (see Hofstede's foreword to this volume).

At the cultural level, Triandis et al. (1986) have identified four dimensions that relate to I/C. They found two dimensions (*family integrity* and *interdependence with sociability*) to be important aspects of collectivism. For individualism, the dimensions of *separation from in-groups* and *self-reliance with hedonism* emerged as important elements. Subsequent research has replicated Hofstede's (1980) results, but suggests that individualism and collectivism are multidimensional even at the cultural level (see, e.g., Chinese Culture Connection, 1987; Triandis et al., 1986; see also Schwartz, Chapter 7, this volume).

At the individual level, Triandis, in Chapter 3 of this volume, describes individualism and collectivism as syndromes. The multidimensional nature of the two constructs has been supported by further conceptual elaboration and empirical verification (see, in this volume, Kim, Chapter 2; Kagitçibasi, Chapter 4; Sinha & Tripathi, Chapter 8; Ho & Chiu, Chapter 9; Cha, Chapter 10; Yamaguchi, Chapter 11; Mishra, Chapter 15; Yu & Yang, Chapter 16).

Interactionism

Although the cultural level and the individual level are separated for conceptual and empirical purposes, they are functionally interrelated (Schwartz, Chapter 7, this volume). Cooley, Angell, and Carr (1933) note that the "whole is a network of interdependent parts, each one of which contributes to the functioning of the entire system" (p. 71). Cultures, through socialization, help to shape the attitudes, beliefs, emotions, and behaviors of individuals who are born into them (Kagitçibasi, Chapter 4, this volume). Although collective entities, by and large, shape individuals' attitudes, beliefs, emotions, and behaviors, they do not determine them. Individuals possess characteristics that are often unique and self-directing. They often accept, select, or reject cultural influences. In addition, individuals contribute to the process of maintaining, synthesizing, and changing existing culture. They cannot be viewed simply as passive recipients of cultural influences. They need to be considered as architects of cultural change. Cooley et al. (1933) state that "a separate person is an abstraction unknown to experience, and so likewise is society when regarded as something apart from persons" (p. 71).

Although a simple one-to-one correspondence between the cultural and individual levels may not exist, these two levels are interrelated. Bond (1988), for example, found a coefficient of congruence of 0.8 between the two levels. Schwartz (Chapter 7, this volume) found similar results and articulates several reasons they are related. Conceptually, individuals and cultures should not be viewed as mutually exclusive entities; rather, they need to be viewed as interactive entities. The degree of correspondence or interaction between the two levels is a research question worthy of further exploration in itself.

These two levels interact through intermediate social structures, organizations, norms, and beliefs (Giddens, 1984; Hofstede, 1980; see also, in this volume, Kim, Chapter 2; Schwartz, Chapter 7; Bierbrauer, Meyer, & Wolfradt, Chapter 12). In every society, institutions (both formal and informal) have been erected to maintain and propagate particular constellations of values, norms, and skills. Rokeach (1973) defines an institution as "a social organization that has evolved in society and has been 'assigned' the task of specializing in the maintenance and enhancement of a selected subset of values and in their transmission from generation to generation" (pp. 24-25). In Confucian societies, for example, families play a central role and serve as a prototype for all other organizations (King & Bond, 1985; see also Kim, Chapter 2, this volume). Individualist cultures, in contrast, use individual "rights" as the central moral and ethical basis upon which to erect institutions (see Kim, Chapter 2). The complex relationship between individual beliefs on one hand and norms, social structure, institution, and culture on the other is articulated in the next section and further elaborated in Chapter 2 of this volume.

Conceptual Integration

Individualism and collectivism are culture-level constructs that represent a rubric of patterned variables. To understand the relationship across different levels of analysis (i.e., individual, interpersonal, societal, and cultural), one must trace the development of individualism or collectivism within a particular culture. In the West, liberalism serves as a foundation for individualism; in East Asian cultures, Confucianism serves as a moral-political philosophy that helps to entrench collectivism. These two philosophies are used here to clarify the relationship across different levels of analysis. (For further analysis, see Kim, Chapter 2, this volume.)

Figure 1.1 provides a schematic representation of individualist societies that support the basic tenets of liberalism. Liberalism represents a moral-political philosophy and a way of life that rejects a "traditional," ascribed,

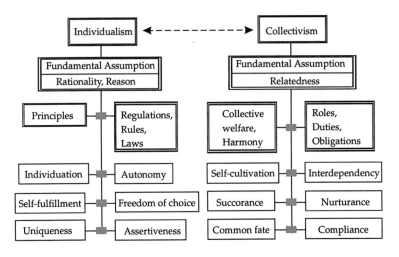

Figure 1.1. Individualism and Collectivism: An Integrated Framework

communal, and "medieval" social order. Liberalism serves as the foundation for individualism and fills a void left by the rejection of arbitrary
authorities and metaphysical explanations. Liberal philosophy assumes
that individuals are *rational* and able to use reason to make personal
choices, and as such they should be given individual rights to choose
freely and to define their own goals. At the interpersonal level, individuals
are considered to be discrete, autonomous, self-sufficient, and respectful
of the rights of others. From a societal point of view, individuals are
considered to be abstract and universal entities. Their status and roles are
not predetermined or ascribed, but defined by their achievements (e.g.,
educational, occupational, and economic status). They interact with others
utilizing rational principles such as equality, equity, noninterference, and
detachability. Individuals with similar goals are brought together into
groups. Laws, rules, and regulations are institutionalized to protect individual rights, with everyone being able to assert his or her rights through
informal or formal channels (such as the legal system). The state is
governed by elected officials whose role is to uphold individual rights and
the viability of public institutions. As a result, in individualist cultures each
person is encouraged to be autonomous, self-directing, unique, and asser-
tive, and to value privacy and freedom of choice.

Collectivism, on the other hand, represents a modification of an ascribed, communal, and "traditional" social order. For example, in East Asian
societies, Confucianism has provided a moral and philosophical basis

for self-construal and social order. As depicted in Figure 1.1, collectivist societies that support the basic tenets of Confucianism prioritize the common good and social harmony over individual interests. All individuals are assumed to be linked in a web of interrelatedness. Individuals are conceived to be embedded and situated in particular roles and status. They are bound by relationships that emphasize common fate. Individuals are encouraged to put other people's and the group's interests before their own. From a societal point of view, duties and obligations are prescribed by roles, and individuals lose "face" if they fail to fulfill these duties and obligations. Concession and compromise are essential ingredients in promoting role-based and virtue-based conceptions of justice. Social order is maintained when everyone fulfills his or her roles and duties. Institutions are seen as an extension of the family, and paternalism and legal moralism (i.e., moral values institutionalized in legal codes) reign supreme. In order to promote the collective welfare and social harmony, individuals are encouraged to suppress any individualist and hedonistic desires. As a result, interdependency, succor, nurturance, common fate, and compliance are important aspects of East Asian collectivism.

Figure 1.1 represents a useful schema for comparing individualism and collectivism. Within a particular culture, however, there are numerous philosophies that compete with one another in inculcating a particular set of values. In the United States, competing philosophies, such as conservatism and fundamentalism, aim to challenge, discredit, and dislodge liberalism. In China, Buddhism and Taoism have traditionally contended with Confucianism as competing moral-political philosophies. In modern East Asia (i.e., China, Japan, and Korea) liberal ideals have penetrated to compete with Confucian philosophy. Each moral-political philosophy, nevertheless, has profound influence in its respective culture and is propagated through the socialization of children.

Research Strategies

In actual research, it is difficult to examine different levels simultaneously. A researcher needs to choose a starting point based on philosophical and scientific grounds. In the area of I/C, there are four reasons it is more parsimonious to start at the individual level rather than at the cultural level. First, all the current data have been collected, through surveys and experiments, at either the individual or the group level, or they represent statistical summaries (see Bond, Chapter 5, this volume). Second, individualism and collectivism represent abstract psychological concepts. They are constructed not to explain single variables, but to explain patterns of events.

As a result, they have been operationalized and measured in various ways. It is thus more parsimonious to conceptualize I/C at the individual level, which allows for explicit operationalization and measurement.

Third, a culture-level analysis requires reductionism. For a particular variable, each culture is reduced to a single datum. Cross-cultural comparisons are then conducted, using culture as the unit of observation. A single datum does not, however, allow cultural variations and complexities to be encoded, and thus cross-cultural comparisons could lead to myopic conclusions. In order to use such procedures, it is important to ascertain whether such reductionist procedures are valid and the degree to which they are valid. Using a summary statistic (such as a mean score to represent a country) becomes more problematic when the data are based on samples of convenience (such as employees of a particular organization or university students) and not on the total population (such as GNP or epidemiological rates) or representative samples (such as Gallup polls). Researchers often assume that these convenient samples represent their corresponding cultures, but the bases of such assumptions are often highly questionable. Within a culture, different samples have been found to vary on I/C (see Schwartz, Chapter 7, this volume).

Fourth, in science, the law of parsimony suggests that we should stay close to the data and make the fewest number of assumptions and abstractions possible. It is more appropriate, based on the individual-level data that we have, to operate at the individual level. Furthermore, it is far more difficult for individual researchers to grasp culture-level phenomena, both heuristically and phenomenologically (see Bond, Chapter 5, this volume). In terms of the personal insights, intuition, and interpretations that are fundamental to science (Holten, 1973), it is far easier to start at the individual level than at the cultural level.

It may be considered scientifically more parsimonious to start at the individual level, but it may not be more fruitful. Individual-level analyses can be of limited scope. Without an overall picture or a map to guide research, it is often difficult to grasp how individual studies relate to one another. In cross-cultural psychology, many researchers have focused on the individual level of analysis. As a result, understanding of culture has been "fuzzy" at best. Hofstede's (1980) I/C dimension provided a direction and a focus for cross-cultural psychologists. This dimension serves as a counterpart to the Human Relations Area Files (HRAF), which have traditionally provided standardized ratings of cultural dimensions based on ethnographies compiled by anthropologists, travelers, and missionaries. The HRAF, however, are based largely upon subsistence economies and have limited utility for industrialized societies. Thus the I/C dimension serves similar functions as the HRAF for industrialized societies.

Better resolutions of I/C could be achieved through a series of collaborative research ventures (e.g., Chinese Culture Connection, 1987; Triandis et al., 1986; see also Schwartz, Chapter 7, this volume). At the same time, researchers have explicated parallel constructs at the individual level (e.g., Kagitçibasi, 1990; Markus & Kitayama, 1991; Schwartz & Bilsky, 1987, 1990; Triandis et al., 1985) and have examined the relationship between the two levels (Bond, 1988; see also, in this volume, Schwartz, Chapter 7; Bierbrauer, Meyer, & Wolfradt, Chapter 12).

Hofstede (1980) also provides a systematic and coherent integration of I/C across various fields (such as sociology, anthropology, economics, management, religion, philosophy, and political science). He notes in his foreword to this volume that his contribution "does not belong to any single social science discipline," and he advocates the development of truly interdisciplinary cross-cultural social sciences. His contribution provides both theoretical and empirical structure for a field searching for its identity.

Two promising trends can be identified that can further unravel the complexities of I/C: the cross-cultural approach and the indigenous approach. Cross-cultural psychology can be described as a blend of *emic* and *etic* approaches (see Hofstede's foreword). In this blending, theories and methods are typically developed in one culture and then transported to and imposed upon another. They are, however, adapted in the other culture to incorporate its indigenous knowledge system. The final results are compared between two or more cultures to verify, revise, or reject an existing theory.

The indigenous psychologies approach upholds the view that each culture needs to be understood in its own reference frame (see Kim & Berry, 1993, for a review). It attempts to document, organize, and interpret behaviors, values, customs, and beliefs of a particular cultural community. Methodologically, it emphasizes the use of natural taxonomies to discover regularities in a particular context. It examines how individuals and groups interact within this context. This information is used as the first step in the discovery of psychological invariants. The second step involves comparing results across different contexts to examine commonalities and variations; this is known as the *cross-indigenous approach* (Enriquez, 1993). From systematic studies of indigenous psychologies, it is possible to look for general principles and universals.

Cross-cultural psychology and the indigenous psychologies approach are complementary, not mutually exclusive (Kagitçibasi, 1992; Kim & Berry, 1993). The main difference lies in the starting point of research. Integration of these two approaches is necessary if we are to discover true psychological universals (Kim & Berry, 1993).

Triandis, in Chapter 3 of this volume, advocates the use of multimethod probes to unravel the multifaceted nature of I/C. Value constructs have been the most popular research tool in this area (e.g., Chinese Culture Connection, 1987; Hofstede, 1980; see also Schwartz, Chapter 7, this volume). Attitudes scales have also been widely used (Hui, 1988; Triandis et al., 1986; see also, in this volume, Yamaguchi, Chapter 11; Bierbrauer, Chapter 12), and experimental methods (e.g., Leung & Bond, 1984; Trafimow, Triandis, & Goto, 1991) and open-ended questionnaires and ethnographic methods have also been used (e.g., Bellah, Madsen, Sullivan, Swidler, & Tipton, 1985; Hsu, 1981; Maday & Szalay, 1976; Wheeler, Reis, & Bond, 1989).

Triandis, McCusker, and Hui (1990) integrated five different methodologies to yield a consistent pattern of results. Similarly, Chan (Chapter 13, this volume) found that three measures of collectivism are intercorrelated and that a summary score of these measures is a more powerful tool than any single measure. A multimethod approach can help to clarify, refine, elaborate, and validate our understanding of I/C.

OVERVIEW OF THE CHAPTERS

This volume contains 19 chapters divided into three sections. In Part I, "Theoretical Analysis," six chapters outline frameworks for further clarifying and advancing the constructs of I/C. In Chapter 2, Uichol Kim reviews the historical antecedents to I/C and examines the influences of ecology, industrialization, and urbanization on the development of I/C in modern societies. He proposes an alternative model of I/C by linking two levels (individual level and the group level) together. Kim outlines three facets of I/C and provides empirical evidence to support his model.

In Chapter 3, Harry C. Triandis suggests that the strength of I/C constructs lies in their ability to provide testable attitudinal, value, and behavioral predictions. He outlines 66 testable hypotheses differentiating individualism from collectivism. Although only a small number of these hypotheses have actually been tested, Triandis reviews a series of empirical studies that provide a systematic and coherent pattern of results. He outlines a strategy for the use of multiple methods for unraveling and verifying the 66 hypotheses outlined in his table. He concludes that although systematic research in the area of I/C is in its infancy, "the extent to which consistency has been obtained across the various methods of the study of the theoretical constructs suggests that there is a really important cultural syndrome that corresponds to I/C."

In Chapter 4, Çigdem Kagitçibasi notes the similarity in the use of I/C to the former modern/traditional dichotomy and deplores the evolutionary stance, especially as it associates individualism with greater cultural complexity. She suggests that individuation and separation are the defining features of individualism and human relatedness is the defining feature of collectivism. She proposes that the psychology of relatedness is a promising area for future research. Kagitçibasi outlines three types of socialization: pattern X (the collectivist model based on communion, interdependence), pattern Z (the individualist model based on agency, independence), and pattern Y (a dialectical synthesis of patterns X and Z). She suggests that rather than a shift from pattern X to pattern Z, as has been assumed by most social scientists, there is a shift from pattern X to pattern Y in developing countries with cultures of relatedness.

In Chapter 5, Michael Harris Bond provides a personal and scientific account of his contribution to the I/C literature. He outlines the usefulness of the culture-level dimension of I/C by providing a map to guide cross-cultural research and linking social psychological phenomena such as conflict resolution, resource allocation, self-serving bias, attribution, in-group bias, and conformity. He suggests that the challenge that lies ahead is in developing individual-level measures of I/C and linking them with psychological phenomena.

John W. Berry provides a theoretical bridge in Chapter 6, linking the ecological perspective that has traditionally focused on subsistence-level societies to the area of I/C that has typically examined industrialized societies. He suggests that societal size (made up of size of local community, settlement pattern, and political and occupational specialization) is systematically related to social conformity. He suggests that personal individualism can be predicted by the ecocultural dimension of societal size. He predicts that as local population units become larger, more differentiated, and more diffuse, individualist tendencies will increase.

In Chapter 7, Shalom H. Schwartz provides a systematic elaboration, extension, and integration of Hofstede's (1980) four dimensions of cultural variation. He points out limitations of previous cross-cultural studies of I/C. By compiling results from 87 samples from 41 cultural groups in 38 nations, he proposes seven culture-level values types: egalitarian commitment, intellectual autonomy, affective autonomy, mastery, hierarchy, conservatism, and harmony. All of these types are mapped in a two-dimensional space, suggesting new cultural dimensions of values.

Part II, "Conceptual and Empirical Analysis," contains six contributions. The first of these is Chapter 8, by Durganand Sinha and Rama Charan Tripathi, who suggest that whereas dichotomous conceptualization of self and social phenomena are common in the West, *coexistence of opposites* is characteristic of the Indian psyche and culture. They review indigenous concepts and literature that support their contention. In Indian culture, the boundaries of the self shift constantly, depending on the context. The self sometimes expands to fuse with the larger collective, but at other moments can completely withdraw from it. The most characteristic feature of the Indian sense of self is that individuals are able to incorporate diverse elements, even if some of these elements are in conflict with one another and appear mutually exclusive. Sinha and Tripathi note that although collectivist values are important in the family setting, in the areas of religion and ethics there is a strong emphasis on the realization of self through self-control and meditation.

In Chapter 9, David Yau-Fai Ho and Chi-Yue Chiu explore the complexity of individualism, collectivism, and social organization in Chinese culture. They outline a conceptual scheme for classifying component ideas from popular Chinese sayings and proverbs. These ideas were administered to a group of subjects in their empirical study. The analysis of the component ideas and the empirical study demonstrate the multidimensional nature of both constructs. Although many individualist ideas were endorsed, collectivism was emphasized more than individualism overall (such as values conducive to integrative social organization and the maintenance of harmony).

In Chapter 10, Jae-Ho Cha examines collectivism in traditional Korean culture and in modern Korea by analyzing the following: travelogues written by foreign observers of Koreans during the years 1870 to 1970, a review of empirical studies done on Korean values since 1945, and survey data collected from younger and older generations of Koreans in the late 1970s. The content analysis of 22 travelogues reveals an emphasis on the family line, dependence on relationships, hierarchy, courtesy, mutual succor, maintenance of tradition, and loyalty to the king. One significant change that occurred in the late 1970s was the emergence of a new ingroup, school, which displaced the role of the extended family and clan. Cha found that despite changes toward individualism, the vast majority of Koreans, both young and old, espouse collectivist beliefs, attitudes, and values in some domain, such as accepting in-group obligations and ingroup favoritism. The younger generation, however, is more likely to be individualistic when it comes to granting autonomy to their children, or when personal goals are in conflict with family or clan.

Susumu Yamaguchi links the study of I/C to the perspective of the self in Chapter 11. He suggests two antecedents to individuals' collective tendency: psychological attachments (i.e., expectation of reward) and fear of rejection (i.e., expectation of punishment). In other words, individuals are motivated to sacrifice their self-interests temporarily for the group as long as they can expect long-term rewards. Similarly, the expectation of punishment by group members may motivate individuals to abandon their personal goals in favor of the group's goal. The consequences of collectivism Yamaguchi outlines include lower need for uniqueness, higher external locus of control, and higher interpersonal sensitivity. By using his Collectivism Scale, he shows that collectivism is systematically related to both antecedents and consequences of collectivism.

In Chapter 12, Günter Bierbrauer, Heike Meyer, and Uwe Wolfradt point out the need to differentiate between norms that exist in a particular culture and a personal evaluation of these norms. Individuals can be aware of norms that are widely shared and that serve to control behaviors of individual members, but may not necessarily value or follow these social norms. Bierbrauer has developed the 26-item Cultural Orientation Scale to distinguish the normative aspect from the evaluative aspect, and has used it in conducting cross-cultural and acculturative investigations.

Darius Kwan-Shing Chan, author of Chapter 13, investigates the interrelationships among three measures of collectivism: "social content of the self," 16 attitude items, and 37 value items. He finds good convergent validity among the three collectivism measures and proposes a method of deriving a summary score, COLINDEX, from the three measures. COLINDEX demonstrates a superior criterion-related validity when compared with any single instrument. Chan's study provides a method of combining various measures to create a single collectivism index.

Part III, "Social and Applied Issues," begins with Chapter 14, by Gyuseog Han and Sug-Man Choe, who examine factors that contribute to in-group and out-group distinctions in Korea. These researchers investigated three markers that are typically used to distinguish in-group members from out-group members: family network and common bloodlines, regional network (i.e., people from the same hometown), and school network (i.e., people from the same school). Han and Choe found that the vast majority (more than 80%) of their subjects participated in one or more network activities. Through a scenario method, they examined 12 different social acts aimed at a director of a company who was initially a stranger. They found that respondents engaged in network activities for pragmatic reasons (i.e., because of social pressure and personal gains) and not necessarily because doing so was consistent with their values or beliefs.

In Chapter 15, Ramesh C. Mishra reports on his investigation of individualist and collectivist orientations across two generations in India. He examined the orientations and values of 100 fathers and sons with varying degrees of education who were living in rural and urban areas. He found that people exhibited both individualist and collectivist orientations and values at the same time. Although young, highly educated, and urban respondents were less collectivist, this effect was largely attributable to their living in an urban area. Highly educated urban respondents were somewhat more individualist, but this difference was not found among highly educated rural subjects. The strength of in-group influence varied according to the nature of the in-group and the decisions. Individualist values such as personal happiness, economic gains, and personal benefits coexisted with collectivist values such as salvation, enduring relationships, and altruism among Mishra's respondents. His results support not the linear modernity model, but the *coexistence* model espoused by Sinha and Tripathi (Chapter 8).

In Chapter 16, An-Bang Yu and Kuo-Shu Yang point out that motivation theories developed in the United States, especially David McClelland's formulation of achievement motivation, are based on individualist assumptions. Within McClelland's model, the goal, incentive values of the goal, standard of excellence, evaluations of one's efforts, and results of one's efforts are defined by the individual. Similarly, the linkages across the domains of culture, socialization, personality, and society are based on individualist assumptions. Such a model reflects an *individual-oriented achievement motivation,* or IOAM. To help describe achievement motivation in Confucian cultures, Yu and Yang propose an alternative model, *social-oriented achievement motivation,* or the SOAM. The most important goals in SOAM are collective good, social harmony, and fulfillment of social obligations. Substantive goals coupled with emphasis on effort, discipline, industriousness, frugality, willingness to make sacrifices, education, achievement, and respect for authorities have contributed to the phenomenal economic success in East Asia. The goal, incentive values of the goal, standard of excellence, evaluation, and fruits of one's efforts are defined and shared by the group.

In Chapter 17, Uimyong Kim suggests that organizations in Japan and Korea are created and perceived as extensions of a family. In these societies, companies and the government encourage paternalism and communalism. To examine the nature of paternalism and communalism in Korea, Kim surveyed personnel managers working for mining and manufacturing firms with more than 100 employees. He found that the vast majority (more than 80%) of the managers strongly endorsed the ideas of paternalism and communalism. Many of their companies provide services to foster paternalism and communalism, which are believed in turn to enhance production, efficiency, solidarity, loyalty, job satisfaction, and social control.

Jai B. P. Sinha and Jyoti Verma provide empirical evidence in Chapter 18 that support received, rather than a general collective orientation, is associated with psychological well-being. They have found that collectivist individuals who receive high social support report an overall sense of psychological well-being. Under conditions of low social support, however, collectivist individuals report lower levels of psychological well-being. This study reveals that although social support received by in-group members can promote psychological well-being, there may be psychological and social "costs" attached to remaining in a tight-knit in-group.

In Chapter 19, Janusz Reykowski explores the effects on I/C of the rapid social and political changes experienced in Polish society in recent years. To some extent, these changes have been associated with increased acceptance of individualism. Reykowski attributes this change in the educated and professional sector of Polish society to "changes in educational structure, social impact, and citizens' experience of the collectivist state's failures." He reviews a comparative longitudinal study conducted in Germany and Poland. For the Polish sample, individualism increased with age; by the age of 17, Polish subjects' individualist tendencies were comparable to those of their German counterparts. In conflict situations, German adolescents showed self-reliance and active problem-solving strategies, whereas Polish adolescents were more likely to depend upon their parents for support. Reykowski notes that the vacillation displayed by the Polish adolescents may reflect a lack of consolidation or the state confusion in Polish society. He suggests that, although individualism may reign supreme, a coexistence model is also a real possibility.

PART I

Theoretical Analysis

2

INDIVIDUALISM AND COLLECTIVISM
Conceptual Clarification and Elaboration

UICHOL KIM

This chapter provides a historical analysis of the development of I/C. First, I present an examination of ecological influences in the development of individualist and collectivist cultures, and then explore the effect of social change on traditional subsistence cultures. I offer also a brief summary of liberalism and Confucianism, as a basis for understanding Western European individualism and East Asian collectivism. Finally, I outline three facets of individualism and three facets of collectivism.

ECOLOGY AND CULTURAL ADAPTATION

Ecology refers to a total pattern of relationships between life forms and the physical environment. Climatic and natural conditions (such as temperature, humidity, water supply, soil conditions, sunlight, and terrain) shape and determine the existence of various types of life forms, including that of human beings (Segall, Dasen, Berry, & Poortinga, 1990). Early in human history, collective units (such as families, clans, and tribes) developed strategies to cope with, and adapt to, their ecology. The unit of survival was the group.

A critical feature of survival in a particular ecological niche rests upon the availability of food supply (Segall et al., 1990). For early humans, the food supplies in mountain areas, jungles, and deserts were often limited. When the supplies were depleted, the people had to move on to other regions. Hunting and gathering tribes were among the first collective units. They subsisted by moving with, or toward, food sources. This type of collective

unit emphasized efficient coordination of activities (such as the division
of labor and the division of territories covered by each hunter) and sharing
of resources (i.e., the successful hunter shared the catch with unsuccessful
members).

Agrarian communities can be considered a second type of collective
unit. In both of these subsistence economies there was a fragile balance
between ecological demands and human intervention. According to Segall
et al. (1990), "Ecological variables constrain, pressure, and nurture cultural forms, which in turn shape behavior" (p. 18). Ecology by and large acted
as a filter that shaped and determined the types of cultures and individuals
that survived.

Migratory tribes that lived in jungles, mountains, and deserts needed
specific sets of skills that were adaptive to their ecological niches. Barry,
Child, and Bacon (1959) found, in their analysis of 104 societies, that in
migratory tribes (hunting and gathering societies with low food accumulation), socialization practices emphasized assertiveness, autonomy, achievement, and self-reliance. As a result, adults in these communities tended to
be self-assured, independent, and venturesome (i.e., individualistic). In contrast, Barry et al. found that in sedentary communities (societies that have
relatively high food accumulation through agriculture and animal hus-
bandry), socialization practices emphasized compliance, obedience, and
responsibility. As a result, adults in these communities tended to be consci-
entious, compliant, and conservative (i.e., collectivistic). These characteristics were developed and passed on to subsequent generations. Values,
norms, and beliefs were institutionalized as cultural molds that served to
mediate between ecological pressures and individual survival.

Paralleling I/C, field-independent individuals tend to be socially independent, autonomous, and distant. Field-dependent individuals are socially
interdependent, more sensitive to social cues, and develop closer interpersonal ties. Paralleling Barry et al.'s (1959) results, Berry (1976) found that
sedentary communities socialize their members to be field-dependent and
migratory tribes socialize their members to be field-independent. These
sets of results highlight consistent patterns of relationship among ecology,
culture, socialization, and individual functioning.

SOCIAL AND CULTURAL CHANGE

From about the sixteenth century, the ecology of Western Europe began
to be altered drastically. Human beings began to exert greater control over
their ecology. Numerous factors contributed to this change: the rise of
international trade, the rise of nation-states, the formation of a merchant

class, rapid development in science and technology, increased agricultural efficiency, industrialization, urbanization, and the rise of capitalism. These changes combined to create a radical shift away from subsistence economies (which are largely determined by ecology) to market economies (which are created by human intervention).

More and more, human interventions buffered ecological influences. For example, people did not have to migrate to find new food sources. They did not have to till their soil to have dinner on the table. They did not have to store their food for the coming winter. They did not have to sew to have shirts on their backs. They no longer needed neighbors' help to put up a barn. They were no longer at the mercy of changing climatic conditions. People instead worked for wages in climate-controlled environments. The money they earned could be used to buy necessary goods and services. It could be deposited with a bank for future use. Currency, especially paper money, acted as an intermediary commodity that allowed the efficient movement of resources.

With the advent of greater agricultural efficiency, coupled with the rise of the nation-states, many serfs and peasants were dislocated from their agricultural communities. They congregated in the newly formed cities, where they were hired by industrial factories that paid wages for their labor. The work involved acquiring skills that reflected the rapid developments in science and technology. For example, machines were introduced for increased production, efficient distribution, and greater profits. These workers were often viewed as extensions of the machines that were used to produce goods and profit.

The lifestyle in the industrial urban centers contrasted sharply with the previous life experiences of the new working class. The traditional agricultural communities represented the gemeinschaft tradition (Tönnies, 1887/1957); families lived in particular communities for many generations, and people knew one another. Relationships were based on collective cooperation and trust. Agricultural production meant that members of a community lived together and worked together. Goods were produced with the main purpose of consumption in the local community. Trust, cooperation, and conservatism were important parts of the daily lives of the people in this type of community.

The industrial urban setting, in contrast, was full of *unrelated* strangers. It represented the gesellschaft tradition (Tönnies, 1887/1957). The relationship workers had with employers was contractual, not based on any long-standing relationship of trust and cooperation. This contractual relationship was fueled by the law of supply and demand. Each individual received a contract and was paid according to the market value of his or her services. The labor was often viewed as a commodity. The interest of the employers in many cases was in profit and not in the welfare of the workers. When demand for labor was low and supply was high, many laborers, including women and children, were exploited. They had to work long hours under miserable conditions. In those settings, there was no one to protect the rights of these unrelated individuals. Tönnies contrasts the situation during the middle ages with the situation in 1935:

> Then there were sympathetic relationships among kinsfolk and old acquaintances, now there are strangers and aliens everywhere; then society was chiefly made up of home- and land-loving peasants, now the attitude of the businessman prevails; then man's simple needs were met by home production and barter, now we have world trade and capitalistic production; then there was permanency of abode, now great mobility; then there were folk arts, music, and handicrafts, now there is science. (cited in Loomis, 1957, p. 2)

Collective action began to appear in protest of the undesirable working conditions and working relationships. New collectives emerged in Europe and in the United States (e.g., unions, employer organizations, and consumer groups). Members of the working class began to organize and lobby for their interests against the ruling class through demonstrations and revolutions. These collective actions brought forth two types of moral-political ideologies: democracy and communism. In Western Europe and the United States, officials are elected to protect the rights and freedom of all citizens. This type of collective represents a shift away from ascribed relationships such as families, communities, and religion and toward individualism, which emphasizes achieved status based on common interests, experiences, and goals (Tönnies, 1887/1957; see also Triandis, Chapter 3, this volume).

Advocates of communism, such as Karl Marx, criticized the capitalist exploitation of workers, dehumanizing aspects of the uncontrolled market economy, and excessive individualism coupled with fierce competition. Marx criticized the capitalist conception of work as a means to an end (i.e., toward greater production and profit; Tönnies, 1887/1957). Marx viewed work as an end in itself. Work was a way of life and tools were seen as extensions of self. Self-identity, self-expression, and meaning of life are found through work. At the collective level, Marx emphasized a fundamental belief that human beings can collectively determine their future and create a utopian society. Individuals need to be educated to achieve this collective end. Marx called for the creation of a collective based on communal ownership and shared goals that curtailed excessive individualism. It meant creating a new economy based on communal ownership rather than individual ownership, a centralized distribution system rather than a distribution system based on the law of supply and demand, and a central bureaucracy rather than democratic representation.

Hofstede (1980) notes that a "capitalist market economy fosters individualism and in turn depends on it" (p. 233). In contrast, "various socialist types of economic order foster collectivism and in turn depend on it, although to various degrees" (p. 233). Communist societies and capitalist societies, however, do share one common characteristic: People are encouraged to separate from their ascribed relationships and to form achieved relationships. The nature of this achieved relation, however, is significantly different in the two societies: One is based on communist ideology and the other is based on individualism.

Individualist societies view in-group loyalty based on ascribed relationships as a hindrance to the development of a more encompassing collective that would protect the inalienable human rights of all citizens. Béteille (1977) notes that a high degree of correspondence exists among political democracy, capitalism, competition, and individualism (cited in Hofstede, 1980). Cultures based on this type of social, philosophical, and political realignment are called "individualistic" (Hofstede, 1980). Kagitçibasi (Chapter 4, this volume) prefers to describe such cultures as "cultures of separateness," because they require separation from ascribed relationships coupled with an emphasis on achieved relationships.

Cultures that maintain ascribed relationships and interpersonal relatedness have also been labeled "collectivistic." Kagitçibasi prefers to describe these cultures as "cultures of relatedness." In cultures of relatedness, ascribed and interpersonal relationships serve as a societal foundation. Maintenance of strong and cohesive in-groups in cultures of relatedness, however, often perpetuates in-group favoritism, ethnocentrism, factionalism, regionalism, and particularism. In-group loyalty often leads to out-group derogation, and in-group cooperation is often coupled with fierce out-group competition (see Han & Choe, Chapter 14, this volume). In-group solidarity often hampers the development and promotion of more encompassing principles, rules, and laws that would protect every individual regardless of his or her group affiliation (see Schwartz, Chapter 7, this volume). These problems arise because of emphasis on particularism rather than universalism (Hofstede, 1991; Parsons & Shils, 1951; see also Triandis, Chapter 3, this volume).

During the process of acculturation to social change, four interesting patterns have emerged. First, although characteristics of individualism in "modern" societies (i.e., driven by the market economy) resemble features of individualism in "traditional" migratory tribes, market-based economies evolved from traditional sedentary communities and not from traditional migratory tribes. One could thus hypothesize that many structural and organizational features of traditional sedentary communities are compatible with the development of modern capitalist societies and that these structural features may still persist (in some form and in varying degree) in these societies. For example, demand and surplus, which are essential features of capitalism, are more likely to appear in sedentary communities. In addition, sedentary communities support relatively large numbers of people, and this means developing viable social institutions that can manage their members (Barry et al., 1959; see also Berry, Chapter 6, this volume). Thus sedentary communities have the three necessary ingredients in place for capitalism: surplus, demand, and viable social institutions. To become full-fledged capitalist societies, however, sedentary communities are required to shift away from subsistence economy toward specialized production that emphasizes surplus and profit, efficient movement of resources, adherence to the law of supply and demand, and social institutions that will protect the viability of the market economy.

Second, Berry and Annis (1974) found that the native peoples in Canada who came from "traditional" migratory communities have had enormous difficulties acculturating into "modern" Canadian society. Native peoples from "traditional" sedentary communities, however, had relatively fewer difficulties acculturating into Canadian society. These results could be interpreted as follows: Although both "traditional" migratory communities and "modern" Canadian society emphasize individualism, the structural and institutional organization of "traditional" sedentary communities is more compatible with "modern" industrialized societies. As a result, native peoples from "traditional" sedentary communities as a whole have less difficulty acculturating into "modern" Canadian society. Within these sedentary communities, however, those individuals who are field-independent (i.e., individualistic) adjust better than those who are field-dependent (i.e., collectivistic) (Berry & Annis, 1974). This result suggests that compatibility at both individual and cultural levels promotes the best possible adaptation.

Third, in Europe and North America, capitalism and communism evolved from within. In Asia, Latin America, and Africa, capitalism and communism were imposed through colonization. In other words, "traditional" communities (i.e., subsistence economies) in these countries were forced to adopt either capitalism or communism. These countries needed to respond to these external colonial impositions. Although many countries are still struggling, attempting to cope with the destructive forces of these impositions, several countries in the Pacific Rim that were traditionally agrarian (such as Hong Kong, Japan, Singapore, South Korea, and Taiwan) were able to develop collective strategies that were compatible with their "traditional" cultural values.

In Japan, for example, some researchers have noted, industrialization, urbanization, and capitalism have not significantly altered the underlying cultural value system that emphasizes human-relatedness (Lebra, 1976; Misumi, 1988; Stevenson, Azuma, & Hakuta, 1986). Although many external features of Japanese culture have changed, the core elements of the culture that emphasize human-relatedness remain strong. Misumi (1988), for example, notes that the phenomenal economic progress of Japan has been achieved because of the maintenance of human-relatedness, and not in spite of it. Although capitalism has altered external features of Japanese culture, capitalism itself was modified to fit underlying Japanese cultural values that emphasize human-relatedness. In a country such as Japan, the ability to respond collectively to both internal and external challenges remains intact. Other countries in the Pacific Rim have developed their own unique strategies to cope with both internal and external demands (see Yu & Yang, Chapter 16, and U. M. Kim, Chapter 17, this volume).

COMPARATIVE ANALYSIS OF LIBERALISM AND CONFUCIANISM

The rise of individualism in Western European countries represents a schism between "traditional" medieval order and liberal ideals. Liberalism extols the virtues of individualism, and Confucianism glorifies collectivism. Table 2.1 provides a summary of key differences between these two moral-political philosophies. The table should be read vertically, and liberalism as a whole should be compared with Confucianism as a whole.

In Western Europe and North America, liberalism became a dominant philosophy that delineates the conception of self and society. From this perspective, individuals are considered to be rational and universal entities. The liberal tradition focuses on the rational individual's rights to choose, define, and search for self-fulfillment freely. The content of self-fulfillment can vary widely, from hedonism to self-actualization. At the interpersonal level, individuals are considered to be discrete, autonomous, self-sufficient, and respectful of the rights of others. Their status and roles are not predetermined by ascribed status, but defined by their achievements (i.e., educational, occupational, and economic status). They interact with others utilizing mutually agreed-upon principles, such as equality, equity, noninterference, and detachability. Individuals with similar goals are brought together into groups. Laws and regulations are institutionalized to protect individual rights, with everyone being able to assert his or her rights through the legal system. The state is governed by elected officials whose role is to uphold individual rights and the viability of public institutions.

Table 2.1 Liberalism and Confucianism: Comparative Analysis

Level of Analysis	Liberalism	Confucianism
Individual level		
Goals:		
individual	self-fulfillment	self-realization
social	assertion of rights	substantive goals
means	freedom of choice	self-cultivation
barriers	external constraints	internal constraints
Nature of self:		
internal	rational	lower versus higher self
boundary	discrete	fluid
entity	autonomous; self-sufficient; goal directed; universalistic	embedded; interdependent; situated; particularistic
Interpersonal level:		
individuals	abstract	relational
orientation	respect	concern
basis	commonality	common fate
status and role	achieved; universalistic	ascribed; particularistic
Societal level:		
Norms and principles	equality, equity; noninterference; detachability	role fulfillment; maintenance of face; social obligations
morality	rights-based	virtue-based
conflict resolution	adversarial arbitration	conciliatory compromise
justice	egalitarianism; procedural	role-based; substantive
order	laws and regulations	roles and duties
institutions	protection of individual rights	familism; legal moralism
state	by people; rational principle; democratic representation	for people; welfaristic; paternalistic

Individual rights are of prime importance, and substantive rights are considered supererogatory (Miller, 1984; Scanlon, 1978; C. Taylor, 1985).

In East Asia, Confucianism became the dominant moral-political philosophy. Confucianism promotes the collective welfare and harmony as its ultimate goal. Individuals must eradicate within themselves any individualist, hedonistic, and selfish desires in order to be considered persons of virtue. Individuals are conceived of as embedded and situated in particular roles and statuses. They are bound by ascribed relationships that emphasize their common fate. Individuals are encouraged to put other people's and the group's interests before their own. From a societal point of view, individuals are considered to be interrelated through their ascribed roles. Duties and obligations are prescribed by their roles, and they lose "face" if they fail to fulfill their obligations as prescribed. Concession and compromise are essential ingredients in promoting a role- and virtue-based conception of justice. Social order is maintained when everyone fulfills his or her roles and duties. Institutions are seen as an extension of the family, and paternalism and legal moralism reign supreme. A ruler is considered to be a father figure who is paternalistic, moralistic, and welfaristic.

CONTRASTING FACETS OF I/C

The following subsections provide schematic representations of I/C at the individual-group level that complement the culture-level analysis of liberalism and Confucianism. With these elaborations I attempt to conceptualize explicitly the relationship between individuals and groups based on a literature review and current contributions. In individualist cultures, boundaries and internal attributes have been described meticulously (Sampson, 1988; Waterman, 1981), but the characteristics of groups are implicit and have not been clearly articulated. In contrast, in collectivist cultures, the boundaries and characteristics of the group have been clearly delineated (Hofstede, 1980; Triandis, 1988b, 1990), but the internal structures and interrelationships among individuals have not been explicitly examined. The following subsections provide descriptive models, not explanatory models, that delineate central features of I/C. They are approximations and are not meant to be exhaustive.

Within the present approach, individualism is defined by an explicit and firm individual boundary between self and others. Individualist cultures emphasize the *I* versus *you* distinction. Figure 2.1 provides a schematic representation of three different facets of individualism.

Aggregate Mode

Figure 2.1A depicts an *aggregate* mode, which is defined by three critical features. First, it emphasizes distinct and independent individuals (solid circles in the figure). Second, individuals need to detach themselves from ascribed relationships, such as family, relatives, community, and religion. Third, rational principles, rules, and norms (dashed circle) provide mechanisms through which unrelated individuals interact with one another.

In the aggregate mode there is the "belief that each of us is an entity separate from every other and from the group" (Spence, 1985, p. 1288).

A. Aggregate Mode   B. Distributive Mode

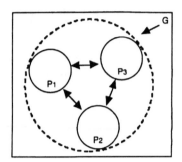   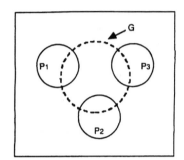

C. Static Mode

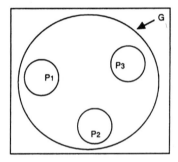

Figure 2.1. Facets of Individualism

NOTE: P = persons; G = group. Solid lines indicate firm boundaries; dashed lines indicate fluid boundaries.

This belief can "lead to a sense of self with a sharp boundary that stops at one's skin and clearly demarks self from nonself" (p. 1288). It is defined by a "reference to one's own internal repertoire of thoughts, feelings, and actions, rather than by reference to thoughts, feelings, and actions of others" (Markus & Kitayama, 1991, p. 226). Sampson (1977) uses the term "self-contained individualism," which emphasizes the values of freedom, independence, self-determination, personal control, and uniqueness. It is characterized by a "firmly individuated self" and "deep and rich interior" (Sampson, 1987, p. 85). Riesman (1961) describes such individuals as "inner-directed types" who are guided by a "psychological gyroscope" (p. 16). Schwartz (Chapter 7, this volume) has found that one aspect of individualism focuses on self-direction and the other on stimulation and hedonism.

Separation from one's ascribed relationships is considered to be a pre-requisite of the development of a firmly individuated self (Bellah, Madsen, Sullivan, Swidler, & Tipton, 1985; Hsu, 1983; Maday & Szalay, 1976; Triandis, Bontempo, Villareal, Asai, & Lucca, 1988; see also Triandis, Chapter 3, and Kagitçibasi, Chapter 4, this volume). From a developmental perspective, individuation and separation from ascribed relationships are considered necessary for healthy human development, whereas interdependent or "enmeshed" individuals are considered pathological (Kagitçibasi, 1990).

The third feature of the aggregate mode is the emphasis on abstract principles. It is a process by which core values and characteristics of a group are abstracted from a specific context and person. It is similar to Waterman's (1981) "normative (ethical) individualism," which emphasizes "universality involving respect for the integrity of others" (p. 764), and Kohlberg's (1969) final stage of moral development. Schwartz (Chapter 7, this volume), for example, has found that individualism is positively correlated with social concern. He notes that "as autonomous selves, individuals in such societies might naturally feel detached from and unconcerned about others" and thus "smoothly functioning social relations require that autonomous individuals internalize the importance of committing themselves to others' welfare and of expressing their concern by taking prosocial action."

In the aggregate mode, individuals interact with others based on such principles as equality, competition, equity, noninterference, and exchanges based on contracts (Bellah et al., 1985; Hofstede, 1980; Leung & Bond, 1984; Shweder & Bourne, 1982; Waterman, 1981). Members of a group are conceived as independent and unrelated individuals, and no one individual enjoys special privileges. Decisions are made equally, based on majority approval. Resources are shared equitably, based on merit and performance. Individuals are "democratically" elected to represent the group, to arbitrate grievances, to oversee the fair distribution of resources, and to implement policies and programs on behalf of the group.

Researchers have found that people from the United States describe their personalities in an abstract and context-free manner (Markus & Kitayama, 1991; Shweder & Bourne, 1982). Such a conception contrasts sharply with the Chinese, Indian, Japanese, or Korean view, which is predominantly concrete, relational, and bound in a particular behavioral context (Maday & Szalay, 1976; Markus & Kitayama, 1991; Miller, 1984; Shweder & Bourne, 1982; Triandis, Bontempo, Leung, & Hui, 1990). A tendency to remain concrete and relational has not been found to be related to differences in educational attainment, literacy, or socioeconomic class,

or to lack of abstraction skills (Shweder & Bourne, 1982). Shweder and
Bourne (1982) note that the emphasis on abstraction is collectively created
and supported in the American culture:

> This abstracted individual, "man-as-voluntary agent," is protected by deeply
> enshrined moral and legal principles prescribing privacy and proscribing
> unwanted invasions of person, property, and other extensions of the self.
> Americans are culturally primed to search for abstract summaries of the
> autonomous individual behind the social role and social appearance. (p. 192)

Shweder and Bourne use the term "egocentric contractual" to describe
American individualism. From this perspective, social relationships are
viewed as derivatives of the autonomous and abstracted individuals. They
interact through mutual consent and contractual relationship. Social situations serve "primarily as standards of reflected appraisal, or as sources
that can verify and affirm the inner core of the self" (Markus & Kitayama,
1991, p. 226).

Distributive Mode

The central difference between the aggregate mode and the *distributive*
mode is the nature of the group. In the aggregate mode, a group is defined
by abstract principles. In the distributive mode, a group is defined by common interests and attributes (see Figure 2.1B); a group "arises by each
member having some similar attributes to every other" (Harré, 1984, p. 930).
The boundaries of a group are defined by commonality and fluidity.
Voluntary organizations, interest groups, and recreational clubs are examples of this type of group. Because the form and degree of participation
is voluntary, permanent loyalty is not demanded from group members.
The group persists if it satisfies the needs and interests of its members. It
dissolves when it fails to do so. In the distributive mode, individuals are
"capable of a rapid if sometimes superficial intimacy with and response
to everyone" (Riesman, 1961, p. 25).

Another feature of the distributive mode is an emphasis on contracts.
A contract defines a relationship between a professional (who provides
services) and a client (who pays a fee for the services). Doctors, lawyers,
accountants, teachers, counselors, and professors provide specialized
services to anyone and everyone in need of those services. Similarly, labor
and management represent collective entities whose relationship is defined by a contract.

Static Mode

A third facet of individualism is the *static* mode (see Figure 2.1C). It consists of two levels: an individual's inalienable rights and institutions, such as the government, that protect freedom and justice for all individuals. The Bill of Rights and the Constitution of the United States, for example, guarantee and protect inalienable rights of all individuals. These rights are seen as the cornerstone of American individualism: "Individual rights are political *trumps* held by individuals"; "individuals have rights when, for some reason, a collective goal is not a sufficient justification for denying them what they wish, as individuals, to have or to do, or not a sufficient justification for imposing some loss or injury upon them" (Dworkin, 1977).

Laws guarantee basic rights to all individuals, regardless of their ascribed or achieved status. These rights cannot be usurped or exploited by second parties (such as powerful adversaries or malevolent agencies). They protect the welfare of the disadvantaged, the defenseless, and the powerless (e.g., minorities, children, and people with disabilities). They guard against the "totalitarian menace" (C. Taylor, 1985) that could oppress, bully, and torture individuals on the behalf of national interests and collective welfare (Berlin, 1967). Rights protect individuals' autonomy and freedom to pursue their own goals (Scanlon, 1978), and institutions are established to protect the rights of all citizens.

Because most individuals are unrelated to one another, they may not always act in responsible, moral, sane, and altruistic ways (Hogan, 1975). They may exploit or commit crimes against one another or against society. Sampson (1977) notes that highly individualist societies may "require strong, autocratic governance to control their appetites" (p. 779). In such societies laws are established so that no one person can step beyond the agreed-upon boundaries. If a person does, he or she is identified, punished, and incarcerated. The legal system, the correctional system, the military, and the Internal Revenue Service are examples of institutions found in the static mode. Everyone in the culture is bound by the same laws and, theoretically, no one enjoys special privileges.

Although the boundaries of the static mode are firm, they are not permanent. Individuals and groups can challenge the boundaries of existing laws and regulations, especially if these boundaries are perceived as infringing upon their rights. The law defining abortion rights in the United States is an example of a law that has fluctuated with time, depending on the political and legal climate.

Facets of Individualism:
Comparative Analysis

The central difference between the aggregate mode and the static mode lies in the fluidity of the group boundaries. Individuals in the aggregate mode are bound by normative and ethical principles, whereas individuals in the static mode are bound by laws. An example provided by R. Brown (1986) highlights the difference between the two: When one sees another person drowning, one is compelled by a normative or ethical principle to help that person; one is not, however, bound by any law to do so. If one makes no attempt to save the drowning person, one has not committed a crime, but has violated a moral principle. Of course, if one takes an active part in the drowning (e.g., by pushing the person into the water), one has both violated an ethical principle and committed a crime punishable by law. When important moral and ethical principles are not widely upheld, they are sometimes formalized into laws (e.g., abortion, incest taboo, and child abuse).

The distributive mode can often resemble the static mode. In the United States, individuals join interest groups to protect and propagate their own interests. If a group is effective in maintaining its viability and competes successfully with other organizations, it can become a dominant group, and it can develop its own subculture with its own socializing mechanisms. Its goals can be in direct conflict with the goals of other individuals and of society. In such instances, members of the society can lose their ability to change the group, and the boundaries of the group lose their fluidity. In the economic sphere, this is called a monopoly. By law, monopolies are not allowed, or, if they do exist, they are under strict governmental control. In the service sector, such groups are widespread. Many professions in the United States (such as the legal and medical professions) have complete monopolies on the services they provide, and they are relatively autonomous and resistant to change (Kleinman, 1980; Zola, 1983). They often serve the interests of their members at the expense of consumers' interests (Kleinman, 1980; Zola, 1983).

Facets of Collectivism

Collectivism is defined by explicit and firm group boundaries. It is considered to be more than the mere sum of individual characteristics. In collectivist societies, one of the most important differentiations made about individuals is whether a person is part of an in-group or an out-group. Collectivist cultures emphasize a *we* versus *they* distinction. The emphasis

A. Undifferentiated Mode

B. Relational Mode

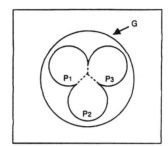

C. Co-Existence Mode

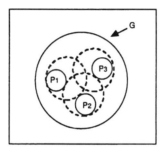

Figure 2.2. Facets of Collectivism

NOTE: P = persons; G = group. Solid lines indicate firm boundaries; dashed lines indicate fluid boundaries.

on collective welfare, harmony, and duties typically applies only to the in-group and usually does not extend to out-groups. The internal structure of collectivism is further elaborated in Figure 2.2.

Undifferentiated Mode

The *undifferentiated* mode is depicted in Figure 2.2A. It is defined by firm and explicit group boundaries, coupled with undifferentiated self-group boundaries. At the cultural level, the culture and personality school represents the undifferentiated mode (e.g., modal personality). Previous definitions of collectivism have focused on this mode (e.g., Hofstede, 1980; Hsu, 1983; Hui & Triandis, 1986; Triandis, 1988b; Triandis, Leung, Villareal, & Clark, 1985). Markus and Kitayama's (1991) interdependent view of self is similar to the undifferentiated mode. An extreme form of collectivism occurs when an individual is governed and defined by an in-group (Triandis, 1988b).

The undifferentiated mode can develop in two ways. From a developmental perspective, an individual who has failed to achieve some degree of individuation and separation and who is defined by an "enmeshed" identity represents this mode. Second, individuals who have previously achieved some degree of individuation and separation but have chosen to give up their self-identity in order to immerse themselves completely in an in-group (such as a religious cult or ideological group) would be another example. In reality, the undifferentiated mode is rare. It is often confused with the relational and coexistence modes.

Relational Mode

Figure 2.2B depicts the *relational* mode. It is depicted by porous boundaries between in-group members that allows thoughts, ideas, and emotions to flow freely. It focuses on the relationship shared by the in-group members. It requires three key features: "the willingness and ability to feel and think what others are feelings and thinking, to absorb this information without being told, and to help others satisfy their wishes and realize their goals" (Markus & Kitayama, 1991, p. 229). Its qualities have been discussed in relation to the concepts of *amae* ("dependence") in Japanese culture (Doi, 1981) and *chong* ("affection") in Korean culture (Choi, Kim, & Choi, 1993).

In traditional Korea, socialization for interdependence starts in the prenatal period and continues throughout the individual's life (see Kim & Choi, in press, for a review). *T'aekyo* ("prenatal care") includes rigorous guidelines for pregnant women outlining desirable and undesirable attitudes, emotions, and behaviors during pregnancy (A. C. Yu, 1984). These prescriptions are based upon a belief that a mother's experience during her pregnancy will directly affect the baby inside her womb and leave lasting impressions on the child. The goal of *t'aekyo* is to heighten awareness of the unique psychological and biological bonds between the mother and the unborn child.

When a child is born, Korean mothers believe, that child needs more than just mother's milk; the child needs symbolic "dew" that comes from the mother. The mother must remain close to the child to indulge the child with this essential psychological nutrient. The belief is that the maternal dew propagates the existence of an unseen but powerful bond between mother and child. Both *t'aekyo* and maternal dew create a strong psychological and emotional bond called *chong* ("affection").

In an open-ended survey, Choi et al. (1993) found that the word *chong* elicited the following associations: sacrifice, unconditionality, empathy, care, sincerity, shared experience, and common fate. *Chong* arises from a close-knit family and friends who spend a long time together and are bound by a common fate. *Chong* does not develop in a contractual, commercial, and rational relationship. Someone without *chong* is described as being conditional, selfish, hypocritical, apathetic, rational, self-reliant, independent, and autonomous. *Chong* is an essential component of the relational mode in Korea.

Although the influence of Confucianism has declined with modernization, some researchers agree that two important features of the relational mode still persist: devotion and indulgence (see, e.g., Azuma, 1986; Ho, 1986; Kim & Choi, in press). Mothers in modern Confucian cultures view unselfish devotion to their children as a critical feature of their personhood and motherhood (Azuma, 1986; Ho, 1986; J. E. Kim, 1981; Lee & Kim, 1979). Choi (1992) found that Korean mothers' personal identities are often defined by their role as mothers. They become closely and intrinsically tied to their children and see their children as extensions of themselves. Children's accomplishments and failures become the mothers' own, and mothers fulfill their own dreams and goals vicariously through their children. Attaining this gratification is one of the most important aspects of motherhood, and it is the most valued meaning that Korean mothers have in raising their children.

In modern Confucian cultures, parents are not discipline oriented in enforcing weaning, bedtimes, and toilet training. They are lenient and indulgent in order for the mother to foster the relational mode:

> The reason for leniency toward the younger child is that he or she is considered to be not yet capable of "understanding things," and therefore should not be held responsible for his or her wrongdoing. . . . It is thought that training cannot be expected to accomplish much for infants or young children; they are viewed as passive dependent creatures who are to be cared for, and whose needs are to be met with little delay or interference. (Ho, 1986, p. 4)

According to Azuma (1986), when a Japanese child is born, the mother remains close to the child to make the child feel secure, to make the boundary between herself and the child minimal, and to meet all of the child's needs, even if that means a tremendous sacrifice on her own part. This type of socialization creates the bond of *amae* ("dependence"). Children's strong dependency needs, both emotional and existential, are satisfied by their mothers' indulgent devotion. As a child grows, he or she senses that it is through the mother that one obtains gratification, security, and love. As the child matures, he or she is motivated to maintain a close relationship with the mother and does so by gradually taking a more active role by pleasing the mother and behaving according to her wishes. Thus the feeling of interdependence helps children to assimilate their mothers' values and beliefs as their own, through an osmosislike process.

The fear of potential separation from the mother is sometimes used in punishment for the child. Psychological and physical distance are often used by mothers to shape or correct children's behavior. Vogel and Vogel (1961) note that in the United States, a much-disliked form of punishment for children is to be "grounded" (i.e., their freedom to leave their rooms or their houses is taken away from them), whereas in Japan they are instead locked out of their homes. This physical distancing symbolizes the psychological separation that is considered to be traumatic to Japanese children.

As Japanese children grow up, they are expected to transfer identification and loyalty from their mothers to other family members, other relatives, particular individuals such as teachers, and larger social groups, such as the companies they work for. A mother's job is to prepare her child for adult life and to become a mediator between the home environment and the external environment (Stevenson et al., 1986). She achieves this goal by gradually inculcating appropriate social values in her child. Socialization for interdependence has also been documented in Chinese culture (Ho, 1986; see also Yu & Yang, Chapter 16, this volume), Indian culture (Kakar, 1978; see also Sinha and Tripathi, Chapter 8, this volume), and Turkish culture (Kagitçibasi, Chapter 4, this volume).

Coexistence Mode

Sinha and Tripathi (Chapter 8, this volume) have coined the term *coexistence* to describe a model that allows diverse, even contradictory, elements to coexist within a culture and within a person (see Figure 2.2C). The coexistence mode separates the private self (as represented in the figure by solid lines) from the public self (as represented by dashed lines). The public self becomes enmeshed with collectivist values, such as family loyalty, in-group solidarity, and national identity. It coexists with the private self, which maintains individualist values of self-cultivation and personal striving. Sinha and Tripathi point out that coexistence appears in all facets of Indian culture: in child-rearing practices, interpersonal relationships, intergroup relations, and public institutions. It does not imply dissonance in the Indian culture. It has been verified in a series of empirical studies in India (Sinha & Verma, 1987; see also Sinha & Tripathi, Chapter 8, and Mishra, Chapter 15, this volume), Poland (Reykowski, Chapter 19, this volume), Turkey (Kagitçibasi, Chapter 4, this volume), and Hong Kong (Ho & Chiu, Chapter 9, this volume).

Doi (1986) notes that in Japanese culture there are two sides to virtually all social phenomena. He uses the following distinctions: *omote* ("face") and *ura* ("mind, heart, and soul"), *soto* ("outside") and *uchi* ("inside"), and *tatemae* ("principles, rules, and conventions") and *honne* ("true intentions, or the inner self"). These terms are related to one another: "*Omote* and *ura* are parallel to the paired concepts of *tatemae* and *honne*, and . . . they represent a psychology corresponding to the distinction between *soto* and *uchi*" (p. 17). Within the psychological space, these contrasting elements coexist as two contiguous principles (Doi, 1986). The relationship between *tatemae* and *honne* can be conceived as the two sides of a coin lying on a table: The public self (*tatemae*) is the visible side of the coin, and the private self (*honne*) is the hidden side. In the Japanese context, the hidden side needs to be inferred or figured out if one is to understand the true nature of the coin.

In public situations, social norms and roles dictate the behavior of individuals. Collective actions need to be orchestrated cooperatively and harmoniously. If an individual's aspirations are not compatible with social demands, he or she is likely to be asked to sacrifice his or her personal interests for group harmony. This does not imply that individuals necessarily agree with the existing social norms. The cultural expectation is that if there are conflicts, individuals must suppress their own desires, locate them within the private domain, and not display them in public. For this reason, East Asian cultures emphasize the maintenance of "face" (*mientze* in Chinese, *ch'emyon* in Korean, *taimien* in Japanese) in public situations. Individuals have particular statuses and roles, and they must fulfill them in socially prescribed manners. Ho (1973) points out that face is lost when a person, through his or her own actions or those of closely related others, "fails to meet essential requirements" that come with his or her social position. Regardless of an individual's desires, face has to be maintained to preserve social harmony.

The respective roles of father and mother are best summarized in a popular Chinese and Korean phrase: "strict father, benevolent mother." Consistent with this role differentiation, fathers in Chinese culture are perceived by their children as autocratic, fearsome authority figures and harsh disciplinarians. Mothers, in contrast, are generally better liked and viewed as more forgiving (Ho, 1986).

Although the father is the head of the family, in reality he does not hold much power. He transfers his *amae* relationship from his own mother to his wife (Befu, 1986). He becomes dependent on his wife and is considered "more burdensome and harder to control than other children" (Azuma,

1986, p. 8). In addition, Japanese fathers spend most of their time in the workplace and socializing with their colleagues after work (Befu, 1986; Vogel, 1963). A father incurs expenses to meet his social obligations outside of the family. Mothers, in contrast, spend most of their time with their children. A mother is responsible for looking after the children and the household, and she frequently sacrifices her own personal interests to benefit the family. For these reasons, unlike mothers, fathers have difficulty developing *amae* relationships with their children and occupy a peripheral position in the family. As a result, conflicts of interest often develop in the allocation of resources, and mothers often develop alliances with their children against fathers (Befu, 1986). Azuma (1986) notes that "in many families the position of the father is peripheral. The formal head of the family, he is accorded respect. However, this respect is symbolic; in reality he does not exert much control" (p. 8).

Although a father is only the symbolic head of a family, he represents a link to the outer world. Through the father, children are linked across time (i.e., through his lineage) and across space (i.e., through his position in a community). It is his responsibility to maintain, propagate, and elevate the position of the family. When making a decision, he must use wisdom and foresight as essential ingredients because his decision affects the family members, his lineage, and his progeny. Children are considered incapable of understanding such a complex process, and thus they are required to obey, respect, and abide by their fathers' decisions. From the children's perspective, this often means sacrificing personal interests for the benefit of the family. Thus fathers represent the outer world, which is governed by the coexistence mode and *tatemae* ("principles, conventions"), and mothers represent the inner world, governed by the relational mode, *amae,* and *honne* ("true self").

Facets of Collectivism: Comparative Analysis

Researchers have often failed to distinguish the undifferentiated mode from the coexistence mode (e.g., Markus & Kitayama, 1991). They have suggested that in Japan, inner opinions, feelings, and attributes are insignificant constituents of self. Markus and Kitayama (1991) remark that "it is the individuals' roles, statuses, or positions, and commitments, obligations, and responsibilities they confer, that are the constituents of the self, and in that sense they are self-defined" and that "one's internal attributes (e.g., private attitudes or opinions) are not regarded as significant attributes of the self" (p. 240). To use the previous analogy, internal attributes represent the hidden side of the coin (i.e., private self) and social demands represent the visible side (i.e., public self). Doi (1986) points out that "*honne* refers to the fact that individuals who belong to the group, even while they consent to the *tatemae*, each have their own motives and opinions that are distinct from it, and they hold these in its background" (p. 37). To obtain a complete picture of a situation, the relationship between what is visible and what is hidden must be considered.

Unlike individualists, who have one self, in some collectivist cultures individuals may have two selves (private and public). Azuma (1986) articulates the need to separate the two different realities that correspond to two different aspects of self. The relational mode is maintained in close relationships: "In interpersonal relationships defined by *amae*, a person may forget about *tatemae* and live with *honne*" (p. 8). In public situations, an individual must be able to "discriminate *uchi* ('inside'), where *amae* will be accepted and rewarded, and *soto* ('outside') where *amae* will not be so readily tolerated" (p. 8). In the relational mode, guilt plays an important role in controlling a person's behavior; in the coexistence mode, shame plays a central role. When we study Japanese culture, we usually tap the *tatemae* self and rarely the *honne* self.

Both the undifferentiated and the coexistence modes accentuate "sameness," and the relational mode emphasizes "oneness." The undifferentiated and coexistence modes prescribe behaviors, through existing norms and expectations, that demand role fulfillment at the expense of individuals' desires, opinions, and ideas. The relational mode, on the other hand, does not necessarily mean sacrificing one's wishes and goals for the in-group. It implies that working together, collectively and harmoniously, is a way of expressing and enhancing oneself. In Japan, for example, children are taught to align the goals of self-fulfillment with the goals of social integration so that both can be met simultaneously (White & LeVine, 1986).

SUMMARY AND CONCLUSION

The three facets of I/C parallel other descriptive categorizations. The syndrome represented by I/C shares characteristics described by other dichotomies: gesellschaft and gemeinschaft (Tönnies, 1887/1957), contractual and familistic relationships (Sorokin, 1948), agency and communion (Bakan, 1966), and independent view and interdependent view (Markus & Kitayama, 1991). These categorizations, along with the current description of facets of I/C, are broad brush strokes outlining a wide range of phenomena. As I noted at the outset of this chapter, these two constructs help to clarify the rather fuzzy construct of culture; allow direct linkage of psychological phenomena to a cultural dimension; help to operationalize the concept of culture; provide more concise, coherent, integrated, and empirically testable dimensions of cultural variation; allow fruitful integration of knowledge; and suggest convergence across different methodologies.

The purpose of this chapter has been to weave a pattern across different levels of analysis: individual, interpersonal, institutional, and cultural. Each facet of I/C is like a thread that is used to weave a pattern. Individualism represents a particular pattern with key moral and philosophical threads that are used to maintain, propagate, and reify a particular social structure and norms. Similarly, collectivism represents a pattern with a different set of moral and philosophical threads that are used to maintain, propagate, and reify a particular social structure and norms. The boundaries within a culture or across cultures, however, are dynamic. Thus the patterns depicted by I/C are crude approximations that need further refinement, elaboration, and validation. Finally, the generic nature of I/C must be contextualized within each culture, and the meaning and phenomenology of experience must be added to the content of I/C.

3

THEORETICAL AND METHODOLOGICAL APPROACHES TO THE STUDY OF COLLECTIVISM AND INDIVIDUALISM

HARRY C. TRIANDIS

The individualism/collectivism constructs (Lukes, 1973) have been discussed in many contexts in the social sciences. For example, in the areas of values (Hofstede, 1980; Kluckhohn & Strodtbeck, 1961), social systems (Parsons & Shils, 1951), morality (Miller, Bersoff, & Harwood, 1990; Shweder & Bourne, 1982), religion (Bakan, 1966), cognitive differentiation (Berry, 1976), economic development (Adelman & Morris, 1967), modernity (Inkeles & Smith, 1974; C. Taylor, 1989), the structure of constitutions (Massimini & Calegari, 1979), and cultural patterns (Hsu, 1983) the concepts that have been used are closely related to I/C constructs.

Individualism is very high in the United States and generally the English-speaking countries (Hofstede, 1980), and has been studied with both historical (Inkeles, 1983) and empirical (Bellah, Madsen, Sullivan, Swidler, & Tipton, 1985) methods. Collectivism can be found in parts of Europe (e.g., southern Italy, rural Greece) and much of Africa, Asia, and Latin America.

The utility of the construct is increasingly becoming clear. For example, Earley (1989) shows that "social loafing" occurs among individualist Chinese but not among collectivist Chinese working in an in-group. But collectivist Chinese "loaf" when they are in an "individual condition" or an "out-group condition." Feldman and Rosenthal (1991) found age expectations of behavioral autonomy in Hong Kong to be different from such expectations in Australia and the United States, as expected from I/C theory.

Radford, Mann, Ohta, and Nakane (1991) found the expected differences between Australian and Japanese decision processes. Han (1990) found that Korean advertising utilizes more collectivist themes and American advertising more individualist themes than the comparison culture. H. P. Brown (1990) sees a counterrevolution, in Britain, away from the socialism of the 1940s and 1950s. The trend is toward more acquisitive individualism, lower influences by groups (e.g., trade unions), and greater tendencies toward self-employment. The list could be made longer, but this sample of studies is sufficient to indicate the variety of interests in the construct.

THEORETICAL APPROACHES

Whereas ecological factor analyses, as used by Hofstede (1980), tend to provide bipolar factors suggesting that individualism and collectivism are opposite poles of one dimension, individual-level factor analyses suggest that the two can coexist and are simply emphasized more or less in each culture, depending on the situation. All of us carry both individualist and collectivist tendencies; the difference is that in some cultures the probability that individualist selves, attitudes, norms, values, and behaviors will be sampled or used is higher than in others.

The current view of I/C theory is that it consists of a set of contrasting elements (see Table 3.1) that operate like ambiguous pictures. Just as in perceptual psychology one might see a "lady" or a "pot" in a particular picture, so a person can sample a collectivist or individualist element to construct a social situation. If individuals in a culture sample collectivist elements most of the time, across most situations, then we call the culture collectivist. If we use more than one way of measuring (e.g., see Chan, Chapter 13, this volume), we can arrive at statements such as "70% of the people in this culture are collectivists, and 30% are individualists." Such statements can be useful when we make predictions about behavior in a culture, because most predictions in social psychology concern samples of individuals in a culture, rather than the behavior of one specific individual.

We can make more clinical predictions if we examine data at the individual level of analysis. Here I use the terms *idiocentric* and *allocentric* for analyses at the individual level that correspond to I/C at the cultural level (see Triandis, Leung, Villareal, & Clark, 1985). This terminology allows quick reference to the idiocentric (who selects mostly individualist solutions) in collectivist cultures and the allocentric (who selects mostly collectivist solutions) in individualist cultures. Such individuals are countercultural, but nevertheless very real. Those who join communes or gangs in individualist cultures and those who migrate from collectivist to individualist cultures because they cannot tolerate the oppression of in-group norms are examples of such countercultural individuals.

In earlier work, I proposed a theory of the self in relation to culture (Triandis, 1989). In that theory, individualist cultures had members whose selves included more private elements (e.g., I am kind, my strengths are few); collectivist cultures had selves with more collectivist elements (e.g., my family expects me to be kind; my coworkers believe that I have few strengths); members of individualist cultures also had public selves with more individualist elements (e.g., people in general expect me to be kind), and those in collectivist cultures had public selves with more collectivist elements (e.g., people in general expect me to be a good family man). Because there are more elements in the private, collective, or public selves in some cultures than in others, the probability that different types of elements will be sampled differs in different cultures.

A theoretical issue of some significance is whether the private and collective elements of the self are in one or two cognitive structures. I assumed that one structure, with different numbers of private and collective elements, was involved (Triandis, 1989). However, my colleagues and I later checked the possibility that two distinct cognitive structures might be operating (Trafimow, Triandis, & Goto, 1991). We found that private and collective self-cognitions are stored in separate locations in memory. This was indicated by the finding that priming a particular aspect of the self increases the retrieval of self-cognitions pertaining to that aspect of the self. Furthermore, the probability of retrieving a self-cognition was greater if the same type of self-cognition had been previously retrieved than if a different type had been previously retrieved.

The broadest theoretical framework for thinking about I/C is that ecology (economic geography, resource availability, subsistence level, and methods of making a living, e.g., hunting, food gathering, agriculture, industrial labor, information services) influences the social structure (number of levels of differentiation, percentage of the population in agriculture, percentage urban, family size, social and geographic mobility) (see, e.g., Whiting & Whiting, 1975). Affluence, derived from the ecology, is reflected in the social structure. An important variable is the number of groups a person can be a member of. Especially important are in-groups, defined as "sets of individuals with whom a person feels similar." The similarity may come from common fate or some other attribute. In general, collectivist in-groups are ascribed (e.g., kin, caste, race, tribe, religion, village, nation), whereas individualist in-groups are achieved (e.g., similar beliefs, attitudes, values, action programs, occupations). Some attributes may be both ascribed and achieved (e.g., nationality) and one is more likely to see a change from ascribed to achieved in individualist cultures (e.g., a person taking the citizenship of another nation).

The more complex the social structure, the greater the number of groups a person may be a member of. Individuals can then join or leave groups according to whether the groups satisfy their personal needs. Individualism is a consequence of (a) the number of available groups (e.g., urban environment), (b) affluence (one does not need groups as much if one is affluent, hence the upper classes in all societies are more individualistic), (c) social mobility, and (d) geographic mobility (if one is mobile, one can change groups more easily, and groups cannot influence individuals as much). Thus the American frontier, migration, and affluence may have been the major determinants of American individualism. In addition, cultural heterogeneity has the effect of exposing people to diverse standards and normative conflicts, which can relegate to the individual the task of deciding which norm to follow. The more individuals rather than groups decide what norms are applicable, the more individualistic is the culture. The mass media are produced in affluent cultures, and thus exposure to the mass media has the effect of exposing individuals to individualist norms. Therefore, the greater the exposure to the mass media, the greater the individualism.

Culture is here defined as the "human-made part of the environment" (Herskovits, 1955), and subjective culture is its subjective aspect, that is, the shared perceptions of the social environment (Triandis, 1972). Subjective culture results in automatic processing of information, because it specifies what is worth noticing, for which the language provides a label; how that is to be evaluated; what are desirable or proscribed behaviors for members of the culture (norms); what are desirable or proscribed behaviors for those holding positions in the social structure (roles); and what are important goals and principles in life (values). Thus, at the cultural level, the analysis of I/C should be done by studying norms, roles, and values.

Corresponding to subjective culture, at the cultural level, are psychological processes such as idiocentrism and allocentrism (Triandis et al., 1985). The analysis at this level requires the study of self-definitions, beliefs, and attitudes, as well as individual norms and values.

When studying values at the cultural level (e.g., Hofstede, 1980), many researchers simply sum the individual responses within cultures, and thus if one has 50 cultures and 30 values, one can compute the 50×30 matrix of correlations among the values (based on 50 observations per variable) and do an analysis. Clearly, this approach ignores individual differences. But is it an adequate culture-level method? There is some doubt that this is the best way to do "culture"-level studies.

An approach that might be better is to ask people in each culture to report what they believe to be the values of members of their culture, for example, to respond to the statement "Most Americans consider *freedom* an important value." The data one gets with this kind of instruction (where each subject is an "informant," in the ethnographer's sense, on his or her own culture) are not identical to the data one gets with the question "What are *your* important values?" A similar approach was used by Bierbrauer and associates in the study reported in Chapter 12 of this volume.

The relative emphasis on individualism/collectivism or idiocentrism/ allocentrism can be seen within a broader framework. In my analysis of subjective culture and in subsequent publications, I have argued that the basic dimensions of social behavior are (a) association versus dissociation, (b) superordination versus subordination, (c) intimacy versus formality, and (d) overtness versus covertness (Triandis, 1972, 1978). Adamopoulos and Bontempo (1986) report evidence that these dimensions have emerged during the course of historical development. Deutsch (1990) uses similar dimensions: (a) cooperation versus competition, (b) inequality-equality, and (c) informality versus formality. Collectivism is character-ized by associative, intimate relations with in-groups and dissociative, formal relations with out-groups. Schwartz (1990) uses self-direction, stimu-lation, hedonism, and achievement, which correspond to individualism and security, restricted conformity, traditionalism, and benevolence, which correspond to collectivism; and universalism (which includes equality) and power (which includes wealth and authority), which corresponds to Deutsch's equality-inequality dimension. Thus a number of different research programs converge in identifying the same patterns of social behavior.

However, the most convincing typology has been presented by A. Fiske (1990), who argues that humans use four models of relating to one another: *Communal sharing* is very much like collectivism, *authority ranking* emphasizes power distance (Hofstede, 1980) or superordination, *equality matching* reflects reciprocity and other such attributes of social relation-ships, and *market pricing* is very similar to individualism. Fiske moves farther than most of the other theorists, conceptually, by showing that any culture can be described using these four universal relational models, and these basic models can generate an infinite variety of social behaviors, because the way each basic model is implemented is unique to each culture.

An essential point in both my own work and Fiske's is the idea that whether one of these models is to be sampled depends on the situation. For example, I may be very individualistic, but when my university gives me the job to represent it at a meeting, I act collectivistically in that setting.

Thus the essential advance from Hofstede's (1980) formulation is that we are both allocentric and idiocentric, and we *sample* cognitive elements that correspond to these relational models differently in different situations. However, in some cultures more situations are sampled allocentrically, and in other cultures more situations are sampled idiocentrically.

There is also the possibility, suggested by Forgas and Bond (1985), that situations are grouped differently (e.g., determined in multidimensional scaling studies) in collectivist and individualist cultures. This is quite plausible and should be explored through studies of the structures of situations in various cultures.

Table 3.1 lists some of the attributes that are more likely to be sampled by idiocentrics than by allocentrics. The table is a composite summarizing several of my studies as well as studies reviewed by Markus and Kitayama (1991). The main conceptual point I am making is that the allocentric elements are likely to be sampled in more situations in collectivist cultures and the idiocentric elements more in individualist cultures. Note that each contrast in this table constitutes a hypothesis that can be tested. For example, under *values,* the table notes that allocentrics should value security more than should idiocentrics. By my count there are 66 testable hypotheses in this table. Only half a dozen of these have been tested so far, thus much work remains to be done.

The list of empirically verifiable attributes in Table 3.1 allows us to measure allocentrism and idiocentrism with multimethod procedures. To the extent that a cultural syndrome is reflected in these attributes, there should be significant positive correlations among them in each culture.

The basic argument is that individuals have in their cognitive systems all the diverse elements presented in the table, but they use these elements with greater or lesser probabilities, depending on the situation and the culture. Thus, for example, I am more likely to use the collectivist elements when I am in a collectivist culture, or when I am interacting with a person I know comes from a collectivist culture; I am more likely to also use the collectivist elements in my family than at work, because I was socialized in Greece with respect to how to interact within the family, and in the United States with respect to how to interact at work. However, the use of these elements becomes habitual (Triandis, 1980b). Once a person develops the habit of using individualist elements, the switch to the use of collectivist elements requires quite a lot of "cognitive work"—that is, the person has to instruct him- or herself to suppress individualist tendencies in that situation. This is similar to a point made by Devine (1989), who shows that stereotypes have both automatic (habitual) and control (information processing) components, and low-prejudiced Americans have learned to suppress the automatic component.

Table 3.1 The Defining Attributes of Allocentrics and Idiocentrics

Allocentrics	Idiocentrics
Cut the pie of experience by focusing on:	
Groups as the basic units of social perception	*Individuals* as the basic units of social perception
Attributions:	
Others' behaviors explained as reflecting norms	Others' behaviors explained by reference to personality traits, attitudes
Success attributed to help from others	Success attributed to own ability
Failure attributed to lack of effort	Failure attributed to external factors (e.g., task difficulty, bad luck)
Self-defined in terms of in-groups, relationships	*Self*-defined as an independent entity
Know more about others than about self	Know more about self than about others
Self is more similar to friends than friends to self	Self is less similar to friends than friends to self
Have few self-linked memories	Have many self-linked memories
Achievement for the group's sake, cooperation, endurance, order, self-control	Achievement for self-glory, competition, exhibition, power
Experience little cognitive dissonance	Experience much cognitive dissonance
Goals: In-group goals have primacy or overlap personal goals	Personal goals have primacy over in-group goals
Emotion:	
Other-focused (empathy), short duration	Self-focused (anger), long duration
Like those who are modest	Like those who are self-assured
Cognitions:	
What makes me the same as my group. Needs of in-group	What makes me different, distinguished My needs, rights, capacity (obligations, contracts)
Cognitions are context-dependent	Cognitions are context-independent
Attitudes: Favor beliefs that reflect interdependence	Favor beliefs that reflect independence, emotional detachment from in-groups
Norms: Favor embeddedness in in-groups	Favor independence from in-groups
Values: Security, obedience, duty, in-group harmony, hierarchy, personalized relationships	Pleasure, achievement, competition, freedom, autonomy, fair exchange
Major calamity:	
Ostracism	Dependence on others.
In-groups: Few, but relationship to them is close, with much concern for their integrity	Many, relationships are casual, little emotional involvement; less willingness to self-sacrifice for the in-group
In-group perceived as more homogeneous than out-groups	In-group perceived as more heterogeneous than out-groups

(*continued*)

Table 3.1 Continued

Allocentrics	Idiocentrics
Harmony required. In-group influences many behaviors, and influence is deep	Debate, confrontation are acceptable
Defined by similarity in ascribed attributes (e.g., kinship, caste, race, village, tribe)	Defined by similarity in achieved attributes (e.g., beliefs, occupation)
Accepted structure: Hierarchical	Egalitarian
Vertical relations more important than horizontal	Horizontal relations more important than vertical
Social behavior: Very different when the other person belongs to an in-group versus an out-group	Only somewhat different when the other person is an in-group versus an out-group member
Difficult to get to be friendly, but relationships are intimate after they are established	Easy entry and exit from groups, but relationships are mostly nonintimate
Cooperation with in-group members; communal exchanges	People appear very sociable but relationships are superficial and depend on social exchanges and contracts
Mutual face saving	Personal face saving
Regulated by in-group norms	Regulated by attitudes, cost-benefit computations, and generalized public norms
Interdependent (e.g., communal bathing)	Independent (e.g., privacy)
Select mates who will maximize family integrity	Select mates who are physically attractive and have "exciting" personalities

Support for This Framework

Indirect evidence that in collectivist cultures people think in terms of groups, whereas in individualist cultures they think in terms of individuals, comes from the work on the perception of in-group/out-group homogeneity/heterogeneity. Triandis, McCusker, and Hui (1990) present evidence that in collectivist cultures in-groups are perceived to be more homogeneous than out-groups. Additional support for this point is presented by Lee and Ottati (1990), who show that American subjects perceive Americans as more heterogeneous than Chinese, whereas Chinese subjects perceive Chinese as less heterogeneous than Americans. The collectivist pattern is contrary to the usual finding in the West (e.g., Quattrone, 1986) that in-groups are perceived as more heterogeneous than out-groups. However, it can be explained by the argument presented by Kashima (1989) and demonstrated experimentally: When people focus on what people have in common within a group (i.e., focus on the group), they see the group as relatively homogeneous; when people focus on the individuals who constitute the group, they see the group as relatively heterogeneous.

The discussion of attributions reflects, in part, the study by Kashima and Triandis (1986), but is also consistent with Bontempo and Rivero's (1992) meta-analysis of cross-cultural studies, which used the Fishbein attitude-behavior model. They found that individualists' behavior is more closely linked to attitudes and collectivists' behavior is more closely linked to norms. I am also willing to speculate that the fundamental attribution error will be stronger in individualist than in collectivist cultures.

The self-definitions reflect the content analysis of responses to 20 statements that begin with "I am . . . ," as reported in Triandis, McCusker, and Hui (1990). It is also consistent with several studies reviewed by Markus and Kitayama (1991). Mitchell and Silver (1990) have shown, experimentally, that people in an individual goal condition are more competitive than people in three other goal conditions (no specific goal, group goal, and individual plus group goal).

The section in the table on major calamity is taken from Markus and Kitayama (1991). Recall that in the United States children are punished by being "grounded," whereas in Japan they are put out of the house! The section on in-groups reflects theoretical arguments presented in Triandis (1988b) and empirical studies reviewed in Triandis (1990). The section on accepted structure reflects the work of Hofstede (1980), who found that collectivism correlated about .7 with high power distance. However, the two dimensions are theoretically distinct, as is reflected in the work of A. Fiske (1990). We need to do a study utilizing the Human Relations Area Files, to check if the link between collectivism and hierarchy is a general finding or reflects the particular sample of countries used by Hofstede.

The table's section on social behavior summarizes studies reviewed in Triandis (1990). The mate selection point is reflected in the work of Buss et al. (1990). Dion, Pak, and Dion (1990) show that people in collectivist cultures pay less attention to physical attraction than do people in individualist cultures, as would be expected from the argument that in individualist cultures people are more hedonistic.

METHODOLOGICAL APPROACHES

A number of studies have already appeared in the literature (Georgas, 1986; Hui, 1988; Hui & Triandis, 1986; Marin & Triandis, 1985; Triandis et al., 1986; Triandis, Bontempo, Villareal, Asai, & Lucca, 1988; Triandis, McCusker, & Hui, 1990). A summary of many of these studies, as well as the related literature, can be found in Triandis (1990). The basic findings, thus far, generally confirm Hofstede's contention that European-derived cultures are more individualistic than Asian or Latin American cultures, and that affluence, social mobility, and small family size are antecedents of individualism. In addition, there is evidence that individualism and collectivism are "cultural syndromes"; that is, beliefs, attitudes, norms, roles, values, and behaviors found in certain cultures converge and also differ in expected ways from beliefs, attitudes, norms, values, and behaviors found in other cultures.

DISCUSSION

The power of I/C theory, as developed in Triandis (1988b), is that it predicts attitudinal, value, and behavioral results in diverse parts of the world (e.g., Gudykunst, Yoon, & Nishida, 1987; Wheeler, Reis, & Bond, 1989). It shows that phenomena that are not obviously linked, such as the greater rejection of out-groups in diverse collectivist cultures than in diverse individualist cultures and the greater difficulties of communicating with strangers in diverse collectivist than in diverse individualist cultures (Gudykunst et al., 1987), follow the same social science laws, just as the behaviors of falling apples and asteroids follow similar physical laws.

The striking similarities in behavior patterns found in very different locations around the world, which apparently have in common only that the cultures are characterized by more collectivist or more individualist behaviors, make the construct quite useful. For example, La Rosa and Diaz-Loving (1988) did an exhaustive study of the Mexican self-concept. The factor that accounted for most of the variance in a factor analysis included these scales: respectful, amiable, decent, amicable, desirable, educated, courteous, and attentive. The similarity to the Greek concept of *philotimos* (doing what the in-group wants one to do; well socialized) is striking.

The essential element of the recommended strategy for further research on I/C is the use of multimethod approaches. We have used systematic observations of behavior (e.g., how frequently people in the street walk alone or with others), asked people to define themselves (e.g., required them to write 20 sentences that begin with the words "I am . . . "), explored the attitudes they have (e.g., do they agree or disagree with "Before taking an important decision it is desirable to consult many of one's friends and relatives"?), and investigated what values they endorse (e.g., had subjects respond to the values list developed by Schwartz, and in individualist samples they endorsed values such as "an exciting life" and "pleasure," whereas in collectivist cultures they endorsed values such as "family security" and "honoring parents and elders"). Wheeler et al. (1989) studied the interactions that occur in Hong Kong and the United States by having subjects keep diaries. Their results are quite consistent with I/C theory. Finally, Triandis, McCusker, and Hui (1990) obtained psychophysical judgments relating social distance (as the x-axis) and the basic dimensions of social behavior mentioned above (as the y-axes) from samples in the People's Republic of China and the United States. It was found that whereas people in the United States and the People's Republic of China were similar in their levels of intimacy toward close relatives and toward people toward whom they experienced much social distance, the PRC sample showed more intimacy toward targets of intermediate social distance (e.g., coworkers) than did the U.S. sample. Also, the PRC sample showed more dissociation, more superordination, and less subordination toward large social distance targets than did the U.S. sample. These results are consistent with the attributes listed in Table 3.1, but much more observational work combined with other methods is in order.

CONCLUSION

All of this work must necessarily be considered as preliminary. There is a need for replication and extension. However, the extent to which consistency has been obtained across the various methods of the study of the theoretical constructs suggests that there is a really important cultural syndrome that corresponds to I/C.

4

A CRITICAL APPRAISAL OF
INDIVIDUALISM AND COLLECTIVISM
Toward a New Formulation

ÇIGDEM KAGITÇIBASI

A massive amount of work has been carried out in the area of individualism and collectivism since 1980, so much so that the 1980s may be called the decade of I/C in cross-cultural psychology. An overview of the literature is provided in a recent article on cross-cultural psychology in the *Annual Review of Psychology* (Kagitçibasi & Berry, 1989), and other reviews are available (e.g., Kagitçibasi, 1987; Triandis, 1990; Triandis et al., 1986; Triandis, Bontempo, Villareal, Asai, & Lucca, 1988). It is important to note that research on I/C has not been limited to any specific behavioral domain, but has covered an astonishingly wide array of domains. Together with a great deal of empirical research, significant attempts at conceptualization and operationalization have also been made. Nevertheless, there is still something elusive about the concepts of I/C.

In this chapter I will attempt to do two things. I will first try to discover the reasons for this elusiveness. In doing this I will point out the problems involved in the current treatment of the topic. Second, I will propose a rather delimited domain of study that I consider promising for a more basic treatment of the topic, namely, the psychology of relatedness. The main part of the chapter, however, is devoted to a critique of the current treatment of I/C.

WHERE WE ARE IN I/C

Essentially, four types of empirical evidence have brought I/C to the fore. First, there appear to be systematic differences among societies, in fact it is possible to rank order societies in terms of where they stand on these variables (e.g., see Chinese Culture Connection, 1987; Hofstede, 1980). Second, subjects from individualist cultures tend to have individualist values and behaviors, and subjects from collectivist cultures tend to have collectivist values and behaviors (Triandis, Chapter 3, this volume). Third, this difference is also found in other psychological processes as well, so that predictions can be made for a wide variety of behaviors (Triandis, Chapter 3, this volume). Fourth, in addition to cultural differences, I/C also shows within culture variability, at the individual level, and therefore can be used in explaining individual/group differences in various psychological characteristics.

Given such high potential for predictive and explanatory use as well as flexibility for use in societal, group, and individual levels of analysis, it is no wonder that I/C has gained such tremendous popularity in recent research. However, together with this great promise of I/C as a wide-ranging and flexible explanatory/predictive construct goes the danger that it is too readily used as an explanation for every behavior studied cross-culturally— a catchall construct.

Cross-cultural psychologists often use culture-level explanations for observed differences in behavior. This is problematic, because culture is too diffuse a concept and therefore a poor independent variable (Segall, 1983) unless its links with behavior are specified in terms of mediating variables (see also in this volume Bond, Chapter 5; Schwartz, Chapter 7). In the absence of refined intervening variables, "what" in culture "causes" behavior is often not clear. Explanations resorting to I/C appear to be particularly prone to this weakness, because the construct is being used so readily, almost synonymously with cultural differences in general. Yet at times it is not clear whether I/C is the relevant antecedent variable for the observed differences in behavior.

For example, it is found that need norm is used more by Indian than by American subjects in allocating rewards (Berman, Murphy-Berman, & Singh, 1985). To conclude from such a finding that it is the greater collectivism of Indian subjects that makes them more prone to use the need norm rather than merit is unwarranted. Such reasoning ignores alternative explanations, such as greater salience of scarce resources for (Greenberg, 1981; Leung, 1988b) or greater sensitivity to poverty of Indian subjects. Thus the high salience and availability of I/C (high face validity?) is as much a source of potential weakness as it is of strength in cross-cultural explanations. It may in fact be the case that the finding of greater need norm use by Indian subjects could be attributable to any of the other antecedents of I/C. However, this is to be demonstrated empirically, not assumed from the start. In fact, Marin (1985; cited in Triandis, 1990), in a review, found I/C to be better than other explanations; but more systematic work of this sort is needed to unravel the antecedents of an observed behavior and to determine their relative importance.

Another attraction of I/C for cross-cultural psychologists is its potential for becoming a universal dimension of variation across cultures (Triandis, 1987). Given its applicability at different levels of analysis—societal, group, and individual—it promises to be a theoretically and practically important construct in our understanding of the cross-culturally varying links among these different levels of analysis. For example, it can be used to develop insights into the relationship between the psychological characteristics of a people and their level of economic development (i.e., the noneconomic factors underlying economic development; Kagitçibasi, 1990). This is an issue that has interested social scientists and others for a long time: the question of why some have made it and others have not. Several psychological concepts have been proposed as key variables to deal with this issue, such as achievement motivation (McClelland, 1961) and individual modernity (Inkeles, 1969; Inkeles & Smith, 1974; Smith & Inkeles, 1966). However, the high hopes put into these key concepts, such as achievement motivation and individual modernity, for enhancing our understanding of the varying levels of development in the world or even for "motivating" economic achievement, have met with some disillusionment. The enthusiasm of the 1960s and the early 1970s has died down almost to the degree of discrediting these concepts as Western impositions (see Yu & Yang, Chapter 16, this volume, for a review). Is I/C going to face the same fate? It is hard to conceive of such an end at this time, when its popularity has soared so high. Nevertheless, there is that potential danger if the concept is used too loosely, as mentioned before. If it is employed to explain everything, it may not be able to explain anything.

PROBLEMS OF CONCEPTUALIZATION

One possible reason for the elusive nature of I/C may be that the research and conceptualization are too recent, in fact ongoing, and thus a certain distancing has not yet occurred. Apart from this, however, a number of problems are apparent in the treatment of the topic that contribute to this elusiveness and the loose, catchall characteristic of the concepts. Some of these problems are rather basic and have to do with general metatheoretical orientations, whereas others are more specific conceptual-methodological issues. One problem has to do with semantics and the value-laden connotations of the terms used.

Semantic Issues

In the social sciences it is hard to create value-free concepts and terminology, because these are not formed in a vacuum but emerge in a sociocultural-ideological context. This can cause conceptual confusion and sensitivities on the part of those who have to use these concepts and terminology. I believe this is particularly troublesome in the case of individualism and collectivism, especially the latter. The original terms *gesellschaft* and *gemeinschaft* (Tönnies, 1887/1957) indeed referred to societal types, and Hofstede (1980; see also his foreword to this volume) identifies the I/C continuum as a dimension of national cultures. Nevertheless, in the hands of psychologists using individual-level analysis, there is a shift, often back and forth, between macro and micro levels, resulting in some conceptual confusion. This is well recognized (see Hofstede's foreword), and other terms have been proposed for use at the individual level, such as *idiocentric* and *allocentric* (Triandis, Leung, Villareal, & Clark, 1985) and *individual loyalties* and *group loyalties* (Kagitçibasi, 1987). Nevertheless, these terms have not caught on to the same degree.

In addition to the confusion caused by the multilevel use of the terms *individualism* and *collectivism*, their value-laden connotations are troublesome. Again, *collectivism* especially carries a pejorative meaning (Lawler, 1980, p. 164); it is associated with conformity to group pressure, crowd behavior, deindividuation, and the like in the social psychological literature and also has negative political overtones (e.g., collective farms). It is unfortunate that the word *collectivism* was used to start with, because it looks like it is here to stay, yet it is not even a "psychological" concept, in the sense of referring to an *individual-level* behavior or cognitive process.

Of course, one reason collectivism carries this negative excess meaning is because most research and researchers view it from a Western or, more specifically, American perspective, from which individualism is highly valued, notwithstanding criticisms (e.g., Sampson, 1977, 1987; Smith, 1993). Such negative connotations can influence interpretation and blur the boundaries between scientific inquiry and ideological thinking. Furthermore, interpretations that are perceived to be value laden (or prejudiced) can create sensitivities and reactions on the part of psychologists from collectivist cultures, thus again pushing the debate beyond scientific limits.

Other Issues

Some other problems of conceptualization that are as yet unresolved have to do with whether individualism and collectivism are polar opposites of a single dimension or are independent dimensions and whether they are situation and target specific or have traitlike generality over situations and targets (Kagitçibasi, 1987). It is important to note here, however, that there is evidence supporting the view that these concepts do not necessarily form opposite poles and may coexist in individuals or groups in different situations or with different target groups (Kagitçibasi, 1987; Triandis, 1990; Triandis et al., 1988; Yang, 1988; see also, in this volume, Sinha & Tripathi, Chapter 8; Ho & Chiu, Chapter 9). Therefore, the common tendency to pit individualism against collectivism and use them as general traits across time and space is not warranted. They should, rather, be treated in probabilistic terms, as, for example, the likelihood of a person or a group of people behaving in individualist or collectivist ways in various situations (Triandis, 1989; see also Chapter 3, this volume).

THE EVOLUTIONARY PROBLEM

The problem of value-laden conceptualization appears to be especially acute in an evolutionary approach to I/C. *Evolution* means the development of more complicated forms (of life) from earlier and simpler forms, and in this sense, what is more developed and comes later in time is better than the less developed and older form. The history of cross-cultural psychology, as well as that of anthropology, is replete with evolutionary views regarding, for example, "primitives' childlike cognition" and assumed fundamental differences among peoples in basic psychological processes (see Cole & Scribner, 1974, for a review). In the history of sociological and anthropological thinking, the classic concept of social evolution, meaning progressive differentiation of function (Durkheim, 1930; Spencer, 1990), has been important. With the rise and fall of modernization theory in the 1960s and 1970s, however, this concept is no longer in common use. It has been more or less abandoned.

Nevertheless, there appears to be a revival of interest in the idea of societal progression on the part of some cross-cultural psychologists. For example, Yang (1988) asks if societal modernization will eliminate cross-cultural psychological differences, and Hofstede (1980) and Triandis (1984, 1988a) consider individualism rather than collectivism to be compatible with social organization, economic development, and cultural and social complexity.

There are two different but related issues here, namely, the parallels between modernization and individualism on the one hand and the assumed progression toward individualism with societal development on the other. I will deal with these in that order.

THE PARALLEL WITH
MODERNIZATION THEORY

After reviewing research conducted with the individual modernity paradigm, Yang (1988) correctly notes the great similarity between core modern characteristics deriving from the 1960s' individual modernity research and "Hofstede's (1980) and Waterman's (1984) individualism on the left pole of the I/C construct, as conceptualized by Hui and Triandis (1986) and Triandis (1987)" (p. 77). Yang's check of some 20 individual modernity traits indeed revealed that about two-thirds reflected individualism. Thus in the 1980s conceptualization of individualism we see a revival of the 1960s modernization paradigm. The implication of this is that, as the antithesis of individualism, collectivism may be expected to be replaced by individualism through the process of modernization. Thus the evolutionary progression view is clearly in the tradition of modernization theory.

It may be useful to recall the socioeconomic context in which modernization theory emerged and its concepts were utilized. In many Third World countries, the 1950s and 1960s marked the beginnings of massive social structural changes, including population growth and the migration of peasants from villages into cities, looking for jobs. Formerly completely isolated people started to be exposed to mass media and urban lifestyles and values. In this context the psychological characteristics conducive to modernization assumed greater interest for sociologists and policy makers. Some of these included positive attitudes toward achievement rather than ascription; freedom from primordial ties and parental authority; participation in secondary groups; interest in participation in national activities, nationalism; openness to innovation; self-reliance and sense of personal efficacy; belief in science rather than religiosity; (future) time orientation, punctuality; individualist orientation; positive attitudes toward education and information; belief in internal control of reinforcement; optimism; flexibility; risk taking; high educational and occupational aspirations; preference for urban life; exposure to mass media; and activism (Dawson, 1967; Doob, 1960; Inkeles, 1969; Inkeles & Smith, 1974; Kahl, 1968; Kagitçibasi, 1973; Smith & Inkeles, 1966).

What modernization theory showed was that psychological orientations adaptive to urbanization emerged in the process of urbanization, and that those groups or individuals who had or developed more of these psychological characteristics adapted better to social change. It had to do, basically, with attitudes that could change with changing environmental demands, rather than with basic psychological processes. Indeed, Inkeles

(1969) found that with every year of formal education, subjects gained three points on the 100-point OM (Overall Modernity) Scale.

With the majority of the populations in many developing countries now living in urban or semiurban conditions and the ready availability of the mass media, many characteristics of the individual modernity syndrome are now commonplace, not novel or even "modern." Furthermore, the individual modernity paradigm was severely criticized (Bendix, 1967; Gusfield, 1967) for pitting modernity against tradition and assuming that the former will replace the latter, considered by some to be in the tradition of social Darwinism (e.g., Mazrui, 1968).

It appears that individual modernity is not a coherent syndrome at all; rather, those characteristics incompatible with the demands of urban living give way to more compatible ones, and those characteristics that are not incompatible with those demands endure even though they may be labeled "traditional" from a Western perspective. There is no overall progression to a higher level of social development, but rather shifts and adjustments in dysfunctional psychological characteristics. In fact, in current sociological thinking the term *modernism* is being used in a very different sense than in 1960s usage. It is not contrasted with tradition, but rather with postmodernism. No progression is assumed from a less to a more "developed" societal state, and "new traditions" are seen to be created in the postmodern era.

The very same analysis applies to I/C. Some aspects of individualism are adaptive to urban living conditions, and they can be expected to become more prevalent with urbanization/industrialization. However, those aspects of collectivism that do not conflict with urban living conditions need not change, or new types of collectivism (or individualism) may be created alternatively or at the same time, and these may coexist (see Sinha & Tripathi, Chapter 8, this volume). After the experience of modernization theory in social sciences, cross-cultural psychologists need not fall again into the trap of "misplaced polarities" (Gusfield, 1967).

Accordingly, the tendency to (over)generalize to many different behavioral domains and to create a "syndrome" may not be warranted in substantive terms, quite apart from the risk of forming a too-loose catchall construct, as mentioned before. Nevertheless, *individualism* and *collectivism* are being used in ways similar to the terms *modernity* and *tradition* (or *conservatism*), respectively. For example, Triandis and his colleagues associate individualism with such diverse factors as cultural complexity, capacity for social organization, economic development, modernity, mobility, low primary group orientation, small family size, using universalistic rather than particularistic exchanges in in-groups, having many in-groups, and even higher cognitive complexity and creativity. Collectivism, on the other hand, is associated with opposite factors, as well as with conformity, low levels of natural resources, ethnocentrism, corrupt governments, "tight" culture, and lower levels of stress-related diseases (Triandis, 1987, 1988a).

Such an all-encompassing typology is problematic on several grounds. First of all, some of the characteristics mentioned may have more to do with socioeconomic development, level of affluence and education, and rural or urban residence than with I/C. Second, some of these generalizations are not based on sound evidence. For example, it may not be collectivism that prevents social organization and public interest, but poverty and low levels of education, because it takes affluence to be altruistic and education to develop public awareness. Indeed, it has also been claimed (e.g., Sampson, 1987; Smith, 1993) that self-contained individualism threatens social harmony and the public good. There is also evidence from earlier studies that in collectivist nations group loyalties often extend far beyond the family and other kin to national loyalties, whereas in the context of individualism individual interests are most important (Gillespie & Allport, 1955; Kagitçibasi, 1970, 1973).

In fact, often the societal characteristics associated with I/C, like those relating to modernization, refer to socioeconomic development levels and make sense mainly at the level of shifts from tribal-agrarian to urban lifestyles, not in urbanized contexts in collectivist and individualist cultures. As I mentioned earlier, rural to urban mobility, even extending into international labor migration, has been going on worldwide since the 1950s, with the resultant concentration of populations in Third World cities. For example, the Turkish population was 80% rural in 1950; today it is only 40% rural. Thus the claim that high mobility is associated with individualism is questionable.

THE CULTURAL COMPLEXITY ISSUE

Inherent in a social evolutionary stance on individualism and collectivism is the association of the former with cultural complexity (Triandis, 1988a, 1989; Triandis et al., 1988). This appears to be particularly problematic given the positive connotation of the word *complex* and the negative one of *simple*. The most recent typology seems to be "simple, collectivist, tight" versus "complex, individualistic, loose" cultures (Triandis, 1988a).

Cultural complexity is an anthropological construct, also used by sociologists, to refer to the level of social development of a collectivity. Naroll

(1956) uses three indicators, craft specialization, organizational ramification, and urbanization, in ranking mostly preliterate and all preindustrial
peoples from the Human Relations Area Files. His main urbanization
indicator is the size of the largest settlement, and he notes that when this
size exceeds 500 people, it facilitates organizational ramification and thus
social development/complexity.

It is obvious that the cultural/social complexity concept, like the modernization concept, makes sense in the passage from isolated tribal, rural,
agrarian preindustrial conditions into nation-states or when comparing
different types of preindustrial societies, such as hunters-gatherers and
sedentary subsistence agriculturists, but not when comparing mostly urban
contemporary nations (see also Berry, Chapter 6, this volume). If, for example, Naroll's size of the largest settlement indicator were to be used,
we would end up ranking Mexico City as the world's most culturally complex society.

Accordingly, the U-shaped relationship between cultural complexity
and I/C (Triandis et al., 1988, p. 324) appears unwarranted. There is research
evidence pointing to higher individualism among hunters, fishers, and
gatherers than among high food-accumulating agriculturists or horticul-
turists, which has been explained in terms of ecologically determined
different socialization patterns (Barry, Child, & Bacon, 1959; Berry, 1976,
1979). However, this has recently been challenged by Billings and Majors
(1989), who worked with two Melanesian Island cultures. They provide
evidence for the existence of both tight (group, collectivist) and loose
(individualist) societies with the same ecological contexts and modes of
subsistence. They did not find appreciable differences between the tight
and loose peoples in terms of group stratification and hierarchy (complexity) either (p. 97). Westen (1985) also questions Barry et al.'s (1959)
interpretation of high individualism among hunters and gatherers and
attributes low individualism in more complex agricultural societies to the
rise of classical religions, which suppress individualism.

If even at this preindustrial level there appears an uncertainty about the
relationship between complexity and I/C, the contention that higher levels
of complexity are associated with individualism stands on very shaky
ground in contemporary societies, which are all highly complex. It seems
absurd, for example, to claim that New Zealanders are more individualistic than Indians or Japanese because New Zealand is more socially or
culturally complex than India or Japan. Any such claim would have to
define very clearly what is meant by *cultural complexity*.

NEED FOR REFINEMENT

The above discussion clearly shows the need to disentangle psychological-level variables relating to I/C from social-normative ones. Paralleling the findings of modernization studies, the social-normative aspects of I/C may be expected to change in response to changing lifestyles, social structural changes, and the like. However, psychological aspects of I/C, which are not directly influenced by social structural changes, may not change. For example, belonging to more than one homogeneous group may be necessitated by urban living and working conditions. However, *how* one relates to other in-group members and how closely one is interconnected with them may remain the same. Thus, for example, work organizations are prevalent in all urban contexts in the world, but whereas such organizations are typically "secondary" groups in Western societies, they assume "primary" group qualities in Japan.

With such conceptual refinement, we may be able to discover those aspects of collectivism that may be expected to change with changing lifestyles (e.g., industrial development) and those others that may not be affected by such changes. Similarly, we may discover if some aspects of individualism can be expected to weaken in the postindustrial era whereas some others may endure.

PSYCHOLOGY OF RELATEDNESS

A promising domain for conceptual and operational refinement is the analysis of basic human relatedness involving such concepts as personal boundaries and dependence/independence. If there are cultural differences in this domain, as claimed, and if such systematic differences in relational behavior can be empirically established and related to distinct antecedent conditions, then we may be getting closer to discovering a psychological aspect of I/C and possibly a universal dimension of human behavior.

It appears to me that there are some basic variations in core personal-interpersonal characteristics irrespective of socioeconomic variations. This is because the converging effects of economic change and urbanization in the world do not act directly upon these psychological-level variables. Focusing on these psychological variables, therefore, helps us to go beyond the common effects of modernization that may mask underlying diversity. The antecedents of these psychological variables in general and the psychology of relatedness, in particular, are the cultures of relatedness and separateness, mediated through socialization and child

rearing. The *culture of relatedness* refers to the family culture and interpersonal relational patterns characterized by dependent-interdependent
relations with overlapping personal boundaries. The *culture of separateness,* on the other hand, reflects the opposite pattern of independent
interpersonal relations, with separated and well-defined personal boundaries (Kagitçibasi, 1987, 1990). A similar conceptualization is used by Markus
and Kitayama (1991) in distinguishing *interdependent* and *independent*
construals of self. Thus this is a psychological conceptualization of culture
and of collectivism and individualism, respectively.

A promising research area for accomplishing the above goal is the examination of early socialization and mother (caretaker)-child interaction.
A good example is Choi's (1992) work on communicative socialization
processes among Korean and Canadian mother-child pairs. This study
points to a fundamental difference between Korean and Canadian mothers'
communicative patterns with their children. Choi found Korean mother-
child interactions to have a "communicative pattern relationally attuned
to one another in a fused state," where the mothers freely enter their children's reality and speak for them, "merging themselves with the children."
The Canadian mothers, on the other hand, were "distinguished by their
effort to detach themselves from the children . . . withdrawing themselves
from the children's reality, so that the children's reality can remain autonomous." This is quite similar to Azuma's characterization of the mother-
child interaction in Japan, where the mother's message to the child is "I
am one with you, we can be and will be of the same mind" (discussed in
Kagitçibasi, 1990, p. 156).

The above differences resulting from Choi's meticulous analysis of
mother-child utterances cannot be the result of socioeconomic status or
education differences, because these were matched. They reflect some
basic cultural differences in the definition of self and other and in the meaning
attached to rearing and interacting with one's child. Even though Choi
does not interpret her findings in terms of I/C, I believe that they are highly
relevant in pointing to some key antecedents of I/C in terms of the psychology of relatedness. More basic research along these lines is needed to
ground I/C firmly within psychological theory.

The above discussion has focused on the significance of cross-cultural
differences in the psychology of relatedness. This is not to say, however,
that there are no commonalities. Elsewhere, I have proposed a model of
family change (Kagitçibasi, 1990) based on the dual common human needs
for agency (autonomy) and communion (relatedness), going back to conflict theories of personality (Angyal, 1951; Bakan, 1966, 1968; Rank, 1945).
Here is a recognition of the coexistence of these two basic conflicting
needs everywhere. However, their expression in behavior, relative to one

another, varies with context. Individualism may be conceived as the expression of the need for autonomy and collectivism as that for relatedness. When viewed this way, the psychology of relatedness would again throw light on I/C at a basic psychological level. Such study would need to assume a dialectic orientation, given the conflicting nature of the two needs involved. Thus an individualism that does not recognize the need for relatedness and a collectivism that does not recognize the need for autonomy would not do justice to the two basic human needs. A dialectical synthesis of the two would appear to be a more optimizing solution.

Accordingly, in the model of the family I have developed, I differentiate three types: X, the collectivist model based on communion (total interdependence); Z, the individualistc model based on agency (independence); and Y, a dialectical synthesis of the two (Kagitçibasi, 1990). Furthermore, relatedness is conceptualized along two dimensions, material and emotional. The individualist model of relatedness (pattern Z) involves independence along both dimensions, the collectivist model (pattern X) involves interdependence along both, and the synthetic model (pattern Y) involves independence along the material and interdependence along the emotional dimensions. In pattern X, parent-child interactions are oriented toward obedience; in pattern Z, autonomy and self-reliance are stressed; in pattern Y, however, both control/dependence and autonomy orientations are seen in child socialization. The last model (Y) is considered a more optimizing model of relatedness (and family), because it integrates the two basic needs for autonomy and relatedness through child socialization. Accordingly, I have predicted a general shift in family and human relational patterns toward this model. A great deal of evidence, which I have reviewed elsewhere (Kagitçibasi, 1990) but cannot dwell upon here, supports this prediction. I can only point to continuing relatedness (collectivist) patterns in some non-Western-industrialized-urbanized contexts, mentioned before, and the search for relatedness in the postmodern society.

An applied research in low-income areas of Istanbul has provided evidence for the coexistence of dependency and autonomy orientations in mothers' child-rearing values (Kagitçibasi, Sunar, & Bekman, 1988). Initial assessments of mothers revealed strong needs for close ties with their children and the valuing of dependence and obedience. A randomly selected group of mothers then participated in a two-year parent education program involving cognitive enrichment and sensitization to the needs of the growing child. The existing close-knit family emotional ties were reinforced, but new values were also introduced encouraging autonomy in children. In the reassessments after the intervention, it was found that subjects in the experimental group valued autonomous behavior in their children more than did those in the control group. Yet both groups continued to encourage relational-dependent behavior in their children and to prefer close emotional ties. A coexistence or synthesis of individualist and relational values was thus made possible through a training program.

Other research also points to the coexistence of individualist and collectivist child-rearing orientations, supporting model Y. For example, Lin and Fu (1990), in a comparison of Chinese, immigrant Chinese, and Caucasian American parents, found the two Chinese groups to be higher than the American group on both parental control *and* encouragement of independence and emphasis on achievement. Also, Phalet and Claeys (1993) found *combined* preferences among modern urban Turkish youth for both loyalty (to the family and the larger group/society) and "self-realization" contrasted with self-realization, alone, among Belgian youth. Similar findings of "social achievement motivation" have been reported from India (Agarwal & Misra, 1986). Research such as that discussed above, focusing again on the psychology of relatedness and looking into new combinations (coexistence, synthesis) of individualist and collectivist orientations, promises to contribute to better conceptualizations in this area (see Sinha & Tripathi, Chapter 8, this volume).

In all likelihood, the thinking and research on I/C will continue throughout the 1990s. Three logical alternative outcomes seem possible at this time. First, the view that commonality is greater than diversity may prevail—that is, that there are no fundamental differences across cultures to warrant a universal human dimension of I/C, that the variations are apparent, not real, and have more to do with content than with psychological processes. This is a more likely outcome if the analyses focus on the most fundamental level, such as the two basic needs, mentioned above. Nevertheless, even at this level the differences in the relative emphasis put on the two basic needs would clearly point to diversity. Similarly, research results such as Choi's (1992) would challenge this view. Also, beyond the basic needs level, it appears unlikely that no systematic differences would be found.

Second, the view that differences are real but temporary may prevail—that is, the convergence hypothesis predicting increasing psychological similarity with economic development, industrialization, and Western-dominated mass media in the world. On the basis of research outcomes this view appears problematic if it is seen in an evolutionary perspective, as a total shift toward individualism with socioeconomic development. As discussed above, such a shift would be more likely in some behavioral domains (directly influenced by socioeconomic development) than in others. On the other hand, from a dialectical perspective, a convergence toward a pattern integrating both individualism and collectivism (relatedness) appears entirely possible.

Third, the view that there are fundamental lasting differences may prevail. Again, it depends on the level of analysis whether this outcome is likely or not. In the face of forces toward convergence, lasting differences would be more likely at the level of the basic psychology of relatedness than in the social-normative aspects of I/C.

It may be argued that these are not necessarily alternative outcomes, but that commonalities will be discovered in some fundamental processes and differences will be forthcoming in others, and also that there will be some shifts toward convergence in line with the common changes in environmental demands. In this chapter I have attempted to analyze the grounds for making these distinctions.

Smaller-range models and theories focusing on delimited areas would be more effective than attempts to formulate all-encompassing theoretical schemes. The psychology of relatedness, covering relational patterns of dependence/independence and personal boundaries, presents itself as a promising area for the cross-cultural psychological study of I/C. It may be an area of research and conceptualization that comes closest to being core I/C. This is because whether the self is defined as separate from others or as partially overlapping with them (i.e., the degree to which self-perception is relational, dependent-interdependent) or individuated (independent) is conceptually more basic than any other aspects of I/C (Kagitçibasi, 1990; Markus & Kitayama, 1991). Whether there are no differences in these basic self-perceptions or significant differences that may or may not converge will have far-reaching implications for all other behavioral aspects of I/C.

What is called for is a second generation of research activity in the 1990s that will build upon the first-generation research of the 1980s and go beyond it. I/C provides a rich conceptual framework and many hypotheses that are testable through empirical research. The critical appraisal I have attempted here is not meant to discourage research in this area; on the contrary, it is a call for better theoretical development through cross-cultural research.

5

INTO THE HEART OF COLLECTIVISM
A Personal and Scientific Journey

MICHAEL HARRIS BOND

> One reason we can see so far is that we stand upon the shoulders of those who have gone before us.
>
> (attributed to Nietzsche)

Uichol Kim has skillfully observed the strategy embodied in the Chinese proverb, "Dripping water bores a hole through stone," and eventually prevailed upon me to write a piece for this timely collection on individualism and collectivism. My reluctance stems in part from the fact that I now seem to hold more questions than answers. These questions are, however, honestly acquired, as they arise from the scientific work I have been doing over the past 20 years. Much of this work has exploited the construct of collectivism and, indeed, various articles authored by me and my colleagues constitute some of the justificatory litany of the field. So perhaps some reflection is in order.

I did warn Dr. Kim that I would adopt a personal approach in this essay. For me this dance with collectivism has been both scientific and personal because it began 20 years ago when I arrived at Haneda Airport in Japan, American Ph.D. freshly in hand. I had crossed the Pacific with my wife, who was employed to teach English conversation, so I was officially designated her "dependent." This reversal of "natural" order appeared to produce considerable consternation among the immigration officers on duty, who quickly assembled around my passport. Much laughter, many in-drawn breaths, and furtive glances in my direction followed. Puzzled, I had landed in the heart of collectivism and have spent my time since then trying to figure out what is going on.

We often end up studying what we most need to know, and it is various scientific themes in this personal exploration that I will attempt to formulate in this piece. I will report developments chronologically and thereby disclose a more psychologically accurate portrayal of a scientist at work. Such a strategy will accord a disproportionate representation to my own work, I know, but living so long in the Orient has educated me out of my individualist pretensions to objectivity. I will reserve that conceit for journal articles.

STAGES IN THE JOURNEY: DISCOVERY

To strive, to seek, to find, and not to yield.
(Alfred, Lord Tennyson, *Ulysses*)

Learning to Play the China Card

My motive for abandoning my home country was religious-spiritual, not academic. In fact I undertook no appropriate training—linguistic, historical, anthropological, sociological, or philosophical—before venturing to the East. In consequence, a whole education awaited me, and I spent a lot of time reading, observing, and questioning cultural mediators (Bochner, 1981) to redress the balance. I am still doing so. As Gabrenya (1988) has astutely observed, such retooling is both humbling and time-consuming, definitely not recommended to those struggling for tenure! Fortunately, I had left the mainstream and was temporarily innocent of those concerns.

In fact, we next moved to Hong Kong, where a further adult education awaited. I had to master a mere 4,000 years of recorded Chinese history, wisdom, and lifestyle before I could speak scientifically with some authority. Fortunately, where I was struggling, many others elsewhere had not even begun. They were as fascinated with things Chinese as they had been with things Japanese. In consequence, they were eager to read about psychological differences between Asians and Americans (usually!).

By this time I had sensibly devoured our discipline's *I Ching*, Brislin, Lonner, and Thorndike's (1973) *Cross-Cultural Research Methods*. It had become my touchstone after I had received some devastating reviews of my early comparative research. Suitably armored, I was enabled to write more acceptable cross-cultural work. This research was bicultural, descriptive, and based on Western instrumentation, but its publication was facilitated by people's fascination with things Oriental (e.g., Bond, Nakazato, & Shiraishi, 1975).

I typically spiced the offerings with local proverbs or *ex cathedra* pronouncements based on my personal judgments about what was happening around me. Now firmly ensconced on the doorstep of the People's Republic, I had learned to "play the China card" with my accumulated wisdom. Few in my audience were familiar with such cards, and in any case the field needed data from Chinese humans, too. I had launched a career, of sorts.

A Conceptual "Eureka!"

Ultimately this Linnaean strategy of accumulating bicultural contrasts was personally unsatisfying. However interesting the problems being studied, a difference was simply an underlying similarity awaiting discovery. And this underlying dimension that united the different data points would enable us to locate the population of other cultures, too, thereby transcending this dust bowl of bicultural empiricism. As a scientist, it was this deck of cards rather than the journalistic China card that I wanted to use.

For me, Hofstede's scholarly tome *Culture's Consequences* (1980) provided the integration I was seeking. There he defined, elaborated, and operationalized four basic dimensions of cultural variation. These dimensions had been empirically identified by a procedure he called "ecological factor analysis" and were based on value surveys administered to 117,000 people in 66 countries. His processing of this extraordinary data set initially yielded scores for 40 countries on these four dimensions. At last, a cross-cultural navigator had an empirically charted map to guide and inform our journey.

The structure hunger of social scientists and the growing importance of an international perspective have combined to elevate Hofstede's work to classic status. For me it was a godsend. It located three Chinese societies, Hong Kong, Taiwan, and Singapore, as neighbors on the dimensions of individualism and power distance, thereby justifying references to "the Chinese" with respect to these dimensions. It also identified other groups, such as the Japanese, that operated according to similar cultural dynamics. We might thus generalize results found with certain country populations to other conceptual neighbors. And further, it allowed us to rationalize our choice of cultural groups in comparative research. All scientists had to do was link the phenomena under investigation to one of Hofstede's four dimensions. Our research could then assume a more hypothesis-driven and cumulative flavor (e.g., Bond, Leung, Wan, & Giacalone, 1985).

More challenging yet, Hofstede's (1980, 1983b) country data points now enabled us to address strong tests of our ideas. We could take a dimension, such as collectivism, relate it to a phenomenon, such as confrontive strategies of conflict resolution, and sample respondents from not two, but four countries. If our reasoning was correct, then the two collectivist cultures would produce similar results and be together different from the two individualist cultures that would themselves be similar. In this way we would avoid capitalizing on the many irrelevant differences that distinguish any two cultures and be more confident that our four-culture pattern of results was in fact based on our hypothesized cultural dimension of interest. This ambitious approach often results in sobering results (see, e.g., Leung, Bond, Carment, Krishnan, & Liebrand, 1990).

The Rapid Ascendancy of Collectivism

The cultural-level contrast between individualism and collectivism has exerted a magnetic pull on cross-cultural researchers over the past 10 years. Hofstede's (1980) other three dimensions, and indeed a fifth subsequently isolated (Hofstede & Bond, 1988), have been relatively ignored. There are many reasons for the lionizing of collectivism:

1. The United States received the highest score on individualism in Hofstede's 40 (and subsequent 53) samples, making it an atypical culture in this important respect. Most social science data have, of course, been produced in the United States. A cadre of social scientists is professionally, emotionally, or politically committed to challenging this American database that many unquestioningly accept as universal truth. Hofstede's data legitimates this challenge empirically.

2. In the course of these challenges, the concept of collectivism becomes elaborated. Of assistance in this development is the extensive literature that has accumulated over the past 100 or so years around the broad contrast between individualism and collectivism: gemeinschaft versus gesellschaft (Tönnies 1887/1957), the self-orientation versus collectivity orientation (Parsons & Shils, 1951), modernization (Inkeles, 1969), and so on. In short, lots of theoretical ammunition was available to unhorse Americocentrism.

3. In psychology, especially social psychology, the timing was right. Numerous respected figures in the field had emerged during the "crisis" period of the 1970s to question the cultural underpinnings of the enterprise (Gergen, 1973; Hogan, 1975; Sampson, 1977, 1981).

4. Harry Triandis plays a key role at the center of the cross-cultural sociogram. He and his colleagues have focused on collectivism in a series of key theoretical (Triandis, 1988b), empirical (Triandis et al., 1986; Triandis, Bontempo, Villareal, Asai, & Lucca, 1988), and integrative (Triandis, 1989, 1990) papers. These scholarly offerings in mainstream outlets galvanized and oriented many of us in the trenches. With increasing attention comes increasing criticism and refinement. My explorations of this conceptional landfall formed a part of some interests and concerns that began to echo around our professional territory.

STAGES IN THE JOURNEY:
EXPLORING THE LANDFALL

> An invasion of armies can be resisted, but not an idea whose
> time has come.
>
> (Victor Hugo, *Histoire d'un Crime*)

Interests

Collectivism in the context of discovery. One invaluable legacy of
collectivism's "discovery" by the field was the currency it accorded to social
scientists writing from within that cultural context (e.g., Doi, 1981; Enriquez,
1988; Hsu, 1953, 1971; Kakar, 1978; Minami, 1971; Nakamura, 1964;
J. B. P. Sinha, 1982). These representations of alternative worldviews then
stimulated empirical work out of these cultural settings (e.g., Misumi, 1985;
Yang, 1981, 1986).

Part of this increased activity from social scientists in collective cultures
was a further healthy step: Many began asking whether new or complementary theories, constructs, and methodologies could be teased from the
collective worldview. Instead of merely applying Western theories or
translating and refining Western instruments and procedures, could non-
Western psychologists not originate such scientific creations from out of
their own cultural legacy? By so doing, they could rebalance the scientific
center of gravity (Bond & Pang, 1991).

A number of such attempts have been made. With respect to theory,
Yang and Liang (1973) have identified and measured both collectivist and
individualist achievement orientation. With respect to construct development, the Chinese Culture Connection (1987) exploited the repository of
emic value terms in Chinese culture to create a value survey that was then
exported to more than 20 countries and validated in various ways (Bond,
1991). Additionally, Yang and Lee (1971) analyzed the Chinese trait lexicon
and subsequently examined the areas of overlap between the Chinese and
English lexicons for assessing implicit personality theory (Yang & Bond,
1990). With respect to methodology, Triandis, Bontempo, Leung, and Hui
(1990) took the implications of collectivist logic seriously and had subjects respond to a values questionnaire in triads, producing joint responses
rather than individual responses. With respect to instrumentation, Zhang
and Bond (1993) acknowledged the importance of the in-group/out-group
distinction for collective cultures and developed a target-specific trust
scale to complement the target-general trust scales developed in the West.

All these are valuable exercises, not only in terms of their scientific
yield but also in terms of indigenous confidence building. Psychologists

outside the mainstream have often responded to their perceived marginality by politicizing the professional arena. The developments noted above, however, represent some of the empirical harvest grown from this discontent and are a productive consequence of internationalizing the psychological enterprise. Their visibility will encourage others to examine the creative potentials of their own cultural heritages.

Is collectivism communion? Bakan (1966) synthesized a basic polarity in human affairs between the task-focused orientation to life, called "agency," and the integrative orientation toward life, called "communion." The publication of Carol Gilligan's book *In a Different Voice* (1982) further focused attention on this fundamental contrast. Many cross-cultural psychologists had been primed by sociopolitical critiques of individualism (e.g., Sampson, 1977) to presume that individuals from collective cultures place a greater emphasis on the harmonizing, prosocial dimensions of human behavior (see also Triandis, 1988b), so we were keen to assess this possibility scientifically.

Our first attempt to test this hypothesis involved manipulating both the task (masculine) and maintenance (feminine) contributions of a target group member to a group project (Bond, Leung, & Wan, 1982). We assumed that collectivist Chinese would accord relatively greater weight to maintenance inputs relative to task inputs than would individualist Americans in assigning grades. This was not the case. The Chinese were simply more egalitarian in assigning grades for *both* types of input. To our surprise, Chinese-style collectivism, at least, did not achieve harmony by emphasizing integrative, feminine contributions, but rather by responding to all inputs with greater moderation.

Our second attempt to link collectivism and communion (Bond & Forgas, 1984) argued that cultural collectivism educates attention (McArthur & Baron, 1983) to those aspects of personality that promote group harmony, namely, agreeableness and conscientiousness (see McCrae & John, 1992). Relative to Australians, Hong Kong Chinese did indeed emphasize these traits when assessing how they would behave toward the described target person.

So the general theme of harmony as underlying collectivist socialization is still viable, although the strategies for achieving this end state may not follow any simple distinction between agency and communion. Indeed, it may be that persons from individualist cultures place no less emphasis on harmony, but rather endorse different strategies for achieving that goal (e.g., Bond, Hewstone, Wan, & Chiu, 1984). We must also remember that Hofstede (1980) identifies a cultural dimension labeled "masculinity-femininity." Surely it would be sensible to examine communion with respect to this hitherto neglected dimension of cultural difference (see, e.g., Leung et al., 1990).

Collectivism as a communication aid. Being a social psychologist, I was often asked to help in orientation programs for expatriates coming to Hong Kong (Bond, 1992). In addition, I had edited a book on the psychology of the Chinese (Bond, 1986). In both activities I found the contrast between collectivism and individualism as defined by Hofstede (1980) and Triandis (1988b, 1990) very helpful in packaging information about Chinese (indeed, Asian) and Western differences. My designation of Chinese as collectivists and Westerners as individualists could be legitimated by Hofstede's country scores.

In capable, synthesizing minds the collectivism construct can be used to integrate a wealth of cross-cultural data from a host of countries (e.g., Triandis, 1990). But such Promethean undertakings remain creative acts of intelligence based mostly on bicultural contrasts. We simply do not have equivalent data from a variety of countries across a variety of behavioral domains that we could submit to a culture-level (or ecological) factor analysis (see, e.g., Smith & Crano, 1977). How ideal it would be to have standardized measures of resource allocation, conflict resolution, self-serving biases, conformity, in-group favoritism, and so on from 40 countries that we could than sift empirically for a country-level measure of behavioral collectivism! As mentioned before, multicultural comparisons selecting various countries from a putative dimension of individualism to collectivism often produce sobering results (see, e.g., Smith, Misumi, Tayeb, Peterson, & Bond, 1989). Fortunately, imaginative theorizers can invoke additional cultural dimensions as a *deus ex machina* to explain away troublesome inconsistencies. However, those of us who harbor healthy suspicions about our verbal creativity find this ability to explain away problems worrisome.

STAGES IN THE JOURNEY:
STUMBLING OVER OBSTACLES

Every wall is a door.

(Ralph Waldo Emerson)

Questions

An individual-level measure of collectivism? I frequently catch myself glibly designating cultures or countries as "collectivist" or "individualist."

When challenged, I defend my labeling by pointing to Hofstede's (1980) map. This mapping is derived, however, from individual value responses, mechanically averaged to yield country scores. These country scores were then factor analyzed to yield country-level factors. Finally, factor scores were calculated for the four factors and a mapping produced.

To me, this procedure has never yielded a satisfactory portrait of *country-level* collectivism (or power distance or uncertainty avoidance or masculinity, for that matter). The problem is that the input to the factor analysis was not country-level in any sense but the statistical. For me a country-level score is one that makes sense only when taken as a single score from that unit. For example, proportion of GNP devoted to education, percentage of women in the workforce, observation of human rights (Humana, 1986), references to freedom in the constitution (Massimini & Calegari, 1979), percentage of deaths owing to coronary heart disease, proportion of the workforce in service industries, and so on—all derive from forces at play within a country as an organic whole. They are not mechanical averages of individual events. A factor analysis of such inputs could yield what, at least for me, would be a satisfactory measure of *country-level* collectivism.

Of course, we would still have to ladder the country-level phenomenon down to individual-level dynamics so that we could continue practicing *as psychologists*. This would be an exciting venture involving appeals to parental socialization, educational practices, legal codes, and so forth. At present, we achieve this laddering by committing the ecological fallacy (Hofstede, 1980, pp. 28-31). This faux pas involves taking a country-level construct, such as Hofstede's individualism, and transferring it to the person level. So it is an easy step to presume that persons from countries identified as "individualist" are "individualist" people (see also Kagitçibasi, Chapter 4, this volume). We are assisted in this word magic by English syntax, which allows the same adjective to refer to both persons and countries.

This step is, however, as illegitimate as it is seductive (Leung, 1989). Hofstede did not provide cross-cultural psychology with individual-level measures of anything. He could have done (Bond, 1988; Leung & Bond, 1989), but scruples about equivalence (Bosland, 1985) stopped him. Triandis et al. (1986) tried, and coined the individual-level terms *allocentrism* and *idiocentrism,* but unfortunately made a small statistical misstep (Leung & Bond, 1989), which they subsequently rectified (Triandis, Chan, Bhawuk, Iwao, & Sinha, 1993). Clearly, however, the perceived need was there, and eventually my own work provided average scores for persons from 22 countries on two universal dimensions from the Chinese Value Survey (Bond, 1988). Schwartz (Chapter 7, this volume) is now in a position to do so with even more cultural groups and a more comprehensive measure of values.

Some combination of the Schwartz value types may provide us with a new operationalization of "collectivism-at-the-individual-level." Of course, it will probably not be called "collectivism," nor will those high on the profile be called "collectivists." Given the connotative baggage freighting such terms as *individualist* and *collectivist* however, more neutral terminology would probably be a blessing!

Other types of individual-level constructs may prove useful, if they can sidestep the problem of cultural equivalence. Elements from Triandis's (1980b) theory, such as self-definitions or affect toward behavior domains, may be useful—or perhaps attitudes toward various targets (Triandis et al., 1986). The essential requirement is that they release us from our thrall to culture-level constructs.

Accept the mainstream challenge? Psychologists from the mainstream (e.g., Clark, 1987; Messick, 1988) have signaled to cross-culturalists what we must do to be taken seriously. In short, they assert that we must find a way to integrate the cultural dimension into theories of behavior. One obvious way is to use values. We know (a) that individuals differ in their value endorsements, (b) that values influence behavior (Feather, 1979), and (c) that people from different cultures differ on average from people of other cultures both in their values and in their behavior. So we can run studies in which both values and behavior are measured in a variety of cultures, then look for pancultural relationships (e.g., Bond, Leung, & Schwartz, 1992).

Note that we must *measure* individual responses to the mediating variable of interest that connects to culture—in this case, values. We cannot appeal to either hypothesized or country-level processes. If we do so, our results will simply not withstand such mainstream skepticism. Of course, the Excalibur in this battle may not be values, popular as the concept is with cross-cultural psychologists (Leung, Bond, & Schwartz, 1993). It may be expectancies for reinforcement associated with the target behaviors. Or perhaps measures of self-efficacy (Bandura, 1982). Whatever, it must be more persuasive than the global, hypothesized concepts we have typically pulled from our cross-cultural suitcases to bedazzle skeptics.

Distinguishing collectivism from modernity? Whatever definition is given, we must attempt to distinguish collectivism from modernity, at both individual and cultural levels. Yang (1988) and Kagitçibasi (Chapter 4, this volume) have carefully documented the empirical and conceptual overlap in these conceptual domains. They are considerable.

For the collectivism construct to be useful, we must find some way to distinguish it from modernization, cultural complexity, urbanization, and other related constructs, for, if individualism is just another name for modernization, cross-cultural psychology may simply be a dinosaur about to sink into the tar pits of time. Cross-cultural differences in behavior may disappear with the march of history.

Attempts at conceptual refinement, such as Kagitçibasi's discussion of relatedness in Chapter 4 of this volume, are important in this regard. Operationally, we may wish to analyze multicultural data, such as those from the Schwartz (1992) project, in such a way as to partial out GNP/capita, degree of urbanization, and the like. Alternatively, one of the value dimensions could be extracted in such a way as to maximize the overlap with modernity. The remaining dimensions of value would then be measures of variation uncontaminated by the shadow of mere modernization. Thereby, we may be able to discern a dimension of relatedness, or whatever, independent of modernization. This result could focus our theoretical speculations in more productive directions for the future.

STAGES IN THE JOURNEY: REMAPPING

> And the end of all exploring
> Will be to arrive where we started
> And know the place for the first time.
>
> (T. S. Eliot, *Four Quartets, Little Gidding*)

Horace Greeley advised, "Go west, young man!" Significantly, if we travel far enough West, we find ourselves in the East. The process of extending the known will lead us full circle to a point where we have exhausted the compass. Returning home after spanning the globe, however, transforms our appreciation of home (Adler, 1975). It is now seen in context, no longer the movie screen for our existence; it is only a chip in a kaleidoscope, one colored stone in a larger mosaic.

For this psychologist, the consequences of an explorer's journey into the heart of collectivism are several. First, I am committed to addressing the questions we have discovered in exploring the landfall: Can we find useful individual-level measures of collectivism? Can we separate these measures from the influence of modernity? Can we develop universal theories of behavior that include a measured cultural component?

Second, I am sustained by the exciting possibility that in so doing we may discover alternative models of socialization for interdependence, as Kagitçibasi (1990; see also Chapter 4, this volume) is heralding. There are, indeed, other possibilities for relationships, and as Gardner Murphy (1969) has maintained, "A human race speaking many tongues, regarding many values, and holding different convictions about the meaning of life sooner or later will have to consult all that is human" (p. 528). The collectivist movement in cross-cultural psychology is fueling just such a consultation. It is a deep pleasure for me to contribute.

Finally, I believe I have become a better scientist. Living abroad has sobered my romanticism about things foreign and sharpened my appreciation of my origins (see, e.g., Waterman, 1981). My hope is that I have achieved some detachment and objectivity in my thinking as a result. Attainment of these epistemological grails requires considerable struggle and involves something more than just the methodological asceticism demanded by our discipline. This rigor is necessary, but it must be alloyed with a sincere desire to appreciate difference in all its facets. So it occurs to me that traveling seriously may constitute some of the best postgraduate training still available!

> Come, my friends,
> 'Tis not too late to seek a newer world.
>
> (Alfred, Lord Tennyson, *Ulysses*)

6

ECOLOGY OF INDIVIDUALISM
AND COLLECTIVISM

JOHN W. BERRY

This chapter addresses the question, How can one account for variations in I/C across cultures and across individuals? One possible way is to link such variations to ecological and cultural factors that may underlie human diversity. This ecological approach would take us beyond countries as units of analysis (which is the level at which most research is now carried out) to a more focused concern with cultural communities and their specific eco-cultural characteristics.

AN ECOLOGICAL APPROACH

The ecological perspective has been used in cross-cultural research for a number of years, both as a general framework for understanding human diversity and as a specific research model for understanding the distribution of particular behaviors. As a general paradigm, it has served a variety of purposes, including strategies for doing research in the fields of cross-cultural psychology (Berry, 1975) and culture and personality (J. W. M. Whiting, 1974), and most recently as the organizing framework for a pair of textbooks in cross-cultural psychology (Berry, Poortinga, Segall, & Dasen, 1992; Segall, Dasen, Berry, & Poortinga, 1990). As a specific model, it has been employed to understand the distribution of a variety of individual behaviors, such as cognitive style (Berry, 1976; Berry et al., 1986; Witkin & Berry, 1975), cognitive development (Dasen, 1974), and conformity (Berry, 1967, 1979).

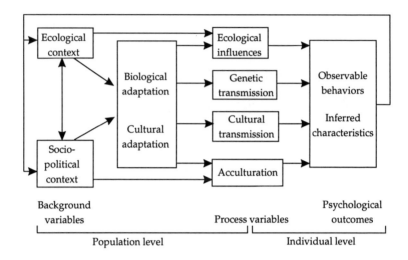

Figure 6.1. Ecocultural Framework for Cross-Cultural Psychology

From the ecological perspective (see Figure 6.1), human populations are considered to be adapted (both culturally and biologically) to their ecological contexts, and individual psychological characteristics are considered to be developed as a function of these ecological, cultural, and biological population variables. Influences on individual development are both direct (from ecological engagement of the person) and mediated (by cultural and biological factors); the latter are carried through cultural transmission (enculturation and socialization) and genetic transmission from the group to the developing individual. In addition to the ecological line of influence on individual behavior, the framework also includes factors that stem from contact with other societies and that produce changes in individuals and their societies. These sociopolitical influences operate through the process of acculturation, and modify (sometimes in substantial ways; see Berry, 1991) the psychological characteristics previously found in the cultural group.

In more detail, the model has been operationalized (e.g., Berry, 1976) with respect to the development of the field-dependent/field-independent cognitive style (Witkin et al., 1962) and the related area of social conformity (Berry, 1967, 1979). This work began with the observation that individuals living in societies that engage their habitat differentially (of particular interest has been the contrast between hunter-gatherers and agriculturalists) tend to require different cognitive and social abilities in order to survive and prosper (Berry, 1966). These "ecological demands" (sometimes referred to as "ecological press") lead to population-level adaptations. Culturally, hunter-gatherers tend to be small in population size, nomadic in settlement style, and "loose" or unstratified in social organization; conversely, agriculturalists tend to live in larger population units and are sedentary and more stratified. These cultural adaptations are transmitted to developing individuals through the process of cultural transmission (both general enculturation and specific socialization practices; see Barry, Child, & Bacon, 1959) so that individuals in a society develop a particular set of characteristic behaviors (the outcome of the model, at the right of Figure 6.1).

In parallel with this set of ecological influences are those that arrive by way of contact with other cultural groups. This sociopolitical context gives rise to the process of acculturation, which also affects the course of individual human development, often in interaction with ecological influences.

With respect to cognitive style and social conformity, hunter-gatherers have been found to be relatively field-independent in their approach to cognition and independent in their social relationships; conversely, agriculturalists have been found to be relatively field-dependent and conforming (Berry, 1976, 1979; Witkin & Berry, 1975). The rationale is that in hunting- and gathering-based societies, there is a need to develop the ability to disembed cue from context, and to analyze and organize spatial information (two of the central features of the field-independent cognitive style). Similarly, a good deal of personal initiative and self-reliance are considered to be valuable attributes in the successful hunter, and appear to be emphasized in hunters' child-rearing practices (Barry et al., 1959). In contrast, agriculturalists need not develop these perceptual-cognitive abilities, and close group living tends to be best served by child training for, and the development of, a more socially responsive and conforming pattern of interpersonal relationships. The influence of contact with other societies (mainly through the impact of formal schooling) has tended to push cognitive styles for all groups in a more field-independent direction, and to induce people to become more independent in social relationships.

Considering acculturation phenomena beyond these cognitive and social domains, there is substantial evidence that hunter-gatherers have greater cultural dissimilarity with the demands of the new ecology (urban, close-group living) (see Berry & Annis, 1974; Berry, Kim, Minde, & Mok, 1987). These difficulties sometimes manifest themselves in psychological and social pathologies (such as anxiety, depression, suicide, homicide, family violence, and substance abuse). This result, based on cultural dissimilarity, seems not to be affected by psychological similarity, because both hunter-gatherers and urbanites tend to share the same relatively field-independent cognitive style.

This brief sketch is intended to serve as a model for the following discussion of I/C, rather than as a full portrayal of either the ecocultural perspective or the research findings with respect to cognitive style or social conformity.

In this chapter, I wish to bring the ecological perspective to bear on the dimension of cultural and behavioral variation that has become known as I/C. In so doing, two problems are immediately apparent. One is that the dimension has come into cross-cultural psychology through the writing of Hofstede (1980), who worked exclusively with samples of subjects who were participating in industrial enterprise; in contrast, much of the previous use of the ecological framework has been with subsistence-level societies, or at least with those in the process of acculturating from such societies. Thus there are *theoretical* bridges that need to be built between these two domains. The second problem is that there is a dearth of *empirical* studies of I/C among preindustrial subsistence-level populations; thus much of the chapter will be concerned with predictions rather than actual results.

A third issue that will be of concern here has already been identified in the I/C literature: the need to keep culture-level and individual-level phenomena distinct. Triandis, Leung, Villareal, and Clark (1985) have proposed that the terms *individualism* and *collectivism* be retained at the culture level of the dimension, but that *idiocentrism* and *allocentrism* be used at the individual level. In this chapter I will retain *individualism, collectivism,* and *I/C* as general terms, but precede them with *societal* or *personal* to make the distinction wherever the context does not make it clear.

ECOLOGICAL DIMENSIONS OF CULTURAL VARIATION

In earlier ecological analyses, I have employed a single dimension (the "ecocultural" dimension) to represent some population variations in subsistence-level societies (Berry, 1966, 1976). This dimension brought together a number of cultural variables that covaried in the anthropological literature and that were theoretically linked to the development of cognitive style and social conformity. These included settlement pattern (nomadic to sedentary), mean size of local community (usual number of local inhabitants), political stratification (number of levels of authority above local residence unit), social stratification (rank and wealth distinction), and family type (extended versus nuclear). A fundamental element of this ecocultural dimension is the *subsistence pattern* of the group, classified as gathering, hunting, agriculture, irrigation, or industrial. One important

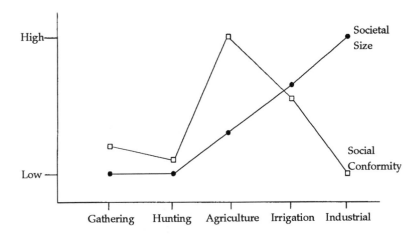

Figure 6.2. Two Dimensions of Cultural Variation by Subsistence Pattern

feature of these cultural factors is that there is a systematic relationship between them and the subsistence strategies employed by each society. Specifically, hunter-gatherers (as noted earlier) tend to be nomadic, live in small population units, are minimally stratified, and have nuclear families; agriculturalists tend to exhibit a contrasting pattern.

Earlier, Murdock (1967) employed a similar single dimension of "cultural complexity," and Pelto (1968) a "tight-loose" dimension. However, about the same time, Lomax and Berkowitz (1972) proposed that there were *two* separable dimension of cultural variation that covaried with subsistence strategy: "differentiation" and "integration" (see also Denny, 1988). Boldt and Roberts (1979; Roberts, Boldt, & Guest, 1990) later proposed that these two dimensions are to be understood as "structural complexity" and "structural tightness." In these two-dimensional conceptualizations the ideas of "many distinctions within a society" (termed here *societal size*) and "close-knit relations within a society" (termed here *social conformity*) are argued to be independent of each other. They are also considered to vary across subsistence strategies (see Figure 6.2) in dissimilar ways, as evidenced in the ethnographic literature (e.g., Lomax & Berkowitz, 1972).

In our current work (Berry, Bennett, & Denny, 1990), societal size is made up of mean size of local community, settlement pattern, political stratification, and occupational specialization. The components are considered to be correlated among themselves, and are related to subsistence strategies in the nearly linear fashion hypothesized in Figure 6.2. Social

conformity is made up of social stratification, socialization emphases ranging
from compliance to assertion (Barry et al., 1959), and obligation to conform
to social norms. These components are also considered to be correlated
among themselves, but are related to subsistence strategy in a curvilinear
way. The variables selected for both dimensions are rooted in the anthropological literature noted above, but, more important, they are considered
to be theoretically predictive of individual cognitive and social development. For example, field-independence and social independence are known
to be found in societies that are high in societal size and low in social
conformity.

I/C AS A DIMENSION
OF CULTURAL VARIATION

Although the general idea that societies vary on a dimension of I/C has
been in the anthropological, sociological, and political literature for a long
time (see, e.g., Billings & Majors, 1989; Kagitçibasi, 1987), it was Hofstede's
major study that brought the idea centrally to the attention of cross-
cultural psychology. In his factor analyses of more than 100,000 respondents across 40 societies, he identified four factors: power distance, uncertainty avoidance, individualism, and masculinity. With respect to I/C,
individualism was linked to national wealth (wealthy countries were more
individualistic), upward social mobility, a developed middle class, nuclear
family structure, and high industrialization and urbanization. More recent
analyses have extended the list of societal correlates of I/C (see, e.g.,
Triandis, Chapter 3, this volume).

LINKAGE OF ECOLOGICAL
AND CULTURAL FACTORS TO I/C

In this section, I attempt to find some linkages between ecological and
cultural variables found in subsistence-level societies and societal I/C. From
these linkages, it is possible to make some predictions through to personal
individualism and collectivism.

It is likely that Hofstede's four dimensions are more relevant to contemporary industrialized nation-states (or at least to societies that have
such an economic sector) than to the subsistence-level societies more usually
attended to by cross-cultural psychology. This situation is a function of
the sample of countries actually involved in Hofstede's study, those countries
where a particular corporation was established. Nevertheless, it may be

possible to find some links to ecological and sociocultural variables in subsistence-level societies if we take the two dimensions outlined earlier into account.

In particular, there is an apparent similarity between the social conformity dimension and some ecocultural antecedents to collectivism. For example, the "compliance" emphasis in socialization (Barry et al., 1959) has been shown to be associated, across subsistence-level societies, with conformity (Berry, 1967, 1979) and with a more field-dependent cognitive style (Berry, 1976; Witkin & Berry, 1975). Both of these involve attention to, and acceptance of, social influence from one's immediate social context (one's primary group and one's in-group). Similarly, the social stratification component of the social conformity dimension places individuals in a hierarchy of social relationships in which differential social rank is likely to be associated with the acceptance of responsibility for those lower down in the social system. Although not identical to the sociocultural underpinnings of societal collectivism as outlined in the literature up until now, there is sufficient similarity to expect that personal collectivism will vary across subsistence-level societies as a function of the social conformity ecocultural dimension, and in parallel with it. For industrial societies (those not at subsistence level), the general expectation is that personal collectivism will be low. However, some exceptions have been reported for societies that have recently made a transition from agricultural to industrial activity (e.g., Japan and Hong Kong). A possible explanation is that earlier-established cultural and psychological characteristics have persisted (e.g., by "cultural lag") into the period of industrialization.

What is the situation for individualism? On the one hand, it is possible to predict inverse relationships across the social conformity dimension. This prediction would be based upon the presumed bipolarity of the I/C construct, where personal individualism is believed to be the psychological opposite of personal collectivism. However, this assumption is increasingly challenged theoretically (e.g., Kagitçibasi, 1987), and such a prediction may very well not hold up empirically in other than industrial societies.

Alternatively, I believe that personal individualism may be better predicted by the societal size ecocultural dimension. Here, as local population units become larger, more differentiated, and more diffuse, individuals have more options for their daily conduct. In such situations, personal rather than collective goals may well guide individuals' behavior; personal beliefs may increasingly replace shared norms as influences on the choices people make.

If this linkage turns out to have empirical substance, then the differential *cross-group* distribution of personal individualism and personal collectivism would provide a theoretical starting point for a reexamination of their differential *within-group* distribution. That is, the apparent opposing relationship between individualism and collectivism found by Hofstede (1980) may be limited to those societies where there are clear differences in the social conformity and societal size characteristics of the cultural group (e.g., in industrial societies, which predominate in Hofstede's sample, and to some extent in agricultural societies). However, where there is similarity in a society on these two ecocultural dimensions (e.g., where both are low, as in hunting and gathering societies, and where both are intermediate, as in irrigation societies), it is possible that individualism and collectivism would not appear as contrasting or opposing values and behaviors.

CONCLUSION

Methodologically, the ecological approach to I/C would be a particularly important demonstration of the value of the cross-cultural method. By showing that a presumed constant psychological relationship varies across cultures in a way that is predictable from known features of those cultures, we could add another notch to our bow in our attempt to convince our colleagues that ecological and cultural contexts are important elements in every psychological equation (Bond, 1988). Theoretically, by showing that individualism and collectivism may not always exist as opposites across cultures, we would provide support for the view that they are not necessarily opposed either within individuals, or as individuals and societies change from agricultural to industrial subsistence strategies. And substantively, patterns of covariation among cognitive styles, social conformity, and personal values could be demonstrated within cultures and shown to be adaptive to ecological context across cultures, information that may be particularly valuable as many societies contemplate transition to an industrial base.

7

BEYOND INDIVIDUALISM/COLLECTIVISM
New Cultural Dimensions of Values

SHALOM H. SCHWARTZ

The usefulness of culture as an explanatory variable depends upon our ability to "unpackage" the culture concept (Rohner, 1984; B. B. Whiting, 1976). In order to do this, it is best to view "culture as a complex, multidimensional structure rather than as a simple categorical variable" (Clark, 1987, p. 461) and to array cultures along interpretable dimensions. Differences in the locations of cultures along these dimensions can then be used to explain differences between cultures in their distributions of behavior patterns, norms, attitudes, and personality variables (Triandis, 1978). This chapter unpackages an aspect of culture by deriving a new set of dimensions of values appropriate for comparing cultures.

The vast majority of cross-cultural studies have compared samples from only two or three cultures, usually operationalized as different nations (see, for example, recent volumes of the *Journal of Cross-Cultural Psychology* and *Journal of Personality and Social Psychology*). But any set of a few samples is likely to be ordered in the same way on a number of different variables that could each be used to explain the phenomenon of interest. One way to overcome this problem of alternative explanations is to compare a substantial number of samples drawn from cultures arrayed along a cultural dimension for which theoretical linkages to the phenomenon have been generated. Then there are likely to be few, if any, alternative variables that array these samples in the same order and also have convincing theoretical links to the phenomenon.

AUTHOR'S NOTE: The research reported here was supported by Grant No. 187/92 from the Basic Research Foundation (Israel Academy of Sciences and Humanities); by Grant No. 88-00085 from the United States-Israel Binational Science Foundation (BSF), Jerusalem; and by the Leon and Clara Sznajderman Chair of Psychology.

Studies that array large numbers of cultures on a priori or at least post hoc dimensions have been reported (e.g., Berry, 1976; Bond, 1991; Buss et al., 1990; Whiting & Whiting, 1975; Williams & Best, 1982). Among the most influential studies of this type is Hofstede's (1980, 1983a, 1991) monumental research on work values in 53 nations or regions. Indeed, Hofstede has provided one of the few empirically and conceptually based sets of cultural dimensions on which contemporary cultures or nations can be arrayed.

Hofstede derived four dimensions along which the dominant value systems in different nations can be ordered. These dimensions are widely accepted and have been used by many researchers to locate and compare cultural groups (e.g., Bond & Forgas, 1984; Gabrenya, Wang, & Latané, 1985; Leung, 1988b; see review in Kagitçibasi & Berry, 1989). In this chapter, I raise several questions relevant to Hofstede's dimensions. I then present an alternative conceptual and operational approach for deriving cultural dimensions of values. Next, I apply this new approach in a study of value priorities in 87 samples from 41 cultural groups in 38 nations. The new culture-level dimensions I derive are then compared with Hofstede's dimensions. Finally, I present scores for one set of national samples on these new dimensions.

The current report provides an ordering of nations on the new value dimensions that can be used in future research. Researchers can use these orderings to select cultural samples strategically. Differences between the samples on psychological and social variables (e.g., perception, modernization) can then be studied as functions of theoretically based cultural dimensions. My collaborators and I are currently studying meaningful patterns in the locations of nations on the cultural dimensions, the factors that may account for them, and their possible consequences.

The Hofstede dimensions. Hofstede sought dimensions of cross-cultural variation in the responses of more than 117,000 employees of a multinational business corporation in 40 nations. Based on an approach that takes the national sample rather than the individual person as the unit of analysis, Hofstede derived what he calls "ecological" and others call "culture-level" dimensions (Leung & Bond, 1989; Shweder, 1973). From his analysis of the intercorrelations among the mean nation scores for each item, Hofstede (1983a, pp. 336-337) derived and defined four dimensions:

- *power distance:* "the extent to which members of a society accept [as legitimate] that power in institutions and organizations is distributed unequally"
- *uncertainty avoidance:* "the degree to which the members of a society feel uncomfortable with uncertainty and ambiguity, which leads them to

support beliefs promising certainty and to maintain institutions protecting conformity"

- *masculinity/femininity:* "a preference for achievement, heroism, assertiveness, and material success as opposed to . . . a preference for relationships, modesty, caring for the weak, and the quality of life"
- *individualism/collectivism:* "a preference for a loosely knit social framework in society in which individuals are supposed to take care of themselves and their immediate families only as opposed to . . . a preference for a tightly knit social framework in which individuals can expect their relatives, clan or other in-group to look after them, in exchange for unquestioning loyalty"

I/C is the dimension that has been used most often as an explanatory variable in subsequent research (summarized in Kagitçibasi & Berry, 1989; Triandis, 1990). Triandis (1990) has elaborated broader conceptualizations of this dimension. He emphasizes more strongly than Hofstede the idea that individualism entails giving priority to personal goals over the goals of the in-group, whereas collectivism entails giving priority to in-group goals over personal goals.

CONCEPTUAL AND METHODOLOGICAL ISSUES IN DERIVING CULTURE-LEVEL DIMENSIONS

I address six issues relevant to Hofstede's dimensions and to culture-level dimensions in general. First, I expand on two issues that Hofstede has noted.

Exhaustiveness of the Value Dimensions

Hofstede recognizes that his four dimensions are not necessarily exhaustive. These dimensions describe basic problems for every society, but there may be "other dimensions related to equally fundamental problems of mankind which were not found . . . because the relevant questions simply were not asked" (Hofstede, 1980, pp. 313-314).

Values suitable for uncovering all four Hofstede dimensions were included in the current value set. Therefore, this research can serve as a check on the replicability of the Hofstede dimensions with a different method of measurement. The analysis may support Hofstede's dimensions, it may suggest that it is appropriate to refine them into finer-tuned dimensions or categories (see Schwartz, 1990), or it may reveal that a different set of cultural dimensions emerges when a more comprehensive set of values is analyzed. The current research seeks a set of universal conceptual dimensions to describe human variety and divergences (Shweder & Sullivan, 1993). Additional emic dimensions are probably needed to characterize unique aspects of particular cultures. However, in the interests of parsimony, it is incumbent on the researcher to demonstrate that an apparently emic cultural variation cannot be represented adequately as a point along a universal dimension.

Without an a priori theory of the fundamental issues that confront humankind, it is difficult to specify the items needed to reveal *all* significant value dimensions of cultural variation. The items included here were taken from a source that improves the chances of approaching an exhaustive set of etic dimensions: a survey developed to measure the content of individual values recognized across cultures (Schwartz, 1992). This content is also likely to reflect the major concerns that groups must face and give expression to as values.

Human values are defined as desirable goals, varying in importance, that serve as guiding principles in people's lives (Kluckhohn, 1951; Rokeach, 1973; Schwartz, 1992). The crucial content aspect that distinguishes among values is the type of motivational goals they express. In earlier work, I derived a typology of the different contents of individual values by reasoning that values represent, in the form of conscious goals, three universal requirements of human existence to which all individuals and societies must be responsive: needs of individuals as biological organisms, requisites of coordinated social interaction, and survival and welfare needs of groups (Schwartz, 1992). In order to cope with reality in a social context, individuals and groups represent these requirements cognitively as specific values about which they communicate.

Ten motivationally distinct types of individual values have been validated (Schwartz, 1992). Each type is briefly defined in terms of its central goal in Table 7.1. A comprehensive set of 56 specific values was generated to represent these types. These 56 values were used in the current research. Specific values represent a value type if the central goal of that type is promoted when people act in ways that express the value or lead to its attainment.

The social and psychological conflicts that arise when people pursue their values give structure to their value systems. For example, the pursuit of achievement values may conflict with the pursuit of benevolence values: Seeking personal success for oneself is likely to obstruct actions aimed at enhancing the welfare of others who need one's help. The total pattern of likely conflicts and compatibility among value priorities yields a structure for value systems that has been supported in cross-cultural work

Table 7.1 Definitions of Individual-Level Motivational Types of Values

Power: social status and prestige, control or dominance over people and resources

Achievement: personal success through demonstrating competence according to social standards

Hedonism: pleasure and sensuous gratification for oneself

Stimulation: excitement, novelty, and challenge in life

Self-Direction: independent thought and action—choosing, creating, exploring

Universalism: understanding, appreciation, tolerance, and protection for the welfare of all people and for nature

Benevolence: preservation and enhancement of the welfare of people with whom one is in frequent personal contact

Tradition: respect for, commitment to, and acceptance of the customs and ideas that traditional culture or religion impose on the self

Conformity: restraint of actions, inclinations, and impulses likely to upset or harm others and to violate social expectations or norms

Security: safety, harmony, and stability of society, of relationships, and of self

(Schwartz, 1992). The 10 value types are organized on two basic bipolar dimensions. Each pole constitutes a higher-order value type that combines two or more of the 10 types. One dimension opposes Openness to Change (Self-Direction and Stimulation) and Conservation (Conformity, Tradition, and Security). The other opposes Self-Transcendence (Universalism and Benevolence) and Self-Enhancement (Achievement and Power). Hedonism is related to both Openness to Change and Self-Enhancement. Although this structure applies to individual values, it can suggest hypotheses for the structure of culture-level values, too, for reasons developed below.

The dimensions measurable with the current value set are likely to be more inclusive of all important dimensions than are Hofstede's. No significant omissions in this set were revealed by a review of the value categories proposed as universal in the social science and humanities literature. Moreover, when researchers in many nations added values they thought might be special to their cultures and missing from the core set of 56, no additional distinct types of values were revealed in analyses of data from these nations. Instead, the added values emerged with the appropriate a priori value types (Schwartz, 1992).

Adequacy of the Sample of Nations

A second limitation noted by Hofstede (1980) is that his dimensions are "based on one specific set of 40 modern nations, excluding, for example, all countries under state socialism" (p. 314). He recognizes that adding other nations might affect the dimensions that emerge. Unless the sample of nations studied is a reasonable representation of the full heterogeneity of cultures, different dimensions may emerge in culture-level analyses of different samples of nations. In the current research, samples from China, Poland, Estonia, East Germany, Hungary, Slovakia, Slovenia, and Zimbabwe were included, thus bringing countries where value systems were influenced by state socialism into the culture-level analysis and partly filling the gap noted by Hofstede.

In individual-level research, the robustness of dimensions can be checked by replicating studies on different samples of respondents. When nations are the unit of analysis, however, this type of check on robustness is much more costly. Hofstede and Triandis report no check of the robustness of their culture-level value dimensions.[1] That is, they did not examine whether the same dimensions emerged when different samples were taken from the same nations and their mean scores subjected to multivariate analyses. To check robustness here, I split the set of the first 60 samples studied into two parallel subsets of 30 samples each. I then performed the same structural analyses in each and compared the dimensions obtained as well as the order of nations on each dimension.

Four issues not raised by Hofstede are also examined here: effect of sample size, historical change, culture-level versus individual-level dimensions, and equivalence of the meaning of values.

Effect of Sample Type

To what extent were the dimensions that Hofstede derived dependent upon the fact that the data were obtained from employees of a single multinational corporation? Did characteristics unique to this type of sample influence the ordering of nations on the dimensions? Would samples of other types yield similar dimensions and orderings?

The difficulty of obtaining representative national samples from many nations makes a strategy of matching samples from each nation a virtual necessity. Reflecting his interest in organizations, Hofstede obtained matched samples of employees of the same large corporation in each nation. To support his dimensions further, he drew on the results of surveys with other samples that appeared compatible with them. Without criticizing Hofstede's choice of sample type or his matching procedure, one can conjecture that other types of samples might yield different dimensions and orders of nations. HERMES, as Hofstede calls the corporation, is a high-technology business employing mainly highly skilled professionals, managers, and technicians. HERMES employees doubtless differed from the general population in their nations not only in their education but in their interest in science and technology and their exposure to "modernizing" forces—qualities likely to affect their values (Inkeles & Smith, 1974; Kahl, 1968).

Furthermore, HERMES employees most likely diverged from the general population more in some nations than in others. The divergence was probably greater, for example, in Third World nations (e.g., El Salvador, Pakistan) than in industrialized Western nations (e.g., Switzerland, United States). Such variability would affect the order of the nations on the dimensions and might even affect which dimensions emerge.

At a minimum, one needs two types of matched samples to replicate the culture-level analyses. The current research was largely based on two types of matched samples—schoolteachers (grades 3-12) and university students. Although no single occupational group can represent a culture, teachers may be the best available group when one is trying to characterize cultural priorities. They play an explicit role in value socialization, they are presumably key carriers of culture, and they are probably close to the broad value consensus in a society. Undergraduate students, like HERMES employees, are more likely to show the influence of exposure to modernizing trends. Students are younger than the population in general, and their priorities may reflect directions in which the culture is changing. I examined whether analyses based on these two types of samples yielded similar orders of nations. Comparisons with a set of occupationally heterogeneous samples from seven nations provided a further check of generalizability.

Historical Change

Hofstede's analyses were based on data gathered from 1967 to 1973. During the two decades since his last sampling, major cultural changes have occurred throughout the world, especially in the Pacific Basin, in Eastern Europe, and among developing nations. Even industrialized Western nations have been described as shifting emphases from materialist to postmaterialist values (Inglehardt, 1977). It is therefore desirable to update our information about the dimensions of cultural variation and the relative positions of different nations on these dimensions. If substantial change has occurred, updated nation scores are critical for current research aimed at testing hypotheses that relate the standings of nations on the cultural dimensions to other variables.

Culture-Level Versus Individual-Level Dimensions

As noted above, Hofstede's dimensions of cultural variation are "ecological" or culture-level dimensions. Unlike individual-level dimensions, which are derived from analyses of the scores of individual persons, culture-level dimensions are based on nation means. More important, the dimensions that organize values have different conceptual bases at the two levels. Individual-level value dimensions presumably reflect the psychological dynamics of conflict and compatibility that individuals experience in the course of pursuing their different values in everyday life (Schwartz, 1992; Schwartz & Bilsky, 1987, 1990). In contrast, culture-level dimensions presumably reflect the different solutions that societies evolve to the problems of regulating human activities, the different ways that institutional emphases and investments are patterned and justified in one culture compared with another.

The culture-level values that characterize a society cannot be observed directly. Rather, they must be inferred from various cultural products (e.g., folktales). Presumably, these cultural products reflect assumptions about the desirable that are built into the institutions of the society and are passed on through intentional and unintentional socialization.

The prevailing value emphases in societies have also been inferred from individual values averaged across members of a society (e.g., Hofstede, 1980; Inkeles & Smith, 1974; Kahl, 1968; Morris, 1956). This approach, adopted here, views individual values as partly a product of shared culture and partly a product of unique individual experience. The commonalities in the intentional and unintentional value socialization to which different members of society are exposed reflect the cultural emphases that support and maintain the social, economic, and political system of the society. The average of the value priorities of societal members reflects these commonalities of enculturation. Individual variation around this average reflects unique personality and experience. Thus averaged values of societal members, no less than folktales or textbooks, can point to cultural values.

The dimensions obtained in individual-level and culture-level analyses are empirically based on statistically independent treatments of the data (Hofstede, 1980; Leung & Bond, 1989; Shweder, 1973). Therefore, the dimensions are not constrained to be similar. This is illustrated by Hofstede's findings for the power distance dimension and the I/C dimension. These dimensions emerged only in the culture-level analysis, based on national means for the value items. When the same items were analyzed at the individual level, based on the responses of individuals within nations, the three power distance items had near-zero intercorrelations. Moreover, the six I/C items formed a different dimension that opposed intrinsic to extrinsic goals (Hofstede, 1980).

Despite their statistical independence, there are theoretical reasons to expect culture-level and individual-level value dimensions to be related conceptually. First, the setting of institutional priorities in a society must take into account the psychological dynamics inherent in human nature and in universal aspects of social interaction. Otherwise, individuals would not function effectively in these institutions. Second, individual members of a society are socialized to internalize values that will lead them to promote the interests and conform to the requirements of cultural institutions. Third, cultural priorities create social reinforcement contingencies that help determine whether conflict or compatibility is experienced when individuals pursue particular sets of values. It would therefore be surprising if the value dimensions identified at the two levels did not overlap somewhat.

To illustrate this argument, consider how a dimension of autonomy versus submission is likely to be found at both levels. Kohn (1969; Kohn & Schooler, 1983) and I (Schwartz, 1992) have identified a dimension we label *self-direction versus conformity* in individual-level analyses within many nations. This dimension contrasts an emphasis on independence of thought and action with an emphasis on restraint of own inclinations in favor of conformity to social expectations. The dimension reflects the fact that trying to behave in ways that simultaneously express autonomy from others and submission to them is psychologically as well as socially incompatible.

Similar dynamics are likely to find expression in the culture-level organization of priorities: Nations with institutional structures conducive to independence (e.g., widespread higher education, religious pluralism, occupations demanding nonroutine decision making, democratic political structures) will foster self-direction values in their citizens. Such institutions will also run more smoothly if citizens give high priority to self-direction versus conformity values. Moreover, in the struggle to attain or maintain sway over cultural priorities, institutional structures that foster self-direction will come into conflict with those conducive to conformity (e.g., limited educational opportunities, a single sovereign religion, routinized and closely supervised occupations, centralized political structures). In sum, the conditions that foster autonomy versus submission at the cultural and individual levels are so similar that we expect similar dimensions to emerge in analyses at both levels.

Equivalence of the Meaning of Values

Do the specific items included in the analyses for deriving culture-level dimensions have reasonably similar meanings in each of the cultures? Comparisons are virtually meaningless if there is no equivalence of meaning (Berry, 1980; Poortinga & Malpass, 1986). Careful back-translation of materials helps, but it hardly ensures equivalence. This issue can be tackled only by identifying the within-culture meanings of items (values) and then examining their conceptual equivalence across cultures. Because Hofstede did not address this issue, the extent to which his items were conceptually equivalent across cultures is unknown. Hence one cannot assess the validity of comparing the scores of the national samples on his dimensions.

To overcome the problem of meaning differences, the current research used only values found to be highly equivalent in meaning in the heterogeneous set of 20 nations in my earlier research (Schwartz, 1992). The conceptual meaning of a value for a sample was assumed to be expressed in the pattern of intercorrelations of its importance ratings with those of all the other 55 values in the value survey. By examining whether a given value showed a similar pattern of correlations with other values in each sample, I determined whether the meaning of that value was similar in the different samples. For 45 values, high consistency of meaning was found (Schwartz, 1992; Schwartz & Sagiv, in press). For these values, cross-cultural comparison is justified because most people in each culture apparently understood them in similar ways.

PREDICTED CULTURE-LEVEL
VALUE TYPES AND STRUCTURE

The culture-level analyses of Hofstede, Kluckhohn and Strodtbeck, and Triandis, and extrapolation from my individual-level values theory, provide bases for predicting the distinct types of values likely to be found in a culture-level analysis and the structure of relations among them. I follow these earlier sources in postulating that cultural dimensions of values reflect the basic issues that social groups must confront. I propose four hypotheses:

1. There is a broad dimension interpretable as a more sharply defined version of I/C. This dimension can and should be refined into more specific types of values to reduce confusions in the literature (Schwartz, 1990). Loosely defined, I/C has received considerable support in culture-level analyses. Its apparent

usefulness for discussing cultural differences suggests that it does reflect an aspect of reality (Hofstede, 1980; Kagitçibasi & Berry, 1989; Triandis, 1990).

The literature on individualism and collectivism emphasizes such contrasts as autonomy/relatedness, separateness/interdependence, egocentrism/sociocentrism, and individualism/communalism (e.g., Bellah, Madsen, Sullivan, Swidler & Tipton, 1985; Bond, 1986; Doi, 1986; Geertz, 1984; Hsu, 1983; Hui & Triandis, 1986; Kagitçibasi, 1990; Kim & Choi, in press; Markus & Kitayama, 1991; Miller, 1984; Sampson, 1989; Shweder & Bourne, 1982; Triandis, Leung, Villareal, & Clark, 1985; see also Sinha & Tripathi, Chapter 8, this volume). These contrasts include two major themes. Assuming the possibility of conflict between personal and group interests, one theme focuses on whose interests take precedence. This parallels my individual-level, higher-order, self-enhancement versus self-transcendence dimension. The second theme focuses on the autonomy or embeddedness of the person vis-à-vis the group. This parallels my higher-order openness-to-change versus conservation dimension.

I consider the autonomy-embeddedness theme the more appropriate emphasis for defining the culture-level dimension related to I/C. This is the more fundamental theme because, to the extent that persons are truly embedded in their groups, conflict of interest is not experienced. It is difficult to label this hypothesized dimension without causing confusion or violating "political correctness." Retaining the I/C label assimilates excess meanings I wish to avoid that are associated with the terms *individualism* and *collectivism.* These terms are also interpreted as pejorative when applied to cultures (e.g., see Kagitçibasi, Chapter 4, this volume). I will label this the *autonomy/conservatism* dimension in an attempt to capture the essence of the culture-level contrast and in hopes of avoiding any judgmental implication.

In cultures at one pole on this dimension, the person is viewed as an autonomous entity endowed with independent rights and desires who relates to others in terms of self-interest and negotiated agreements. This view is expressed in values favoring autonomy of individual thought, feeling, and action (e.g., curiosity, creativity, varied life). At the opposite pole, the person is viewed as a part of the social fabric whose significance derives from his or her participation in and identification with the group in carrying on its shared way of life. This view finds expression in values favoring propriety and harmony in interpersonal and person-to-group relations (e.g., moderate, social order, security, reciprocation of favors). Because this is a bipolar dimension, values whose pursuit is likely to disturb propriety and harmony (e.g., excitement, adventure, enjoying life) will be opposed to conservatism values and express autonomy. Conversely, values that constrain individual thought, feeling, and action (e.g., self-discipline, obedience, honoring elders) will be opposed to autonomy values and express conservatism.

    2. In every society, people must manage their interdependencies with one another. There is a culture-level value dimension that reflects the way societies procure and/or enforce the necessary consideration for the welfare of others and coordination with them in the course of coping with interdependencies. One pole of this dimension is related to the use of power.

This hypothesized culture-level value type is based both on my finding that power is a universally recognized value type at the individual level, apparently reflecting a basic human problem with which societies must cope, and on Hofstede's finding of a power distance dimension at the culture level. This value type should express the preferred degree of hierarchical relations in society. It is likely to include the values that formed my individual-level power type (e.g., wealth, authority, social power).

This value type should be more closely related to the conservatism than to the autonomy values type. This is because the hierarchical allocation of fixed roles is more compatible with cultures where persons are viewed as enacting ascribed roles built into the social fabric than with cultures where persons are viewed as autonomous individuals with the right to seek their own level. The very high correlation between power distance and collectivism reported by Hofstede (1980, 1983a) suggests that such a value type might not be distinguishable from autonomy/conservatism. However, because I define the latter in terms of embeddedness in group rather than in terms of individual versus group interests, I expect this hierarchy type to be distinguishable.

    3. There is a culture-level value type that emphasizes actively mastering the environment and changing the world (expressed in such values as success, ambition, daring). This recalls the mastery pole in Kluckhohn and Strodtbeck's (1961) man-nature orientation and is related to Hofstede's masculinity dimension. It is the societal response to the problem of eliciting individual productivity, reflected at the individual level in the achievement value type, that emphasizes assertive achievement and success. Mastery is likely to be adjacent to the power/hierarchy type, with which it shares the broad concern for self-enhancement.

    4. There is a culture-level value type that includes values that express concern for the welfare of others and emphasize harmony with nature (e.g., social justice, equality, protecting the environment). This type is the societal response to the problem of eliciting prosocial action. The existence of such a type is suggested by the existence of individual-level value types—benevolence

and universalism—that are responses to the same issue. This type is also suggested by the femininity pole of Hofstede's masculinity dimension. Benevolence, universalism, and femininity all emphasize caring for the weak and the quality of life. Kluckhohn and Strodtbeck (1961) distinguish one component of this type, harmony with nature, which they postulate to be opposed to mastery. These approaches, taken together, suggest that this set of values forms a broad self-transcendence value type, opposed to mastery and hierarchy.

The four hypotheses stated above can be reframed into two broader hypotheses regarding the relations between the content and structure of values at the cultural and individual levels.

Content

The same set of four higher-order value types that organizes individual-level value systems (Schwartz, 1992) also organizes culture-level value systems. Stated operationally: A spatial representation of the intercorrelations among the 45 single values is partitionable into four broad, interpretable regions. Each region includes the values that share an emphasis on one of the following: (a) openness to change, (b) conservation of the status quo, (c) self-enhancement, (d) self-transcendence in favor of others' interests.

The theoretical basis for postulating similar broad value types at both levels, despite their statistical independence, has been elaborated above. In brief, the cultural and individual levels are conceptually related because (a) psychological requirements of individuals place constraints on the ways institutions must be structured in order to be effective and (b) cultural priorities influence both the content of individual socialization and the social reinforcement contingencies that individuals experience in the pursuit of their values.

Structure

The basic structural organization of values into competing types is similar at the cultural and individual levels. Just as the four higher-order value types form polar dimensions at the individual level, because of the psychological and social incompatibility of pursuing them simultaneously for the individual (Schwartz, 1992), so they form polar dimensions at the culture level, because of the conflicts that would arise were institutions structured to emphasize and promote them simultaneously.

Specifically, if a nation's institutional structures promote the pursuit of openness-to-change values, they must downplay the importance of conservation values, and vice versa. This is necessary in order to ensure consistent socialization and reinforcement of behavior and to foster smooth institutional functioning. For these same reasons, there must be a trade-off between emphasizing self-enhancement versus self-transcendence values in the way institutional structures are organized and in the implicit messages these structures convey. Operationally, these conflicts should be expressed in the locations of the four broad regions in a spatial representation of value intercorrelations: openness-to-change values in a position opposite conservation values, self-enhancement values in a position opposite self-transcendence values.

In sum, two culture-level dimensions, consisting of opposing value types, are hypothesized:

1. Autonomy versus Conservatism (parallel to individual-level Openness to Change versus Conservation, and closest to the core idea of I/C)
2. Hierarchy and Mastery versus Egalitarian Commitment and Harmony With Nature (parallel to individual-level Self-Enhancement versus Self-Transcendence)

METHOD

Samples

Data were gathered during the 1988-1992 period from 86 samples drawn from 41 cultural groups in 38 nations. Some 80% of the sample included between 150 and 300 respondents, with 4 smaller samples (minimum 76) and 11 larger (maximum 1,868). The samples came from every inhabited continent and included speakers of 30 different languages and adherents of 12 religions as well as atheists.[2]

The culture groups were differentiated mainly by nationality. Although nation and culture do not necessarily overlap, the set of groups studied doubtless comprises a large variety of diverse cultures, and it is diversity that is critical for identifying dimensions. Moreover, the dimensions proposed are intended for use in research on modern cultures that are most often represented as national groups. The locations of national samples along the dimensions indicate cultural value contents that can be interpreted as cultural contexts for psychologically interesting variance in behavior.

The individuals who made up the 38 samples of schoolteachers teach the full range of subjects in grades 3-12 of the most common type of school system in each nation. For the 35 samples of university students, respondents were selected to cover a wide range of majors. Twelve general samples of adults with widely varied occupations and two adolescent samples were also included. In 26 nations, both teacher and student samples were obtained from the same regions. Gender ratios in the samples reflected those in the populations from which they were drawn. As gender effects on values were very small compared with national differences, differences in gender ratios had no significant impact on the results reported below.

Value Survey

The theoretical rationale for this survey instrument, details of its construction, and some of its psychometric properties are described in Schwartz (1992), Schwartz, Antonovsky, and Sagiv (1991), and Schmitt, Schwartz, Steyer, and Schmitt (1993). In order to express directly the definition of values as guiding principles in the life of a person or group, the survey asks respondents to rate each value "AS A GUIDING PRINCIPLE IN MY LIFE," using a scale from 7 (*of supreme importance*) to 0 (*not important*) and −1 (*opposed to my values*). Included are 56 single values selected to represent 11 potentially universal types of individual-level value types. A short explanatory phrase further specifying the meaning of each value follows it in parentheses. In some nations, up to 10 emic values were added, interspersed among the core 56 values.

Procedure

The survey was administered in the respondents' native languages, based on back-translations that were further checked with native speakers. Responses were anonymous, and background questions appeared at the end of the questionnaire. In about two-thirds of the samples the survey was administered to groups, in most other samples to individuals, and in a few mail surveys were used.

Analyses

All analyses reported here were performed at the Hebrew University, Jerusalem. As noted above, only the 45 values demonstrated to have cross-culturally consistent meanings for individuals (Schwartz, 1992) were included in the current analyses. For each of the samples, the mean importance rating of each of these values was computed. The intercorrelation matrix of Pearson correlations between the mean importance ratings of the values was analyzed with the Guttman-Lingoes smallest space analysis (SSA) (Guttman, 1968). This technique represents the values as points in multidimensional space such that the distances between the points reflect the empirical relations among the values as measured by the correlations between their importance ratings. The greater the conceptual similarity between two values, the more related they are empirically, and hence the closer their locations in the space.

I interpreted the SSA by using a "configurational verification" approach (Davison, 1983). That is, I interpreted the configurations of substantively related points that emerged to form regions and the arrangement of these regions in the space relative to one another. The hypotheses regarding the different value types were tested by examining whether it was possible to partition the points that filled the two-dimensional projection of the space into distinct regions that reflected these value types. When two or more of the elements in a substantive facet (the value types here) are in conceptual opposition to one another, wedgelike regions emerging from a common origin are predicted (Levy, 1985; Shye, 1985). The hypotheses regarding the structure of oppositions and compatibility among the value types were tested by examining whether the regions obtained formed a pattern of polar oppositions and of adjacencies corresponding to the hypothesized relations among the types.

To identify distinct regions that reflect the a priori value types, I sought spatial concentrations of the values expected to constitute each value type. I then drew boundary lines that connected the values located at the outer edges of these concentrations. Overlap between region boundaries was avoided (Lingoes, 1977, 1981). Partition lines placed between these boundaries divided the total space into regions for testing the hypotheses. Because this was the first attempt to identify a full set of culture-level value types, I also examined the spatial configuration in an exploratory manner: I looked for regions constituted of values that might form meaningful types that were not predicted.

Once the culture-level value types were established, scores for the priority given by each sample to each type were computed: The importance ratings for all the single values included in a type were averaged. These scores were corrected for sample differences in scale use by subtracting from each sample's scores the average rating that the sample gave to all 56 values. The scores were then rescaled to reflect the original -1 to $+7$ importance scale by adding to them the average rating given to all 56 values across all samples.

RESULTS AND DISCUSSION

Culture-Level Value Types

Figure 7.1 presents the two-dimensional solution of the SSA based on 86 samples. Before I present a discussion of the specific value types identified, consider the overall pattern of relations among the values, which reflects how they discriminate among nations. As hypothesized, culture-level values are organized into the same two basic dimensions that organize individual-level values: (a) The values in the upper-right quadrant largely express conservation of the status quo (e.g., family security, social order). They are opposed to the values in the lower-left quadrant, which largely express openness to change (e.g., creativity, varied life). (b) The values in the lower-right quadrant largely express self-transcendence to promote the interests of other persons and the natural world (e.g., social justice, unity with nature). They are opposed to the values in the upper-left quadrant, which largely express self-enhancement to promote own interests regardless of others' interests (e.g., ambitious, wealth). Thus the same broad, basic conceptual principles govern the organization of values at the individual and the culture levels, despite the statistical independence of the analyses.

Partition lines have been drawn in Figure 7.1 to form regions that correspond to the hypothesized value types. The space could, of course, be partitioned into broader or more fine-grained regions. The decision to distinguish these seven regions was based on three criteria: fit with the a priori hypotheses, meaningfulness and interpretability of each region, and replication of regions including the same single values when different subsets of samples were analyzed separately. All the seven value types that were identified fit the predictions. Each value type is labeled to reflect its core conceptual content.

Conservatism. The culture-level value type on the upper right, labeled "Conservatism," is constituted precisely of those values likely to be important in societies based on close-knit harmonious relations, in which the interests of the person are not viewed as distinct from those of the group. All of these values emphasize maintenance of the status quo, propriety, and avoidance of actions or inclinations of individuals that might disturb the traditional order. These are sociocentric values, appropriate in settings where the self lacks autonomous significance but has meaning as part of the collectivity (Miller, 1984). Cultures that emphasize Conservatism values are primarily concerned with security, conformity, and tradition.

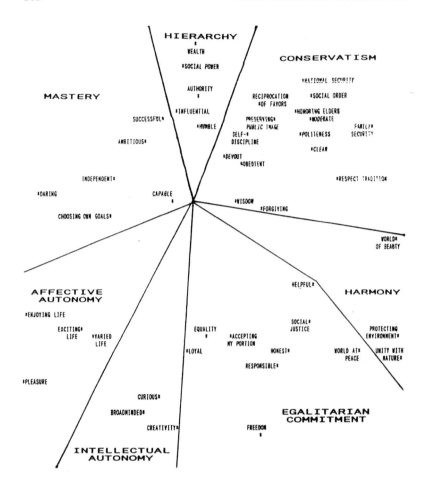

Figure 7.1. Culture-Level Value Structure Based on 86 Samples
From 38 Cultures: Two-Dimensional Smallest Space Analysis

Intellectual and affective autonomy. Opposite Conservatism, as hypothesized, are those values likely to be important in societies that view
the person as an autonomous entity entitled to pursue his or her individual
interests and desires. Two related aspects of Autonomy values appear to
be distinguishable: a more intellectual emphasis on self-direction and a
more affective emphasis on stimulation and hedonism. The mean priority
scores for the Intellectual and the Affective Autonomy value subtypes are
correlated across cultures ($r = .49$), and they are strongly negatively correlated with priority scores for the Conservatism value type, whether con-

sidered separately ($r = -.74$ and $-.80$, respectively) or combined as a general Autonomy value type ($r = -.89$).[3] The strong negative correlation suggests that, when the loose I/C concept is narrowly understood as Autonomy versus Conservatism, a polar opposition may exist that is not found for broader definitions of the I/C concept (Schwartz, 1990; Triandis, 1990).

Hierarchy. As hypothesized, a distinct region of values that express a preference for Hierarchy emerges closer to Conservatism ($r = .34$) than to the combined Autonomy index ($r = -.28$). The value "humble" falls in this region, together with the power values from which it was consistently distant in individual-level analyses (Schwartz, 1992). This location of humble reinforces the interpretation of the culture-level Hierarchy value type as emphasizing the legitimacy of hierarchical role and resource allocation. This value type forms the hypothesized broad self-enhancement region together with the next type, Mastery, the type with which it is correlated most positively ($r = .41$).

Mastery. The values in this region emphasize active mastery of the social environment through self-assertion. Although this value type and the Intellectual Autonomy type both include values that represent self-direction at the individual level, these two culture-level value types are not related ($r = -.02$, n.s.). Mastery values promote active efforts to modify one's surroundings and get ahead of other people, whereas Intellectual Autonomy values emphasize flexibility of thought and feeling but not active social behavior. Mastery is related to Affective Autonomy ($r = .37$) because the two types share an emphasis on stimulating activity.

All the Mastery and Autonomy values, and some of the Hierarchy values, presume the acceptance of the individual's pursuit of personal interests as legitimate. Might it be better to view all these value types as a general individualism type? For several reasons, I think not. On conceptual grounds, the Mastery and Hierarchy values are a pole of one of the two basic dimensions (self-enhancement), and the Affective and Intellectual Autonomy values are a pole of the other basic dimension (openness to change). On empirical grounds, these value types are also distinct. Mastery, as noted, is related only to Affective and not to Intellectual Autonomy; and Hierarchy is correlated negatively with both Affective ($r = -.17$, n.s.) and Intellectual Autonomy ($r = -.35$). Moreover, the correlation of Mastery with Conservatism is considerably less negative than the correlations of either type of Autonomy with Conservatism ($r = -.26$ versus $-.80$ and $-.74$). Finally, the correlations of Mastery and Hierarchy with the two value types discussed next are very different from the correlations of Affective and Intellectual Autonomy with these two types.

Egalitarian commitment. A region of values that express transcendence of selfish interests emerges opposite to the Hierarchy and Mastery types, as hypothesized. I label this type Egalitarian Commitment because the values that constitute it exhort voluntary commitment to promoting the welfare of other people (e.g., social justice, responsible, loyal). This is a social commitment that can occur among equals. It must be present for societies of autonomous individuals to function smoothly. Among people who share status obligations and kinship ties, adherence to such values is assumed and is not left to voluntary decisions that must be encouraged by cultural value exhortation.

Almost all the values that constitute this type are from the individual-level benevolence or universalism types, as anticipated. An interesting exception is "freedom." The location of this value in the Egalitarian Commitment region was replicated in analyses of subsets of samples. Thus the patterns of associations for freedom are different at the cultural (national) and individual levels. In nations where freedom receives high average ratings as important, values that emphasize protecting the welfare of others are also attributed high importance, but striving for mastery and wealth are disvalued. At the individual level, in contrast, persons who rate freedom as high rather than low in importance emphasize values that promote their own independence of thought and action but give no special emphasis to the welfare of others.[4]

Egalitarian Commitment is negatively correlated with Hierarchy ($r = -.67$) and with Mastery ($r = -.36$). These correlations reflect the expected opposition of self-transcendence and self-enhancement values. Egalitarian Commitment is negatively correlated with Conservatism ($r = -.54$) and positively correlated with Intellectual ($r = .41$) and Affective ($r = .21$, $p. < 05$) Autonomy. These correlations contradict the pattern one would expect were the autonomy/conservatism dimension very similar to the I/C dimension described by Triandis (1990): People in individualist societies are emotionally detached from in-groups (other than close family) and place their personal goals ahead of those of the in-group, whereas people in collectivist societies are emotionally attached to their in-groups and concerned with promoting their welfare.

The negative correlation of Egalitarian Commitment with Conservatism cannot be explained by reference to a tendency of "collectivists" to disregard the welfare of all but in-group members, because a number of Egalitarian Commitment values (loyal, helpful, responsible) largely govern relations with in-group members. This negative correlation and the positive correlation of Egalitarian Commitment with Autonomy indicate that valuing emotional attachment and promotive interaction with others is not the unique hallmark of societies in which so-called collectivist values are given priority over individualist values. I argue next that emotional attachments and promotive interaction are important in all societies, but their nature is different.

In societies where Autonomy values prevail (many so-called individualist cultures), it is necessary for institutions to socialize and exhort individuals to act as voluntary contributors to the collective good. As autonomous selves, individuals in such societies might naturally feel detached from and unconcerned about others. Smoothly functioning social relations require that autonomous individuals internalize the importance of committing themselves to others' welfare and of expressing their concern by taking prosocial action. These social requirements are expressed in the priority given to Egalitarian Commitment values, values that emphasize emotional attachment to and active concern for the welfare of others in close interaction (e.g., helpful, loyal, responsible) and in wider groups (e.g., equality, social justice, freedom).

In societies where Conservatism and perhaps Hierarchy values prevail (many so-called collectivist cultures), in contrast, emotional attachments are inherent in the binding, often ascribed, relationships of close interdependence. Interaction is expected to preserve these relationships. To the extent that people experience themselves and are viewed as parts of a collectivity rather than as autonomous individuals, there is little need for cultural emphasis on voluntary prosocial action of persons toward one another (hence the negative correlation with Egalitarian Commitment values). That people will act toward close others in accordance with Egalitarian Commitment values can be taken for granted. One is "naturally" helpful, loyal, and concerned for the welfare of members of the in-group. People are exhorted, instead, to act in conventional ways that avoid upsetting or harming others and that preserve the welfare of the in-group as traditionally defined—that is, to express Conservatism values.

Harmony. This culture-level value type, emphasizing harmony with nature, is found opposite Mastery, just as Kluckhohn and Strodtbeck (1961) postulate. It relates most closely to Egalitarian Commitment ($r = .39$), with which it forms the broad self-transcendence region. "World at peace," "social justice," and "helpful" could also be placed in Harmony, suggesting that this value type involves social harmony as well.[5] Its correlations with the Conservatism (–.16, n.s.), Affective Autonomy (–.16, n.s.), and Intellectual Autonomy (.31) value types indicate that it is virtually orthogonal to the autonomy/conservatism dimension. Harmony values presume no particular stance regarding the autonomy of the person, but they stand in opposition to value types that promote actively changing the world through self-assertion and exploitation of people and resources (Mastery, −.52; Hierarchy, −.56).

Cultural-Level Value Structure

The seven value types form an integrated structure of relations that is reflected in the SSA analysis in Figure 7.1. Value types whose simultaneous emphasis in a culture promotes smooth and coherent social action are located in adjacent regions. Competing value types whose simultaneous pursuit would lead to cultural contradictions and disruptions of social action emanate in opposite directions from the center of the figure. The compatibility or contradiction among value types is largely the result of the inherent stances on four issues mentioned in passing above:

- view of the person as an autonomous entity who enters voluntarily into relationships versus an entity who lacks autonomous significance and finds meaning only as part of a collectivity of interdependent, mutually obligated others (Intellectual and Affective Autonomy and Egalitarian Commitment versus Conservatism)
- preference for equal versus hierarchical treatment of people and allocation of resources (Egalitarian Commitment versus Hierarchy and Mastery)
- preference for change versus preservation of and fitting into the social and material environment (Mastery and to some extent Affective Autonomy versus Harmony and to some extent Conservatism)
- acceptance of the legitimacy of pursuing selfish individual or group interests versus transcending self and in-group interests in favor of others (Mastery and Hierarchy versus Egalitarian Commitment and Harmony)

Robustness of the Culture-Level Value Types

To test the robustness of the value types and the structure of relations among them, separate culture-level SSAs were run on two matched, heterogeneous subsets of 30 samples each. Multiple samples from a single nation were assigned to different subsets, and equal numbers of teacher and student samples were allocated to each.

In both subsets, the same seven types of values identified in the overall SSA emerged in distinctive regions. In subset 1, 43 of the 45 single values were located in the same region as in the overall analysis. In subset 2, 42 of the 45 values were located in the same region. This small number of changes in locations of single values can be expected by chance alone (Schwartz & Sagiv, in press). Equally important, the order around the circle of the seven value types found in both subsets was identical to that found in the overall analysis. Thus the same basic polar dimensions and sets of oppositions and compatible elements organized the values in both subsets and in the overall analysis. In sum, these cross-validations show that the conceptual content of the value types, the specific items that constitute them, and the structure of relations among them are robust.

Comparisons With the Hofstede Dimensions

How does the order of nations on the current types compare with their order on the Hofstede dimensions? Before this question can be answered, it is necessary to establish whether Hofstede would have found his four dimensions in the analysis of his data had he included only the nations included here. Duplication of the intercorrelations that Hofstede reported among his dimensions, using his data only for the nations also studied here, would imply that similar dimensions would have been found with the more limited subset of nations. In support of this conclusion, Hofstede's intercorrelations were indeed duplicated in our reanalysis of his data.

For example, the two strongest intercorrelations that Hofstede reported were for individualism (IDV) $\times$ power distance (PD) ($r = -.67$) and for IDV $\times$ uncertainty avoidance (UA) ($-.35$). Similar correlations were found using only the nations in which we obtained teacher data ($-.70$ and $-.13$, respectively) or the nations in which we obtained student data ($-.75$ and $-.15$, respectively). The two weakest intercorrelations that Hofstede reports, PD $\times$ masculinity (MAS) ($.10$) and IDV $\times$ MAS ($.00$), were also very similar ($.12$ and $.03$, respectively, for nations in the teacher set; $.12$ and $-.02$, respectively, for nations in the student set). Thus the main patterns of intercorrelation in Hofstede's full set of nations were replicated in the reanalysis with the current subset. Consequently, comparisons using this subset of nations are legitimate.

Table 7.2 presents correlations between the importance ratings of the value types derived here and the ratings reported by Hofstede (1983a) for his four dimensions. Correlations in the teacher sample columns are based on the 23 nations that overlap with Hofstede for the teacher samples, and those in the student sample columns are based on the 22 nations that overlap for student samples. In both analyses, Hofstede's IDV dimension is positively correlated with my Autonomy value types (Affective and Intellectual) and negatively correlated with my Conservatism value type. These correlations were expected, but the positive correlation of IDV with Egalitarian Commitment in both samples was not. The latter correlations reinforce my argument that a strong cultural emphasis on voluntary action to benefit others is compatible with a view of the person as an autonomous agent, not as an embedded member of a collectivity.

National wealth (GNP per capita in 1970) explained most of the variance in Hofstede's IDV index ($r = .82$) across 40 nations. GNP accounts for considerably less variance in the value dimension most similar to I/C using the new value types. This dimension is formed by computing the difference between the scores on my combined Intellectual and Affective Autonomy value types and my Conservatism type. The correlations of 1988 GNP with this autonomy/conservatism dimension is .40 (n.s.) for the teacher subset and .57 for the student subset.

The lesser magnitude of these correlations compared with those in Hofstede is not the result of the inclusion of a particular subset of nations from Hofstede's full set. Recalculating the correlation of IDV with GNP, using Hofstede's data only for this particular subset of nations, duplicated the original correlation of IDV with GNP reported by Hofstede for his total set (.87 teacher subset; .81 student subset). Thus I conclude that GNP accounted for more than twice as much variance in IDV across nations around 1970 as it does in autonomy/conservatism in our data around 1990. The substantially weaker association with GNP probably reflects conceptual and measurement differences between Hofstede's version of the dimension and my own and also a historical weakening of the association between national wealth and this type of culture-level dimension.

Hofstede's PD dimension shows a pattern of correlations virtually the opposite of IDV in both analyses. The strong negative correlation between PD and IDV, coupled with their opposing patterns of correlation with the value types here, reinforces the possibility, acknowledged by Hofstede (1980), that PD and IDV are opposing poles of a single dimension. The absence of a correlation between my Hierarchy value type and Hofstede's PD is open to various interpretations. Most probably, it reflects a difference between the concepts. The Hierarchy values emphasize the legitimacy of using power to attain individual or group goals in general. The PD items refer quite narrowly to legitimacy of power inequality in employee-boss relations.

The substantial correlations of IDV and PD with the Autonomy and Conservatism value types indicate similarity in the rankings of nations in the two studies. This is striking in light of the passage of some 20 years between the studies and the use of different empirical measures and different samples of respondents. Still, the proportion of variance shared by the ratings of nations in the two studies indicates that they are far from identical; it ranges from about 25% to 70%, depending on the index used. Hence it makes a considerable difference which set of ratings is used to order nations for current research.

Table 7.2 Correlations Between Hofstede Value Dimensions and Schwartz Culture-Level Value Types

	Hofstede Dimensions							
	Teacher Samples (N = 23)				Student Samples (N = 22)			
Schwartz Types	IDV	PD	UA	MAS	IDV	PD	UA	MAS
Conservatism	-.56*	.45*	-.25	-.02	-.66*	.70*	-.32	-.08
Hierarchy	-.51*	.27	-.08	.15	-.22	.06	-.32	.32
Mastery	-.24	.26	.25	.56*	-.19	.28	.22	.39
Affective Autonomy	.46*	-.45*	.20	-.10	.85*	-.83*	.07	.10
Intellectual Autonomy	.53*	-.35	.21	.13	.48*	-.49*	.13	.07
Egalitarian Commitment	.51*	-.37	.27	-.23	.45*	-.47*	.37	-.23
Harmony	.18	.01	.43*	.10	.26	-.17	.29	-.09
Autonomy: Affective + Intellectual	.54*	-.47*	.21	.01	.81*	-.79*	.11	.09

NOTE: IDV = individualism, PD = power distance, UA = uncertainty avoidance, MAS = masculinity.
*$p < .05$, one-tailed.

The positive correlation of UA with the Harmony value type fits what one would expect, as do the weaker positive correlations with Egalitarian Commitment. The positive correlation of MAS with the Mastery value type also fits expectations, as do its negative correlations with Egalitarian Commitment. The relatively low magnitude of these correlations suggests, however, that the conceptual content measured by these Hofstede dimensions and by the value types is quite different, and/or that the nations have changed considerably in 20 years on the UA and MAS dimensions. In any case, the key conclusion is that the results of research will be seriously affected by choosing to order nations according to the new types or according to Hofstede's dimensions.

NATION SCORES ON
THE CULTURE-LEVEL VALUE TYPES

The above analyses provide the justification for using the seven culture-level value types to compare nations in future research. To sum up: These value types are conceptually meaningful, grounded in the literature, and empirically validated. The theorized structure of conflicts and compatibility among the types is confirmed, as is the existence of two basic dimensions that organize them. The value types and structure are robust across two different subsets of nations. The value types show a reasonable pattern of associations with Hofstede's dimensions, and they also show the theoretically predicted pattern of conceptual relations with the individual-level value types. Finally, the values included in these analyses and in computing the scores for each type have been found to have equivalent meanings across cultures (Schwartz, 1992; Schwartz & Sagiv, in press).

The number of nations for which mean importance scores are available for comparison is growing. Table 7.3 lists national scores for researchers who might wish to use them. In order to reduce possible impacts of factors other than nation-culture on the reported means, Table 7.3 presents only the means obtained from the samples of teachers. The data reveal interesting differences not only between nations but also between cultural areas broader than single nations. Space considerations preclude discussion of these differences here. I comment only on a few results that highlight differences between the current findings and the order of nations that has been used in research based on Hofstede's findings.

First, these data do not support a view of the United States as a highly individualist nation, if *individualism* refers to a conception of the person as autonomous relative to the group. The U.S. sample is not especially high on the Autonomy types or low on Conservatism. It is relatively high

on Mastery. This supports a view of the United States as having an entre-
preneurial culture in which mastering and controlling the environment are
central goals. Confidence in these conclusions is strengthened by the fact
that the two U.S. student samples show similar value profiles relative to
other student samples.

Second, the mainland China samples are especially high on the importance attributed to Hierarchy and Mastery values, low on the importance
of Egalitarian Commitment values, and average on the autonomy/conser-
vatism dimension. These data suggest that China is not a prototypical
collectivist society, if *collectivism* refers to a conception of the person as
deeply embedded in the collectivity without legitimate autonomous interests. The notion of China as a culture that legitimates hierarchical differentiation is supported, and the major hallmark of this culture is an emphasis
on entrepreneurship within highly regulated relationships (see Elliott, 1989;
Gibney, 1991; Redding & Wong, 1986; Yang, 1986).

Third, samples from Western European nations (e.g., France) are located closest to the Autonomy pole of the autonomy/conservatism dimension. Hence, if individualism is understood primarily in terms of cultural
assumptions about the autonomy/embeddedness of the person, these are
the most individualist nations. Note that these samples are also especially
high on the importance they attribute to Egalitarian Commitment values.
Thus these are cultures in which individuals are viewed as autonomous
but subject to legitimate expectations to concern themselves voluntarily
with the welfare of their fellow citizens (Schwartz & Ros, 1994).

Finally, the sample from Singapore shows a profile that is closest to the
pure Hofstede conception of collectivism, high in Conservatism and
Hierarchy and low in Autonomy and Mastery. However, for most nations
high in Conservatism (e.g., Malaysia, Taiwan, Poland), their locations on
other value types do not fit Hofstede's conception. This demonstrates that
a clear understanding of the value aspects of their culture requires a
different dimensional analysis from what I/C permits.

To what extent do the schoolteacher samples studied reflect the general
priorities in their cultures? The validity of the orderings of nations on the
value types presented here as bases for future research depends upon the
answer to this question. At the opening of this chapter, I suggested why
teachers may be the optimal occupational group to represent a culture.
Hofstede (1980) defends his results by arguing that even if the samples in
a set are atypical, it "does not matter so long as they are atypical in the same
way from one country to another." Although we cannot assess this contention for Hofstede's dimensions, some empirical evidence is available
on the new value types. Two types of assessment were undertaken: compari-

Table 7.3 Mean Importance of Culture-Level Value Dimensions in 38 Teacher Samples (corrected for differences in scale use)

Conservatism		Affective Autonomy		Intellectual Autonomy	
Israel-Druze	4.51	France	4.41	Switzerland (Fr)	5.33
Malaysia	4.46	Switzerland (Fr)	4.24	France	5.15
Bulgaria-Turks	4.43	East Germany	4.16	Slovenia	5.03
Singapore	4.38	West Germany	4.03	Spain	4.90
Estonia-Rural	4.37	Denmark	4.01	West Germany	4.75
Isr-Christ Arab	4.36	New Zealand	3.98	Japan	4.68
Isr-Muslim Arab	4.33	Spain	3.97	Finland	4.62
Taiwan	4.31	Greece	3.96	Italy	4.60
Poland	4.31	Zimbabwe	3.85	Denmark	4.58
Slovakia	4.28	Slovenia	3.76	Guangzhou (PRC)	4.58
Slovenia	4.27	United States	3.65	East Germany	4.47
Turkey	4.27	Thailand	3.62	Hungary	4.44
Estonia-Urban	4.26	Israel-Jews	3.62	Netherlands	4.44
Thailand	4.22	Portugal	3.54	New Zealand	4.36
Zimbabwe	4.21	Japan	3.54	Israel-Jews	4.31
Shanghai (PRC)	4.10	Netherlands	3.51	[China (comb)	4.27]
Israel-Jews	4.08	Finland	3.51	Shanghai (PRC)	4.25
Hebei (PRC)	4.07	Australia	3.50	United States	4.20
Australia	4.06	Hebei (PRC)	3.46	Mexico	4.20
Hong Kong	4.04	Guangzhou (PRC)	3.45	Brazil	4.13
Mexico	4.03	Hungary	3.34	Portugal	4.12
Hungary	3.97	[China (comb)	3.32]	Australia	4.12
[China (comb)	3.97]	Brazil	3.30	Turkey	4.12
Brazil	3.97	Isr-Muslim Arab	3.27	Greece	4.09
United States	3.90	Isr-Christ Arab	3.27	Poland	4.09
Japan	3.87	Turkey	3.25	Hong Kong	4.08

Finland	3.84
Italy	3.82
Portugal	3.76
Guangzhou (PRC)	3.75
New Zealand	3.73
Greece	3.68
Netherlands	3.68
Denmark	3.64
East Germany	3.50
West Germany	3.42
Spain	3.42
France	3.35
Switzerland (Fr)	3.25

Hierarchy

Hebei (PRC)	3.98
Guangzhou (PRC)	3.78
[China (comb)	3.70]
Shanghai (PRC)	3.36
Thailand	3.32
Turkey	3.30
Isr-Muslim Arab	3.17
Zimbabwe	3.14
Bulgaria-Turks	3.07
Isr-Christ Arab	2.93
Japan	2.86
Taiwan	2.85
Israel-Druze	2.83
Hong Kong	2.83

Mexico	3.23
Taiwan	3.21
Malaysia	3.16
Israel-Druze	3.16
Bulgaria-Turks	3.13
Poland	3.13
Hong Kong	3.11
Shanghai (PRC)	3.09
Estonia-Urban	3.08
Singapore	3.04
Estonia-Rural	3.03
Italy	2.95
Slovakia	2.76

Mastery

Guangzhou (PRC)	4.84
Hebei (PRC)	4.76
[China (comb)	4.73]
Zimbabwe	4.62
Shanghai (PRC)	4.57
Greece	4.53
Malaysia	4.34
United States	4.34
Mexico	4.34
Japan	4.27
Portugal	4.25
New Zealand	4.23
Isr-Muslim Arab	4.22
Isr-Christ Arab	4.21

Thailand	4.08
Malaysia	4.07
Israel Druze	4.07
Isr-Muslim Arab	4.07
Slovakia	4.03
Hebei (PRC)	4.01
Taiwan	3.93
Estonia-Urban	3.93
Zimbabwe	3.82
Isr-Christ Arab	3.80
Bulgaria-Turks	3.78
Estonia-Rural	3.69
Singapore	3.68

Egalitarian Commitment

Portugal	5.62
Italy	5.57
Spain	5.55
Denmark	5.52
France	5.45
Netherlands	5.39
West Germany	5.37
Greece	5.35
East Germany	5.29
Finland	5.26
Switzerland (Fr)	5.19
New Zealand	5.15
Turkey	5.12
United States	5.03

Table 7.3 Continued

Hierarchy		Mastery		Egalitarian Commitment	
Singapore	2.75	Hong Kong	4.18	Estonia-Rural	5.02
East Germany	2.69	Switzerland (Fr)	4.18	Mexico	4.99
Israel-Jews	2.69	Israel-Druze	4.16	Slovakia	4.98
Brazil	2.64	Brazil	4.16	Australia	4.98
Poland	2.53	East Germany	4.16	Estonia-Urban	4.96
Malaysia	2.43	Spain	4.11	Brazil	4.92
Hungary	2.42	Taiwan	4.11	Isr-Muslim Arab	4.88
United States	2.39	Slovakia	4.09	Isr-Christ Arab	4.88
New Zealand	2.38	Australia	4.09	Hungary	4.87
Australia	2.36	Italy	4.08	Israel-Druze	4.86
Mexico	2.35	West Germany	4.07	Hong Kong	4.85
West Germany	2.27	Israel-Jews	4.06	Bulgaria-Turks	4.83
Netherlands	2.26	Bulgaria-Turks	4.04	Poland	4.82
Switzerland (Fr)	2.20	Poland	4.00	Singapore	4.79
Estonia-Rural	2.18	Thailand	3.99	Israel-Jews	4.78
France	2.16	Netherlands	3.98	Japan	4.69
Slovakia	2.11	Denmark	3.97	Taiwan	4.68
Portugal	2.08	Hungary	3.96	Malaysia	4.66
Spain	2.03	Singapore	3.93	Shanghai (PRC)	4.65
Finland	2.03	Turkey	3.90	[China (comb)	4.49]
Greece	2.01	France	3.89	Zimbabwe	4.48
Estonia-Urban	2.00	Slovenia	3.76	Hebei (PRC)	4.46
Denmark	1.86	Estonia-Urban	3.73	Slovenia	4.36
Slovenia	1.76	Estonia-Rural	3.64	Guangzhou (PRC)	4.35
Italy	1.69	Finland	3.63	Thailand	4.34

Harmony

Italy	4.80	France	4.31	Guangzhou (PRC)	3.83
Slovenia	4.72	Portugal	4.29	Singapore	3.72
Mexico	4.67	Turkey	4.26	Hebei (PRC)	3.71
Estonia-Urban	4.65	Taiwan	4.17	[China (comb)	3.71]
Finland	4.54	Denmark	4.16	United States	3.70
Estonia-Rural	4.53	Poland	4.10	Shanghai (PRC)	3.63
Spain	4.53	East Germany	4.08	Israel-Druze	3.50
Hungary	4.51	Japan	4.07	Malaysia	3.50
Switzerland (Fr)	4.50	Australia	4.05	Zimbabwe	3.42
West Germany	4.42	Brazil	4.02	Hong Kong	3.34
Slovakia	4.40	New Zealand	3.99	Isr-Christ Arab	3.28
Greece	4.39	Netherlands	3.98	Isr-Muslim Arab	3.05
Bulgaria-Turks	4.32	Thailand	3.93	Israel-Jews	3.01

sons of the orderings of nations when using teacher samples with the orderings using (a) student samples and (b) heterogeneous adult samples.

For 26 nations, data were available from both teacher and university student samples in the same cities or regions. To assess how much the order of nations on each value type was affected by the kind of sample studied, the scores based on the teacher samples and on the student samples were correlated across the 26 nations. Moderately rather than extremely high correlations would be expected because there is considerable variation across nations in the social, educational, and economic bases of selection into universities, and hence in the ways students are atypical for their countries.

Pearson correlations for each value type were as follows: Conservatism, .77; Hierarchy, .59; Mastery, .53; Affective Autonomy, .63; Intellectual Autonomy, .75; Egalitarian Commitment, .68; Harmony, .65. Thus the order of nations on each value type was substantially similar whether the data came from teacher or from student samples. We also compared the order of nations on the two basic dimensions that organize the culture-level value types: For Conservatism versus Autonomy (Affective + Intellectual), the correlation between the orders based on teacher and student samples was .83. For Transcendence (Egalitarian Commitment + Harmony) versus Enhancement (Hierarchy + Mastery), it was .71.

For a diverse set of seven nations (China, Estonia, Finland, France, Holland, Israel, and Japan), data were also available from heterogeneous samples roughly representative of the national adult urban populations. Scores on the two basic culture-level value dimensions from these samples were also correlated with those from the teacher samples across these seven nations. The correlations were .70 for Conservatism versus Autonomy, and .90 for Transcendence versus Enhancement. Thus, on both basic dimensions, the order of nations based on using two very different kinds of samples was similar. In sum, the two sets of findings provide considerable support for the generalizability of the order of nations found with the teacher samples.

CONCLUSION

In *Culture's Consequences*, Hofstede (1980) shows the way toward unpackaging the culture concept into a set of interpretable etic dimensions on which specific nations and cultures can be compared. The current research has derived a new set of culture-level dimensions that summarize seven distinct value types. Not surprisingly, the two sets of dimensions, though related in some respects, are quite different. The current dimensions are based on different theoretical reasoning, different methods, a different set of nations, different types of respondents, data from a later historical period, a more comprehensive set of values, and value items screened to be reasonably equivalent in meaning across cultures.

Considering all of these differences, the fact that a dimension similar—though far from identical—to Hofstede's individualism was found speaks powerfully to the usefulness of this basic idea for comparing cultures. It is not surprising that so many researchers have found I/C an appealing rubric for thinking about cultures. I have argued that the value concepts we use should be defined and operationalized more narrowly and precisely and that much is to be gained in conceptual clarity by doing so. Most important is to distinguish two dimensions confounded in the I/C literature: a dimension opposing conceptions of the person as autonomous versus embedded or related (Autonomy versus Conservatism), and one opposing pursuit of personal goals versus collective goals (Mastery and Hierarchy versus Egalitarian Commitment and Harmony).

Given their theoretical grounding and empirical support, the new value types and dimensions are arguably the most fitting etic indexes currently available for cross-cultural research. In order to use the nation scores on these value types effectively to represent the cultural dimensions of interest, researchers should select samples from nations that are spread across a substantial part of the range of scores. If this is done, findings compatible with the order predicted from the order of samples on the culture-level dimensions can be explained more confidently by cultural variation in values, and alternative explanations can more readily be rejected.

I have proposed and validated culture-level value types here, and I have addressed individual-level value types in earlier work (Schwartz, 1992). There is a danger of confusion regarding when to use which types. The culture-level types are appropriate when one seeks to understand how differences between cultures in their symbol systems, institutions, rates and styles of behavior, and so on are related to cultural value emphases. If one's interest is in how the cultural value context relates to differences across cultures in themes in popular media, political structures, or prevalence of attribution styles, for example, one should use the culture-level types. Theoretical linkages can be generated to interpret associations between sample means on one or more of the culture-level types and sample differences on such variables.

The individual-level types should be used when one seeks to understand how differences between individual persons in beliefs, attitudes, or behavior are related to individual differences in value priorities. Thus, for example, if one is interested in how people's values relate to their political involvement and attitudes, their perceptions of justice, or their aggression toward out-group members, one should use the individual-level types. In order to determine how generalizable the individual-level process is across cultures, one would replicate such individual-level studies in several nations or cultural groups.

Hofstede's (1980) work points to fruitful kinds of questions worth exploring with the new culture-level value types and dimensions. On the one hand, he sought possible antecedents of national scores on the value dimensions in ecological, technological, social, and economic factors. On the other hand, he probed possible consequences of national scores on the dimensions by examining associations with strategically chosen social structural, normative, attitudinal, and behavioral variables. This type of research is currently under way with the new culture-level value types and dimensions.

Thus far, our culture-level dimensions have been validated empirically through the use of sample means of self-report data. As Triandis, McCusker, and Hui (1990) have argued, it is crucial to use multiple methods to probe cultural differences. Because the value dimensions are clearly specified, it should be feasible to generate alternative methods to measure their importance in different cultures (content analysis of documents, behavioral observation, and so on). Moreover, it should be possible to test whether the same clearly specified dynamic structure of compatibility and oppositions among culture-level value types is also observed when such alternative methods are used.

Of course, it would be a mistake to regard the current findings as the final word on culture-level value dimensions. First, the sample of nations studied, however broad, may exclude some whose inclusion would affect the dimensions and structure of oppositions. Second, heterogeneity of culture within some nations makes it desirable to include multiple samples from these nations. It is encouraging that the three teacher samples from across China had quite similar profiles, as did the two student samples from two regions of the United States and the three student samples from three regions of Japan, but this is not sufficient. As additional samples are added to the pool, reanalyses will reveal what modifications, if any, are required in the value dimensions.

Finally, over the course of history the factors that influence cultural value priorities undoubtedly undergo change. Therefore, it is necessary to undertake a study of this type anew periodically. Because the current dimensions are grounded theoretically in universal aspects of social and psychological organization, however, there is hope that they will show considerable stability over time. Consequently, the dimensions may be used as a stable grid upon which to examine historical change in cultural value priorities.

NOTES

*The contributions of the following persons in gathering data are gratefully acknowledged: Ruth Almagor (Israel); Klaus Boehnke (East Germany, Fiji); Gabriel Bianchi (Czechoslovakia); Edna Bonang (Indonesia); Michael Bond (Hong Kong); Bram Buunk (Holland); Bartolo Campos and Isabel Menezes (Portugal); Agnes Chang (Singapore); Rolando Diaz-Loving (Mexico); J.-P. Dupont and F. Gendre (Switzerland); Andrew Ellerman and Norman T. Feather (Australia); Johnny Fontaine (Belgium, Indonesia); Adrian Furnham (England); James Georgas (Greece); Suzanne Grunert (Denmark); Judith Howard and Melanie Moore (United States); Sipke Huismans (Holland); Sumiko Iwao (Japan); Saburo Iwawaki (Japan); Maria Jarymowicz (Poland); Çigdem Kagitçibasi (Turkey, Bulgaria); Leo Montada (Germany); Kathleen Myambo and Patrick Chiroro (Zimbabwe); Toomas Niit (Estonia); Henri Paicheler and Genvieve Vinsonneau (France); Wu Peiguan (China); Darja Piciga (Slovenia); Penkhae Prachonpachonuk (Thailand); Mark Radford (Japan); Sonia Roccas (Italy); Maria Ros and Hector Grad (Spain); Jose Miguel Salazar (Venezuela); Osamu Takagi (Japan); Alvaro Tamayo (Brazil); Giancarlo Tanucci (Italy); Harry Triandis (United States); Shripati Upadhyaya (Malaysia); Antti Uutela, Martti Puohiniemi, and Markku Verkasalo (Finland); Zsuzsa Vajda (Hungary); Colleen Ward (New Zealand); Louis Young (Taiwan); Wei Zhi-Gang (China). My thanks also to Galit Sagie and Lilach Sagiv for their aid in analyzing the data and for their comments on earlier drafts of this chapter, together with Anat Bardi, Marina Barnea, Eetta Prince-Gibson, and Sonia Roccas.

1. Hofstede interprets two factor analyses reported in later publications as replications of his culture-level dimensions (Hofstede & Bond, 1984; Hoppe, 1990). Judging the similarity of factors is problematic, so interested readers had best consult these sources themselves. For example, Hofstede and Bond (1984) report only two values ("exciting life" and "world of beauty") as loading on the factor purported to replicate I/C. These values hardly represent a dimension essentially concerned with person-group relations.

2. Further details on sample characteristics are available from the author.

3. All correlations reported in this chapter are significant ($p < .01$) unless otherwise indicated.

4. Because "accepting my portion" does not fit the interpretation placed on Egalitarian Commitment, it was not included in the computation of importance scores for this type. Statistical analyses suggested that this value has no well-defined meaning at the culture level.

5. As I have noted elsewhere, the assignment of values to discrete types is necessary to establish reliable indexes for research (Schwartz, 1992). However, because values form a continuum of related goals around the circular structure, those near regional boundaries express the goals of both adjacent types to some degree.

PART II

Conceptual and Empirical Analysis

8

INDIVIDUALISM IN
A COLLECTIVIST CULTURE
A Case of Coexistence of Opposites

DURGANAND SINHA
RAMA CHARAN TRIPATHI

The use of dichotomies is a heuristic device popular in the West, especially in psychological descriptions of individuals. A host of exclusive descriptive categories, such as extroversion versus introversion, tough-minded versus tender-minded, form-bound versus form-labile, have been used frequently in personality descriptions. Such dichotomous categories are also common in characterizations of nations and cultures. Though this device is convenient, it produces stereotypical and distorted pictures of complex social reality. When a whole culture or society is pigeonholed in dichotomous categories such as masculine/feminine, active/passive, or loose/tight, subtle differences and qualitative nuances that may be more characteristic of these social entities are glossed over. Such descriptive labels evoke unduly fixed and caricaturelike mental impressions of cultures or societies rather than representative pictures of their complexities. Also, when cultures are presented in black-or-white terms, not only does this cloud our understanding of them, but it inevitably leads to our making good/bad comparisons.

In this chapter we will argue that both individualist and collectivist orientations may coexist within individuals and cultures. How these orientations interact and the conditions under which they surface in the same culture are likely to provide us with far greater insights into that culture and its consequences than would categorizing the culture as either collectivist or individualist (see Kagitçibasi, Chapter 4, this volume). To illustrate our point we will focus on the culture with which we are most familiar, that of India. Hofstede (1980) originally predicted that India would occupy a very low point on his Individualism Scale. In fact, India scored 48, compared with 91 for the United States and 12 for Venezuela. Yet Hofstede went on to characterize it as a collectivist culture. This categorization has some how gotten stuck to the Indian culture (Chinese Culture Connection, 1987; Sinha & Verma, 1987).

I/C as a descriptive category is inappropriate for designating Indian culture and social reality for two main reasons. First, the Indian psyche, which is a reflection of Indian social reality, is highly complex; contrasting values and basic propensities often coexist, and Indians display a high "tolerance of dissonance" (Chaudhuri, 1966; D. Sinha, 1979, 1988a). Second, as has been pointed out by Roland (1984), J. B. P. Sinha (1982), and Ramanujan (1990, p. 47), the Indian selfhood is so constituted that the typical way in which an Indian responds and reacts is "contextual." Though values occupy a high place in the cognitive-emotional structure of an average Indian, in actual practice they seem to be conditioned by the exigencies of the situation. We will elaborate both these points further in the discussion below.

In the Indian psyche, as well as in Indian modes of behavior, juxtaposition of opposites has been frequently observed and commented upon by travelers, writers, social scientists, and historians. To some extent, historical circumstances have greatly contributed to this feature of the Indian psyche. Down the ages, instead of assimilation and integration of diverse cultural influences, what seems to have taken place in India has been a kind of coexistence of disparate elements without any synthesis. The country has been exposed to many cultural influences through invasions from its northwestern frontier. In most European countries, various cultural groups inhabiting the same territory for years have merged into homogeneous and cohesive systems, but nothing like this has occurred in India in spite of the unique capacity of Hinduism to incorporate often hostile elements into some kind of a unique sociocultural structure. In India, enormous numbers of dissimilar people with distinct cultures had to find a way of living together, and they have coexisted rather than merged. Neither a "melting pot" mechanism nor a "social blending machine" seems to have operated on the Indian scene.

The lack of homogenization in Indian culture and religion has been the result of a mechanism that can best be described as a process of "enfolding" or "engulfing" that has operated over centuries to deal with incoming diverse cultural elements. Hinduism did not absorb the influx of influences from outside into a unique and unified system, but it *engulfed them,* to use Schulberg's (1968, p. 17) expression. Groups coming into the country with their own customs, cultures, and lifestyles lived apart or amicably side by side with those who were already there. There occurred a kind of *cultural coexistence.* The process has also been described as *encompassing* (Dumont, 1970), in which seeming contradictions of thoughts and actions, instead of leading to confrontation, are tolerated, balanced, accommodated, and integrated (Marriot, 1976). The Indian strategy is not one of resolving conflict but of juxtaposing opposites, which is often perceived as synthesis. This is often reflected in the tolerance of dissonance (or contradictions) that appears to be a paradoxical characteristic of the Indian psyche and that has often been commented upon by observers. For example, Ramanujan (1990) remarks:

> When Indians learn, quite expertly, modern science, business, or technology, they "compartmentalize" these interests (Singer, 1972, p. 320ff); the new ways of thought and behavior do not replace, but live along with older "religious" ways. Computers and typewriters receive *ayudhapuja* (worship of weapons) as weapons of war did once. The modern, the context-free, becomes one more context, though it is not easy to contain. (p. 57)

COEXISTENCE OF CONTRADICTIONS

The coexistence of contradictions is reflected in various facets of Indian culture and behavior, and historians, social scientists, and other writers have commented on it (for a fuller account of the coexistence model of the Indian psyche, see Sinha & Tripathi, 1990). Koestler (1960) remarks about Indian's basic predisposition of "indifference to contradictions" and "the peaceful coexistence of logical opposites." Mehta (1962) notes the simultaneous coexistence in Hinduism of "all gradations of beliefs, from the crudest to the most highly refined" (p. 130). Looking at all the degradation, squalor, and misery of slum life in Calcutta, Lapierre (1986, p. 75) has wondered how the people there can remain good humored, with radiant expressions. Carl Jung (1978) made some perceptive comments after his visit to India:

> I have, so it seems to me, observed the peculiar fact that an Indian, in as much as he is really Indian, does not think, at least not what we call "think." He rather perceives the thought. . . . It is true that the logical processes of India are funny, and it is bewildering to see how fragments of Western science live peacefully side by side with what we, short-sightedly, would call superstitions. Indians do not mind seemingly intolerable contradictions. If they exist, they are a peculiarity of such thinking, and man is not responsible for them. He does not make them, since thoughts appear by themselves. The Indian does not fish out infinitesimal details from the

Universe. His ambition is to have a vision of the whole. He does not yet know that you can screw the living world up tightly between two concepts. (p. 101)

The historian Basham (1971, p. 3) in his famous book *The Wonder That Was India*, has talked about the Indian people's "love of ease and comfort" (*aram* culture), which has been inculcated by bounteous nature, as well as of a capacity for sustained effort and hard work that has produced gigantic temples, marvelous feats of architecture, and immense irrigation works. Contemporary Indian work behavior is characterized by the attitude of *chalta hai* ("it goes on like this"): a virtual absence of work ethos and general inefficiency, casualness, and procrastination. On the other hand, the same people display the highest level of work culture when working abroad or when confronted with "big" tasks. Tripathi (1990) reports studies of Indian work organizations that were found to display a mixed set of values said to be characteristic of both Western and non-Western societies. Thus a belief in detachment was found to coexist with materialistic orientation, collectivism with individualism, and humanism with power orientation. Sinha and Sinha (1990) also have observed a "dissonance" in Indian work culture in which the highest ideal of work (as embodied in Indian scripture) stands side by side with lower examples of depravity in work behavior. There is eulogization of the ideal along with tolerance of the profane. Two systems and two distinct concepts of work coexist and are exemplified in Indian work life.

There are contradictions galore when one looks at the mythological "heroes" and "models" portrayed in the two great Indian epics, the *Ramayana* and the *Mahabharat*. If one is looking for a model to emulate that is perfect in every respect, with no blemish, neither the *Mahabharat* nor even the *Ramayana* is able to furnish such a character. The greatest heroes in the two epics have their weaknesses. And, conversely, the villains possess many virtues worth emulating. Every character has compulsions, justifications, ambitions, virtues, and weaknesses. If these characters are reflective of the Indian psyche in any way, they indicate that in the Indian mind conflicting tendencies coexist and seldom are resolved. The actions of the characters reflect their inner contradictions: Even in conflicts, the lines between friends and enemies are blurred. The heroes talk with and seek advice from their "enemies" during battle intervals. In contemporary times, Gandhi, through his technique of *satyagraha,* demonstrated very much the same—that there are no opposite sides in a conflict. For example, though Gandhi engineered and led the famous strike in the calico mills of Ahmadabad, the mill owner used to look after his comforts and welfare, and constantly sought his advice. Gandhi, on his part, praised the mill owner in the most laudatory terms (D. Sinha, 1987).

In philosophy and ethics, similar juxtapositions of contradictory elements are to be found where *dharma* (duty) and *moksha* (salvation) coexist with pursuit of wealth (*artha*) and sexual satisfaction (*kama*) as constituents of cardinal virtues. Material wealth and worldly pleasures are considered illusory (*maya*), and spiritual values and otherworldliness are emphasized. At the same time, how much sexual pleasure is cherished can be gauged from the most elaborate treatise on the art of love that the ancient seer has given to posterity, the *Kama Sutra*.

Even the conceptualization of well-being in ancient Indian treatises on medicine reflects the same point. In the context of health and well-being of the individual, the balancing of opposite tendencies and elements is emphasized (D. Sinha, 1990). Imbalance (*asantulan*) is the cause of illness, and avoidance of extremes is vital to humans' well-being. According to Caraka, the preponderance of *qunas* or the humors called *vayu* (wind), *pitta* (bile), or *kapha* (phlegm), the imbalance of which results in disease, are variable conditions, and cure or healing requires restoration of normal conditions of the body or the mind. Both positive and negative elements are present at the same time. The factor of *sama,* or having elements in right or natural quantities, is considered essential for health. All along, the adoption of a middle path (*madhyama*) has been emphasized. Thus a healthy being is equipoised both in pleasure and in pain, in success and in failure. What is significant for functioning is not the extremes, but the middle range. It is the ambiguous middle area, and not the extremes or the dichotomies, that is vital. To give an analogy from music, the beauty of playing the sitar lies not so much in producing the true notes, but in *mirh* (i.e., the delicate nuances between the two adjacent notes). It appears that the Indian has the propensity to function in the "gray area," or between the opposites.

It is this coexistence of opposites all through Indians' lives and culture that is considered to be the cultural and psychological root of their anxiety. An average Indian is "caught in a chaos of conflicting patterns, none of them wholly condemned but no one of them clearly approved and free from confusion" (D. Sinha, 1962, p. 34). Such contradictions and odd paradoxes are in evidence in the sociopolitical plane, where, to give a few examples, Gandhian *sarvodaya* goes hand in hand with building of highly complex technoindustrial society, cottage industry with mass production, and *ahimsa* (nonviolence) with the worst kind of social violence (D. Sinha, 1962, p. 35).

Instances of coexistence of contradictions in Indian life and psyche have led Chaudhuri (1966), a sharp observer and critic of Indian character, to designate Indians as "Janus Multifrons," torn by internal psychological struggles. He refers to the creation of double consciousness, each complete and coherent, but capable of shutting out the other when one is dominant. He talks of the "terrible dichotomy" of the Hindu personality, where a large number of antithetical though connected traits that shape behavior coexist: a sense of solidarity with an uncontrollable tendency toward diversity, collective megalomania with self-abasement, extreme xenophobia with abject xenolatry, authoritarianism with anarchic individualism, violence with nonviolence, militarism with pacifism, possessiveness with carelessness about property owned, courage with cowardice, cleverness with stupidity. As Kapp (1963) points out, there remains "an unresolved dualism within the present human situation which explains the paradoxical coexistence in one culture system of contradictory value orientations and actual behavior pattern" (p. 18).

In view of the above, it is not surprising that various analysts of Indian behavior and child rearing have often emphasized features that are contradictory. Whereas one refers to indifference and less affection between parents and children than in the West (Carstairs, 1957, p. 168), others stress closeness and high participation in adult life by children (Minturn & Hitchcock, 1966; W. S. Taylor, 1948). Weaning has been found to be a very traumatic experience for Indian children (Carstairs, 1957, p. 158) as well as a transition accompanied by no signs of emotional upset (Minturn & Hitchcock, 1966, p. 321). D. Sinha (1962) has highlighted many contradictory practices in Indian child rearing and socialization. These conflicting behavior patterns do not represent mere errors of judgment on the part of observers, but evidence of the paradoxical nature of the reality itself. It is therefore not surprising that Western scholars, used to thinking in terms of logically exclusive categories and disjunctures, fail to understand and appreciate the Indian social reality.

CONTEXTUAL NATURE
OF VALUES AND BEHAVIOR

A second, but related, aspect of the Indian psyche is that values and reactions are *contextual* rather than *textual*. Indians switch gears constantly according to the situation, thereby displaying many frequently contradictory facades. This is true not only on the political plane—where practical and pragmatic considerations are bound to be dominant, often producing bizarre "compromises"—but also in spheres where purely moral and ethical issues are involved. Moral values occupy a very high place in Indian life, but in their actual behavior, Indians do not appear to operate in abstract and absolute ethical terms; rather, actions are conditioned by the exigencies of the situation. Though truth has a very high place in the Indian moral code, its practice is bound by context. Thus, as one popular Indian adage goes, "One should speak the truth; one should speak what is pleasant; and one should *not* speak the truth if it happens to be unpleasant."

Similar is the case relating to the social code prescribed for taking food or drink that has been "polluted" by being touched by persons of low caste. According to tradition, high-caste individuals are enjoined not to drink water or partake of food touched by those of low caste. But exceptions to this "prohibition" are straightaway provided; for example, one may have such food or drink when one is on a journey or traveling in a conveyance such as a boat or a cart (*apaddharma*). "Rightness" and "wrongness" appear to be determined by the context in which the behavior takes place. Here, unlike in the Western tradition, which concentrates on the textual and the individual, the entire emphasis is on the contextual and the relational. The action or behavior by itself is not to be judged; it is the context in which it is made that determines the ethical meaning. As Roland (1984) remarks, "Correct behavior is much more oriented towards what is expected in specific contexts of a variety of roles and relationships, rather than any unchanging norm for all situations" (p. 174). In this context, Ramanujan's (1990) observation is very pertinent:

> I think cultures [may be said to] have overall tendencies (for whatever complex reasons)—tendencies to *idealize,* and think in terms of, either the context-free or the context-sensitive kind of rules. . . . In cultures like India's, the context-sensitive kind of rule is the preferred formulation. Manu explicitly says: [A king] who knows the sacred law, must imagine into the laws of caste (jati), of districts, of guilds, and of families, and [thus] settle the peculiar law of each. (p. 47)

In fact, as J. B. P. Sinha (1990a) points out, two opposite sets of values coexist, one pertaining to one's own group and the other for the eyes of others. In interpersonal relationships, the norms and values for in-group members are different from and sometimes opposite to the norms for outsiders. In-group behavior is characterized by shared needs, beliefs, values, and goals. The members cooperate, make sacrifices, and protect each other's interests, and show what Roland (1984) has called "affective reciprocity." J. B. P. Sinha (1990a) notes that "the interaction patterns with the outside members, however, are strikingly different," and "the ingroup members compete with the outside members rather than cooperate, exploit rather than sacrifice, manipulate rather than help, fight rather than accommodate" (p. 37).

Ambiguity of role models and values among Indian youth (D. Sinha, 1979) is evidenced not only in the high degree of diversity in their choices of role models and "heroes" to be emulated, but also in the fact that they give a high proportion of "uncertain" and "undecided" responses when confronted with questions about situations of social-moral transgression. These are considered to exemplify the dichotomies inherent in the Indian personality and situation, being instances of the "compartmentalization" (Singer, 1972) that characterizes a society in a state of transition (Dawson, 1963).

In a study that examined the dynamics of interrelationships at the intergroup level in a rural setting and focused on the modes of interconnection between cooperation and competition, Jha, Sinha, Gopal, and Tiwary (1985) observed the coexistence of the two that was crucial for the occurrence of events at any level of social structure. The primacy of one over the other depended upon the sociohistorical and cultural and context. Not only did the two opposite processes, cooperation and competition, operate together, their primacy was governed by situational factors. This complex operation may appear paradoxical and bizarre to outsiders, but it is a characteristic way of functioning at the group level so far as the Indian setting goes.

I/C AND THE INDIAN CULTURE

The aspect of the coexistence of opposites so characteristic of the Indian psyche is amply evident with respect to I/C. Before detailing the same, we should note that Craka, the famous ancient *guru* of the Ayurveda system of medicine, recognized individualist and collectivist orientations in conceptualizing personality topology. Based on the preponderance of the three *qunas* (qualities) of *sattva, rajas,* and *tamas*, Craka suggested 16 classifications of human nature. Of the seven types in which *sattva* predominates, two are indicative, respectively, of individualist and collectivist orientations. The *aindrasattva* type is energetic, powerful, unfatigued by activities, and given to religious, economic, and pleasure-giving activities. The *kaubera-sattva* type is fond of family life, given to performance of religious and secular duties, and favors and chastises fellow beings according to their merits and demerits.

Two important factors constituting collectivism are family integrity and interdependence. It is said that Indians are collectivists so far as orientation to family is concerned. In support of this claim, existence of extended family and the important role played by family and kinship ties are cited. However, research concerning valence and psychological proximity to family among older and younger generations has revealed that there is a mix of both individualist and collectivist orientations in family life. From the empirical evidence that is available in this context (D. Sinha, 1979), it is clear that, unlike the older generation, who regard "near" and "other" relations also as parts of the family, among the young there is a distinct trend toward nuclearization, that is, greater individualist orientation. The young tend to define the family in narrower and more restricted terms than do their elders. A mix, however, is there, because the "joint" family is still perceived as fulfilling many needs of the individual. Many of the younger generation are not prepared psychologically to break away completely from the advantages of extended family. Attitudinally, at least, the individual is going nuclear, but without losing the benefits of kinship and extended family living (D. Sinha, 1988b). The individualism of nuclear family structure is juxtaposed with the collective advantages of extended family ties.

In religion and ethics, some essential features of Hindu religious practices and ethical tenets indicate clearly the strong individualist strand present in them. There are infinite varieties of religious tenets and forms of worship permitted in Hinduism; most are based on the individual. Unlike in Semitic religions, there is no central revelation of God, no one messenger of that revelation; no one central religious book is considered the ultimate authority in all religious matters, and no single code of commandments or laws exists for regulating behavior. There is enormous heterogeneity of beliefs and practices, ranging all the way from strict monism to monotheism, to dualism, pantheism, and near-paganism, and even atheism. Regulation of behavior through conformity to group or social norms, which is an important aspect of collectivist orientation, is all but absent. At least the pressure for conformity is much less than what obtains in Islam, Judaism, or Christianity. The individual has the widest range of choices, making any kind of collectivist conformity meaningless. One can believe in an absolute reality, or in many gods, or be an atheist, and still remain a Hindu. Individuals are permitted to follow whatever forms suit them, according to their *samskara* (basic predisposition), *karma* (past actions), and inclinations. The variety is so great and individuals' choices so unlimited that it almost seems there is no such religion as Hinduism. Worship, again, is entirely a matter of individual preference. An entire range of choices is available among the innumerable forms that the gods and goddesses are said to have assumed. As it has been put in Bengali, worship is to be done in a corner, in one's mind, and in the forest (*kone, mane,* and *vane*). Congregational worship is not particularly important, and collectivist forms such as *kirtan* and mass prayers are of recent origin. As far as Indian religion goes, the feature that stands out is strong individualism.

The same is true of Hindu ethics. The importance of individuals' own conduct and behavior has been emphasized. The law of *karma*—that is, the doctrine of "As you sow, so shall you reap"—which still pervades the belief system of Indians, is all-powerful. *Karma* is a force generated by one's actions; it is accumulated and stored by the individual in his or her past lives (*sanchita*), and it is already bearing fruit owing to the individual's actions in the past (*praradha*). It is constantly being acquired and accumulated as a result of actions during the individual's present life (*sanchiyamana*). Thus the individual is the master of his or her own destiny. Any present evil and suffering are consequences of one's own past actions. There is rarely any idea of collective sin for which the entire community is responsible and has to suffer, as found in Judeo-Christian religions (e.g., biblical stories of punishment by famine and pestilence). There is hope for a better future for the individual if he or she adopts the rightful path. There is room for individual effort and personal endeavor (*purusartha*).

In Hindu culture there is a belief that the root cause of bondage is an individual's own ignorance, and he or she can achieve liberation from the world by acquiring true knowledge of reality. Attainment of *vivekajnana* (discriminative knowledge) is an essential condition for liberation. The discipline that is considered essential and prescribed for its attainment is, again, based in the individual. Among other things, it consists of a life of self-control and meditation. Thus, whether one take Jainism, Buddhism, or the orthodox Hindu system of thought, one has the central place in the entire scheme of religion and ethics. In collectivist cultures, group goals are said to have primacy over individual goals, whereas in individualist cultures personal goals have primacy over in-group goals. As far as the Indian ethical goal of liberation is concerned, though it is the *summum bonum* (the ultimate goal to be shared by all), it is one that is attainable through personal effort. That is, liberation is the goal for everyone, but it is individualistic in the sense that it is attainable only through personal endeavor. Everyone can achieve the ultimate goal for and by him- or herself. The two strands coalesce. Strong emphasis is put on the realization of the self, although one is also told to transcend the self in the interest of larger social good.

A series of studies done on competition versus cooperation have found Indians to score high on the former and low on the latter. When asked to make wagers on their own behalf and on behalf of partners, U.S. subjects were found to do better when they bet on behalf of their partners, whereas Indian subjects did better when they bet on their own behalf and were allowed to keep the money (L'Armand & Pepitone, 1975). They also did better when they bet on behalf of their caste group members. In another study that examined bargaining behavior in India, the United States, and

Argentina, competition motivation was found highest among Indians (Druckman, Benton, Ali, & Berger, 1974). Similarly, in a maximizing differences game, Indians were found to be more competitive than Canadians (Carment, 1974). Indians have also been found to be more competitive when they are in the "top-dog" position than when they are in the "underdog" position (Alcock, 1975). As Tripathi (1988, p. 226) has observed, the form of collectivism found in Indian society is a mix of individualism and collectivism that is conditioned by many values and contingencies.

A STUDY OF THE COEXISTENCE MODEL

In developing the questionnaire used in the study reported below, we adopted a different strategy.[1] Instead of giving only individualist and collectivist statements, we provided three alternative statements pertaining to the situation given in each item. One was how an individualist would respond, the second was a collectivist's response, and the third was a mix of the two. In the third alternative, individualist and collectivist elements were blended where the juxtaposition consisted of contradictory elements. In other words, the mix provided a position in which the subject could have something of both the orientations at the same time, but the natures of the two elements were often conflicting, so that one could not always have both at the same time. The third alternative was in consonance with the coexistence model we have proposed above for the Indian psyche and cultural system.

We constructed 22 items centering on some of the factors that have been identified with I/C syndrome, including family integrity and orientation, interdependence, self-reliance, personal achievement and group consideration, and cooperation and competition. We used a variety of social and personal situations that an individual is likely to face in day-to-day life to prepare the three alternatives that were offered on each item. The situations pertained to decision making on various matters, work behavior, facing personal problems, the value of friendship, family interrelationships, personal freedom, ability, achievements, personal happiness, concern for others, and the like.

We administered the questionnaire, at three sessions, to a total of 82 English-medium undergraduates of a university in North India. We then conducted a qualitative analysis of the responses based mainly on the frequencies of choices made by the subjects among the three sets of alternatives indicating individualist, collectivist, and mixed orientations. Each subject was designated as displaying one of the three orientations, depending on most frequent choices among the three alternatives on the 22 items.

The results of the study support our contention that Indian culture contains the coexistence of opposites: Mixed orientations were overwhelmingly found. A total of 86.6% of subjects displayed mixed orientations; 12.2% were individualists and only 1.2% showed collectivist orientations. In their second choices, 64.5% of subjects showed individualist orientations, followed by 23.2% collectivist and 12.3% mixed.

Itemwise analysis of the frequencies of choices made also support the above findings (see Table 8.1). On 17 of the 23 items, the highest frequency was always of the mixed type. Individualist orientation was most frequent on only 5 items, and there was only 1 instance of collectivist orientation being most frequent. Looking into the items on which there were higher frequencies for individualist choices, we found that they pertained to situations concerning personal problems, achievement, and basis of choice in voting (one question asked whether the respondent would vote on the basis of candidate's ability or personal relationship or both, and another asked about voting on the basis of the candidate's ability or caste or both; in both cases, the majority of respondents opted for ability as the basis for voting). Similarly, when asked what motivated them more to work, 45 out of 82 respondents chose competition and personal achievement, compared with 6 who opted for cooperation and sharing. However, a sizable proportion (31 of 82 respondents) said that a mix of both the factors would motivate them to work. The only item on which collectivist orientation appeared to be prominent concerned a purely personal relationship issue: reaction to a person who was once close becoming distant.

DISCUSSION

As the above account of the Indian psyche indicates, Indian behavior is highly complex. Contradictions often coexist, and the stances individuals take are not usually the result of value considerations in absolute terms; rather, reactions are often conflicting and contextual, and situational contingencies operate in a powerful manner. Individualism and collectivism often coexist in individuals' behavior, and, as we have observed, the cultural system reflects both these elements as well.

The Indian form of collectivism contains strands of individualism. Tripathi (1988) explains at some length this apparent paradox that characterizes the Indian orientation:

Table 8.1 Distribution of the Three Modes of Responses on Individual Items

Theme of the Item	Individualist	Collectivist	Mixed
1. Health and disease: consult a doctor versus members of family	12	2	68
2. Voting: own concern versus family solidarity	25	4	58
3. Career: own inclination versus advice of parents/friends	13	1	68
4. Vital matters: decide oneself versus discuss with friends	39	6	37
5. Staying with parents: loss of personal freedom versus would not mind it	2	12	68
6. Voting: ability versus friendship	47	2	33
7. Guests: avoid versus would not mind	4	19	59
8. Interest in problems of others: perceived as interference versus social support	4	15	63
9. Personal problems: struggle on my own versus discussing with others	53	6	23
10. Own happiness versus others' happiness	22	4	56
11. Feeling of loneliness: if family not around versus no such feeling	13	16	53
12. Skill/ability versus congenial coworker	16	1	65
13. Being successful versus being helpful	11	4	67
14. Cooperation versus competition	6	8	68
15. Loss of affective closeness	10	39	33
16. Independence versus dependence	16	2	64
17. To get work done: importance of procedure versus knowing people	18	7	57
18. Concern about opinions of others	22	18	42
19. Solving problem on own versus looking for guidance and support	20	10	52
20. Cooperation versus personal achievement	45	6	31
21. Work: done at any cost versus not at the cost of friendship	11	15	56
22. Voting: ability versus caste	68	3	11

He is revengeful yet forgiving. He acts to protect family honor, yet does not mind killing his own kith and kin if called upon by his *dharma*. He is called upon to engage in *karma* but not seek fruit of it. However, these apparently contradictory values and attitudes are integrated in one scheme by him on the basis of some higher moral principle. An Indian is, therefore, not surprised or shocked by the coexistence of things which are mutually contradictory, either in his own mind or in reality. (p. 321)

The most important distinction between Indian and Western minds, Tripathi (1988, p. 322) points out, lies in the ways boundaries are laid down that define mental structures. In the Western mind, boundaries appear to be more stable and fixed—self and environment, mind and matter, subjective and objective, material and spiritual, secular and religious, and so on. The Indian mind, on the other hand, is governed by boundaries that are constantly shifting and variable. The self sometimes expands to fuse with the cosmos, but at another moment it may completely withdraw itself from it. The self and in-group have variable boundaries. The self does not relate to the in-group but is included in it. In the Western mind, such dichotomies are complete. The self and in-group are taken as two different entities, each having its own boundaries. The self is then related to its in-group by forging links with the group. Thus, as Tripathi (1988) points out, "In the Indian society, I/C act like figure and ground. Depending on the situation, one rises to form the figure while the other recedes into the background" (p. 324).

The Indian culture and psyche are neither predominantly collectivist nor individualist in orientation. Their distinguishing feature is that they incorporate elements of both orientations. Though these elements often conflict with one another and appear mutually exclusive, Indians endeavor to incorporate both orientations in their preferred modes of behavior. They try to have the best of both and frequently display a mixture of collectivist and individualist modes at the same time. Therefore, it is erroneous to label the Indian cultural system as collectivist; if it is collectivist at all, there is still plenty of individualism to be found there.

NOTE

1. We are grateful to Ms. Anshu Mehra, junior research fellow, Department of Psychology, Allahabad University, for her assistance in the preparation of the questionnaire.

9

COMPONENT IDEAS OF INDIVIDUALISM, COLLECTIVISM, AND SOCIAL ORGANIZATION
An Application in the Study of Chinese Culture

DAVID YAU-FAI HO
CHI-YUE CHIU

Individualism and collectivism are exceedingly complex concepts, central to debates over how society is to be organized. To the extent that this complexity is not addressed, research efforts will be misguided or incomplete. An examination of the empirical literature reveals that there is a pervasive tendency to treat individualism and collectivism as opposite ends of a single continuum along which cultures or individuals are differentiated (see Kagitçibasi, Chapter 4, this volume). Typically, the investigation takes the form of convenient oversimplification: individualist versus collectivist cultures, or "individualists" versus "collectivists." To do justice to the two concepts, a reassessment of their scientific status is in order.

This chapter is divided into two main parts. First, we explore the complexity of individualism, collectivism, and social organization and propose a conceptual scheme for classifying the component ideas of these concepts. In the second section, we report on two studies of Chinese culture. Study 1 classified and statistically analyzed popular Chinese sayings pertaining to the concepts of individualism, collectivism, and social organization, using as analytic tools the conceptual schemes we present in the first part

AUTHORS' NOTE: We gratefully acknowledge the financial support we received for the present research from the University of Hong Kong.

of the chapter. Study 2 investigated relations among components of I/C, attitude, and personality variables.

SCHEME OF CLASSIFICATION

We have attempted to identify the component ideas common to the diverse conceptions of I/C by consulting authoritative sources in the history of these ideas (e.g., Lukes, 1973). We then developed a comprehensive scheme for classifying components of the constructs of individualism and collectivism, guided by the following three propositions (see Kagitçibasi & Berry, 1989; Schwartz, 1990). First, individualism and collectivism are multidimensional constructs; each embodies a constellation of component ideas. Second, the two constructs should not be construed as opposite ends of a continuum. Rather, they are distinct; one is not reducible simply to the antithesis of the other. There is no necessary contradiction in holding individualist and collectivist views at the same time. Third, individualism and collectivism have different implications for social organization. To understand these implications, it is necessary to analyze the distribution of responsibilities, obligations, and conflicting interests among individuals within defined target groups.

Our resulting scheme, which call the Components of Individualism and Collectivism (CIC), is presented in Table 9.1. The CIC comprises 18 components, each of which pertains to both individualism and collectivism. Related components are combined into more inclusive major components, of which there are five:

1. Values (Components 1-4)
2. Autonomy/Conformity (Components 5-8)
3. Responsibility (Components 9 and 10)
4. Achievement (Components 11 and 12)
5. Self-Reliance/Interdependence (Components 13-18)

Another scheme, the Components of Social Organization (CSO; presented in Table 9.2), comprising eight components, was constructed independent of the CIC. All these components are important in social organization; admittedly, however, the list is by no means complete, let alone comprehensive. A bipolar construct, integrative versus nonintegrative organization, is introduced in the CSO. Integrative organization is based on principles that emphasize the sharing of leadership and responsibility, altruism, public morality, group discipline, harmony, and hierarchical loyalty; nonintegrative organization, in contrast, negates those principles.

Table 9.1 Components of Individualism and Collectivism

Individualism	Collectivism
Values:	
1. Value of the Individual/Group	
The intrinsic worth of the individual; the ultimate moral principle of the supreme and intrinsic value of the individual human being.	The supremacy of the group or collective; the principle that the value or survival of the collective takes precedence over that of the individual.
2. Human Development	
Self-realization or self-actualization; each person develops to his or her fullest potential; individual self-development and self-cultivation.	Collective development and actualization.
3. Individuality/Uniformity	
Individuation, individuality, and uniqueness of the individual.	Uniformity, conformity to an ideal, and model emulation.
4. Identity	
Individual identity, defined by personal attributes; self-identity defined by self-concept.	Collective identity, defined by group membership.
Autonomy/Conformity:	
5. Self-Direction/Conformity	
Self-assertion or autonomy; individual makes independent judgments and decisions; nonconformity, assertion, and conflict.	Conformity to societal or group norms, compliance, and harmony.
6. Right to Privacy (Is the individual entitled to privacy?)	
People should mind their own business; privacy should be respected. The notion of a private existence within a public world, within which the individual is free from interference to do and think whatever he or she chooses.	One's business is also the business of the group; friends should be concerned with each other's personal matters. The notion that the collective is able and entitled to know, even regulate, what individuals do and think in private; or that what individuals do and think in private may be subject to public scrutiny.

(continued)

Table 9.1 Continued

Individualism	Collectivism
7. Personal Privacy (Should personal matters be kept private or made public?)	
Keep personal matters private.	Personal matters may be made public. Public sympathy solicited; public invited to "uphold justice."
8. Affiliation	
Prefers to be alone; values solitude.	Prefers the company of others.
Responsibility:	
9. Ethical-Legal Responsibility (Who is held responsible for one's actions?)	
Individual responsibility: The individual alone is held morally and/or legally responsible for what he or she does.	Collective responsibility: Others with whom the individual is associated are also held responsible. Perhaps the entire group is held responsible for the actions of its individual members.
10. Consequences of One's Actions (Who is affected by one's actions? Both positive and negative consequences included.)	
The individual actor alone is affected.	The whole group; others with whom the actor is associated are affected.
Achievement:	
11. Individual/Group Efforts	
Do things by oneself; single-handed efforts. Emphasis on individual initiative; achievement through independence.	Do things together. Collective efforts are superior.
12. Competition/Cooperation	
Attainment of excellence and/or achieving goals through competition.	"Unity is strength." "Ten thousand people with a single purpose." Cooperation is the best way to achieve goals. Achievement through conformity.
Self-Reliance/Interdependence:	
13. Self-Reliance/Interdependence (Who is responsible for the individual's well-being?)	
Self-reliance; individual responsibility for well-being.	Interdependence and mutual help. Each individual's well-being depends upon the well-being of the group; the group assumes responsibility for the well-being of each of its members.

14. Individual/Group Interests

Fulfillment of individual needs and interests. Actions are guided by self-interests. (Does not necessarily imply selfishness or disregard for or violation of the interests of others.)

Fulfillment of obligations. Collective goals take precedence. Actions are guided by consideration of group interests.

15. Security

To be sought in the individual's strength.

To be found in the group's solidarity and integrity.

16. Economic Individualism/Collectivism

Private ownership of property; individual's wealth not shared. Reward depends on individual performance.

Public or communal ownership; sharing of wealth; egalitarianism.

17. Political Individualism/Collectivism

Political system meant to satisfy individual needs. Political control over the individual circumscribed. Individual rights protected by law.

Political system meant primarily to preserve the collective, be it the state or the political party. Individual rights secondary to collective prerogatives.

18. Religious Individualism/Collectivism

Religious beliefs and salvation are highly personal; the individual needs no intermediaries. Emphasis is on the individual's personal relationship with the divine.

Participation in group worship. Personal salvation linked to the salvation of others. Membership in a religious institution is essential.

Table 9.2 Components of Social Organization

Nonintegrative Organization	Integrative Organization
1. Responsibility for Group's Actions (Who is held responsible? Relates to CIS Component 9.)	
The leadership; those who make the decisions or give the orders.	The entire group (i.e., every individual member). Responsibility is shared.
2. Consequences of Group's Actions (Who is affected? Relates to CIS Component 10.)	
Those in the lower strata or in disadvantaged positions.	The entire group.
3. Responsibility for Group's Well-Being (Who should assume responsibility? Relates to CIS Component 13.)	
The leadership.	The entire group (i.e., every individual member). Responsibility is shared.
4. Selfishness/Altruism (Relates to CIS Component 14.)	
Devoted primarily or exclusively to one's own interests, and/or disregarding the interests of other people (regardless of whether they are members of one's own group).	Concerned with others and devoted to humanity. Not motivated by self-interests.
5. Public Morality and Civic-Mindedness	
Public morality secondary to considerations of interpersonal relations. Civic-mindedness not emphasized.	Public morality primary. Civic-mindedness emphasized.
6. Group Discipline	
"A pile of loose sand." Lack of group discipline, organization, solidarity, or cohesiveness.	Disciplined, organized, and cohesive.
7. Conflict/Harmony	
Expressions of conflict allowed or condoned; conflicts viewed as natural.	Emphasis or insistence on the maintenance of harmony.
8. Locus of Loyalty	
Loyalty or allegiance to the immediate group of which one is a member (e.g., family or clan) takes precedence over that to the larger collective (e.g., nation).	Loyalty or allegiance to the larger collective takes precedence.

EMPIRICAL STUDIES OF CHINESE CULTURE

We conducted two studies aimed at contributing to a better understanding of individualism, collectivism, and social organization. The first was a culture-level study; the second, an individual-level study. The conceptualization of I/C follows the analysis described above.

Study 1: Content Analysis of Chinese Popular Sayings

A distinctive part of cultural beliefs comes to us in the form of pithy oral expressions: proverbs, saws, maxims, adages, aphorisms, epigrams, and apothegms, all of which may be subsumed generically under the category of "popular sayings." These sayings are particularly interesting because they represent succinct formulations of experience that have been handed down from generation to generation and are widely regarded as time-honored wisdom. Popular sayings are also culture specific in origin. In short, collectively they constitute a crystallization of cultural beliefs.

It occurred to us that the CIC and the CSO could be applied to a content analysis of Chinese popular sayings, in an attempt to shed light on an important question: To what extent do Chinese cultural beliefs affirm or negate the component ideas of individualism and collectivism, and of integrative/nonintegrative social organization?

Method

Pilot study. In a preliminary analysis of 2,056 Chinese popular sayings, we identified 97 sayings as affirming collectivism and 60 as affirming individualism, of which 17 affirmed self-reliance; out of 27 sayings pertaining to self-interests, 4 were affirmative, 17 were negative, and 6 were neutral. This pilot study suggests that it would be profitable to conduct a more comprehensive analysis.

Interjudge agreement. Three psychology students were trained as judges to compile and sort Chinese popular sayings. After training, the judges worked separately, but cross-checks were conducted at various stages of compilation and sorting. Disagreements, when identified, were discussed until uniformity of opinions was reached. Interjudge agreement was examined using 30 sayings as items to be sorted into 104 cells (as explained below). The results were satisfactory: Between-pair agreements of 100%, 90%, and 90% among the three judges were obtained.

Compilation. The first step was to compile a comprehensive collection of Chinese popular sayings. Fortunately, compendiums of Chinese sayings are available for this purpose. We consulted seven compendiums considered to be among the most comprehensive, and obtained an initial pool of 20,799 items. These popular sayings are often used in everyday speech and thus have contemporary significance.

The second step was to select only those sayings expressing evaluative or prescriptive (or proscriptive) beliefs. According to Rokeach (1968, p. 113), three kinds of belief can be distinguished: *descriptive* or *existential* beliefs, which concern factual matters and can be considered either true or false; *evaluative* beliefs, in which the object of belief is evaluated as good or bad; and *prescriptive/proscriptive* beliefs, which advocate courses of action or states of existence as desirable or prohibit actions or states considered undesirable. We followed this distinction, eliminating sayings expressing descriptive or existential beliefs. In the case of identical or nearly identical sayings appearing in more than one compendium, only one was retained. Complete agreement among the three judges was required before a saying was eliminated. After elimination, a final item pool of 9,995 sayings was left for further analysis.

Sorting. A total 379 sayings (3.79%) from the final item pool were judged to be related to CIC components, and 79 (0.79%) to CSO components. Each of the 379 CIC sayings was sorted into one, and only one, of 72 categories, according to the following procedure.

It should first be noted that the CIC comprises 36 (2 × 18) categories. A dichotomous variable, affirmation/negation, was introduced, applicable to each of these categories. A saying judged to affirm, advocate, or endorse the idea belonging to a CIC category was considered positive; a saying judged to negate, disavow, or be opposed to the idea was considered negative. Each saying had to be considered either positive or negative (in logical terms, disjunctively). This expanded the number of CIC categories to a total of 72 (2 × 36). An illustration using four sayings (translated into English) judged to pertain to the Individual/Group Efforts component (Component 11; see Table 9.1) may serve to make clear how the sorting worked.

1. *Individualism affirmed* (I+): Rather than having three or four people to steal a cow, better to steal a dog alone.
2. *Individualism negated* (I−): A single hand clapping, though fast, makes no sound.
3. *Collectivism affirmed* (C+): Better to have many people to work and fewer people to be fed.

4. *Collectivism negated* (C–): With too many dragons, drought will come; with too many people, chaos will result.

Similarly, each of the 79 sayings judged to be related to CSO components was sorted into one, and only one, of 32 (2 × 2 × 8) categories.

Results and Discussion

The frequencies of the CIC and CSO categories or cells, numbering 104 (72 + 32) in total, are presented in Table 9.3. Of the 379 CIC sayings, a larger proportion pertain to collectivism (52.8%) than to individualism (47.2%), and a much higher proportion express affirmation (78.1%) than negation (21.9%). The proportion expressing affirmation is greater for collectivism (82.5%) than for individualism (73.2%). It may be observed that many of the cells have small or zero frequencies. However, the cell frequencies of the five major (combined) components are sufficiently large for statistical analysis.

Log-linear analysis. The categorical data on the CIC combined components form a three-dimensional (2 × 5 × 2) contingency table with three variables: affirmation/negation (A), component ideas (C), and individualism/collectivism (I). Hierarchical log-linear analysis was applied, and maximum likelihood estimates of expected cell frequencies were computed for different models.

The marginal associations and partial associations, computed from differences between likelihood ratio chi-square values between models, show the three-way interaction to be significant (A × C × I = 34.13; $p <.05$), and all three two-way interactions were significant at the .05 level (A × C = 51.55; A × I = 4.79; C × I = 63.71; $p < .05$). Accordingly, the fully saturated model was accepted as the only one that would fit the highly complex data structure. The three-way interaction means that the association between any two of the three variables varies across the layers of the third variable. Together, the two-way interactions mean that the association between any pair of two variables is significant, even when the third variable is controlled. For instance, affirmation/negation is associated with individualism/collectivism, even when the variable component ideas is controlled. Moreover, because of the three-way interaction, the association varies across layers of this variable.

To describe more fully the complex data structure, we computed measures of association between two variables for different layers of the third variable (presented in Table 9.4). It may be observed that affirmation/

Table 9.3 Frequency Distribution of Chinese Sayings in Components
of Individualism/Collectivism and Social Organization

Rank	Component	*Individualism and Collectivism* TF	I+	I–	C+	C–
1	Self-Reliance/Interdependence	67	41	2	20	4
2	Individual/Group Efforts	67	7	20	25	15
3	Consequences of One's Actions	60	8	0	50	2
4	Self-Direction/Conformity	54	10	14	28	2
5	Individuality/Uniformity	46	34	3	5	4
6	Economic Individualism/Collectivism	18	8	0	6	4
7	Competition/Cooperation	16	0	3	13	0
8	Ethical-Legal Responsibility	15	7	0	7	1
9	Individual/Group Interests	12	7	2	3	0
10	Right to Privacy	8	1	1	3	3
11	Affiliation	5	0	1	4	0
12	Human Development	4	4	0	0	0
13	Personal Privacy	3	3	0	0	0
14	Value of the Individual/Group	2	1	0	1	0
15	Identity	1	0	1	0	0
16	Political Individualism/Collectivism	1	0	1	0	0
17	Security	0	0	0	0	0
18	Religious Individualism/Collectivism	0	0	0	0	0
	Combined components					
1	Self-Reliance/Interdependence	98	56	5	29	8
2	Achievement	83	7	23	38	15
3	Responsibility	75	15	0	57	3
4	Autonomy/Conformity	70	14	16	35	5
5	Values	53	39	4	6	4
	Total	379	131	48	165	35

Rank	Component	*Social Organization* TF	NO+	NO–	IO+	IO–
1	Conflict/Harmony	33	0	8	24	1
2	Selfishness/Altruism	31	5	1	20	5
3	Public Morality and Civic-Mindedness	5	1	0	1	3
4	Responsibility for Group's Well-Being	4	1	0	3	0
5	Group Discipline	3	0	0	3	0
6	Responsibility for Group's Actions	1	1	0	0	0
7	Consequences of Group's Actions	1	0	0	1	0
8	Locus of Loyalty	1	0	1	0	0
	Total	79	8	10	52	9

NOTE: TF = total frequency; I+ = individualism affirmed; I– = individualism negated; C+ = collectivism affirmed; C– = collectivism negated; NO+ = nonintegrative organization affirmed; NO– = nonintegrative organization negated; IO+ = integrative organization affirmed; IO– = integrative organization negated.

Table 9.4 Measures of Association for Two-Way Tables

Interaction	r	V	C	U
A × C (controlling for I)				
Individualism	—	63*	53*	19*
Collectivism	—	28*	27*	04*
A × I (controlling for C)				
Values	34*	34*	32*	10*
Autonomy/Conformity	–44*	44*	40*	15*
Responsibility	09	09	09	02
Achievement	–47*	47*	42*	17*
Self-Reliance/Interdependence	19*	19*	19*	03
C × I (controlling for A)				
Affirmation	—	54*	47*	14*
Negation	—	33	31	06*

NOTE: r = Pearson's r; V = Cramer's V; C = Contingency Coefficient; U = Uncertainty Coefficient (symmetric). A = affirmation/negation; C = component ideas; I = individualism-collectivism.
*$p < .05$.

negation is more strongly associated with component ideas in the case of individualism than collectivism (A × C interactions), and I/C is more strongly associated with component ideas in the case of affirmation than negation (C × I interactions).

Of greater theoretical interest is the variation of the association between affirmation/negation and individualism/collectivism across the combined components. The measures of association are significant at the .05 level, except for Responsibility (and the uncertainty coefficient for Self-Reliance/Interdependence). The sign of Pearson's r is reversed for two of the five combined components, Achievement and Autonomy/Conformity, reflecting the fact that the two cell frequencies in the I– category involved are quite large (see Table 9.3). The percentages expressing negation are higher for individualism, but lower for collectivism, on these two combined components. In this connection, it should be noted that the A × I interaction is much weaker than the other two-way interactions.

Social organization. The frequency distribution of CSO cells is also rather uneven. A clear majority of the sayings pertain to two components: Conflict/Harmony (33) and Selfishness/Altruism (31). As expected, harmony is strongly emphasized, and conflict is disavowed. Likewise, altruism is strongly valued. Yet the pattern is not unambiguous: A number of sayings, though small in number, affirm selfishness and negate altruistic values. In view of the large number of cells with very small or zero frequencies, no statistical analysis was undertaken.

Conclusion

Overall, the results of Study 1 conform to the expectation that Chinese culture is more collectivist than individualist. Compared with individualism, collectivism is more strongly affirmed and less strongly negated. The strength of affirmation or negation depends very much on the component idea concerned. The negation of individualist values is particularly strong on components pertaining to achievement and autonomy.

Yet individualism is by no means negated. As a matter of fact, the number of sayings affirming individualism far exceeds that of sayings negating it, particularly on components pertaining to self-reliance and values affirming the individual person. The numbers of sayings affirming individuality (34) and self-reliance (41) are considerable (see Table 9.3). This should occasion pause in those accustomed to thinking of Chinese culture as anti-individualist.

The data indicate that altruism and the maintenance of harmony stand out among Chinese cultural beliefs concerning social organization; both are strongly affirmed.

Study 2: An Analysis of Collectivism in Chinese Society[1]

The purpose of Study 2 was to investigate the nature of collectivism in Chinese society. Measures of components of individualism and collectivism were developed, and their associations with collectivist orientations specific to different role relationships, traditional values, and personality were investigated. The study focused primarily on the definition of the self-other relationship, a major component of both individualism and collectivism identified in the CIS.

Method

Subjects. The subjects were 158 (64 male, 94 female) Hong Kong university students who agreed to participate. All subjects had been exposed to some concepts of psychology.

Measuring instruments. Several instruments, all written in Chinese, were used. The Chinese Popular Sayings (CPS) scale consists of 35 normative statements pertaining to individualism and collectivism derived from the content analysis of Chinese popular sayings (Study 1, described above). The 35 items were randomly selected from 379 sayings judged to pertain to components of individualism and collectivism. The CPS was scored on a 7-point scale, ranging from 1 (*strongly disagree*) to 7 (*strongly agree*). A principal-axis factor analysis of the 35 CPS items was performed. The scree test clearly indicated that three factors were to be extracted, accounting for 13.6%, 10.9%, and 6.5% of the total variance, respectively. To facilitate interpretation, an orthogonal rotation, using the varimax method, was performed. Following the criterion that the factor loading should exceed .40, there were 7, 7, and 6 items in the three factors, respectively.

The first factor is labeled Self-Reliance. Examples of items in this factor, translated into English, include the following: "Rather than to ask for help, better rely on oneself"; "One accepts the consequences for what one does." The second factor is labeled Self-Interest. Included in this factor is what may be called economic individualism: separate ownership of property, with wealth and rewards not being shared. Examples of items include "If people were not selfish, men would be thieves and women prostitutes" and "As close as brothers are, property should be separately owned." The third factor is labeled Cooperation. Examples of items include "A single hand can hardly make a sound" and "If two persons are united with a single purpose, soil turns into gold."

Three scales were then constructed, each comprising the unweighted items loaded on the corresponding factor: Self-Reliance, Self-Interest, and Cooperation. It should be noted that self-reliance and economic individualism are among the component ideas of individualism, and cooperation is a component idea of collectivism delineated in the first part of this chapter. Accordingly, Self-Reliance and Self-Interest are treated as measuring aspects of a person's individualist orientation, and Cooperation as an aspect of collectivist orientation.

The Individualism-Collectivism Scale (INDCOL Scale), developed by Hui (1988), comprises six subscales purporting to measure a person's collectivist orientation toward target groups: spouse, parents, kin, neighbors, friends, and coworkers/schoolmates. This scale should be interpreted as measuring the extent of sharing, control, and involvement in self-other relationships; it does not measure other components of collectivism identified in the CIC. Responses were scored on a scale ranging from 1 to 6.

The Chinese Value Survey (CVS), developed by the Chinese Culture Connection (1987), measures 40 traditional Chinese values (e.g., harmony with others; reciprocity of greetings, favors, and gifts; solidarity with others; noncompetitiveness; and valuing close, intimate relationship). Subjects were asked to rate the importance of each value on a Likert-type scale ranging from 1 to 9.

Table 9.5 Component Ideas: Means, Standard Deviations, Deviations From the Mean, Reliabilities, and Factor Loadings

Variable	n	Mean	SD	d	r	F1	F2
Self-Reliance	144	4.59	0.64	0.92	77	−44	61
Self-Interest	144	3.36	0.74	−0.86	74	−42	07
Cooperation	144	4.69	0.66	1.05	67	−03	87
Spouse	71	3.14	0.57	−0.63	39	33	−24
Parent	71	3.47	0.46	−0.07	53	74	10
Kin	71	2.93	0.76	−0.75	74	64	02
Neighbor	71	3.08	0.68	−0.62	72	61	−16
Friend	141	3.93	0.62	0.69	54	47	41
Coworker	141	4.27	0.50	1.54	51	00	31
Chinese Value Survey	82	6.26	0.90	1.40	93	—	—
Extraversion	87	12.39	4.20	—	79	—	—
Neuroticism	87	10.81	4.83	—	83	—	—
Lying	87	8.60	3.20	—	64	—	—

NOTE: n = number of subjects who completed the scale; means refer to group averages divided by the number of items, except for Extraversion, Neuroticism, and Lying; d = deviation of the scale midpoint, expressed in SD units; r = coefficient alpha; F1 = loadings on Factor 1; F2 = loadings on Factor 2 (n = 71).

Three scales from the Eysenck Personality Questionnaire (EPQ), translated into Chinese by Eysenck and Chan (1982), were used: Extraversion, Neuroticism (or Emotionality), and Lying (or Social Desirability).

Procedure. All measuring instruments were group administered during class time. The CPS was administered to all 158 subjects, who were then divided into two groups. Subjects in Group 1 (28 males and 43 females) were given the INDCOL Scale in its entirety; subjects in Group 2 (36 males and 51 females) were given the Friend and Coworker INDCOL subscales, the CVS, and the three EPQ scales. No time limit was imposed. Not all subjects completed the measures given to them, resulting in some missing data. The subjects were fully debriefed after the administration.

Results

The means, standard deviations, and reliabilities (coefficient alphas) of all the variables are shown in Table 9.5, and the correlation matrix is shown in Table 9.6. We begin interpreting the data by inspecting scale reliabilities, Lying, and its relations with the other variables. The reliabilities were acceptable, except for the Spouse subscale (a result reported by

Table 9.6 Correlation Matrix of Variables

Variable	1	2	3	4	5	6	7	8	9	10	11	12
1 Self-Reliance												
2 Self-Interest	.17*											
3 Cooperation	.33*	-.05										
4 Spouse	-.21*	-.21*	.20*									
5 Parent	-.22*	-.33*	.13	.17								
6 Kin	-.25*	-.22*	.03	.23*	.44*							
7 Neighbor	-.31*	-.21*	-.11	.27*	.48*	.40*						
8 Friend	-.07	-.21*	.16*	.04	.43*	.38*	.19					
9 Coworker	.02	-.21*	.15*	-.14	-.07	.02	-.08	.27*				
10 Chinese Value Survey	.07	-.12	.17	—	—	—	—	.04	-.01			
11 Extraversion	-.18	.00	.02	—	—	—	—	.16	.04	-.04		
12 Neuroticism	.10	.25*	.02	—	—	—	—	.02	-.05	.03	-.08	
13 Lying	.10	-.05	.11	—	—	—	—	-.12	-.02	.25*	-.20*	-.06

*$p < .05$, two-tailed (adjusted for differing pairwise df).

Hui, 1988). The low reliability of this subscale was probably in part a result of the fact that most of the subjects were unmarried. Lying was not significantly correlated with the other variables, except for its negative correlation with Extraversion and positive correlation with CVS. These results suggest that faking did not present a problem. The correlation between Lying and CVS probably reflected the influence of social desirability on both measures. However, the CPS scales and the INDCOL subscales did not seem to be confounded by social desirability.

Deviations of the mean from the midpoint of the scale, expressed in units of the standard deviation, were computed (the d statistic in Table 9.5). Substantial positive d values (absolute magnitude exceeding 0.50) were obtained for Self-Reliance, Cooperation, Friend, Coworker, and CVS; substantial negative values were obtained for Self-Interest, Spouse, Kin, and Neighbor (t-test results showed that all deviations were significant at the .05 level). The deviation was the largest for Coworker, amounting to 1.54 units. Of course, the d values are a function of the contents of the scale items, though apparently not of social desirability. With this caveat, two points can be made: (a) Both self-reliance, a key component of individualism, and cooperation, a component of collectivism, tend to be endorsed; and (b) the degree to which collectivist orientation is endorsed varies according to relationships—it tends to be endorsed for relationships with friends and especially coworkers, but not for those with the spouse, kin, and neighbors.

These results are consistent with those obtained in other studies. A similar pattern of deviations from the midpoint across the INDCOL subscales may be seen in the data obtained by Hui (1988, Table 1). In Study 1, we found that a substantial number of Chinese popular sayings affirm self-reliance and altruism (construed as the opposite of selfishness); achievement through cooperative group efforts tends to be affirmed, but achievement through individual efforts is negated rather strongly.

Bivariate analysis. An inspection of the correlation matrix reveals the following patterns, bearing in mind that the magnitude of the correlations was, on the whole, rather small (see Table 9.6).

1. Self-Reliance was significantly correlated with Self-Interest and Cooperation in the positive direction; Self-Interest was not correlated with Cooperation. This result indicates that individualist and collectivist orientations are not mutually exclusive or antithetical to each other. A person may or may not endorse the values of self-reliance and cooperation at the same time.

2. Intercorrelations among the six INDCOL subscales were rather low, ranging from −.14 to .48. This indicates that, to a large extent, the subscales do not measure the same dimension, and supports the contention that Chinese collectivism is relationship or target specific.

3. None of the three CPS scales and the two INDCOL subscales, Friend and Coworker, was significantly correlated with the CVS. This result means that a person's individualist or collectivist orientation cannot be predicted from his or her global attitudes toward traditional values alone.

4. Neither Extraversion nor Neuroticism was significantly correlated with the CPS scales, the INDCOL subscales, or the CVS; the exception was the correlation between Neuroticism and Self-Interest—which should not be surprising, considering that less-than-optimal interpersonal relations are implied in both. The results suggest that, within the confined conditions (e.g., sampling) of the present study, holding individualist, collectivist, or traditional Chinese values bears little or no relation to personality functioning.

5. Self-reliance correlated significantly with the Spouse, Parent, Kin, and Neighbor subscales in the negative direction. Cooperation was significantly correlated with the Spouse, Friend, and Coworker subscales in the positive direction. This pattern of results indicates that a cooperative orientation tends to be associated with a greater, and a self-reliant orientation with a lesser, involvement with others. Again, the association varies across self-other relationships. Self-Interest correlated significantly with all six INDCOL subscales in the negative direction. Thus, as expected, the stronger the self-interest, the lesser the involvement with others, regardless of the relationship involved. These results provide an indication of the validity of the three CPS scales.

Factor analysis. Factor analysis was used to explore further the patterning of relations among variables pertaining to individualism and collectivism, namely, the three CPS scales and the six INDCOL subscales. The subjects were from Group 1. Two factors were extracted from principal-axis factoring with oblique (oblimin) rotation, accounting for 29.1% and 21.2% of the total variance. The correlation between factors was −0.17, indicating that they are orthogonal to each other. The factor loadings are given in Table 9.5.

Factor 1 is named Interdependent Relational Orientation; variables with a loading exceeding .30 are Self-Reliance (negative), Self-Interest (negative), Spouse, Parent, Kin, Neighbor, and Friend. It reflects the connection between interdependence (negation of self-reliance and self-interest) and the collectivist orientation specific to close, affective self-other relationships based on blood or marriage ties, friendship, or residential location. Factor 2 is named Cooperative/Self-Reliant Relational Orientation; variables loaded on this factor are Self-Reliance, Cooperation, Friend, and Coworker. It reflects the connection between cooperative, yet self-reliant, attitudes and the collectivist orientation specific to voluntary and instrumental self-other relationships. It should be noted that Friend appears in both factors, suggesting that friendship may entail interdependence as well as cooperation and self-reliance. Coworker/classmate relationships are, however, clearly differentiated from those with spouse, parents, kin, and neighbors.

Discussion

The data obtained in Study 2 may deepen our understanding of the changing interpersonal relationships in Hong Kong society. The changes may be gauged by the intensity of reciprocal involvement in different self-other relationships. The evidence suggests that voluntary and instrumental relationships are gaining ascendancy while relationships based on blood or marriage ties or on residential location are waning—a reversal of the traditional pattern. It is consistent with the findings reported by Ho, Hong, and Chiu (1989), which point to a decline in the acceptance of traditional filial piety and departure from family-matrimonial traditionalism in Hong Kong and Taiwan. These developments give credence to the emergence of voluntarism as one of the consequences of societal modernization.

Yang (1986) contends that, as a result of societal modernization, Chinese character is changing in the direction of an increasingly individualist and decreasingly collectivist orientation. If so, one would expect these changes to be strongly reflected in the present study, because they are generally more pronounced among the better educated. The lowered intensity of reciprocal involvements in close, affective relationships found supports the contention that the collectivist orientation is declining. Yet this finding is contradicted by other results: the continued rejection of self-interest, the endorsement of cooperation, and the heightened intensity of reciprocal involvements in voluntary and instrumental relationships. Thus individualist and collectivist tendencies may coexist in the process of societal modernization, just as they did in traditional China. We would resist the temptation of interpreting the endorsement of self-reliance as indicative of a movement toward the individualist orientation, inasmuch as self-reliance has long been valued in Chinese culture. Rather, we interpret the cooperative yet self-reliant orientation as an exemplary synthesis of individualist and collectivist values.

GENERAL DISCUSSION

Three main conclusions may be reached from the work presented in this chapter. First, overall, Chinese culture is indeed more collectivist than individualist. However, within Chinese culture both individualist (e.g., self-reliant) and collectivist (e.g., cooperative) values are endorsed, although individualist values given to self-interest tend not to be. This finding, based on a study of individuals (Study 2), is consistent with findings based on a content analysis of cultural products (Study 1). In another study, Hui (1988, p. 22) found that Chinese university students actually scored lower than American university students on the INDCOL Scale. This result should be interpreted with caution, because the scale's cross-cultural comparability has not been demonstrated, as Hui admits. It is nevertheless a rather odd result, inasmuch as the INDCOL Scale purports to measure collectivism. Taken together, these results underscore how misleading it is at the individual level of analysis to classify Chinese people indiscriminately as collectivists, just as it is at the cultural level to characterize Chinese society globally as collectivist or anti-individualist. Our evidence indicates that Chinese culture may be characterized as predominantly collectivist as well as anti-individualist on only one of the five major components, namely, Achievement (Study 1).

Second, the evidence consistently supports the contention that Chinese collectivism is specific to role relationships (Study 2). A person's individualist or collectivist orientation depends on the self-other relationship involved, and is not predictable from his or her global attitudes toward traditional values. Furthermore, it does not appear to be associated with personality functioning. The evidence suggests that voluntary and instrumental relationships are gaining ascendancy, and relationships based on blood or marriage ties or on residential location are waning.

Third, Chinese culture places strong emphasis on altruism and the maintenance of harmony (Study 1), values presumed to be conducive to integrative social organization. In the context of the current debate surrounding I/C, these values would appear attractive to those concerned with the excesses and misdirection of individualism in the self-contained form Sampson (1988) has characterized. It is tempting to link the emphasis on harmony in particular to collectivism, inasmuch as both aim for group solidarity.

The Confucian ideal of harmony runs afoul of family dynamics. This should lead us to reconsider the Conflict/Harmony component of the CSO. Expressions of conflict are classified as nonintegrative, and the maintenance of harmony is classified as integrative, in accordance with the Confucian view of social order. However, it may be argued that expressions of conflict serve an integrative function; moreover, insistence on the maintenance of harmony, without giving opportunities for conflicts to be voiced and resolved, sows the seeds of nonintegration. The Confucian view is static; it does not recognize the value of conflict and provides no channels for its resolution. When underlying conflict does come into the open, as it has periodically in Chinese history, it tends to assume violent forms.

From a methodological perspective, the two studies presented in this chapter demonstrate the necessity of recognizing the multidimensional nature of individualism and collectivism in research. The strength of affirmation or negation may vary greatly across components of these two constructs (Study 1). Hence it is important to delineate the pattern of affirmation/negation across components. The results also show that individualist or collectivist beliefs within a culture may not constitute a coherent constellation (see Schwartz, 1990). For instance, across the major components of individualism, self-reliance, individual responsibility, and individualist values are predominantly affirmed, but individual achievement is predominantly negated in Chinese culture. Another conclusion supported is that individualism and collectivism should not be construed as a dichotomy or two opposing value constellations, that is, as opposite ends of a single continuum. Within a given culture, both individualist and collectivist beliefs are likely to be held or rejected.

It is important to distinguish here between dimensionality and polarity. Researchers have treated individualism and collectivism as multidimensional constructs, but as polar opposites on each dimension. Consequently, a high individualist attribute would imply a corresponding low collectivist attribute on the same dimension, and vice versa. Conceptually, however, the two constructs are distinct across dimensions. It is entirely conceivable for a culture to display highly individualist as well as collectivist attributes on a given dimension. Empirically, we have shown this in Study 1 (Table 9.3): Within two major components, Self-Reliance/Interdependence and Responsibility, both individualist and collectivist beliefs are predominantly affirmed. Methodologically, therefore, it is better to represent each of the two constructs on multiple unipolar dimensions.

NOTE

1. Study 2 was based on a reanalysis of data gathered by Chiu (1990).

10

ASPECTS OF INDIVIDUALISM AND COLLECTIVISM IN KOREA

JAE-HO CHA

This chapter presents a social psychological study of the Korean people from the perspective of the I/C continuum. It is my hope that this exploration will bring out various aspects of collectivism shown by the Korean people and thus broaden the base of the current understanding of I/C. Triandis (1988b) defines collectivism as the tendency for a group of people to place "great emphasis on (a) the views, needs, and goals of the ingroup rather than of oneself, (b) social norms and duty defined by the ingroup rather than behavior to get pleasure, (c) beliefs shared with the ingroup rather than beliefs that distinguish oneself from ingroup, (d) great readiness to cooperate with ingroup members, and (e) intense emotional attachment to the ingroup" (p. 74). The purpose of the chapter is to depict the nature of collectivism as it exists within Korean culture.

I focus here on the culture-level *emic* perspective rather than the individual level by examining the historical changes in values, beliefs, and behavior of the Korean people in the past 100 years as they relate to the I/C dimension. The analysis is based on three empirical studies: first, an archival study, based on analysis of travelogues written by foreign observers of Koreans during the period 1870 to 1970 (Cha, 1980, 1993); second, a survey of the attitudes and beliefs of younger and older generations of Koreans (Cha, 1980); and third, a review of empirical studies done on Koreans' values since 1945 (Cha, 1986, 1990).

AUTHOR'S NOTE: I would like to express my gratitude to Professor Uichol Kim for initiating my work on the topic of collectivism and providing me with useful materials for this chapter. I am also indebted to Miss Jeewon Cheong for the help she provided during the preparation of the manuscript. Belated thanks go to Professors Byongchik Ahn of the Department of Economics and Kwangkyu Lee of the Department of Anthropology, Seoul National University, for the materials they generously made available for archival study in 1979.

The data for the first two studies were collected as a part of a larger interdisciplinary project titled "A Study on the Continuity and Discontinuity of Korean Culture," sponsored by the Korean Social Science Research Council. Within these studies, I have focused on the topic of the personality and consciousness of Koreans. These two studies were an effort to tackle the amorphous problem of determining the cultural changes that have taken place over a period of 100 years in Korea. This chapter is essentially an integration of the data from the three studies described above using the framework of collectivism among the Korean people. The first study is valuable because it covers an extended period and because it deals not only with values and beliefs, but also with *behaviors* of the Korean people. The second study, by contrast, deals with one particular period of time, focusing on values and beliefs but not behavior.

The first two studies were conducted in 1979. The first (the archival study) examined 22 travelogues written about the Korean people by visiting foreigners from the mid-1800s to the 1970s. These 22 volumes were selected on the basis of whether they contained direct references to the Korean people. The list of books examined is given in the preliminary report (Cha, 1980). Those books containing mostly secondhand observations or evaluations rather than descriptions of the Korean people and those containing mostly records of incidents were eliminated. The final selections were not entirely free of borrowings from other sources, but such references could usually be identified and were sorted out.

Travelogues by foreign visitors were chosen as data sources because these writings—by American, British, French, Japanese, and Russian visitors to Korea—tended to be very specific and detailed. Also, the travelogues were fresh in the sense that the observations found in them were made by cultural outsiders. Ignorance on the part of the visitors to Korea did often lead to gross misinterpretations of specific episodes, but the advantages of using outside observers, albeit foreigners, were great enough to overshadow whatever disadvantages this approach had. The different frames of reference of the foreign observers brought forth new insights that might have escaped the notice of the native.

Each of the travelogues was perused, and every reference to the Korean people, whether about their values, beliefs, attitudes, or behaviors, was transcribed verbatim on a card. Transcriptions ranged in length from a single line to several lines. Elimination of cards containing information not particularly relevant to psychology left 1,218 cards. These constituted the final data set. Each card contained, in addition to the quoted passage, the source, the time period in which the observation was made, and the social class of the Korean person described, when identifiable.

The writings were divided into three historical periods: the precolonial period (before 1910), the colonial period (1910-1945), and the postliberation period (1945-1970s). The social class categories used were as follows: the *yangban* class (the ruling class, made up of the literati and military officers), the commoner class, and a general category for characteristics not unique to any one class.

The cards were sorted first by time period and then by social class. Then, within each of the resulting 9 piles (3 time periods multiplied by 3 social class categories) each card was sorted into one of three categories, depending on the content of the passage: motive/value, belief/attitude, or behavior. The final stage of analysis involved sorting cards within each of these 27 piles (9 × 3) according to similarity of content. This resulted in a list of category names representing content groupings or types for each domain (motives/values, beliefs/attitudes, and behaviors). Finally, the category names found for the three time periods were listed (Cha, 1980); these were then compared across time periods to estimate the extent of social change. (I conducted all sorting myself.)

In the following section, I review collectivism in traditional Korean culture and then present a discussion of collectivism in contemporary Korea and the changes it has undergone. Finally, I briefly discuss theoretical and methodological issues that are implied by these three studies.

COLLECTIVISM IN
TRADITIONAL KOREAN CULTURE

The collectivism (and individualism) of traditional Koreans can be examined by looking at their values, beliefs, and behavior. Supporting evidence for the following discussion is based exclusively on archival data (Cha, 1980).

I/C as Revealed in Values of the Korean People

A total of 27 value categories were extracted from archival materials concerning Koreans living approximately 100 years ago. Of these categories, 7 appeared to be confined to the upper classes (the middle and *yangban* class); these are shown in Table 10.1, classified according to level (individual, familial, societal) and category (individualist, collectivist, mixed). I have used the three-way classification of values into individual, familial, and societal values in earlier work based on the same set of data (Cha, 1990).

Table 10.1 Classification of Traditional Values

Level	Individualist	Collectivist	Mixed
Individual	*material pleasures,* hearty eating and drinking, *longevity*		money/wealth, avoidance of misfortune and death, a carefree life, **scholarly pursuit,** harmony with nature, power/high office, **taciturnity,** cleanliness, longevity, *recognition*
Familial		*family or blood,* filial piety, many offspring, sons, ancestors	
Societal		*old ways,* dependence, fraternity/heartfulness, hierarchy, **peace with poverty,** politesse	

SOURCE: Based on data from Cha (1980).
NOTE: Values shown in italics are those considered unique to the upper classes (*yangban*); values in boldface type are those considered to be instrumental in character (Rokeach, 1973). Not shown are four values not clearly related to the I/C dimension: nature, Chinese letters, white color, and peace.

Individual, family, and society correspond to the three focuses for which values are intended.

Differentiating between familial and societal levels presented a special problem; it was done mainly through exclusion of values that are clearly familial. Some of the values were not easily classified as individualist or collectivist, and for these it was necessary to take into account the cultural contexts from which they were taken. For example, "hearty eating and drinking" was classified as an individualist value because the context in which this behavior was mentioned indicated that it was a pleasure-seeking behavior, and thus clearly individualist (see Triandis, Chapter 3, this volume).

The results of the classification are presented in Table 10.1, which shows several things. First, the number of familial values was relatively small compared with the numbers of individual and societal values. Second, the familial and societal values contain collectivist values and no individualist values. Third, individualist values were found only at the individual level, but their number was quite small compared with what were labeled "mixed values," which made up the majority of the individual values. Most of the mixed types could be classified as *latently* individualist values. This implies that as recently as 100 years ago, the Korean culture contained a sizable number of latently individualist values. Fourth, not all of the 27 value categories are part of contemporary Koreans' verbal culture. Only 9 of the 27 values (categories) were frequently mentioned either in conversation or in writings by 1979. The values of hearty eating and drinking, material pleasure, old ways, and dependence were rarely found in the verbal culture.

The mixed values contained both individualist and collectivist concerns. They are the value equivalent of reversible figures in perception. The cultural context in which these values are embedded appears to exert a critical influence on meaning. Typical of the mixed type are the values of wealth, high office, and avoidance of misfortune and death. In an industrialized society, these could clearly represent individualism. But in a traditional society, an individual's attaining a high office or acquiring great wealth was celebrated by the entire clan or town (see Table 10.2). Confucian writings extol making a name in the world as an important means of bringing honor and renown to one's clan, a great achievement in the way of filial piety. Scholarly pursuit is a means to high office and hence contains an element of collectivism.

Because these values will ultimately shed their collectivist connotations as the society proceeds toward industrialization, they can be called *latently individualist values.* One implication of latently individualist values is that they are expected to survive better than truly collectivist values. They would, of course, undergo certain transformations, such as redefinition of category boundary, in order to survive.

It must be noted that the family or clan is at the core of the concept of collectivism (Hofstede, 1983b, 1991). Thus to say that family-related values are central to the traditional Korean value system is merely to assert that there is an element of collectivism in the Korean value system. It does not tell us what characterizes collectivism in Korea. In order to determine the specific aspects or features of collectivism in Korea, one has to look at the specific values subsumed under the rubric of family (and societal) values. As we have seen, there were such values as filial piety, many offspring, importance of ancestors, and family or bloodline.

There are other values that do not belong to the family level and yet are indicative of collectivism. Although values such as dependence, hierarchy, courtesy, old ways, and "heartfulness" or fraternity do not by themselves define collectivism, they do constitute elements of collectivism within the context of traditional Korean culture. Therefore, along with family-level values, these values can be said to define the characteristics of Korean collectivism. Although these values are related to family and hence are labeled collectivist values, there are other values that do not belong to the family level and yet are indicative of collectivism (e.g., values of dependence, hierarchy, courtesy, *chong* or "affection," and fraternity).

The characteristics of collectivism in the traditional Korean culture can be described as follows: (a) dependence in interpersonal relationships, (b) hierarchy in the groups, (c) courtesy, (d) affection or a sense of interpersonal attachment, (e) family or bloodline, and (f) old ways or tradition. All of these are tied together by the central concern for family or clan and local community. Evidence from other sources supporting some of these aspects of Korean collectivism will be presented below.

Collectivism as Revealed in
Beliefs and Attitudes of the Korean People

The original catalog of beliefs and attitudes compiled for this study contained 132 categories. The categories were collapsed on social class because in the belief/attitude domain the placement of a category into one of the social classes was often difficult. Because a number of categories were duplicated in two or three social class groupings, collapsing over social class groupings reduced the number of categories to 68 (Cha, 1980). This list was sifted through for beliefs/attitudes that are interpretable in terms of I/C. A total of 42 such belief/attitude categories were identified. Examples of beliefs/attitudes that were excluded as irrelevant are as follows: despisement of artisans and craftsmen, despisement of entertaining women, low regard for military men, survival of the spirit after death, and mountains as sacred objects.

The 42 selected beliefs/attitudes were then classified according to level and category (collectivism versus individualism). The general criterion used in the category grouping was that each belief/attitude category be related to a concern for in-group or collectivity or lack of such a concern. Any belief/attitude showing distrust or hatred toward symbols of collectivity or a concern for pleasure were classified as individualist. Low regard for labor related to earning a livelihood was, however, classified as collectivist, because such an attitude was thought to reflect an attitude of dependence rather than a concern for pleasure.

The beliefs and attitudes judged as being related to collectivism were caring for own parents, respect for parents, respect for elders, obedience to superiors, respect for the *yangban* class, ancestor worship, importance attached to ancestral graves, having offspring to inherit ancestor rites, loyalty to the king, and an exaggerated sense of importance attached to anything Korean. Items that were less obviously related to collectivism, but perhaps more important for understanding the unique nature of collectivism in Korea, included chastity required of widows, secluded life required of women, disdain for stinginess, primacy of friendship over money, the tendency to regard money lending (instead of giving it) as a sinful act, the belief that a payment is a token of appreciation for help received rather than a compensation for services rendered, the belief that an act of helping others in need is bound to be rewarded, the belief that independent actions hurt friendship and foster disorder, fear of independent action, and lack of an idea of individual rights.

These results show that collectivism in Korea can be characterized in terms of (a) filial piety; (b) obedience to parents, the elderly, and the *yangban* class; (c) loyalty to the king and things that are Korean; (d) ancestor worship; (e) sacrifices required of women (for the benefit of the family clan); (f) a strong norm for mutual succor; and (g) fear of independent action. The last two categories are apparently related to the value of dependence.

Collectivism as Revealed in
Behaviors of the Korean People

There were a total of 84 categories (items) in the behavior catalog (Cha, 1980). The following are clearly interpretable in terms of collectivism:

1. willingness to help others in difficulty regardless of their in-group status
2. ancestor worship
3. courtesy
4. obedience, loyalty, and compliance with authorities
5. deference to parents (e.g., refraining from smoking in the presence of parents)
6. running a number of mutual-aid organizations
7. farmers working together when the work can be done by one
8. the whole village or town turning out to welcome home a resident who has just passed the civil service examination and many people looking after that person until he is given an official position
9. wives working self-effacingly for their husbands

Behaviors less obviously related to collectivism are as follows:

10. tendency to suppress emotions and reluctance to say what one thinks
11. telling lies to get oneself out of predicaments
12. indifference to others' rights and what others think
13. tendency to invade others' privacy and general intrusiveness
14. appealing to government offices to adjudicate some disputed matter or to hear personal grievances

15. government officials' tendency to confound private matters with what is official

16. absence of thankfulness

Summary and Discussion of the Archival Data

The above-described examination of values, beliefs/attitudes, and behaviors shown by traditional Koreans for evidence of collectivism revealed many specific features that are characteristic of, if not unique to, Korean collectivism. Some of these specific features reappear throughout the different panels of the values data, the beliefs/attitudes data, and the behavior data. The above review also points up the necessity of making a distinction between the more obvious features and the nonobvious features of collectivism.

In order to determine specific features that are consistently associated with collectivism in traditional Korean culture, the main findings from the three panels of data are juxtaposed in Table 10.2. One can see from the table that family line is the core around which some of the features are grouped. Many offspring, ancestor worship, filial piety, and even sacrifices required of women (e.g., widows forbidden to remarry, wives not allowed out of the house) are but part of this core feature. Collectivism in traditional Korean culture is also characterized by an emphasis on dependence on relationships, hierarchy, courtesy, mutual succor, maintenance of tradition, and loyalty to the king and things Korean.

Of the characteristic features of Korean collectivism cited above, hierarchy can be seen to reflect Hofstede's (1980) power distance dimension. Courtesy, tradition maintenance, and dependence can be considered to reflect Hofstede's uncertainty avoidance dimension. Love of nature and valuing of *chong* (affection or tenderheartedness) can be seen to reflect Hofstede's masculinity/femininity dimension. Of the many specific features discussed above as indicative of collectivism in traditional Korea, only concerns for family line, many offspring, ancestor worship, filial piety, communal support for success, and mutual succor can be clearly related to collectivism. In terms of Hofstede's four dimensions, this cursory analysis suggests that the traditional Korean culture was high on power distance, high on uncertainty avoidance, feminine, and collectivist.

If one conceives of the collectivism of traditional Korean culture as centered on family or clan (there is a Korean word, *kamun,* that literally means house gate or house and the meaning of which encompasses both family and clan), then a question arises concerning the relationships among family line, many offspring, filial piety, and ancestor worship. The answer

Table 10.2   Specific Features of Collectivism in the Traditional Korean Culture: Values, Beliefs/Attitudes, and Behaviors

Values	Beliefs/Attitudes	Behaviors
Dependence	fear of independent action; lack of the notion of individual rights	grievances settled through a third party; intrusive and not respecting others' rights
Hierarchy	obedience to and respect for parents, elders, and the *yangban* class	obedient, loyal, and compliant to authorities
Courtesy		suppressing emotions and keeping thoughts to self; not being frank; restrained affective display
Heartfulness/ fraternity	mutual succor norm; friendship more precious than money; one gets paid for helping and not for work	willing to help even strangers; running mutual-aid organizations; group work; thanklessness; group support for success; confusing what is official with what is personal
Family line	offspring to inherit ancestor rites	
Many offspring	women are for bearing children	
Ancestors	ancestor worship; importance attached to ancestral graves	ancestor rite; take pains in upkeep of ancestral graves
Filial piety	filial piety	deference to parents
Loyalty	loyalty to the king and things Korean	
Sacrifice of women	sacrifice required of women	wives' self-effacing work for husbands

is that ancestors, parents, and offspring form a family line. A clan normally includes many relatives who are connected to the family through the ancestors. It is clear that family or clan was not the only locus of loyalty in traditional Korea. Villages and towns or, more generally, communities, and, to a lesser degree, the king as the symbol of the country, also served as focal points of loyalty.

Hofstede (1980) found that power distance is highly correlated with collectivism. Consistent with his results, hierarchical concern was an important and integral part of collectivism in traditional Korea. One can see that the basis of hierarchy varied according to the distance of the in-group from the self. Within the family and clan, it was the ancestral line. Within a community, the basis was social class, and in the society at large, it was official rank. Whereas these were specific to different circles of intimacy or in-groups, there were generic bases of hierarchy that applied to all in-groups: age and gender. It must be noted that all these markers or bases

of hierarchy have the characteristics of being concrete, easily identifiable, and to a large degree immutable. One can see, therefore, that there
is an element of uncertainty avoidance in the selection of these bases of
hierarchy.

If hierarchy stands for the vertical dimension of in-group relationships,
dependence and *chong* are the glue that binds individual members together in traditional Korea (see Kim, Chapter 2, this volume, for further
discussion of this point). The Five Cardinal Principles of Confucianism,
which have been widely accepted in Korea, extol the following virtues:
love between father and son, *loyalty* between sovereign and subject, *deference* between husband and wife, *order* between the elderly and the young,
and *trust* among friends. Four of the five principles are concerned with
maintaining hierarchy, and the fifth with a horizontal relationship. All the
bases of hierarchy mentioned earlier make appearances in the Five Cardinal
Principles: ancestral line, age, gender, and rank.

There are, in colloquial conversation, familiar terms related to and
reflective of collectivism in traditional Korea. Some of these are directly
related to collectivism, and others are related to less obvious manifestations of collectivism. Those directly related to collectivism include *kamun*
(family clan), *uiri* (obligations or duties, with implied self-sacrifice), *ye*
(courtesy), *chong, bunsu* (one's own station in life), *ch'inbun* (personal closeness), *uichi* (dependence), and *ch'ung-hyo* (the dual principles of loyalty
to country and filial piety). *Ye, bunsu,* and *ch'ung-hyo* are principally related
to hierarchy, whereas *chong, ch'inbun,* and *uichi* are principally related
to dependence, or the horizontal relationship. The remaining terms are
related to both hierarchy and dependence. The term *nunch'i* (other-aware-
ness, or situation sensitiveness) is related to courtesy (*ye*), but belongs to
more indirect manifestations of collectivism. As Table 10.2 shows, there
were other indirect manifestations, such as intrusiveness and disregard
for individual rights, thanklessness, and confusion of the official with the
personal.

COLLECTIVISM IN CONTEMPORARY KOREA

The following discussion of the nature of collectivism in contemporary
Korea and the nature of the changes that have occurred in collectivism
since the turn of the century is based on a survey study of two generations
of Koreans (Cha, 1980, 1993) and a review of value studies done in Korea
since 1945 (the liberation of Korea) (Cha, 1986). With respect to the survey
study, new analyses of the original data were made specifically for this
chapter.

Current Status

In a questionnaire containing 177 items dealing with values, beliefs, and attitudes (Cha, 1980), 32 items related to collectivism were selected, and the mean was calculated. In addition, responses to these 32 items were factor analyzed (Cha & Cheong, 1993). The original list of 177 items was constructed with a view to sampling a diverse set of beliefs found commonly in the daily lives of contemporary Koreans. For most of the items, the question was in the form of a choice between two opposing beliefs or attitudes. The opposition tended to be between a traditional attitude and a modern attitude.

The respondents were married adults in two age groups: in their 20s ($N = 300$) and in their 50s or older ($N = 300$). In each of these age groups, gender and education/residence area (less than primary school/rural, junior high school/urban, college or above/urban) were controlled so that the two age groups were equal in composition with respect to the other two variables. There were 50 subjects in each of the 6 cells (2×3) within each age group.

Data were collected through direct interviews with the respondents in their homes. The urban samples were from Seoul, and the rural samples were taken from several rural hamlets in the provinces. Samples from small rural hamlets (simply sampling districts) were chosen based on convenience, but once chosen, the entire population of a particular district of the required age and sex was interviewed before a new district was added. This way, the study ensured that each cell in the design represents a "population" of some intact sampling district. This procedure was followed in order to control possible biases that an incidental sampling might introduce into the data. Because the primary concern of the study was the generation of more accurate data on epoch effects, the control variables of gender and education/residence were used to help separate genuine epoch effects from observed age effects. These two control variables were selected because they were thought to be the variables exerting the greatest influence on beliefs and attitudes.

Factorial Dimensions of Collectivism

Factor analysis was conducted separately for each age group. For the younger group, three orthogonal factors appeared. Factor 1 is labeled Acceptance of Relational Obligations, reflecting acceptance of collectivity. A significant aspect of this factor is that it provides empirical evidence, for the first time, that important in-groups in contemporary Korean culture are family, clan, and school. That school background serves as a basis for an in-group in Korea has been suggested by many social scientists, but only the present analysis provides empirical evidence that this is so. The particular item that provides this information also shows that collectivism is associated with an avoidance of competition or deference to other in-group members, especially to superiors.

Factor 2 was labeled In-Group Favoritism and was related to a contrast between acceptance and rejection of favoritism based on personal relationships and discriminatory protection based on personal distance. A surprising finding was that a favoritism-accepting attitude was associated with an attitude of expediency, in which one scrambles for one's own interests at the risk of hurting friendship. The favoritism-accepting attitude was also associated with an acceptance of continuation of family line (rather than parental pleasure) as a reason for having children. Factor 3 was labeled Family-Centeredness (family versus country).

Within the older samples only two orthogonal factors were found. Factor 1 was labeled Dependent Relationship. The items with high loading on this factor did not show any overlap with similar items of Factor 1 (Acceptance of Relational Obligations) found for the younger group, but did show considerable overlap with the younger group's Factor 2 (In-Group Favoritism). Thus the older group's Factor 1 was basically an in-group favoritism factor, but with more emphasis on the dependent relationship between parent and child. The latter emphasis makes it a symbiosis factor also. The factor contains an element of protective attitudes toward own children and favoritism toward school alumni. The fact that two of the factor's representative items dealt with preferential treatment of school alumni confirms the earlier conclusion that school background constitutes an in-group focus in contemporary Korea.

Factor 2 of the older samples closely overlapped with Factor 3 (Family-Centeredness) for the young group. An examination of the representative items revealed subtle divergences between the two factors. The other-directedness component found in the younger samples was largely absent. Instead, a "value of children" component (Fawcett, 1972), contrasting family line and parental pleasure (shown in two items), was added. The country (collectivist) end of the factor continuum coincided with affirmation of continuation of family line as a reason for having children.

Of the three factors found in the younger samples, only Factors 1 and 2 are clearly related to the I/C continuum. These two factors indicate that, at least for young Koreans in their 20s, willingness to accept obligations endemic to extended relations and acceptance of in-group favoritism constitute two important aspects of collectivism. Of the two factors found with the older samples, only Factor 1 (Dependent Relationship, or symbiotic attitude) is clearly related to collectivism, but this factor was found to overlap with In-Group Favoritism found for the younger samples. This means that two of the five characteristics outlined by Triandis (1988b) have been confirmed by the study.

The fact that only one factor, instead of two, is found in the older samples suggests that acceptance of in-group obligations was taken for granted, and that is why it did not appear as a separate factor. This of course assumes that older Koreans are generally more collectivist than younger Koreans. The appearance of two factors in the younger group means that the young Koreans are divided on the issue of recognizing in-group obligations and on the issue of in-group favoritism. The single factor (Dependent Relationship) found with the older samples suggests that older Koreans are divided on the issue of autonomous versus dependent parent-child relationships.

**Effects of Sociodemographic Variables
on Collectivism: Analysis of Factor Scores**

Within each age group, factor scores were computed and groups (based on gender and education/residence) were compared on these factor scores. Within the young group, male and female groups did not differ in the in-group obligation aspect of collectivism (Factor 1), but the education/ residence variable produced a significant effect ($F = 32.39$, $df = 2/294$, $p < .001$). Those in the most "modern" group (college or above/residency in Seoul) were most individualist (or least collectivist); those in the least modern group (primary school or below/rural residency) were least individualist (or most collectivist). The intermediate group (junior high school or below/residency in Seoul) fell in between. The other two factors, In-Group Favoritism and Family-Centeredness, showed similar effects of modernity ($F = 12.79$, $df = 2/294$, $p < .001$; $F = 21.41$, $df = 2/294$, $p < .001$, respectively). The more a group was modern, in terms of education received and place of residence, the less discriminatory and more family centered (instead of being country centered).

There was an interesting curvilinear relation in the case of In-Group Favoritism. This curvilinear trend was evident in both the male and female samples. The intermediate modern group (urban/low education) was most protective (discriminatory), and the most modern group (urban/high education) least protective. The least modern group (rural/low education) was intermediate. This means that between the low- and middle-class people living in Seoul there was a sharp difference in attitude with regard to the practice of in-group favoritism. Of the three factor scores, only the third showed a significant gender difference ($F = 16.44$, $df = 1/294$, $p < .001$), with the male group being more country centered (patriotic) than the female group.

Within the older samples (50 years or older), there was a positive relationship between modernity (education received and place of residence) and rejection of symbiotic dependence (Factor 1). That is, the more modern a group was, the more it tended to reject symbiotic parent-child relations ($F = 14.18$, $df = 2/294$, $p < .001$). There was a significant gender difference, with the male respondents being less accepting of dependent relations than the female respondents ($F = 14.19$, $df = 1/294$, $p < .001$). The modernity variable was positively related to Family-Centeredness. The more modern a group was, the more it tended to favor the nuclear family as against country or clan. It is important to realize that in this dimension the opposition was between modern family (in which parents are an inseparable part) and country/clan, not simply between family and country.

The survey data show that for Koreans in the late 1970s collectivism came to include a new in-group in addition to family and clan: school. The significance of extended family or clan has declined greatly in recent years, especially in the 1970s, when the country was well on the way to industrialization. It appears that school has taken over the place that was occupied by extended family or clan. The decline of the value of clan or *kamun* is apparent in the differences between younger and older generations in their beliefs and attitudes. As I have noted elsewhere:

> The above findings show that the younger generation is in a word steeped in individualist thoughts to a greater extent than the older generations are and that they are steadily moving away from clan- or family-centered thoughts and toward society-centered thoughts. And the findings also show that the younger generation is more concerned with problems of social justice and equality than the older generations. (Cha, 1980, p. 57)

DISCUSSION

Despite changes toward individualism, the fact remains that Koreans in both age groups were on the whole collectivist in absolute terms as determined on the basis of their beliefs/attitudes. This conclusion is further supported by the results on an item that asked respondents directly whether they thought the ideals of loyalty (to country) and filial piety are important in today's society. The proportions of respondents supporting these ideals were 75% and 86% for the younger and older groups, respectively.[1]

Detailed findings from the survey data allow more specific conclusions. They indicate that Koreans, including those in their 20s, are still collectivist when it comes to accepting in-group obligations and in-group favoritism, but individualist when it comes to granting autonomy to their children and when family or clan is pitted against self-improvement, or when, as a reason for having children, personal pleasure is pitted against continuation of family line.

More direct evidence on the changes of collectivism through different periods of time comes from the archival study. The sources of data were classified into three groups: those dated before 1910 (the precolonial period), those falling between 1910 and 1945 (the colonial period), and those dated after 1945 (the postliberation period). The first change relevant to collectivism was a weakening of the tendency to confuse public matters with personal matters among bureaucrats; this was observed in the first period. This change signaled a receding of collectivist thinking. A clearer shift toward individualism occurred during the second period, in the 1920s. During this time, the change was in the economic sphere. It was observed that those who made money working in Japan began to show anxiety lest other less fortunate fellow countrymen should come to them and freeload. Such an attitude is in sharp contrast to the traditional hospitality of Koreans and is in violation of the norm of mutual succor. Another change observed during that period was a surge in patriotic feelings (loyalty to country) that coincided with growing resistance among Koreans to Japanese colonial rule.

The following changes were observed in the third period: lack of courtesy toward strangers; decrease in kindness and hospitality; greater equalization of power between husbands and wives; emergence of the nuclear family and retreat from the ideal of extended family; weakening of hierarchy; weakening of traditionalism, including xenophobic ideas; decrease in localism; increase in patriotism; resurgence of the ideals of loyalty and filial piety; and increase in the awareness of public order. These are just some of the changes noted that are thought to be relevant to collectivism. From this list of diverse changes, we can perceive three distinct trends: (a) decline in traditional collectivism and concomitant increase in individualism, (b) displacement of the locus of loyalty away from clan and community to nuclear family and country, and (c) weakening of the vertical structure or hierarchy. It is noteworthy that these changes came at a time when materialistic ideas and values were rising and people began flaunting newly acquired riches (Cha, 1980).

Decade-by-decade tracing of changes is possible within the postliberation period, because within a few years after the end of the Korean War (1953) empirical studies of values and beliefs began to appear in Korea

(Cha, 1986). Soon after the liberation, reflecting partly the newly gained political independence of the country and partly the influence of Americans who came to Korea as part of the occupation army, the value of freedom emerged and immediately became popular. It became a permanent part of Korea's value system. But the 1950s were marred by the Korean War, and materialistic values such as money, power, status, and expediency became dominant. The values of freedom and materialistic values are not directly related to collectivism, but they tended to foster competition and thereby promote individualism. During this decade, most Koreans were still scrambling for a living, and there was precious little to be had in the way of food, clothing, money, or jobs.

In the 1960s, after the student uprising toppled Syngman Rhee's autocratic government, only to be replaced by a military government, Korea's march toward industrialization got under way in earnest, and by the end of the decade, a modicum of success was achieved. It was under these circumstances that values such as patriotism, self-reliance, diligence, national prosperity, happy home, small family, love, and gender equality came into prominence. In fact, the first four of these values were actively promoted by the military government. The values of the 1960s all suggest the erosion of collectivism based on extended family and clan. In fact, values related to traditional collectivism, such as many offspring, son preference, and dependence, underwent significant decline during this period. This decline continued well into the 1970s (Cha, 1979).

In the 1970s, as the people's standard of living reached a level never before dreamed, values such as diligence and wealth began to wane and gave way to less materialist values. It was during this period that the rise of individualism was most noticeable. The value of individual rights rose, and the traditional values of loyalty and filial piety declined. At the same time, the populace's social consciousness reached a high point. Such values as social justice, equality, human rights, and social welfare became common. Here one finds evidence, for the second time, that as extended family and clan recede from the scene of collectivism, they are replaced by society at large (or some segment of it, such as school), which then becomes the new rallying point of collectivism. Also, the value of hierarchy underwent a steady erosion.

Finally, in the 1980s, the values of health and enjoyment of life as well as values indicative of affiliation motives increased, and the value of patriotism decreased. Here we may be witnessing a new level of individualism in Korea. This new brand of individualism, which is apparent as yet only among Korea's young people, does not even admit the value of country.

The above description should make it clear that the past 100 years have seen the continued weakening of collectivism in Korea. But a closer examination reveals that at each stage of weakening there was a new and deeper involvement, whether voluntary or involuntary, of the people with a capitalist economy. One can surmise that emerging individualism at first was largely confined to the economic sphere, and later extended to the social and political spheres (e.g., individual freedom, individuality, individual rights, privacy). In any case, as the survey study of two generations reported in this chapter has shown, despite the continued advancement of individualism that today is interwoven in much of Koreans' lives, by the end of the 1970s Koreans remained largely collectivist rather than individualist in absolute terms.

The beliefs/attitudes catalog for the postliberation period contained two entries, namely, a concept of closed and exclusionary *woori* (we) and fear of deviating from *woori*. These items came from foreign visitors who were in Korea in the 1970s. The catalogs for the earlier periods contain no references to *woori*; this may be because this attitude associated with the word *woori* becomes palpable only in conversations with Koreans. It is possible that the records of the earlier travelers relied mostly on visual observations rather than on verbal exchanges with the natives. The fact that the word *woori* was used at all in the 1970s, and with a meaning so peculiar that it is taken notice of, is another indication that collectivism was alive and well as late as the beginning of 1980s.

SOME THEORETICAL
AND METHODOLOGICAL NOTES

The following brief comments bear on the theoretical and methodological issues suggested by the studies reported in this chapter.

The nature of the in-group. The first issue has to do with the conception of collectivism as defined in terms of in-group. For a person living in a culture, do all in-groups serve as equally significant foci for collectivism? Or, put differently, does the in-group in an individualist society carry the same meaning as the in-group in a collectivist society? Can we say that a person is exhibiting collectivism just because he or she, as a member of a social club in a highly individualist society, displays loyalty to the club? If the answer is affirmative, how is one to distinguish the concept of group cohesiveness from that of collectivism? One recent study showed that the expression *woori* (we), commonly seen as expressing collectivist sentiments, is more likely to be used against someone with a coorientation (Newcomb, 1953) but at the same time with higher status than oneself (Cha & Park, 1991). Such findings suggest an involvement of hierarchy or power distance in collectivism (Hofstede, 1980).

The transient nature of collectivism. Another related question concerns the historical nature of cultural collectivism. Collectivism of a given society may move irreversibly in one direction, toward greater individualism, and in this sense collectivism of the cultural variety may be a one-time phenomenon. Within a collection of cultures, interculture variations in this characteristic may grow or diminish at different times. It is possible that this characteristic may emerge as an ecological factor (in Hofstede's sense) when the interculture variation becomes large. I am suggesting that the ecological factor of collectivism may be time-bound.

This notion, which may be called the *transient factor hypothesis,* can be generalized to the individual level. This notion of psychological factors can be tested by comparing in two groups the variance of the item scores that represent a factor that appears in one cultural group but not in another. For example, Factor 1 of the younger group (in the survey study) did not appear in the older group. If standard deviations of the items showing highest loadings on this factor (Acceptance of Relational Obligations) were compared between the two age groups, and if the hypothesis is true, the score variance in the older group would be smaller. As expected, 12 of the 14 possible comparisons (7 items × 2 genders) were in the expected direction.

NOTE

1. In one study that used college students as subjects, of the two ecological factors found to be related to collectivism, Koreans ranked second highest in terms of collectivism among 22 countries on a factor that had to do with moderation and curbing one's desires and tenth on one that had to do with harmony and tolerance of others (Chinese Culture Connection, 1987). In another study done by Hofstede (1983b), Korean adults ranked eleventh in terms of collectivism in a group of 50 countries. As near as I can ascertain, Hofstede collected his data between "around 1968 and around 1972" (p. 294).

11

COLLECTIVISM AMONG THE JAPANESE
A Perspective From the Self

SUSUMU YAMAGUCHI

It has now become a platitude that the Japanese are collectivistic. Cross-cultural studies (e.g., Hofstede, 1980) have shown that the Japanese are more collectivistic than Westerners, and there is a large body of literature both by Western authors (e.g., Reishauer, 1978; Vogel, 1979) and Japanese authors (e.g., Araki, 1973; Hamaguchi, 1977; Hamaguchi & Kumon, 1982) that refers to the Japanese as collectivistic. Japanese researchers seem to agree that the Japanese are collectivistic (Hamaguchi & Kumon, 1982), although their opinions may be split on whether collectivism is respectable or not. Araki (1973), for example, criticizes Japanese collectivism, stating that the Japanese are taught to meet the demands of their group and adjust themselves to the group from birth. He argues that by always behaving in accordance with the group's decisions, the Japanese have lost their individuality; he calls this behavioral tendency "dependent." On the other hand, Hamaguchi (1982) notes that Japanese collectivism does not mean total conformity to the group, and that people commit to their group expecting benefits from the group to come later.

JAPANESE COLLECTIVISM

Japanese collectivism has often been attributed to characteristics that are assumed to be unique to the Japanese or Asians. Hamaguchi (1977),

AUTHOR'S NOTE: I would like to thank Anthony G. Greenwald, Uichol Kim, and Harry Triandis for their valuable comments on an earlier version of this chapter. Comments by three anonymous reviewers were also very helpful.

for example, stresses the importance of personal relationships in Japanese culture. According to Hamaguchi (1982), what appears to be collectivist behavior from a Western individualist perspective can be reduced to *kanjinshugi* (i.e., a tendency to put importance on person-to-person relationships). *Kanjinshugi* is characterized by three features: interdependence, mutual reliance, and respect for person-to-person relationships without consideration of costs and benefits. Most research on Japanese collectivism, including that conducted by Araki (1973) and Hamaguchi (1977, 1982), however, has been based upon speculation or, at best, personal observation by the respective researchers.

APPROACHES FROM
THE PERSPECTIVE OF SELF

With the recent development of psychology of the self, important theoretical contributions have been made by several researchers (e.g., Crocker & Luhtanen, 1990; Markus & Kitayama, 1991; Triandis, 1989). Markus and Kitayama (1991) assume that people in different cultures differ in their understanding of themselves, others, and the relationships among people. They propose that degrees of separation or connectedness among individuals vary across cultures. The understanding that individuals are not separate but connected to each other is called the *interdependent construal* of the self and is supposed to be shared by the Japanese as well as other Asians. Markus and Kitayama successfully argue, supported by empirical evidence, that an interdependent view of the self, as contrasted to an independent view of the self, affects the individual's cognitions, motivations, and emotions. Their work is important in understanding individuals' collectivism, because group harmony bolstered by healthy interpersonal relationships among in-group members is an important ingredient of collectivism (Triandis, 1990).

Triandis (1989) argues that people differ in the probability that they will sample different aspects of self (i.e., the private, public, and collective self) (see also Baumeister, 1986; Greenwald & Pratkanis, 1984). He asserts that people in collectivist cultures sample the collective aspect of the self more often than the other aspects. He has empirically verified his contention by comparing undergraduate students of Asian backgrounds with those of Northern European backgrounds at the University of Hawaii, using Kuhn and McPartland's (1954) "who am I" test. As expected, the mean percentages of sentences referring to a social category were significantly higher for the Asian Americans compared with the Euro-Americans in his sample. These results indicate that people from collectivist cultures sample the collective self more often than do people from individualist cultures.

If the collective self is sampled more frequently, more elements of the collective self become salient (Triandis, 1989). Hence the individual's membership in the group becomes more salient, which in turn leads him or her to behave differently in in-group and out-group situations. Researchers have found significant differences between in-group and out-group behaviors in collectivist cultures compared with individualist cultures (e.g., Gudykunst, Yoon, & Nishida, 1987; Leung & Bond, 1984; see also Han & Choe, Chapter 14, this volume). Such results indicate that a person's self-definition as a member of a group determines how he or she acts in social situations. It seems quite plausible that persons' collectivist behavior is mediated by their self-definition as members of a social category.

Crocker and Luhtanen (1990) propose the existence of collective self-esteem in individuals, which is differentiated from personal self-esteem. Collective self-esteem is defined as the motivation to maintain a positive social identity, which is an aspect of individuals' self-concept deriving from their membership in a social group(s). Crocker and Luhtanen's formulation is an extension of social identity theory (Tajfel, 1982; Turner 1982), which posits that a person is motivated to maintain a positive social identity, or what Crocker and Luhtanen call collective self-esteem. Based upon the assumption that collective self-esteem functions like personal self-esteem, they predicted that high collective self-esteem subjects would engage in in-group-enhancing biases or distortions when faced with a threat to their collective self-esteem. Consistent with their prediction, they found that high collective self-esteem subjects changed their evaluations of average- and below-average scorers depending on their own performance on the Social-Cognitive Aptitude Test in order to maintain or enhance their collective self-esteem.

The three lines of research discussed above suggest that the self is a very useful concept for understanding persons' collectivist behavior. In this chapter, I will approach individuals' collectivism from the perspective of the self, and will describe a scale for measuring individual differences in collectivism (Yamaguchi, 1990c). Finally, I will present empirical evidence on individual collectivism among the Japanese.

THE PRESENT APPROACH

The self has been conceptualized by theorists in psychology as consisting of more than one system. Freud (1940/1964) argues that personality

CONCEPTUAL AND EMPIRICAL ANALYSIS

is composed of three systems: the id, the ego, and the superego. According to William James (1890), the self can be divided into another three parts: the material self, the social self, and the spiritual self. Gordon Allport (1943) proposes eight aspects of the self. These theoretical analyses and recent empirical work in social psychology have led Greenwald and his associates to identify three motivational facets of the self: the public self, the private self, and the collective self (Greenwald & Breckler, 1984; Greenwald & Pratkanis, 1984). Each of these facets is thought to be motivated by favorable evaluation from a significant audience. The public self attempts to gain a favorable evaluation from important others (e.g., parents or authority figures). The private self is more individualistic and motivates the person to act to obtain a positive self-evaluation according to internal standards. The collective self seeks to gain favorable evaluation from a reference group by fulfilling a particular role and helping to achieve the goals of the group. Until recently, the collective self had received the least attention among the three facets of the self, but researchers have now begun to explore it.

There is no consensus on the definition of *collectivism* among Japanese researchers (Hamaguchi & Kumon, 1982) or Western researchers. Triandis (1989), for example, defines collectivists as those who "either make no distinctions between personal and collective goals, or if they do make such distinctions, they subordinate their personal goals to the collective goals." In earlier work, I have defined persons' collectivism as the tendency to give priority to the collective self over the private self, *especially when the two are in conflict* (Yamaguchi, 1990c). Collectivists are those who weigh collective goals more heavily than private goals, especially when the two come into conflict. This definition raises some interesting questions about antecedents and consequences of persons' collectivism.

ANTECEDENTS
OF PERSONS' COLLECTIVISM

The above definition of persons' collectivism highlights the possibility that the interests of all facets of the self are not necessarily satisfied simultaneously. Based on ego-task analysis, Greenwald and Pratkanis (1984) suggest that subjects in experiments on conformity are put in a dilemma that pits the public self against the private self: Subjects have to jeopardize approval from an audience when they stick to their personal standards. When working in a collective situation, one may well find that the pursuit of personal goals (i.e., the task of the private self) is at variance with group goals (i.e., the task of the collective self). If one chooses to work for the group, abandoning personal goals, then one's behavior is collectivist.

Taking the above line of reasoning, the following question emerges: What underlies persons' self-sacrifice? In my own work, I have suggested two reasons for the dominance of the collective self over the private self: psychological attachment (i.e., expectation of reward) and fear of rejection (i.e., expectation of punishment) (Yamaguchi, 1990c). Individuals may temporarily sacrifice their self-interest for a group so long as they can expect rewards from the group in the long run. The expectation of punishment by group members can also motivate an individual to abandon personal goals in favor of those of the group. Such reasoning would explain why a group member feels obliged to work for personally undesirable group goals; he or she may anticipate a negative outcome for behaving otherwise. This reasoning suggests that collectivism among individuals is accompanied by a tendency to expect either positive or negative outcomes of interactions with others.

CONSEQUENCES
OF PERSONS' COLLECTIVISM

Persons' collectivism is also thought to be responsible for other individual differences (Yamaguchi, 1990c). First, collectivists are expected to hesitate in making unique personal choices on their own. By definition, collectivists give priority to group goals, and they should withhold their personal opinions and preferences when these are at variance with those of their group. When they conform to group standards they cannot logically be unique relative to their group members. Such behavioral patterns would weaken individuals' motives for being unique. Second, the collectivist tendency would also affect individuals' perceptions of locus of control. Collectivists are supposed to withhold personal opinions and choices in favor of those of the group, and they do not gain a feeling that reinforcements are the results of their own choices. Thus collectivists are expected to acquire the expectation that reinforcement is not contingent upon their own actions. Third, collectivism among individuals should make them sensitive to the needs of other group members. If they are inattentive to the needs of other group members, collectivists will be unable to gain favorable reputations as group members. Thus collectivists are expected to regulate the expression of their opinions and emotions so that they will not make fellow group members unhappy (i.e., they emphasize harmony in the in-group). These expectations about antecedents and consequences of individuals' collectivism are schematically described in Figure 11.1.

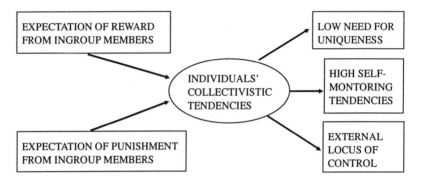

Figure 11.1. Hypothesized Antecedents and Consequences of Persons' Collectivism

In Chapter 3 of this volume, Harry Triandis provides an extensive list of cognitive, emotional, and behavioral tendencies that accompany persons' collectivism as well as their individualism. Later in this chapter, I will discuss how persons' collectivism is related to consensus estimates and interpersonal attraction in the group. Specifically, I will argue that consensus with other members of the group is more important for collectivist members than for their noncollectivist counterparts. I will also argue that collectivists' preference for the equality principle results in their unfavorable attitudes toward particularly able members in the group.

OPERATIONALIZATION OF PERSONS' COLLECTIVISM AND RELEVANT INDIVIDUAL DIFFERENCES

We need a device to measure persons' collectivist tendencies and conceptually relevant individual differences when we attempt to test the model described in Figure 11.1. In previous work, I have developed a scale to measure collectivism among individuals as defined above (Yamaguchi, 1990c). The Collectivism Scale consists of 10 items describing behavioral choices that favor group goals in situations where group and personal goals come into conflict (see the appendix to this chapter). The other individual differences that are expected to accompany a person's collectivist tendencies can be measured by established scales. Expectations of reward or punishment in interaction with group members can be measured using Mehrabian and Ksionsky's (1974) Affiliative Tendency Scale and Sensitivity to Rejection Scale. These scales were developed to measure individual differences in expectations regarding reward or punishment in the presence of others. Because in everyday life individuals' reinforcing agents are usually group members (e.g., those in the family, peer group, and work group), individuals' scores on these scales may be appropriately used as indices of how much reward and/or punishment the individuals would expect from the group.

The strength of the need to be unique from others can be assessed by Snyder and Fromkin's (1977) Need for Uniqueness Scale. These researchers have shown that people differ in the extent to which they want to be different from others in opinions and behaviors. The concept of perceived locus of control was first introduced by Rotter (1966), who developed an individual difference measure of the perceived locus of control. More recently, Kanbara, Higuchi, and Chimizu (1982) have proposed a new Locus of Control Scale that they claim has better reliability. I have adopted Kanbara et al.'s scale to measure individual differences in the degree to which people expect reinforcements as a result of their own actions (Yamaguchi, 1990c). The tendency to be attentive to others' needs in the group can be measured using Snyder's (1974) Self-Monitoring Scale, which is intended to tap an individual's tendency to regulate the expression of opinions and emotions in response to others' needs. The Self-Monitoring Scale is also expected to measure individuals' expressive behavior in group situations.

Thus it is hypothesized that the Collectivism Scale should be correlated with established scales in the following ways: (a) a positive correlation with the Affiliative Tendency Scale, (b) a positive correlation with the Sensitivity to Rejection Scale, (c) a negative correlation with the Need for Uniqueness Scale, (d) a negative correlation with the Locus of Control Scale, and (e) a positive correlation with the Self-Monitoring Scale.

EMPIRICAL EVIDENCE

In this section I present some empirical evidence found in several studies I have reported on in more depth elsewhere (Yamaguchi, 1990c).

Reliability of the Collectivism Scale

In Study 1, the Collectivism Scale was administered to 609 undergraduate students who constituted six samples. Respondents used a 5-point scale to indicate the extent to which each item described them. As can be seen in Table 11.1, the results reveal that the scale is highly reliable

Table 11.1   Descriptive Statistics and Reliability Coefficient (Alpha) for Samples

Sample	Male	Female	Mean	SD	Alpha
1		67	28.28	6.09	.85
2		171	27.74	5.76	.82
3	110		26.53	5.86	.79
4		156	28.28	6.73	.85
5	32	28	25.84	5.91	.77
6	34	11	26.91	7.03	.88

(Cronbach's alpha ranged from .77 to .88). In addition, when the scale was readministered to 75 respondents about three months after the first administration, the test-retest reliability was also high ($r = .71, p < .001$). In factor analyses, the variance explained by the first factor ranged from 75% to 96% of the common variance. The scree plots for the sample indicate a one-factor solution for the Collectivism Scale.

In Study 3, I found the Collectivism Scale to be independent of response bias, owing to acquiescence and social desirability (Yamaguchi, 1990c). In that study, I reversed half of the original items while attempting to preserve their meaning (see the appendix to this chapter). The correlation between the original scale and the reversed items after a one-month interval was substantial and significant ($r = .73, p < .01$). This correlation is larger than the test-retest reliability and thus indicates that the scores are not affected very much by the reversed items. The correlation between the Collectivism Scale and the Social Desirability Scale was very small and nonsignificant ($r = .08$).

Personality Correlates of Persons' Collectivism

In Study 1, respondents were administered the individual difference measures described above as well as the Collectivism Scale. They also rated items on two scales relevant to the conception of the self: the Self-Consciousness Scale (Fenigstein, Scheier, & Buss, 1975) and the Self-Esteem Scale (Rosenberg, 1965). The Collectivism Scale and the Locus of Control Scale (Kanbara et al., 1982) were originally provided in Japanese; my own translations into Japanese were used for all the other scales employed in the study.

The correlations of the Collectivism Scale with the conceptually relevant individual differences measures are as follows. The Collectivism Scale was positively correlated with the Affiliative Tendency, Sensitivity

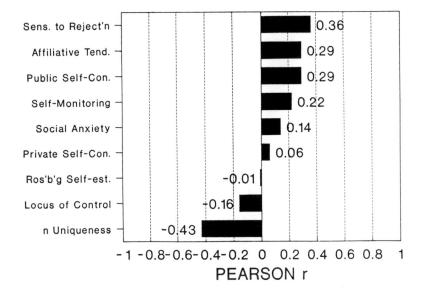

Figure 11.2. Average Correlations Between the Collectivism Scale and Other Scales

to Rejection, and Self-Monitoring Scales. It was negatively correlated with the Locus of Control and Need for Uniqueness Scales. The Collectivism Scale was positively correlated with the Public Self-Consciousness subscale.

Although these results are generally consistent with the present conceptualization of collectivism, the product-moment correlation coefficients varied with the sample. Therefore, I used a meta-analysis technique developed by Mullen and Rosenthal (1985) to test the overall significance of the correlations between the Collectivism Scale and the other scales. The average rs are given in Figure 11.2, which indicates that persons' collectivism is associated with high affiliative tendency ($p < .01$), high sensitivity to rejection ($p < .01$), low need for uniqueness ($p < .01$), more external locus of control perception ($p < .01$), and high self-monitoring tendencies ($p < .01$). Because these relationships had been expected from the present conceptualization of collectivism, one can conclude that the Collectivism Scale has construct validity.

In addition to the predicted correlations, the Collectivism Scale was found to be positively correlated with the Public Self-Consciousness subscale. However, this finding is not surprising, because collectivists are assumed to be attentive to group members, and group members are part of the public. It can also be seen in Figure 11.2 that persons' collectivist tendencies are independent of their self-esteem.

Age and Collectivism

Triandis (1989) suggests that people become more individualistic in affluent societies. He reasons that in a complex and affluent society people attain financial independence, which in turn leads them to be socially and emotionally independent. He suggests that people in affluent societies tend to give priority to personal goals over in-group goals. On the other hand, in developing countries people need to be interdependent. It is quite common in developing countries that people need to share limited resources with others. In such economic situations, people can hardly be independent of others.

Japan was not very affluent until relatively recently. In the years immediately after World War II, the Japanese people faced great poverty; many Japanese starved to death during that period. Because Japan has recently achieved substantial economic success, it is to be expected that Japanese can now afford to be more individualistic than before. The effects of affluence would likely be most prominent among younger Japanese, because they did not experience the poverty that previous generations endured. Furthermore, older Japanese have been influenced by their society's collectivist atmosphere more than have their younger counterparts. On the other hand, for the same reason, older people in individualist societies are expected to be more individualistic than younger people (H. C. Triandis, personal communication, 1990). Finally, education in Japan has changed drastically since World War II, from a totalitarian system to a more democratic system in which students are allowed to behave more individualistically.

The above line of reasoning suggests that older Japanese should be more collectivistic than younger Japanese. To test this hypothesis, I administered the Collectivism Scale to 36 older students taking correspondence courses in Tokyo (Yamaguchi, 1990a). Their collectivism score (mean age = 43) is positively correlated with their age ($r = .54$, $p < .0001$).

Consensus Estimate and Collectivism

In 1943, Wallen reported an interesting phenomenon that was later named the "false consensus effect" (Ross, Greene, & House, 1977). In May 1941, Wallen asked 237 female college students to estimate the percentage of students on their campus who believed that the United States would be at war with Germany by midsummer of 1941. The students were also asked if *they* believed the United States would be at war with Germany by midsummer of that year. Wallen then compared the respondents' percentage estimates with their own judgments on the outbreak of war, and found that the respondents tended to expect relatively high consensus among other students on the campus and that they tended to believe, erroneously, that a high percentage of students would agree with them on the issue. This trend was also found with other issues, such as attitudes toward the Selective Service Act and the Saint Lawrence Seaway Project.

More recently, Ross et al. (1977) conducted a series of experiments to show that people tend to overestimate the relative commonness of their behaviors and opinions. Studies on false consensus have pointed out both cognitive and motivational determinants of consensus estimates (for reviews, see Marks & Miller, 1987; Mullen et al., 1985).

In my own work, I reasoned that consensus with the majority of the in-group would be more important for collectivist members than for noncollectivist members (Yamaguchi, 1990c). Thus to the extent one is collectivist, one comes to believe that one's choices are shared by the majority of the group. By thus persuading themselves, collectivists are happy and not required to change or suppress their personal choices. In Study 2, I tested this hypothesis by giving 177 female students a fictitious decision-making situation. They were given a booklet titled *Survey on a Social Issue,* which contained the following decision-making problem. They were asked to imagine that their country was under threat of nuclear attack and that there were 12 people who were striving to get into a fallout shelter that could accommodate only 6 people; a descriptive list of the 12 candidates was given.[1] Each subject was then asked to decide, within 15 minutes, which 6 people were to be accommodated in the fallout shelter and why. After making her decisions, each subject was asked to make three consensus estimates:

1. What percentage of students would make the same choices based upon the same principles she had used? (indicated on a 100-point scale)
2. What percentage of students in the college would choose the same 6 people she had chosen? (indicated on a 100-point scale)
3. How many students in the college would choose the same 6 people she had chosen? (indicated on a 6-point scale)

The subjects' answers to these questions were standardized within each scale and then summed to yield a consensus estimate index. Pearson product-moment correlation of the consensus estimate index with the collectivism score was significant ($r = .17$, $p < .03$). The subjects with higher collectivism scores tended to give higher consensus estimates. The results confirmed the expectation that the individuals' collectivist tendency was positively correlated with their consensus estimate concerning their choices. In this study, no relationship was found between consensus estimate and individuals' level of self-esteem ($r = .00$) or need for uniqueness ($r = -.07$).

Interpersonal Attraction in the Group and Persons' Collectivism

People in collectivist cultures have been found to prefer the equality principle to the equity principle when it comes to the distribution of outcomes of group work. Leung and Bond (1984) report that collectivist Chinese students preferred to distribute a reward equally among in-group members more than did their American counterparts, liked the allocator who distributed the reward equally better among the in-group members than the allocator who used the equity principle, and rated equal distribution as being as fairer than equitable distribution. It is assumed that persons with stronger collectivist tendencies will favor the equality principle over the equity principle when they distribute group reward among in-group members.

Individuals' collectivist tendencies have also been found to be related to interpersonal relationships in a group (Yamaguchi, 1990b). In a series of studies, I asked female college students how easy they felt it would be to get along with the highest scorer, the average scorer, and the lowest scorer on a psychology test (Yamaguchi, 1990b). Findings indicated that the highest scorer was less liked than the average scorer. These results may indicate that collectivists prefer the equality principle on an ability dimension as well as on a reward-distribution dimension. Particularly able members can lower the self-esteem of other group members and disturb group harmony.

I tested this expectation in Study 5, in which an intelligence test was administered to female undergraduate students (Yamaguchi, 1990b). Before they received their marks on the test, they were asked to rate how easy it would be to get along with the highest scorer, the average scorer, and the lowest scorer. The highest scorer was less liked than the average scorer or the lowest scorer. As predicted, the subjects' collectivist tendency was found to be negatively correlated with their evaluation of the likability of the highest scorer ($r = -.30$, $p < .03$). Collectivists favor situations in which even mental abilities are distributed equally in the group. This tendency may be attributable to collectivists' emphasis on group harmony.

CONCLUSION

Collectivism is defined as a tendency to weigh group goals more heavily than personal goals when the two are in conflict. This definition is based upon a theoretical analysis of the literature that was formally presented in Greenwald's (1982) ego-task analysis. Data from more than 600 respondents have confirmed that the Collectivism Scale is reliable and unidimensional. The Collectivism Scale has also been found to correlate with other established scales as predicted from the present conceptualization of collectivism, supporting the validity of the scale.

Use of the Collectivism Scale has shown so far that persons' collectivism is related to their age, consensus estimates, and interpersonal attraction in a group. Several predictions about behavioral characteristics of collectivists can be drawn from the present conceptualization of collectivism. First, because collectivists give more weight to group goals than to personal goals, they should conform to the group's opinion to a greater extent than noncollectivists. Second, it seems plausible that a collectivist who cannot be a good member of the group would leave the group, even though that means sacrificing the benefits of staying in the group. In other words, a collectivist will try not to be a burden on other group members. One may voluntarily leave the group when one's membership might cause the group much loss or when one's behavior might harm the group's reputation. Third, it may also be predicted that collectivists will hesitate to express opinions before knowing the opinions of others. As collectivists try to conform to the majority's wish, it would be embarrassing for them to show their unique opinions. It would be safer for collectivists to express their opinions later, at which time they can agree with others. Thus collectivists should prefer to hear others' opinions before expressing their own. Fourth, it would also be interesting to ask whether collectivists give priority to the collective self over the public self when the two are in conflict. If this is the case, collectivists may tell lies in public for the sake of their group. Politicians, for instance, may lie publicly for the sake of their parties or other interest groups.

Theoretically, the present analysis of collectivism is based upon the assumption that there is a superordinate system that regulates the relationships among the three facets of self. It is assumed that the relative dominance of the collective self over the private self is governed by the expected outcome: Collectivists are assumed to be sensitive to both reward and punishment from the group. In this sense, the superordinate system may function like id within Freud's framework or diffuse self in Greenwald's analysis. Diffuse self is, according to Greenwald and Pratkanis (1984), "in some senses, a pre-self, a condition of not distinguishing sharply between self and others, with behavior hedonically guided toward positive affective states."

Although the Collectivism Scale was originally meant for use with the Japanese, it is at least potentially applicable to other cultures as well, because it is constructed to measure the tendency to give priority to the collective self over the private self. This tendency is expected to be shared to some extent by members of more individualist cultures; it would be interesting to apply the Collectivism Scale in such cultures.

APPENDIX:
COLLECTIVISM SCALE ITEMS

Parentheses contain negatively worded items, which are to be used in the half-reversed version of the Collectivism Scale (Yamaguchi, 1990c).

1. I sacrifice self-interest for my group.
   (I don't sacrifice self-interest for my group.)
2. I act as fellow group members would prefer.
   (I don't think it necessary to act as fellow group members would prefer.)
3. I stick with my group even through difficulties.
4. I maintain harmony in my group.
5. I respect the majority's wish.
   (I don't change my opinions in conformity with those of the majority.)
6. I support my group, whether they are right or wrong.
   (I don't support my group when they are wrong.)
7. I respect decisions made by my group.
8. I remain in my group if they need me, even though dissatisfied with them.
9. I avoid arguments within my group, even when I strongly disagree with other members.
   (I assert my opposition when I disagree strongly with the members of my group.)
10. I make an effort to avoid disagreements with my group members.

NOTE

1. The descriptions of the 12 persons were adopted from Benjamin and Lawman (1981) and modified for Japanese subjects.

12

MEASUREMENT OF NORMATIVE AND EVALUATIVE ASPECTS IN INDIVIDUALISTIC AND COLLECTIVISTIC ORIENTATIONS
The Cultural Orientation Scale (COS)

GÜNTER BIERBRAUER
HEIKE MEYER
UWE WOLFRADT

The growing interest in the construct of I/C in recent years is reflected in some promising theoretical developments (e.g., Triandis, 1989) and empirical results (e.g., Brislin, 1990). Despite the concept's great popularity in cross-cultural psychology, there is a lack of research instruments suitable for differentiating between individuals or groups both within and across cultures. In past research, normative views and evaluative views have often been confounded. This may be in part a result of the fact that the definitions of norms and values in the social sciences are vague and often contradictory. This chapter provides conceptual refinements and a more concise instrument for the measurement of cultural orientations.

A major step toward the measurement of I/C was the development of the INDCOL Scale by Hui (1988). This scale consists of 63 items that cover six social targets: spouse, parents, kin, neighbors, friends, and cowork-

AUTHORS' NOTE: The study was in part supported by a grant from the Volkswagen-Stiftung. Numerous people were involved in various phases of this project. They all deserve my sincerest thanks. Jutta Bott and Rüdiger Volkmann collected and prepared the data for Study 2. Heike Meyer and Uwe Wolfradt collected the data for Study 1 and 3 and worked on the data analysis for all three studies.

ers. The items measuring collectivism tap into attitudes, feelings, beliefs, and behavioral intentions related to solidarity and concern for others. Although this scale has been used in several studies to discriminate various cultural groups (e.g., Leung, 1987), the concept and the scale need further refinement, for the methodological and conceptual reasons enumerated below.

First, the INDCOL Scale consists of items that tap into individual values or behavioral intentions, such as "I would help if a colleague at work told me that he/she needed money to pay utility bills." Most items focus in some way on conflicts between personal and in-group goals. Cultural norms, values, or goals, however, which are important elements in the differentiation of cultures, may go beyond the immediate realm of the in-group (e.g., social justice and peace). These norms and values are not represented in the INDCOL Scale.

As discussed in the literature, the I/C and idiocentric/allocentric dichotomies are regarded as reflecting both normative and value assessments (e.g., Hofstede, 1980; Triandis, 1989). They are supposed to reflect both common practices in a target culture and preferences expressed by individuals. Future studies should clearly separate the two levels of analysis: (a) the degree to which certain practices are normative in a particular culture, and (b) the personal evaluations of respondents concerning these practices.

Second, facets and elements of the I/C constructs are not clearly articulated in the INDCOL Scale. According to Hui and Triandis (1986), collectivism can be defined as "a cluster of attitudes, belief and behaviors toward a wide variety of people" (p. 240). An inspection of the INDCOL Scale shows that most of the items are normative in character, with a strong value judgment (e.g., "It is reasonable for a son to continue his father's business"). Several items refer to beliefs (e.g., "My musical interests are extremely different from my parents'") or behaviors (e.g., "I practice the religion of my parents"). Hofstede (1980) measured individualism by asking respondents how important certain work goals were for them, reflecting a strong value overtone. Thus not only is the I/C dimension conceptually confusing, it is unclear how it should be measured.

The perception of norms and the personal evaluation of these norms do not necessarily coincide. Take, for example, the item "It is reasonable for a son to continue his father's business." This statement may be approved because it is an economic necessity or because it is the consequence of a cultural prescription. At the same time, it may be rejected or valued by an individual respondent for personal reasons. It is thus necessary to distinguish between perceived cultural norms (what is practice or normative in a given culture) and an individual's evaluation of these norms (what a person likes or dislikes).

Part of the above-mentioned problem is in definition. Both in common parlance and in academic language, norms and values seem to have different meaning. Norms are defined as widely shared standards of conduct that are suitable for controlling the behavior of members of society. They reflect society's expectancies of individuals' behavior, and those who transgress norms are liable for social sanctions. Values, on the other hand, are desirable standards of orientation in a person's life. Cialdini, Reno, and Kallgren (1990) distinguish norms with regard to their descriptive meaning (what is typical or normal) and with regard to their injunctive meaning (what ought to be done). They conclude that the two meanings of norms are easily confused, because what is approved is often what is typically done. Hofstede (1980) distinguishes the normative aspect of values (what is desirable) and the deontological aspect (what ought to be desired). This definition of norm includes a value aspect, and the definition of value includes a normative aspect.

Taken together, the above considerations lead us to suggest the following distinction between norms and values: Norms reflect the perceived degree to which certain behaviors or practices are common in a given culture. Values, on the other hand, involve personal evaluations of the behavior or practice in question and thus reflect the degree to which the latter are desirable or not.

Third, the separation between norms and the degree of acceptance of these norms is particularly important when one deals with persons whose identities are influenced by two cultures (e.g., foreign students or migrants). Asian foreign students living in Germany may find it appropriate for German students to disregard the advice given by their parents, but may find the same behavior inappropriate within the context of their native countries. In order to understand better the psychological and cultural values of acculturating groups, it is necessary to measure independently the perceived normative patterns and personal evaluations of these norms. We expect that acculturating individuals may change their evaluations of certain normative practices in their cultures of origin because of their experience in the new culture, but should not change their perceptions of norms and practices in their cultures of origin.

Fourth, for distinguishing cultural groups for the assessment of their individual- and group-level data, the INDCOL Scale is too long. For research purposes, a much shorter instrument is desirable. Finally, most of the comparisons made so far with the INDCOL Scale sampled respondents from the United States and various parts of Asia. To assess the validity of both the INDCOL Scale and other scales, it is necessary to collect data from other parts of the world.

Three consecutive studies were carried out to assess the validity of the INDCOL Scale and to develop a shorter instrument that measures cultural norms and values separately. The first two pilot studies serve to validate the German version of the INDCOL Scale and to create the Cultural Orientation Scale (COS), which selected the most discriminating items from existing scales. Students who are currently in Germany representing various cultural backgrounds (i.e., German, Iranian, Korean, and Turkish) participated in these studies.

STUDY 1

Procedure

Subjects. A total of 126 students (71 males and 55 females) took part in the study. The average age was 24 years, ranging from 18 to 35; 67 of the students were German, 33 were Turkish, and 26 were Iranian. The average length of residence in Germany for the latter two groups was 11 years, ranging from 1 to 25 years.

Instruments. Subjects completed the German version of the INDCOL Scale, which was translated by highly competent bilinguals who took the problems of linguistic equivalence into account. After completing the INDCOL Scale, subjects completed the Short Scale 1, which contained eight items that were based on the construct identified by Sinha and Verma (1987). These items tapped into various aspects of family life (e.g., "How often do people in your native country take care of a sick relative rather than go to work?").

Results

Cronbach's alpha for the German version of the INDCOL Scale for the Turkish and Iranian group (T/I) was .74; for the German group (G) it was .69. The results in Table 12.1 show that the Turkish and Iranian subjects are more collectivistic than German subjects as measured by the INDCOL Scale and Short Scale 1. Because the Turkish and Iranian subject groups did not differ significantly, their scores were combined.

Short Scale 1 seems to be an instrument sensitive enough to distinguish individuals from two acculturating groups from native German students.

Table 12.1 Mean Ratings on the INDCOL Scale (63 items) and Short Scale 1
(8 items)

| | Germans (N = 66) | | Turks/Iranians (N = 57) | | |
	M	SD	M	SD	t
INDCOL Scale	3.80	.43	3.97	.38	2.31*
Short Scale 1	3.73	.66	4.85	.58	9.75***

| | Turks (N = 29) | | Iranians (N = 25) | | |
	M	SD	M	SD	t
INDCOL Scale	3.99	.43	3.94	.32	n.s.
Short Scale 1	4.92	.49	4.77	.67	n.s.

NOTE: The scales ranged from 0 = disagree to 7 = agree. The higher the mean, the higher the degree of perceived collectivism.
*p < .05, two-tailed; ***p < .001, two-tailed.

Table 12.2 Interrelations Among INDCOL Subscales and Short Scale 1 Across
All Three Culture Groups

	Total Sample (N = 126) r	Germans (N = 67) r	Turks/Iranians (N = 59) r
INDCOL (total)	.38***	.07	.48**
Spouse	.18*	.08	.41*
Parents	.31***	.17	.58***
Kin	.29***	.14	.58***
Neighbor	.37***	.08	.36**
Friends	.09	.08	.59***
Coworker	.03	−.13	.40**

*p < .05; **p < .01; ***p < .001.

Unlike the Germans subjects, the Turkish and Iranian subjects strongly identified with their families, as revealed by the correlations in the various subscales of the INDCOL Scale and Short Scale 1. This is in line with suggestions of various writers that the family is a strong determinant of collectivism (e.g., Hui, 1988; Sinha & Verma, 1987). Table 12.2 shows that although the correlations between Short Scale 1 and the various INDCOL subscales are highly significant, a similar pattern was not obtained for the German sample.

STUDY 2

A second study was carried out to check whether Short Scale 1 differentiates among subjects from various cultural backgrounds. Furthermore, in this study we attempted to measure separately the perceived normative levels and the personal values of the respondents.

Subjects. The sample consisted of 37 Germans, 41 Lebanese, and 28 Kurds (all male). The average age was 28 years, ranging from 18 to 50. None of the respondents had a college education. The Lebanese and Kurds were asylum seekers who had been living in Germany for an average of 21 months. Subjects were paid the equivalent of $13 for participating in the interviews, which were conducted in their native languages.

Instrument. The subjects responded to Short Scale 2, which is a 14-item scale measuring I/C. The items were partly based on Short Scale 1 and partly based on a scale developed by Sinha and Verma (1987). Five items examined the degree to which a subject believed that a certain behavior in his culture is common or practiced. In addition, each subject was asked to express the degree to which he approved or disapproved of this practice. Thus subjects were asked to rate an item on both normative and evaluative levels. This allows the measurement of cultural orientation in regard to subjects' cultures of origin and the culture of the host country. In addition, subjects' personal evaluations of the behaviors in question were assessed. Furthermore, four additional items were included that measured individuals' attitudes toward the family.

Results

As expected, on an 11-point Likert-type scale ranging from 0 (never or bad) to 10 (always or good), the German subjects had a significantly lower mean, 4.17, than the two other cultural groups, Lebanese ($ML = 7.22$) and Kurds ($MK = 7.28$) ($t(1, 104) = 17.37, p < .001$, two-tailed). Because the two latter groups did not differ significantly, they were combined for all further analyses. Reliability of the scale was acceptable (α total $= .86$; α G $= .61$; α L $= .33$ and α K $= .46$). Analyses of variance for the single items showed higher collectivism scores for Lebanese and Kurds that are in most cases significantly different from the scores of the German subjects.

STUDY 3

Development of the Cultural Orientation Scale (COS)

Based on the items of Short Scale 1, Short Scale 2, and the INDCOL Scale, we developed a new scale measuring general cultural orientation, with separate assessment of normative and evaluative aspects (see the appendix to this chapter). Highly reliable items from the three scales were included in the new scale (reliability >.30 for the INDCOL Scale and >.40 for the two Short Scales; see Torgerson, 1958). We selected 13 items that met the above criteria. Because each item was presented to measure both normative and evaluative aspects independently, the final scale consisted of 26 items. Each normative assessment was followed by a corresponding evaluative assessment. The new instrument is called the Cultural Orientation Scale (COS).

Subjects. In this study, the Cultural Orientation Scale was administered to Korean and German students. It was predicted that Korean students would score higher on collectivism than German students. It was further predicted that Korean students would be less "collectivistic" the longer they stayed in Germany. The sample consisted of 27 Korean students (23 male and 4 female) and 29 German students (18 male and 11 female). Korean students, who were recruited from two German universities, were administered the questionnaire in German. The Korean subjects' self-reported competence in German language was at least "average." The majority of the Korean students came from Seoul. Their average age was 28 years, ranging from 23 to 35. Their average length of residence in Germany was 2.8 years. The average age of the German sample was 23 years, ranging from 19 to 32. All participants were approached individually and asked for their cooperation.

Results

As expected, the COS differentiated significantly between the Korean and German samples. On a 7-point scale, the scores for the Korean subjects showed a significantly higher mean of collectivism (MK = 4.77) than their German counterparts (MG = 3.68) (see Table 12.3). The internal consistency of the scale (α total = .82) was acceptable (α G = .56; α K = .70).

The correlations between the normative items and the evaluative items differed according to the cultural group. The Pearson correlation is .30 ($p < .10$) for the German group and .51 ($p < .01$) for the Korean group.

Table 12.3 Mean Ratings for the Cultural Orientation Scale Across Culture Groups

	Germans (N = 29)		Koreans (N = 27)		
	M	SD	M	SD	t
Cultural Orientation Scale (26 items)	3.86	.32	4.77	.49	8.11***
Normative items (13)	3.81	.32	4.75	.48	8.62***
Evaluative items (13)	3.92	.47	4.79	.65	5.69***

NOTE: The scale ranged from 1 = disagree to 7 = agree. The higher the mean, the higher the degree of perceived collectivism.
***$p < .001$, two-tailed.

Table 12.4 Mean Ratings for the Cultural Orientation Scale for Korean Students According to Length of Residence

	1 Year (N = 8)		2-8 Years (N = 19)		
	M	SD	M	SD	t
Cultural Orientation Scale (26 items)	5.16	.32	4.61	.46	3.59**
Normative items (13)	5.05	.43	4.63	.45	2.28*
Evaluative items (13)	5.27	.45	4.58	.62	3.21**

NOTE: The scale ranged from 1 = disagree to 7 = agree. The higher the mean, the higher the degree of perceived collectivism.
*$p < .05$; **$p < .01$, two-tailed.

For the Korean subjects, there was a greater degree of correspondence between perceived norms and values. This fact is part of the syndrome that characterizes collectivist cultures.

The normative and evaluative assessments show similar differences in the expected direction. Because the scale was designed to measure the degree of perceived norms and evaluations of acculturating groups with regard to their home countries, we expected that during the process of acculturation the assessments of these individuals would shift toward the perceived norms of their host country. As shown in Table 12.4, this is indeed the case. The Korean students who had stayed from two to eight years in Germany became significantly less collectivistic compared with the Koreans who had stayed in Germany for less than one year. This is true for both normative and evaluative assessments, although to a lesser degree with regard to normative assessments.

GENERAL DISCUSSION

The theoretical conceptualization of the I/C dimension and the empirical findings of Hofstede (1980), Hui and Triandis (1986), and others are basically supported. In all our studies, subjects who come from collectivist cultures (i.e., Iran, Korea, Lebanon, and Turkey) showed higher scores on collectivism than did subjects from Germany.

Recent criticism of the I/C distinction made it necessary to go beyond the realm of individual and in-group interest to focus on perceived norms and personal values. The latter distinction enables researchers to measure perceived practices and norms in a target culture and a host culture independently. This distinction is particularly important for a better understanding of individual psychological and cultural orientations, as well as adaptation of acculturating groups, whose cultural identities may be influenced by two cultures, depending on the degree of integration in their host country. The development of the Cultural Orientation Scale is a first step toward reaching this goal. Because the scale is relatively short, it can be used for a variety of research purposes.

As the various contributions to this book attest, the concept of I/C is highly controversial. For some writers (e.g., Sinha & Tripathi, Chapter 8, this volume), the concept is too global to deal with the varieties of cultural patterns in a given society; for others (e.g., Schwartz, 1990), the concept focuses exclusively on the conflict between individual and collective interests and leaves no room for values that express desirable goals in a culture. The studies reported in this chapter address some of these problems. The content and form of the forces that we call culture can be understood only through conceptual refinements that have not been traditionally or rigorously applied. Previous questionnaires and scales have confused perceived cultural norms and the personal evaluation of these norms; we believe it is important to distinguish and measure these two aspects separately.

As expected, the correlation between these two measures for subjects from individualistisc cultures is lower than for those from collectivistisc cultures. One facet of individualism seems to be relatively less agreement between norms and their evaluative content. This could be caused by alienation or anomie. Alternatively, the distinction between "loose" and "tight" cultures can be applied. According to Triandis (1989) and others, in loose cultures a wide variety of norms and deviant behavior is tolerated, whereas tight cultures demand that individuals conform to in-group norms. Collectivism and cultural tightness are closely related (Triandis, 1989). Thus the proposed distinction allows further investigation of the degree to which perceived norms and values may coincide at the cultural level and the degree to which both may change separately or together when individuals move across cultures.

Although the Cultural Orientation Scale differentiated between the two cultures sampled in the predicted direction and is partly based on previously validated instruments, further work is necessary to link the scale with additional constructs and dimensions (such as conservatism and modernism) in order to confirm the present findings. Future research is being planned to investigate the implications of such concepts.

APPENDIX:
CULTURAL ORIENTATION SCALE (COS)

1. How often do teenagers in your native country listen to their parents' advice on dating?

1	2	3	4	5	6	7
not at all	very rarely	rarely	sometimes	often	very often	always

2. What do you think of teenagers in your native country listening to their parents' advice on dating?

I think this is

1	2	3	4	5	6	7
very bad	bad	rather bad	neither good nor bad	rather good	good	very good

3. How often do people in your native country share their ideas and newly acquired knowledge with their parents?
4. What do you think of people in your native country sharing their ideas and newly acquired knowledge with their parents?
5. How often do people in your native country listen to the advice of their parents or close relatives when choosing a career?
6. What do you think of people in your native country listening to the advice of their parents or close relatives when choosing a career?
7. How often do people in your native country talk to their neighbors about politics?
8. What do you think of people talking to their neighbors about politics?
9. How often do people in your native country refuse to take the advice of their friends on how to spend their money because they may consider this a personal matter?

10. What do you think of someone in your native country refusing to take the advice of friends on how to spend his or her money?

11. If someone in your native country is together with friends or colleagues, how often does he or she do exactly what he or she wants to do, regardless of what the others think?

12. What do you think of someone doing exactly what he or she wants to do, regardless of what friends and colleagues present may think?

13. How often do children in your native country live at home with their parents until they get married?

14. What do you think of children in your native country living at home with their parents until they get married?

15. Do people in your native country often find it annoying when visitors arrive unannounced?

16. What do you think of people in your native country being annoyed when visitors arrive unannounced?

17. How often do people in your native country take care of a sick relative rather than go to work?

18. What do you think of people choosing to take care of a sick relative rather than go to work?

19. How often do people in your native country consult their family before making an important decision?

20. What do you think of people consulting their family before making an important decision?

21. How often do people in your native country discuss job- or study-related problems with their parents?

22. What do you think of people in your native country discussing job- or study-related problems with their parents?

23. Do people in your native country often feel lonely when not with their brothers, sisters, or close relatives?

24. What do you think of people in your native country feeling lonely when not with their brothers, sisters, or close relatives?

25. Would someone in your native country feel insulted if his or her brother had been insulted?

26. What do you think of someone in your native country feeling insulted because his or her brother had been insulted?

13

COLINDEX
A Refinement of Three Collectivism Measures

DARIUS KWAN-SHING CHAN

Since the development of the INDCOL Scale by Hui (1988), numerous studies have attempted to measure the I/C construct at both the cultural level (e.g., Triandis et al., 1986; Triandis, McCusker, & Hui, 1990) and the individual level (e.g., Triandis, Leung, Villareal, & Clark, 1985; Yamaguchi, Chapter 11, this volume). Although many of these studies have used attitude items to measure the constructs (e.g., Hui, 1988; Hui & Triandis, 1986; Triandis et al., 1986; Triandis, Bontempo, Villareal, Asai, & Lucca, 1988), there is a need to devise different methods and to adopt multi-method approaches.

As Campbell and associates point out, assessing construct validity depends on the processes of testing for a convergence across different measures or manipulations of the same construct (which is known as convergent validation), and testing for a divergence between measures or manipulations of related but conceptually different constructs (which is known as discriminant validation) (see, e.g., Campbell & Fiske, 1959; Cook & Campbell, 1979). Thus, in order to examine either or both convergent and discriminant validity, researchers must employ more than one method in the validation process.

Since the work of Campbell and Fiske (1959), the importance of using multimethod approaches has been reiterated in the social science literature. For instance, Brinberg and McGrath (1985) argue that every research method is flawed, and that only through the use of multiple methods can researchers offset those flaws and thereby reduce the uncertainty associated with research findings based on a single method. D. W. Fiske (1986) notes that research findings obtained from single methods often fail to replicate (see, for example, Amir & Sharon, 1987), whereas findings established with multimethod approaches do much better. Campbell (1986) further suggests that a multimethod approach is essential in social science research because traditional positivism usually leads to dead ends. In addition, use of a single method usually leads to fragmentation in the social sciences. Consistent with the notion of using multimethod approaches in social science research, studies on I/C have started using different methods to measure the construct (e.g., Triandis, Chan, Bhawuk, Iwao, & Sinha, 1993; Triandis, McCusker, & Hui, 1990). Preliminary results suggest that many of these measures have satisfactory convergent validity.

With the increasing number of methods proposed in the collectivism literature, two methodological concerns have become important. First, in attempting to take a multimethod approach, and given limited resources in conducting cross-cultural research, researchers need a way to decide which specific methods are best or optimal for measuring collectivism. The second concern is, given results from a number of valid collectivism measures, how such results can be combined to obtain a reliable and valid summary-type score useful for testing theoretical predictions. For instance, how can we compare an allocentric person from an individualist culture with an idiocentric person from a collectivist culture? Should we equate them? Or should we just "crudely" treat them as individualist and collectivist, respectively? In a sense, it is a question of how precisely the existing methods can measure the construct. In this chapter I will argue that a summary score derived from several collectivism measures is desirable for making more refined and powerful comparisons at both the cultural and individual levels, given that the collectivism measures are reliable and valid.

This chapter reports on the results of a cross-cultural study that was designed to address this second concern. The study is part of a program of research on the effects of culture on concession-making behaviors in negotiations (see Chan, 1991). It will (a) test cultural differences in collectivism using three different collectivism measures; (b) examine the convergent validity of these collectivism measures; (c) propose a method of deriving a summary score, COLINDEX, from the three measures; and (d) demonstrate the criterion-related validity of COLINDEX.

METHOD

In the study described here, American subjects were considered, on the average, as individualistic, and Hong Kong Chinese were considered, on the average, as collectivistic, based on Hofstede's (1980) and other cross-cultural studies (e.g., Chinese Culture Connection, 1987; Hui, 1988; Leung, 1987, 1988a). In a sense, the test on cultural differences in the construct is confirmatory. Subjects were undergraduates attending the University of Illinois in the United States and the Chinese University of Hong Kong. A total of 120 male subjects, 60 from each culture, participated in the study.

MATERIALS

The three collectivism measures were first written in English, and then translated into Chinese by two bilingual Chinese.

Measure 1: Social content of the self. This is an adaptation of the Kuhn and McPartland (1954) method (see Triandis, McCusker, & Hui, 1990). Subjects were requested to complete 20 sentences that began with the words "I am . . ." as if they were talking to themselves. Each subject's responses were content analyzed by considering whether each response was linked to some social entity (e.g., a group or a demographic category) with which the subject might experience common fate. For example, "I am American" refers to a nation, and "I am Roman Catholic" refers to a religion, whereas "I am independent" or "I am intelligent" does not refer to any specific group. The percentage of each subject's responses that were linked to social entities was noted and called the %S score (i.e., the number of responses that were linked to social entities in proportion to the total number of responses each subject made). Previous research has found that the mean %S score of collectivists is consistently higher than that of individualists (Triandis, McCusker, & Hui, 1990).

Measure 2: Attitude items. Sixteen attitude items that were similar to Triandis's attitude items (see Triandis et al., 1986, 1988) were used as a second measure. In this task, subjects were asked to indicate, on a 7-point scale, if they agreed or disagreed with the attitude items. Half of these items could be classified as collectivistic, such as the items loading on the Family Integrity factor (e.g., "Aging parents should live at home with their children"), and half were individualistic, such as the items loading on the Self-Reliance factor (e.g., "I would rather struggle through a personal problem by myself, than discuss it with my friends").

Measure 3: Value items. Thirty-seven of Schwartz's (see Schwartz & Bilsky, 1987, 1990) 56 value items were used as a third measure. Subjects were asked to judge these value items on the extent to which they constituted "a guiding principle in my life" on a scale ranging from *not important* (0) to *of supreme importance* (7) (an option of *I am opposed to it* [–1] was available for those who considered it appropriate). Collectivist values include those items relating to Security, Conformity, and Tradition. Individualist values include those items relating to Self-Direction, Stimulation, and Hedonism.

RESULTS

Reliability of the Collectivism Measures

Measure 1. Four raters (psychology students), two from each culture, content analyzed subjects' responses to the 20 items that were written in the raters' first language. Interrater correlation for the %S score was .95 for the American sample and .96 for the Hong Kong sample.

Measure 2. Three items, two collectivistic and one individualistic, were deleted from subsequent analyses because of low reliability. Of the remaining 13 items, the 6 collectivist items were averaged to form a collectivist index (COLLAT) and the 7 individualist items were averaged to form an individualist index (INDAT) from this attitude measure (see the appendices to this chapter). Given that there is concern about the assumption of unidimensionality of collectivism (e.g., Kagitçibasi, 1987; Schwartz, 1990), these separate indices of individualism and collectivism allow us to examine the unidimensionality of the construct discussed below. Cronbach's alpha on COLLAT was .46 for the American sample and .41 for the Hong Kong sample. The alphas on INDAT were .51 and .53 for the two samples, respectively. These alphas were relatively low and suggest that these indices may be only moderately sensitive in measuring the construct. Possible explanations are presented in the discussion section below.

Measure 3. Again, separate indices were created. Six value items relating to Security, Conformity, and Tradition were averaged to form a collectivist index (COLLVA) and seven items relating to Self-Direction, Stimulation, and Hedonism were averaged to form an individualist index (INDVA) from this value measure. Cronbach's alpha on COLLVA was .84 for the American sample and .78 for the Hong Kong sample. The alphas on INDVA were .74 and .73 for the two samples, respectively.

Cultural Differences in the Collectivism Measures

As hypothesized above, American subjects were considered more individualistic and Hong Kong subjects more collectivistic. Indices derived from the three measures were tested across the two cultural groups.

Measure 1. The %S score was hypothesized to be lower for individualists than for collectivists. As expected, the mean scores were 15% for the American sample ($N = 58$) and 29% for the Hong Kong sample ($N = 56$). The difference was highly significant, $F(1, 112) = 15.76, p < .001$.

Measure 2. A separate one-way analysis of variance (ANOVA), using culture as the independent variable, was performed on each COLLAT and INDAT. A significant culture main effect was found for both dependent variables. First, Hong Kong subjects scored higher in COLLAT than did American subjects ($Ms = 5.08$ versus 4.53, $F[1, 110] = 15.26, p < .001$), showing that Hong Kong subjects were more collectivistic than American subjects. Second, American subjects scored higher in INDAT than did Hong Kong subjects ($Ms = 4.28$ versus 3.63, $F[1, 110] = 17.02, p < .001$), showing that American subjects were more individualistic than Hong Kong subjects.

Responses to attitude items are often contaminated by response sets (Hui & Triandis, 1989), especially in cross-cultural comparisons. To control for response sets, different methods have been suggested in the literature (e.g., Hui & Triandis, 1989; Leung & Bond, 1989). One possible way is to standardize each subject's responses individually within the scale. That is, the mean response of each subject is set to zero and the standard deviation is one. Even though there was no evidence of response sets in the present study, all the subjects' responses were standardized within the scale (i.e., across the 16 items) in order to check whether the above cultural differences were caused by response sets. The analysis was performed again on the standardized data. As expected, the culture main effect was significant for both dependent variables and the patterns were basically the same as those obtained from the raw data: Hong Kong subjects scored higher in COLLAT than did American subjects ($Ms = .369$ versus $-.01$, $F[1, 110] = 28.82, p < .001$), and American subjects were higher in INDAT than Hong Kong subjects ($Ms = -.15$ versus $-.40$, $F[1, 110] = 13.819$, $p < .001$).

Measure 3. Two separate ANOVAs, using culture as the independent variable, were performed on COLLVA and INDVA, respectively. A signifi-

Table 13.1   Correlation Among the Three Collectivism Measures

	%S	COLLAT	INDAT	COLLVA	INDVA
%S	1.00				
COLLAT	.28**	1.00			
INDAT	−.21*	−.79**	1.00		
COLLVA	.08	.21*	−.18*	1.00	
INDVA	−.29**	−.34**	.33**	−.56**	1.00

NOTE: Standardized data were used for calculating the correlations. Correlations obtained by using the raw data were found to be similar to those presented in this table.
*Significant at the .05 level (two-tailed); **significant at the .01 level (two-tailed).

cant culture main effect was found for INDVA. American subjects scored higher on INDVA than did Hong Kong subjects, (Ms = 4.92 versus 3.76, $F[1, 110]$ = 39.54, $p < .001$), showing that American subjects endorsed individualist values to a greater extent than did Hong Kong subjects. No culture main effect was found for COLLVA.

The analysis was performed again on the standardized data. Consistent with the above results, the culture main effect was found only for INDVA. American subjects were higher in INDVA than Hong Kong subjects (Ms = .011 versus −.17, $F[1, 110]$ = 10.30, $p < .005$).

Convergent Validity of the Collectivism Measures

Consistent with previous research, cultural differences in the three collectivism measures provided support for the hypothesis that American subjects were more individualistic and Hong Kong subjects were more collectivistic. In order to examine whether these three methods converge in terms of measuring the cultural construct, the five indices (%S, COL-LAT, INDAT, COLLVA, and INDVA) were correlated with one another. Specifically, the intercorrelations between the three collectivist indices (%S, COLLAT, and COLLVA) were expected to be positively correlated with one another and, similarly, the two individualist indices (INDAT and INDVA) were expected to be positively correlated.

Based on Hofstede's (1980) conception of a unidimensional construct of collectivism, the collectivist indices were expected to be negatively correlated with the individualist indices. However, as mentioned above, there is also concern about this assumption of unidimensionality of collectivism (e.g., Kagitçibasi, 1987; Schwartz, 1990). Table 13.1 presents the correlations that were obtained.

All the correlations were in the expected direction and were significant beyond the .05 level, except that between %S and COLLVA (r = .08). Specifically, correlations between the collectivist indices and those between the individualist indices were all positive, whereas those between the collectivist and individualist indices were all negative. Such a pattern of correlations provides support for a unidimensional construct of I/C.

Recall that the %S score was derived from an operant measure, whereas the other two methods were basically respondent measures (McClelland, 1980). The correlations, especially those between %S and the other indices, suggest that these different methods converge and are complementary to one another. Given the different natures of the methods, these correlations suggest that the three methods as a whole are satisfactory measures of collectivism and individualism.

Derivation of COLINDEX
From the Three Collectivism Measures

Three different scores were used to form a single, composite collectivism index (COLINDEX): (a) the %S score obtained from Method 1 of the collectivism measures described earlier, (b) the collectivism score (the mean of COLLAT and COLLVA), and (c) the individualism score (the mean of INDAT and INDVA). The distribution of each of the three scores was "trichotomized" and then the scores of 1, 2, and 3 were assigned to each third of the first and second distributions. That is, the more collectivistic the person, the higher the assigned score. The assignment of scores was reversed for the third distribution. That is, the more individualistic the person, the lower the assigned score. This reversal for the individualism score was based on the above finding that the individualist indices were consistently found to be negatively correlated with the collectivist indices.

COLINDEX was then obtained for each subject by summing the three assigned scores. It ranged from 3 (very individualistic) to 9 (very collectivistic). Note that this way of combining the various measures weighs each measure equally and deals with the differences in the scale value of the three different measures.

Criterion Validity of COLINDEX

To check the criterion validity of a measure, it is necessary to have certain "known" groups representing the construct under investigation.

Table 13.2 Distribution of the COLINDEX in the Two Samples (in percentages)

| | COLINDEX | | | | | | |
	3	4	5	6	7	8	9
American (N = 57)	8.8	28.1	21.1	24.6	8.8	7.0	1.8
Hong Kong (N = 56)	7.1	8.9	7.1	14.3	23.2	21.4	17.9

Satisfactory criterion validity of the measure is achieved if one can identify the membership of a respondent by knowing *only* his or her score on that measure. In this study, nationality was used as the criterion for classification. Previous studies have consistently shown that American respondents are among the highest in individualism scores and Hong Kong respondents are collectivistic (e.g., Chinese Culture Connection, 1987; Hofstede, 1980; Hui, 1988; Leung, 1987, 1988a).

Subjects were "reclassified" according to COLINDEX. Seven of them were deleted because of missing data on one or more of the collectivism measures. Table 13.2 presents the distribution of COLINDEX in each sample. Specifically, approximately 60% of American subjects were on the individualist side (scoring 3, 4, or 5) and only 18% of them were on the collectivist side (scoring 7, 8, or 9). An exact reversal was found for Hong Kong subjects: Approximately 23% of them scored 3, 4, or 5, whereas 63% scored 7, 8, or 9. If those scoring a 6 (the midpoint) in COLINDEX were deleted from the analyses, an even more salient reversal was obtained: 77% of American subjects were on the individualist side and 23% on the collectivist side, whereas 27% of Hong Kong subjects were on the individualist side and 73% on the collectivist side.

A discriminant function analysis that used COLINDEX as a single predictor and nationality as the criterion variable correctly classified 73% of the total sample (expected by chance is 50%). This classification result is better than any of those obtained by using only one collectivism measure. For instance, the discriminant analysis using the %S score as the predictor correctly classified 62% of the total sample. In addition, the discriminant analysis that used the %S score, COLSCORE, and INDSCORE as three different predictors correctly classified 75% of the total sample, which is very comparable to that obtained by using COLINDEX alone. This suggests that the derivation of COLINDEX from these three scores is satisfactory in summarizing the three scores without losing much power.

DISCUSSION

As expected, consistent cultural differences in the three collectivism measures were found in the study reported here. These differences replicate previous finding that American respondents are more individualistic and Hong Kong Chinese are more collectivistic. The detailed examination of the convergence of the various indices derived from the three measures provides promising support for their use as collectivism measures.

One point worth noting is the relatively low reliability coefficients (Cronbach's alphas) on the attitude measure. One possible explanation is that these attitude items tap the construct across very different aspects of life. For instance, they range from what one looks for in a job to where one prefers to live. Although this diversity of items can certainly increase the generality of the construct, the scale is less likely to be highly internally consistent because of the very different domains of life these items reflect (unless the construct under investigation is so basic that it is manifested in every aspect of life). In fact, Cronbach's alphas reported in studies using these types of attitude items in the collectivism literature are, in general, relatively low (see, for example, Hui, 1988; Leung & Iwawaki, 1988; Triandis et al., 1993), usually within the range of .50 to .70.

In a sense, this problem of generality versus internal consistency is a conflict of essentials. Measures that attempt to increase either criterion virtually guarantee a lower level of the other. For instance, one way to increase the internal consistency of the attitude scale is to measure a specific aspect of collectivism, such as the individual's preferences in a work setting, with several similar items. However, each such measure would refer to only one in-group or setting (e.g., family, work, religion, politics, education, entertainment). Only through the use of multiple measures can we offset these flaws.

Perhaps even more important is the utility of the summary score—COLINDEX. As mentioned earlier, it is always desirable to use multimethod approaches to measure collectivism. However, it is also desirable to have a single index so that subjects can be classified conveniently. The present study provides a method of combining various measures to create a single collectivism index. Compared with using any one of the three collectivism measures, results from the discriminant analyses show that COLINDEX is superior in terms of the percentage of the sample it classifies correctly. This provides empirical support for the use of multimethod approaches. In addition, the results of the discriminant analyses suggest that using COLINDEX alone is comparable, again in terms of its hit rate, with using all three measures together. This shows the utility of COLINDEX as a summary score of various measures.

As I mentioned in the opening of this chapter, the study reported here is part of a program of research on the effects of opponents' concession patterns, relationship between negotiators, and culture on concession-making behaviors in an integrative bargaining task (see Chan, 1991). In that research, based on the difference in the in-group/out-group distinction proposed by I/C theory, it was hypothesized that the difference in the level of concessions made when negotiating with a friend versus a stranger would be larger for collectivists than for individualists. In the study, we obtained the predicted results when we asked subjects from the United States and Hong Kong to negotiate with either friends they brought with them to the experiment or strangers. In addition to the analyses using nationality as the cultural variable, subjects were "reclassified" as individualist or collectivist according to COLINDEX. The analysis was again performed by using this alternative cultural variable, and the same pattern of cultural differences was found. These results provide additional support for the use of a summary score to perform more powerful tests of the theory.

APPENDIX A

Collectivist Attitude Items

1. What I look for in a job is a friendly group of coworkers.
2. Children should live at home with their parents until they get married.
3. Aging parents should live at home with their children.
4. When faced with a difficult personal problem, one should consult widely one's friends and relatives.
5. I would help within my means if a relative told me that he/she is in financial difficulties.
6. I like to live close to my good friends.

Individualist Attitude Items

1. I tend to do my own things, and most people in my family do the same.
2. When faced with a difficult personal problem, it is better to decide what to do yourself, rather than follow the advice of others.
3. The most important thing in my life is to make myself happy.
4. I like to live in cities, where there is anonymity.
5. I would rather struggle through a personal problem by myself, than discuss it with my friends.

6. What happens to me is my own doing.
7. Aging parents should have their own household.

APPENDIX B

Collectivist Value Items

1. Honor of parents and elders (showing respect)
2. Social order (stability of society)
3. National security (protection of my own nation from enemies)
4. Self-discipline (self-restraint, resistance to temptation)
5. Politeness (courtesy, good manners)
6. Obedience (fulfilling duties, meeting obligations)

Individualist Value Items

1. Pleasure (gratification of desires)
2. Creativity (uniqueness, imagination)
3. A varied life (filled with challenge, novelty, and change)
4. Being daring (seeking adventure, risk)
5. Freedom (freedom of action and thought)
6. Independence (self-reliance, choice of own goals and interests)
7. An exciting life (stimulating experiences)

PART III

Social and Applied Issues

14

EFFECTS OF FAMILY, REGION, AND SCHOOL NETWORK TIES ON INTERPERSONAL INTENTIONS AND THE ANALYSIS OF NETWORK ACTIVITIES IN KOREA

GYUSEOG HAN
SUG-MAN CHOE

The boundary of the in-group varies from culture to culture. In collectivist societies, in-groups are defined through tradition, whereas in individualist societies, people create their own in-groups (Hsu, 1971). Perhaps the most prevalent "we" networks involve family, region, and school. These networks are traditional and informal in that their primary purpose is to promote communal relationships among members. When people are connected through these networks, they treat others as members of "we." Once people are regarded as being within the boundary of "we," they incur instant closeness, assume social interdependence, and consequently give more favor to others in the group. To a great extent, network ties serve as an important building block of the social relationship. The most prevalent networks that permit and even encourage particularistic social influence are those of family, region, and school.

People related through family networks share common bloodlines. The narrowest boundary of the family network is the nuclear family; this boundary can be broadened to encompass the extended family, more distant relatives, the clan, and the ethnic group. As the boundary broadens, the

AUTHORS' NOTE: We would like to express sincere gratitude to the anonymous reviewers and to Dr. Uichol Kim for their suggestions and comments.

intensity of the interaction and the feeling of "we-ness" diminishes. Korean people regard those who share the same great-great-grandfather in the father's line or the same grandfather in the mother's line as their relatives (Hong, 1989). These relatives know each other well and many maintain close personal ties because of frequent meetings and traditional values encouraging family ties. At times, the "family network" refers to this narrow circle. Nevertheless, in Korea, the most common unit of social network based on bloodline is the clan, whose members identify with an ancestor who lived hundreds or sometimes more than a thousand years ago. The membership of a clan can range from hundreds to hundreds of thousands. Usually, a clan of such large scale encompasses people nationwide. Nevertheless, awareness of belonging to the same clan seems enough to change interactional patterns.

The regional network is composed of people from the same "hometown." In Korea, 47% of people tend to identify their township (*ree* or *myun*) as their hometown; 25% regard their county in this way, and another 25% regard their province as their hometown (Hong, 1989). Regional network organizations are formed and operated in major cities in almost all provinces. Membership is provided unconditionally to those who are from the same hometown.

School networks are composed of alumni. The importance of school networks in Korea was first noted in studies on the social origins of high-ranking officials of the Yi dynasty (Lee, 1988). During this dynasty, high officials preferred appointing to government positions those who studied under the same tutor. This tradition, to a certain degree, continues to the present.

Like it or not, almost everyone in Korea belongs to several networks, though the levels of participation vary considerably among individuals. Many merely attend meetings and pay annual dues. Few even contribute to the assets of the network organizations. Such network activity is the normal pattern of life in Korean culture. Networks serve two major functions. First, network connections smooth social interaction. It would be safe to assume that such facilitation occurs in the early phase of interaction. Second, network activities serve to enlarge individual social relationships by supplying common ties to those similar social backgrounds. In this sense, network activity serves personal interest. Traditionally, network activity has been viewed as a manifestation of the collectivist culture of the Korean people, but network activity may also arise from individualist concerns.

The investigation reported in this chapter was conceived to answer the following questions. First, how is interactional intention influenced by the awareness of belonging to the same network as another? Our present concern lies in whether network sharing makes any difference to interactional intentions. To be more specific, we asked, *to what extent does sharing of networks make behavioral intentions different?* and *does a multiple sharing of networks have an additive effect?* Another question we asked is, *what are people's attitudes toward network activities?* Comparison of people's attitudes and activities would yield clues about their real motives for network activities. Although we began with a few suppositions, as stated above, we carried out the analyses in an exploratory manner, posing no a priori hypotheses to test.

METHOD

Respondents

A total of 263 men and 238 women of adult age were interviewed. All were residents of Kwangju, and the South Cholla region of Korea.[1] Subjects were selected through a stratified cluster ratio sampling procedure to represent the adult population of the area. The variables used for stratification were sex and residence (rural and city) and the cluster unit was the *dong* or *myun* (the smallest administrative block of local government). In each cluster, 10 to 12 people were randomly sampled. The purpose of the sampling met with reasonable success with respect to age, education, and monthly income.

Procedures

The present study was done as part of a field survey conducted in March 1989. Trained student interviewers visited respondents' homes to administer the questionnaire. Respondents worked through the questionnaire in a self-paced manner, and interviewers helped them to complete it. The questionnaire took about 30-40 minutes to complete.

The questionnaire was designed to investigate network-prone attitudes and network activities. We measured the attitudes with five statements:

1. People should help each other if they belong to the same network.
2. In formal matters one should serve all people equally regardless of network relationship. (reverse scored)
3. In hiring somebody, networks should play a role.
4. We should actively participate in network organizations.
5. We should not blame the elderly for their adamant insistence in discussion.

Respondents indicated their levels of agreement/disagreement on 4-point Likert-type scales.

Network activities were measured by three questions:

1. How many times did you attend the network meeting during the past five years?
2. What amount did you donate to network organizations?
3. How many *kyes* are you a member of?

A *kye* is an informal organization that gives mutual financial assistance among villagers in traditional Korea. Nowadays, *kyes* are organized not only among villagers but also among close friends for the purpose of mutual help. Membership in a *kye* signifies a deep involvement in relationships with other *kye* members. The above three network activity questions were repeated for each of the three networks.

Toward the end of the questionnaire, a page was attached in which a vignette asked the respondent to assume the role of a supervisor working for a midsize company. The vignette was constructed to represent a typical situation many people experience in real life. Some respondents saw the following vignette:

> Working in a well-established midsize company, I happened to meet a director of another section in a recent committee meeting. I got the impression that he was very able and competent. Since I kept silent at that meeting, I am not sure whether the director even remembers me. During lunch break yesterday, I heard while chatting with colleagues that the director is from *the same town* in which I was raised.

Employing a three-way factorial between-subjects design, we varied the italicized phrase by manipulating network relevance to make up eight different experimental conditions. The three independent variables were whether the director and "I" are family network-related or not, hometown-related or not, and fellow alumni or not. These items were completely crossed with each other, yielding eight cells.

Although it is of interest to compare the effects of different networks and various combinations individually, our primary interest was to determine whether network relationships make any difference and whether the difference would be predictable from the multiplicity of the relationships. For this reason, the number of respondents assigned to each experimental condition was adjusted to balance the cell size. Other than that, the eight different types of vignettes were randomly distributed.

The dependent variable for this experiment was the intention of acting out various types of behavior toward the director. The behavior list included 12 different socially distant acts (see Na, 1988):

1. try to work in the same section
2. introduce myself
3. provide personal reference if asked
4. join his social club
5. consult him on a private matter
6. try to help him
7. defend him from criticism
8. help him to get a promotion
9. ask a favor on a private matter
10. associate with him privately
11. vote for him in an election
12. avoid meeting him

The respondents rated their intentions on a 5-point scale for each act (from *definitely yes* to *definitely no*).

RESULTS

Demographic Characteristics

A total of 38 cases were excluded from the analysis because of incomplete answers on the items of current interest. This deletion occurred without apparent bias across experimental conditions. Therefore, 467 cases (247 men and 220 women) were included for the analysis of the experiment. The youngest respondent's age was 20 and the mean age was 39.7 ($SD = 12.1$ years). The average amount of formal education was 9.4 years ($SD = 4.1$), and the average monthly income was 530,000 won (about \$760; $SD = 385,000$ won). About 60% (276 cases) were city residents and 40% (191 cases) were rural residents.

Interpersonal Intentions

To find a meaningful way to combine the 12 items of interpersonal intentions, we ran a principal factor analysis. Because only one factor showed up (accounting for 98% of the common variance total), we simply

Table 14.1   Intention as a Function of Network Multiplicity: Means and Standard Deviations

	None		Single		Double		Triple	
	M	*SD*	*M*	*SD*	*M*	*SD*	*M*	*SD*
Interpersonal intentions	2.60	.68	2.46	.60	2.38	.60	2.30	.55
Number of respondents	118		121		118		110	

NOTE: Scale value 1 is *definitely yes* and value 5 is *definitely no.* Therefore, a smaller number means more favorable intentions toward the target person than does a larger number.

made an aggregate score of the 11 items. The twelfth item was dropped from the analysis because it had no relationship to the general factor. Cronbach's alpha for this aggregate scale score was .82.

Taking this score as a dependent variable, we carried out a $2 \times 2 \times 2$ ANOVA.[2] Only the main effect of regional network appeared, $F(1, 308) = 8.84, p < .01$. This main effect means that people show less distant social acts toward hometown-related people ($M = 2.53$, $SD = .65$) than toward hometown-unrelated people ($M = 2.32$, $SD = .56$). No interaction effects were significant.

Because our primary interest was the effects of network multiplicity, we collapsed the eight experimental conditions into four. These four are the no-network-related cell, the single-network-related cell, the double-network-related cell, and the triple-network-related cell. To compare mean differences in behavioral intentions among the four conditions, we performed an ANOVA for the aggregate variable. The main effect of network multiplicity was significant, $F(3, 463) = 5.10, p < .01$. The means are provided in Table 14.1.

The Student-Newman-Keuls test of multiple range on the main effect revealed that the differences are mostly between the no-network and the double- or triple-network conditions, meaning people show a greater tendency toward such behavior if the other has double- or triple-network relations to them than if the other is unrelated. As can be seen in Table 14.1, however, intentions of acting favorably show a monotonic increase (decrease in numbers) as the network multiplicity increases. Therefore, one could conclude that network relationships make interactions flow more smoothly in Korean culture. The evidence is strong enough to conclude also that the more networks both interactants share, the more smoothly the interaction proceeds.

To analyze the effects of the respondents' characteristics on the aggregate score, we took the demographic variables (sex, age, education, residence, and income) and divided all respondents into subgroups. Crossing each of these new grouping variables with the network multiplicity variable, we carried out five two-way ANOVAs. We found no interaction effects in any analysis. Some main effects of the grouping variables appeared. They indicate that men rather than women ($F[1, 459] = 3.31$, $p < .07$),[3] rural residents more than city residents ($F[1, 466] = 12.86$, $p < .001$), the older group rather than the young adult group ($F[3, 451] = 14.26$, $p < .001$), the less educated rather than the highly educated ($F[3, 448] = 2.93$, $p < .05$), and the low-income earners rather than the high-income earners ($F[2, 448] = 3.07$, $p < .07$) were more likely to show friendly actions toward the target person.

Network-Prone Attitude

We used five statements to measure people's attitudes toward the networks. Because of the moderately positive correlations among the attitude measures, we simply added up the scores (Cronbach's alpha for this 5-item attitude scale is .47). A correlational analysis showed that this attitude is positively correlated with age ($r = .35$, $p < .001$), but negatively with education ($r = -.35$, $p < .001$) and with income ($r = -.22$, $p < .001$). A correlation between this attitude and the aggregate score of behavioral intentions showed that those scoring high on the attitude scale tend to show warm intentions toward the other ($r = -.32$, $p < .001$). Rural residents were shown to be higher on this attitude scale than were urban residents, $F(1, 459) = 12.9$, $p < .001$. In summary, stronger network-prone attitudes were observed for the older generation, the less educated, the poor, and rural residents. A regression analysis measuring the relative importance of the effects of these variables pointed out that age is the strongest variable; education, residence, and income follow, in that order.

Network Activities

Network activities were measured by frequency of attendance, contributions (including fees), and the number of memberships in *kyes*. Because of great variation of ranges between the variables, we dichotomized each response into 0 or 1. Table 14.2 shows the percentages of respondents who were coded as 1 according to this scheme. As can be seen in the table, family network appears as the most prominent network, followed by

Table 14.2 Percentages of People Participating in Each Network Form

		Type of Network	
Activities	Family	School	Region
Join in the members' kye	45.7	41.9	37.2
Attended meeting once or more	37.7	36.2	20.0
Paid fees or contributions	32.0	32.2	15.3

Table 14.3 Various Effects on Network-Prone Attitude and Network Activity

	Attitude		Activity	
Variable	Standardized Beta	Unique Variance	Standardized Beta	Unique Variance
Age	.21***	.04***	.10*	.006
Education	−.17***	.12***	.23***	.04***
Urban/rural	.11**	.01**	—	—
Income	−.08	.006	.07	.004
Sex	—	—	−.34***	.17***
R^2 total		.18		.22

NOTE: The variables of urban/rural and sex were treated as dummies: 0 for urban, 1 for rural; 0 for male, 1 for female.
*$p < .05$; **$p < .01$; ***$p < .001$.

school and then region. The most typical network activities involve *kyes*. A large-scale network (e.g., family or school) usually has a number of informal *kyes* that individual members with close relationships are encouraged to join. A typical *kye* has 50 or fewer members. These data indicate that Koreans tend to maintain smaller circles inside the network.

Other analysis showed that 82.8% of the respondents are engaged in network activities (only 17.2% reported no activities at all), 31.2% of respondents participate in one kind of network, another 31.3% in two kinds, and 20.3% in all three kinds. It also showed that 59.6% of all respondents are engaged in family networks, 50.9% in school networks, and 44.2% in regional networks.

To analyze individual activity level, we added up the three dichotomized values for each network and finally totaled them to use as the synthetic variable of overall activities. Individual values, therefore, could range from 0 to 9, 0 indicating no activities at all and 9 indicating very high activities. The summated network activity score ranged from 0 to 9, with an average of 2.97. A correlational analysis revealed that this activity level is positively correlated with education ($r = .29$, $p < .001$) but not with the network-prone attitude. We carried out a regression analysis to see the effects of demographic variables on this activity level. This analysis showed that men and the more educated are most likely to participate actively in network organizations (see Table 14.3). This group has a broader range of social activities than do their counterparts. Though age was the most important factor determining the network-prone attitude, age affected network behavior only slightly.

Attitude/Behavior Discrepancy

The above analysis reveals an interesting phenomenon, that network activity is not at all predictable from network-prone attitude. How can this anomaly be explained? The discrepancy might be a result of different levels of specificity (i.e., the attitude items were not about specific acts of participation, whereas the activities items were stated more specifically). However, a more plausible explanation, based on the theory of reasoned action (Fishbein & Ajzen, 1975), would attribute the discrepancy to the strong norm of traditionalism operating in the society. Many respondents listed social pressures from their surroundings as reasons for participating in network organizations. Some 40% of the respondents chose this option to describe their reasons for joining family networks; 25% chose it to explain their joining regional networks, and 17% mentioned it regarding school networks. Therefore, social pressure and informal norms encourage people to engage in network activities.

Another supplementary explanation is that network activities may serve people's personal interests. Goal-oriented behavior can occur without the support of attitudes or subjective norms. To see whether the organizations are used as ways to achieve individual goals, we asked respondents to rate on a 3-point scale how much benefit they receive from participating in each network organization. We summed the responses for the three networks. Examining the relationships among the strength of the attitude, the level of the activities, and the amount of benefit, we discovered that the attitude-benefit correlation ($r = .04$, $p > .40$) and the attitude-behavior correlation ($r = -.08$, $p > .05$) were insignificant, and that only the behavior-benefit correlation was statistically significant ($r = .22$, $p < .001$). This means that network activity increases with the benefits that the networks generate. It can be concluded that people engage in network activities not because of the values or beliefs they hold, but because of their personal interests and the social pressures they feel.

DISCUSSION

The research presented in this chapter is concerned with interactional intentions as influenced by network multiplicity. The field experiment shows that network relationships tend to facilitate smooth social interactions. The data also indicate additive effects of network multiplicity: the more networks people share, the more smoothly the interaction flows. This result supports Triandis (1988b) theory that in a collectivist society interactions are significantly affected when the other is an in-group member. This result can also be accounted for by social identity theory (Tajfel, 1982), which would argue that in-group/out-group distinction is responsible for interactional intentions. At present, clear demarcation is not possible.

Interestingly, however, the type of network made little difference in this study. The analysis of a three-way factorial treatment yielded only the finding that sharing a regional network changed or affected interactions. This should not be taken as evidence of the importance of regional network over family and school networks. Other data certainly indicate that the most important network is the family network (see Table 14.2). Therefore, the main effect of the regional network seems to result from other reasons. Considering the network organizations operating in the area of the present survey, it is more likely that people feel closer to each other when connected through a regional network than through either a family or a school network. That is, the latter two types of networks vary a great deal in size and cohesiveness. For example, sharing the same family name may mean little to those who belong to clans with a thousand members. Therefore, it is more proper to conclude, from the analysis of network multiplicity, that Korean people treat others more warmly when they are related by network, regardless of network type.

The analysis of network-prone attitude shows that in general people with traditional values are friendlier to others. This has close relevance to Hui's (1988) finding that in Chinese culture, where interpersonal harmony is a dominating value, the need for social approval is positively related to collectivist attitudes. The same seems to hold in Korean culture; the present study shows that people with strong network-prone attitudes display friendly intentions regardless of who the other is. Theoretically, it would be expected that network-based differential behaviors would be more typical of people with highly collectivist attitudes (Triandis, 1988b). The present data, however, fail to show such pattern. This result poses a problem because collectivists are not to be equated with warm interactionists.

Collectivists are concerned with interpersonal harmony only in in-group interactions. A relevant theoretical concept is interpersonal orientation (IO), theorized by Rubin and Brown (1975) and developed by Swap and Rubin (1983). High IO people tend to focus on the relationship itself, whereas low IO people focus on their gain. It was found that women and high IO people are more concerned with interpersonal harmony than with performance (Swap & Rubin, 1983; see also Leung & Bond, 1984). Interpersonal harmony seeking is widely observed in individualist cultures as well as in collectivist cultures. In fact, Hofstede (1980) reports a positive relationship between individualism and affiliation need (see also Triandis et al., 1988).

To clarify this anomaly, it is helpful to distinguish affiliation need from the need for intimacy (McAdams, 1982). Separating these two needs, Wheeler, Reis, and Bond (1989) hypothesized that collectivists are relatively high in intimacy need and individualists are high in affiliation need. They confirmed this hypothesis by finding that collectivists are more self-disclosing than individualists. The network-prone attitude scale of the present study apparently failed to tap the intimacy need. The scale construction of I/C would benefit by incorporating this distinction.

Although a network-prone attitude is stronger in the "traditional" segments of the population (the old, the less educated, and low-income earners), network activities are more prevalent in the "modern" segments of the population (the more educated and the men). In premodern societies, networks provided protection and social identity to their members in exchange for loyalty. There was a strong "we" feeling among the members. Individuals were inseparable from and emotionally dependent on their groups (Hofstede, 1980, p. 221). Currently, however, many traditional values are in conflict with new values. In general, people in modern societies are educated to observe the new norms of modernity (i.e., democracy and rationality). Given that formal education facilitates individual modernity (Inkeles & Smith, 1974; Segall, Dasen, Berry, & Poortinga, 1990), it is no wonder that these people do not approve of network-prone values and have become more idiocentric (Triandis, Leung, Villareal, & Clark, 1985). Consequently, the operation of traditional norms is restricted to the informal domains of social life.

There is, however, no clear line between formality and informality in social life. Old customs do not disappear if they still serve useful functions. This explains why network-based discrimination remains prevalent as an interpersonal phenomenon in spite of public denouncements. Although the discrimination served both group and individual interests in the premodern era, the present study indicates that discrimination arises today largely from individual concerns and serves mainly individual interests. This individualist gain, however, may further serve the interests of the network group in aggregate. In this regard, network-based discrimination has features of both individualism and collectivism.

As Kagitçibasi argues in Chapter 4 of this volume, attitudinal changes may serve an adaptive function for modern segments of the population. But behavioral changes are not necessary, because attitude and behavior do not have identical adaptive values. People may have become more individualistic in attitude. These idiocentric people in collectivist cultures feel ambivalent about traditional norms. Nevertheless, most people in such cultures show behavior that complies with the norms. Many theorists argue that collectivism is more typical in the traditional sector and individualism more typical in the modern sector (e.g., Triandis, 1988b; see also, in this volume, Kagitçibasi, Chapter 4; Berry, Chapter 6). If I/C refers to a mind-set and attitudes, the present research provides supportive data to those theorists. It reveals, however, severe limitations in using I/C as an analytic scheme for complex social activities. As Triandis (1980b) conceptualizes, behavior is a function of social factors (norms, roles, and interpersonal agreements), attitudes toward the behavior, and perceived consequences of the behavior. The study of complex social behavior may arrive at misleading conclusions unless those factors are given due consideration.

NOTES

1. The city of Kwangju is a metropolitan area located in the center of the province of South Cholla, which covers the southwestern part of the Korean peninsula. The economy of the region is based primarily on agriculture and fisheries.
2. For each condition approximately 40 cases were randomly selected; thus 316 cases were used for this analysis.
3. Degrees of freedom for the error term were not the same for different missing cases from analysis to analysis.

15

INDIVIDUALIST AND COLLECTIVIST ORIENTATIONS ACROSS GENERATIONS

RAMESH C. MISHRA

Psychological studies have presented overwhelming evidence of behavioral differences between people from collectivist contexts and those from individualist contexts. Triandis (1988a) indicates that changes in individualist and collectivist orientations may take place with migration, religious changes, and changes in conditions of affluence and education. Generational differences have not been implicated in these analyses. Although modernization theory claims that industrialization and economic development necessitate individuals' progress toward individualism, that claim has been questioned (see, e.g., Kagitçibasi, Chapter 4, this volume).

Continuing collectivist culture and familial values in highly developed countries such as Japan (Iwawaki, 1986) has been presented as evidence against the assumptions of modernization theory. However, looking at the general trend of urbanization and nucleation of families and the weakening of traditional institutions of socialization in India over the past two decades (D. Sinha, 1988b), it is likely that the younger generation exhibits fewer collectivist orientations and values than the older generation.

The purpose of the study presented in this chapter was to examine, through an analysis of outlooks and values, the individualist and collectivist orientations of younger and older generations of Indian people of different residential and educational backgrounds toward certain aspects of their lives. In light of some of the previous discussions and empirical findings in this area, it was hypothesized that (a) people in general would exhibit both individualist and collectivist orientations and values at the same time, (b) people of the younger generation would have fewer collectivist

orientations and values than would the older generation, and (c) higher
levels of education and urban residence would reduce collectivist orientations and enhance individualist orientations.

METHOD

Subjects were 200 males (fathers and sons) sampled from the Varanasi
district of eastern Uttar Pradesh in India. The Varanasi region is predominantly agricultural, but the city is considered to be the most ancient city
of India, and people belonging to this region take pride in the fact.
Consequently, the forces of current sociocultural changes have not been
able to make their way very far into the traditional lifestyle of the people
in the region.

The subjects sampled belonged to two age groups (young and old), each
comprising 100 subjects. For both age levels, an equal number of highly
or better educated and less educated subjects of urban and rural residential
background were selected. The total sample was distributed in a 2 (age) × 2
(residence) × 2 (education) factorial design, with 25 subjects in each group.

Certain criteria were used for selecting the subjects. Individuals between 18 and 25 years of age were treated as young; those above 45 years
were regarded as old. Sons and their fathers represented these groups. On
the average, there was a difference of 27.6 years between the two age
groups. Differences observed in people's perceptions and reactions to various
social events in a small survey of the population under study formed the
basis of constituting the two generations in terms of these chronological
ages. Rural people were those who had permanent residence in villages
approximately 30-40 kilometers from the main city. Urban subjects were
those who lived continuously in the city for a period of at least five
years. Graduates of universities and colleges were regarded as better
educated; those who had schooling up to higher secondary level or below
formed the less educated group. All the subjects belonged to the upper
caste Hindu group and were almost homogeneous with regard to other
sociocultural variables. A full description of sample characteristics is
given in Table 15.1.

Instruments

Drawing upon ideas developed by Triandis (1988a), a new measure
of I/C was developed. Based on a pilot study, six decision areas and six
individuals/groups were identified as being considered important by the

Table 15.1 Sample Characteristics

	Young				Old			
	Rural		Urban		Rural		Urban	
	LE (N = 25)	HE (N = 25)	LE (N = 25)	HE (N = 25)	LE (N = 25)	HE (N = 25)	LE (N = 25)	HE (N = 25)
Mean age	20.7	23.3	22.7	22.4	48.5	52.8	50.2	48.0
Mean years of schooling	7.6	14.6	8.7	15.8	6.8	14.2	7.5	14.8
Mean years of city residence	0	0	8.2	11.4	0	0	10.9	14.5
Mean years of village residence	20.7	23.3	14.5	11.0	48.5	52.8	39.3	33.5
Married	22	24	25	20	25	25	25	25
Unmarried	03	01	0	5	0	0	0	0
Joint family	18	22	15	16	19	21	13	18
Nuclear family	7	3	10	9	6	4	12	7
Service	6	9	9	4	7	17	9	14
Self-employment	5	4	10	12	3	7	16	11
Agriculture	14	12	0	0	15	1	0	0

NOTE: HE = highly educated; LE = less educated.

people in the region. The decision areas represented were marriage, job, children's education, medical treatment, selling of property, and buying of household goods. The in-groups included wife, children, parents, friends, relatives, and neighbors. The subjects were asked to consider all of the decision areas in turn and to indicate the individuals/groups they considered important for decisions in those areas. They were also asked to indicate whether they considered themselves of any importance for decisions in those areas. The presence or absence of such linkages was marked. The number of linkages denoted the extent to which an individual was immersed in the pool of his in-group, and this served as the measure of collectivism. The number of absences of linkages indicated the extent to which an individual was free of the influences of in-groups (a measure of individualism). Score range on this measure was 0 to 36.

A list of a number of values discussed by Rokeach (1973) and Bond (1988) was given to a group of experts, who were asked to indicate whether each of the values exhibited the "concern of an individual" or the "concern of a group." Based on these judgments, a set of 10 individualist and 10 collectivist values was created. These values are presented in Table 15.2. The subjects were asked to indicate the importance of each of these values on a 5-point scale ranging from *very much important* to *not at all important*. A subject could obtain a score between 1 and 5 on each value. A follow-up study using these scales on a selected sample ($N = 60$) from the earlier participants revealed that the value judgments were fairly stable ($r = .93$ and $.88$ for the collectivist and individualist values, respectively) over a period of about 25 weeks.

Both the measures (of I/C and of values) were prepared and administered in the subjects' own language (i.e., Hindu). The subjects' willingness to participate in the study had been fully ensured well before they were approached with the tools described.

RESULTS

Mean scores on this measure (Table 15.2) indicate that all the groups were placed between Q^1 and Q^3 points on the scale. If these are taken as cut points for individualism and collectivism, respectively, then the findings indicate a moderate degree of collectivist orientation among the people in the sample in general, although there are differences in the levels of these orientations according to the age, residence, and education.

A three-way ANOVA (Table 15.3) revealed the main effects of age, education, and residence to be significant ($F = 35.10$, 9.61, and 72.81,

Table 15.2 Mean Scores on the Individualism/Collectivism Measure

	Young		Old	
	Highly Educated	*Less Educated*	*Highly Educated*	*Less Educated*
Rural				
Mean	19.56	21.72	21.52	23.20
SD	4.36	3.35	3.67	3.37
Urban				
Mean	14.08	20.80	18.16	26.20
SD	3.24	4.33	4.36	2.86

respectively; $p < .01$), suggesting variations in the degrees of individualism and collectivism among the subjects with regard to these factors; however, the age × residence interaction revealed greater generational difference in urban than in rural settings ($F = 7.67, p < .01$) and rural/urban difference was more evident in the young people in the sample than in the old.

The residence × education interaction ($F = 25.08, p < .01$) revealed a more enhanced effect of education for urban than for rural subjects. Thus rural/urban difference was enhanced with higher education. Generational differences between better and less educated subjects were more or less of the same order. The overall conclusion seems to be that collectivist orientation does not rule out the presence of individualism. Whereas urbanization tended to reduce the level of collectivism among the members of the young generation, higher education tended to reduce it among people of urban residence. Such variable relationships of I/C with age, education, and residential characteristics of subjects indicate that the orientations are not stable across all sections of Indian society.

In order to examine the linkages of individualist and collectivist orientations with in-groups and decision areas, I reanalyzed subjects' responses (Table 15.4). A 7 (in-groups) × 6 (decision areas) ANOVA on pooled data revealed that there was a significant interaction between these variables ($F = 22.26, p < .01$), although the main effects were also significant (in-group, $F = 382.42, p < .01$; decision area, $F = 77.53, p < .01$). The effects of age, education, or residence were not examined here (although such effects are quite likely to be in evidence in these situations). However, the general picture that emerged was quite complex, and this necessitated the computation of several one-way ANOVAs according to in-groups and decision areas. These analyses yielded highly significant F ratios for each decision area and for each in-group.

Table 15.3 ANOVA Results on Different Measures: F Ratios

Measures		Individualism/Collectivism		Individualist Values		Collectivist Values	
Source of Variance	df	MS	F	MS	F	MS	F
Age	1	499.28	33.06**	0.00	0.00	477.40	40.43**
Residence	1	154.88	10.26**	98.00	8.49**	616.00	52.17**
Education	1	1142.42	75.65**	1800.00	155.97**	852.84	72.22**
Age × residence	1	103.68	6.87**	1393.92	120.79**	954.84	80.86**
Age × education	1	5.78	0.38	786.32	66.58**	3.64	0.31
Residence × education	1	408.98	27.08**	98.00	8.49**	59.40	5.03*
Age × residence × education	1	16.82	1.11	288.00	24.96**	43.24	3.66
Error: Within	192	15.10		11.54		11.81	

*p < .05; **p < .01.

Table 15.4 Individualism/Collectivism: Mean Scores of In-Group Salience in Various Decision Areas

Decision Areas	Self	Wife	In-Groups Children	Parents	Friends	Relatives	Neighbors	Overall
Marriage								
Mean	.91	.90	.68	.86	.47	.31	.33	.64
SD	.20	.28	.18	.26	.20	.09	.10	.31
Job								
Mean	.94	.73	.48	.80	.53	.28	.11	.56
SD	.16	.19	.18	.23	.20	.13	.04	.31
Children's education								
Mean	.90	.88	1.01	.54	.43	.23	.15	.59
SD	.20	.26	.31	.22	.17	.12	.12	.38
Medical treatment								
mean	.88	.86	.87	.73	.69	.58	.36	.71
SD	.18	.24	.26	.24	.18	.16	.20	.27
Selling property								
Mean	.77	.74	.94	.81	.86	.57	.39	.73
SD	.27	.22	.29	.27	.26	.16	.21	.29
Buying households								
Mean	.51	.91	.39	.38	.27	.36	.13	.42
SD	.19	.27	.17	.18	.12	.14	.08	.10
Overall								
Mean	.82	.84	.73	.69	.54	.39	.25	
SD	.24	.24	.11	.28	.27	.19	.17	

A posteriori comparisons on Duncan's test revealed that except for the issues of marriage (on which difference between self and wife was not significant) and medical treatment (on which difference between wife and children was not significant), the mean scores of various in-groups differed significantly for all decision areas. Generally, the analysis indicated that friends, relatives, and neighbors were not as important in decisions as were wife, children, and parents, although the salience of these also differed significantly, particularly in the context of decision areas.

More or less similar results were found with Duncan's test for differences pertaining to decision areas. The salience of children, parents, friends, relatives, and neighbors differed significantly across all decision areas. On the other hand, the salience of self did not differ between the decision areas of marriage and medical treatment. Wife's salience did not differ between the decision areas of job and selling of property or between marriage and buying household goods. Parents' salience did not differ between job and selling of property. Besides these few nonsignificant differences among decision areas, the rest of the comparisons were significant. On the whole, it was evident that selling of property occupied the highest place in the hierarchy of decision areas in which the salience of in-groups was generally recognized. Medical treatment appeared next to that, and marriage was the third decision area in which in-groups were reported to be important.

With regard to in-group differences, it was also evident that wife, although an important person in overall decisions, was considered more important for the decision areas of buying household goods, marriage, and children's education. Children were considered more important in decisions regarding their education, the selling of property, and medical treatment. Parents were more important in decisions regarding marriage, selling of property, and job. Friends were more important in decisions regarding selling of property, medical treatment, and job, although relatives and neighbors were given most salient places in relation to the selling of property and medical treatment. Especially noteworthy is the parallel between the salience of wife and self in different decision areas.

Value Measures

The initial analysis on these measures was based on the pooled scores of samples of the 10 collectivist and 10 individualist values, respectively. The mean score for individualist values (32.20) was found to be significantly higher than that obtained for collectivist values (30.84) (F [1, 398] = 5.58, $p < .05$). This indicated that subjects in general shared individualist values somewhat more strongly than they shared collectivist values.

Samplewise comparisons of individualist and collectivist values revealed that young (F [1, 198] = 21.88, $p < .01$), urban (F [1, 198] = 11.19, $p < .01$), and highly educated (F [1, 198] = 108.39, $p < .01$) samples had significantly greater individualist than collectivist dispositions; the less educated sample showed greater collectivist than individualist disposition (F [1, 198] = 28.11, $p < .01$). The strength of these values did not differ significantly in the samples of rural residence and old generation.

Differences in the strengths of collectivist and individualist values in relation to the factors of age, education, and residence were also analyzed separately. The mean scores of different groups are given in Table 15.6. On the individualist values there was a complex interaction among variables (see Table 15.3, middle column). The multiple interaction effect was significant. Age × education, age × residence, and education × residence effects were also significant. Among the main effects, only education and residence were significant. Thus, although age was not a significant variable in terms of its main effect, it was a major factor influencing the value of orientations of highly educated people in the rural sample, and of less educated people in the urban sample. In the former case, the older people shared individualist values more strongly than did the younger people; the opposite was true in the latter case—the younger people exhibited stronger individualist values than did the older people. In general, highly educated and rural people exhibited individualist values more strongly than less educated and urban people, respectively.

With regard to collectivist values, a three-way ANOVA (see the right-hand side of Table 15.3) revealed the main effects of age, education, and residence to be significant; however, these effects were not independent of the levels of other factors. Thus the effects of age and residence were more evident in rural than in urban samples; on the other hand, rural/urban difference was more evident among less educated people, and also among those belonging to the older generation.

These findings indicate that although collectivist values differ widely across generations, individualist values generally tend to be shared equally by young and old people. Educational and residential background contribute significantly to differences in values. There is not much change in the hierarchical pattern of values, but their strengths seem to be altered considerably by these factors.

Regression Analyses

Besides general information on age, residence, and education, for each subject information was also available on some other relevant variables,

Table 15.5 Mean Scores of Groups on Individualist and Collectivist Values

Groups	Individualist Values		Collectivist Values	
	Young	Old	Young	Old
Rural:				
Highly educated				
Mean	31.80	38.60	26.04	34.16
SD	3.25	2.70	3.06	3.39
Less educated				
Mean	28.72	32.48	31.92	38.72
SD	3.42	3.26	4.21	3.28
Urban:				
Highly educated				
Mean	34.68	35.72	28.92	26.44
SD	4.03	3.69	2.45	2.30
Less educated				
Mean	33.60	22.00	30.76	30.68
SD	3.68	2.24	3.95	3.84

such as years of schooling, years of city residence, years of village residence, marital status, family structure, and occupation (see Table 15.1). Multiple regression analyses were done separately on each measure to examine the relative contribution of these variables to individualism/collectivism, individualist values, and collectivist values. As there was no theoretical basis to determine the hierarchical order of variables, a stepwise regression was preferred (see Table 15.6). The outcomes revealed that schooling and village residence were significant predictors of subjects' individualist and collectivist orientations. These accounted for approximately 31% of variance in scores; the contribution of schooling in the total variance was approximately 21%. Although the level of schooling was negatively correlated with collectivist orientation, village residence was positively correlated, suggesting that a lower level of schooling and longer stay in a village are more likely to promote collectivist orientation.

Using the same variables when the regression outcome for individualist values was examined, years of schooling and years of city residence were found to be significant predictors of these values. Both accounted for approximately 28% of variance in scores. The contribution of schooling was approximately 26% in the total variance. Schooling correlated positively with individualist values, whereas city residence correlated negatively. Thus, although the importance of individualist values increased with higher level of education, their importance tended to decrease with longer periods of stay in the city.

Table 15.6 Multiple Stepwise Regression Analyses on the Various Measures

Variables		Simple Beta	R	F
Individualism/collectivism				
years of schooling		−.42**	−.45	48.74**
village residence		.41**	.37	8.09**
family structure		.07	.06	1.57
marital status		.06	.17	1.03
age		.11	.29	0.57
Multiple R	.57			
R^2	.32			
Individualist values				
years of schooling		.53**	.51	74.17**
years city residence		−.14*	−.07	5.08*
marital status		.06	.01	0.82
family structure		.03	.08	0.19
age		.02	.01	0.17
Multiple R	.53			
R^2	.28			
Collectivist values				
years village residence		.75**	.43	29.33**
years of schooling		−.34**	−.39	33.82**
age		−.37**	.30	7.23**
marital status		−.09	.03	2.56
Multiple R	.58			
R^2	.34			

$*p < .05; **p < .01.$

Regression analysis on collectivist values revealed years of village residence, years of schooling, and age to be significant predictors of scores on this measure. These variables accounted for approximately 33% of variance in scores. Village residence contributed approximately 18%, and schooling contributed approximately 12% in the total variance of scores. Village residence was positively correlated with collectivist values, whereas schooling and age were correlated negatively with scores on this measure.

DISCUSSION

The findings of this study reveal no high degree of either collectivism or individualism on the part of the people under consideration. Although young, highly educated, and urban people in this sample tended to be less collectivistic, it was mainly the orientation of young people that was significantly influenced by urban residence, reflecting a kind of generation gap owing to urbanization. Similarly, higher education, with which the orientation of urban people tended to shift somewhat toward individualism, did not lead to much change in the orientation of rural people. The strength of in-group orientation also varied according to the groups concerned and the context of decisions. On the whole, lower level of education and village residence appear to be reliable predictors of individualism and collectivism.

The analysis revealed the existence of both individualist and collectivist values among people at the same time, though the former were held somewhat more strongly than the latter. Personal happiness was the most dominant value of all the groups under study; almost equally important were personal benefits and economic gains. On the other hand, in the category of collectivist values, salvation and enduring relationships were given a prominent place by old, rural, and less educated people, whereas the young, urban, and highly educated subjects attached greatest importance to altruism. Enduring relationships and salvation also found important places among the values of these groups. Although higher education and shorter period of stay in a city were the reliable predictors of individualist values in a global manner, village residence, low education, and young age were significant factors governing collectivist values. Despite such variations, the findings reveal that individualist values such as personal happiness, economic gain, and personal benefits can coexist with collectivist values such as salvation, enduring relationships, and altruism among people. The Indian psyche is generally reported to be full of paradoxes and the juxtaposition of opposites (for a detailed description, see Sinha & Tripathi, Chapter 8, this volume).

Higher education appeared to be a significant factor in predicting a lower level of collectivism among the people in this study; the variance accounted for by this variable was greater than other factors. However, the association of the effect of education with individuals' residential background was so strong that with higher education, the orientation of urban individuals alone appeared to be individualistic. The orientation of rural people tended to remain collectivistic despite higher education. In contrast to this tendency, the less educated subjects were found to be collectivistic, irrespective of their rural or urban background.

An explanation for the different role of higher education for rural and urban subjects may be given in terms of different sociocultural demands placed on individuals in rural and urban settings. Highly educated individuals living in urban sectors may be able to afford to show less concern for others in certain decisions partly because of the unshared nature of their economy (based on wages) and partly because they are staying away from home, at a distance from the larger network of family and relatives. On the other hand, embeddedness in various subgroups and the larger network of relationships is the most salient feature of rural life. Agriculture, which constitutes the major source of the economy of rural people, is very much a shared enterprise. A highly individualist orientation in this setting would appear to be a nonfunctional form of behavior. One's parents, friends, neighbors, and relatives all need to be given due importance in decisions regarding certain issues if one is to avoid various conflicts in day-to-day life.

On the other hand, when the issues were of a more personal nature and relatively free of the local context (such as issues concerning values), the young and old, highly educated and less educated, rural and urban all tended to show dispositions for both individualist and collectivist values, with some differences in the strengths of the values and less in their hierarchy. Evidence for the existence of contrasting values among people in the Indian sociocultural context is not surprising. D. Sinha (1969) has reported such contrasting orientations among villagers in northern India. In describing a happy life, the respondents in this study gave answers in which both materialistic and spiritual orientations coexisted. Although the orientations were found to vary with the personal situations of the villagers, the dominant theme that emerged from the underdeveloped villages was centered on the pursuit of minimum physical necessities and/or fantasizing about a luxurious lifestyle.

Analysis of generational differences revealed a more or less similar trend in results. The changing priorities of life with increasing age may be one reason for differences in in-group orientation between the young and old samples in this study. On the other hand, a significant decline in collectivist orientation of the younger generation with urbanization indicates the possibility that priorities may also vary considerably between rural and urban environments. Upbringing in a liberal family atmosphere and greater susceptibility to the effects of mass media seem to be factors promoting individualist orientations among younger people in urban as compared with rural environments. It appears that rural and urban residence represent separate dimensions, each of which contributes to behavioral development among individuals in unique ways.

Some studies reveal well-being of family to be a dominant concern of Indian people (D. Sinha, 1969; Mishra & Tiwari, 1980; Roy & Srivastava, 1986). This is regarded as *dharma* (sacred duty) of a *grihastha* (householder) in India. Even in studies in organizational settings, the family seems to occupy an important place (J. B. P. Sinha, 1980), and domestic happiness is given a high rank by Indian managers of different age levels (Katju, 1986). The prevalence of such family orientation among Indian people has often led to the belief that Indians have a collectivist orientation. In fact, there is a fair match between the characteristics of Indians and those theoretically proposed to be present among people in collectivist societies (Triandis, 1988a). However, studies indicate that this may not always be true (Sinha & Verma, 1987), and it has been argued that the collectivist orientation of Indian people tends to remain confined to the level of family unless the occasion demands that it be expanded. The Indian form of collectivism seems to contain some streaks of individualism (Tripathi, 1988). Thus the evidence in support of a collectivist orientation among Indians is almost mixed. Even in the Hofstede (1980) survey, Indians were found to be below the median on the dimension of collectivism. Slightly greater in-group orientation among the people in this study does not necessarily mean that they are collectivistic. Tripathi (1988) has argued that such orientations are generally used as strategies for enhancing one's own or one's family's position in society or for providing standards of comparison that allow one to reflect on one's own personal situation rather than on the situation of the group. A moderate level of collectivism with enough flavor of individualism displayed in the orientations and values of the people in the present study substantiates some of these arguments. An attitude favoring the coexistence of individualism and collectivism for dealing with the apparent conflicts between strong traditionality and requisite modernity seems to be the most likely outcome for people in India. This likely outcome is what this study demonstrates.

16

THE NATURE OF
ACHIEVEMENT MOTIVATION
IN COLLECTIVIST SOCIETIES

AN-BANG YU
KUO-SHU YANG

What motivates people in East Asian societies to achieve? McClelland and his associates concluded in the 1960s that East Asians and other non-Western groups were less motivated to succeed than Americans and Europeans. However, the fact that East Asian economies have grown rapidly over the past 20 years belies McClelland's conclusions. How could East Asian economies outperform North American and European economies if East Asians are not motivated to succeed? The answer to this question is not that East Asians are lazy, but rather that McClelland and his associates have assumed that Western middle-class values should motivate East Asians. In contrast, we believe that Confucianism, with its emphasis on cooperation in the family, motivates East Asians much more powerfully than do Western middle-class values, with their emphasis on individualism. By reviewing recent literature on the relationships among East Asian economic development, modernization, and Confucianism, evaluating McClelland and his colleagues' model of achievement motivation, and developing two scales to measure the characteristics and content of Chinese achievement motivation, we will seek to elucidate the culture-specific nature of achievement motivation in East Asian societies.

EAST ASIAN ECONOMIC DEVELOPMENT,
MODERNIZATION, AND CONFUCIANISM

The rapid economic development of Taiwan, Hong Kong, Korea, Singapore, and Japan has led many researchers to investigate the causes of the East Asian *economic miracle* (Hicks & Redding, 1983; Hofheinz & Calder, 1982; Redding, 1990). There are two types of theoretical approaches that explain economic development in East Asia. The first emphasizes the importance of economic policies and legal systems in these societies; the second stresses the influences of social structure and cultural values. Redding (1984) points out that politics and law, economics and geography, and society and culture are all important factors, and that interactions among these factors influence economic development. He suggests that favorable societal-cultural conditions were prerequisites of the economic development of East Asia. Meeting these requirements enabled East Asian governments to design appropriate political and economic policies that led to economic development despite geographic disadvantages (see Hwang, 1988).

Influences of Societal-Cultural Factors

Confucian ethics. If societal and cultural factors were prerequisites of political and economic development in East Asia, then what is the relationship between Confucianism—the dominant value system in Japan, Korea, and Taiwan—and economic growth? Kahn (1979; Kahn & Pepper, 1979) suggests that what he calls the "Confucian ethic" caused the Japanese, Korean, and Taiwanese economies to grow rapidly. He points out that all three of these societies stress interdependent socialization practices, self-control, education and skill learning, and the fulfillment of occupational, familial, and societal obligations. In a similar vein, Hofheinz and Calder (1982) state that economic success in this region can be attributed to Confucianism. According to these authors, Confucianism attaches great importance to the welfare of one's family or clan, emphasizes the importance of children's education and achievement, encourages industriousness and frugality, shows a willingness to make sacrifices, and instills the responsibility of respecting one's duty.

Confucian philosophy presupposes that the life of each individual is only a link in that person's family lineage, that an individual is the continuation of his or her ancestors, and that the same reasoning can be applied to the individual's offspring. The ultimate concern of a person's life is not to pursue salvation in the next life, but to expand and preserve the prosperity and vitality of his or her family in this life. In order to achieve these objectives, an individual has to work hard to accumulate resources, suppress selfish desires, be frugal, and save money to meet the needs of his or her family. Emphasizing the importance of people interacting with one another, Confucianism provides a basis for achievement motivation (Hwang, 1988).

Vulgar Confucianism. Berger (1983) proposes "vulgar Confucianism" to explain East Asian modernization. He argues that Christianity caused the West to modernize, and Confucianism has played a similar role in East Asia. Vulgar Confucianism prizes respect for authority, unconditional sacrifice for the family, and hard work. For Berger, these vulgar Confucian values and beliefs explain the high levels of productivity in East Asian economies.

After reviewing Western literature on the relationships among economic development, modernization, and Confucianism, Yang and Cheng (1987) divide East Asian cultural values into four groups of factors: family, group, job orientation, and disposition. Family factors include family and clan responsibilities and obedience to one's elders. Group factors include accepting the hierarchical structure of society, trust in and obedience to authority, and a commitment to the solidarity, harmony, and norms of the group. Factors related to job orientation include education, skill learning, hard work, and frugality. Disposition factors include austerity, calmness, humbleness, and self-control.

The internal structure of Confucianism. Hwang (1988) has investigated the relationship between Confucianism and modernization in East Asia from the perspective of social psychology, and asserts that the following questions can be answered only by considering cultural values: "Why do East Asian entrepreneurs have such high levels of achievement motivation?" "Why are these entrepreneurs especially good at business organization and management?" "Why do East Asian people emphasize education, hard work, and frugality?" He suggests that there are three major concepts in Confucianism that are closely related to modernization: benevolence, the practice of moral virtue, and benefiting the world. These three major values are found in East Asian societies, and they are responsible for rationalizing and deifying the pursuit of technology, knowledge, and skills, which not only benefit an individual's family, group, society, and country, but also ultimately transform a traditional society into a modern one (Hwang, 1988, 1991).

Huang (1987) holds similar views. He considers the family clan system to be the foundation of Confucian ethics and values as well as the power behind economic development in modern East Asia. Confucian ethics have influenced intellectuals to be reputable, to honor their parents, and to achieve glory first and wealth second. These values, such as filial piety and loyalty, are exemplified in the *Three Character Classic.*[1] In traditional society, such motivation could be fulfilled through an official career. In modern society, a strong motivation to excel remains, but specific achievement goals have shifted from careers in government service to careers in business. Although some goals of achievement in modern society differ from those in traditional society, Confucian ethics still play an important role in nourishing the achievement motivation of Chinese people.

How does Confucianism shape economic development and modernization in East Asia? Although both Chinese and Western scholars repeatedly point to the key role of Confucianism, few if any have offered a precise description of the process by which Confucianism motivates Chinese, Japanese, and Koreans to achieve and thereby transform their societies. In our view, Confucian ethics teach individuals to value the collective welfare of the family more than individual welfare. Moreover, Confucianism expects the individual to value education and skill learning, to practice self-discipline, and to respect authority. These teachings instill a spirit of diligence that not only motivates individuals to achieve, but also increases productivity.

RESEARCH ON ACHIEVEMENT
MOTIVATION IN THE WEST

Development of the concept. McClelland's theory of achievement motivation is based on Murray's (1938) need theory. Murray defines need for achievement as an "individual's desire to accomplish something hard; to master, manipulate, or organize physical objects, human beings, or ideas; to do this as rapidly, and as independently as possible; to overcome obstacles and attain a high standard; to excel one's self; to rival and surpass others; and to increase self-regard by the successful exercise of talent" (p. 164). Emphasizing that achievement motivation arises out of learning, McClelland and his associates have proposed an affective arousal model of achievement motivation.

Instrument and methodology. McClelland, Atkinson, Clark, and Lowell (1953) assert that each individual has his or her own standard of excellence, and that achievement motive is an impulse to meet with that standard. Furthermore, they regard achievement motivation as a desire or need that exists as an implicit personality variable on the preconscious or unconscious level in an individual's mind. McClelland and his colleagues adopted the Thematic Apperception Test (TAT) developed by Murray (1943) to measure an individual's need for achievement.

Defining the three major criteria of achievement imagery, McClelland, Atkinson, Russel, and Lowell (1958) point out what they call "unique achievement," achievement that emphasizes personal success. *Personal success* refers to achievements that an individual values, and this kind of achievement can fulfill the individual's desire for self-actualization. Moreover, the individual determines subjectively the degree of terminal value or incentive value of this achievement goal. In other words, according to McClelland et al., one characteristic of achievement motivation is that the individual determines the achievement goal independently. An individual pursues achievement to glorify him- or herself, and the incentive value of any goal is determined by the individual's preference for or evaluation of that goal. Another identifying criterion of achievement imagery in McClelland et al.'s scoring system lies in the definition of success or failure in achieving a goal according to the results of competition with certain standards of excellence. This criterion shows that an individual determines the achievement's standard, and that success or failure depends on that person's judgment.

Cross-cultural comparisons. Maehr and Nicholls (1980) assert that in order to define achievement motivation, one must first identify different meanings of achievement in different groups or cultures. They propose that cultural differences exist in the definition of achievement and concepts of success/failure. *Success* and *failure* refer not to concrete incidents, but to a person's subjective perception of whether a goal has been achieved or not achieved. In a study on the meaning of success/failure in the United States, Japan, Iran, and Thailand, Salili and Maehr (1975) found cross-cultural differences. Thais, for example, believe that success is closely related with "respect for others" and "tradition." For Americans, the concepts of "free will" and "realism" are emphasized as being major components of "success." A study by Fyans, Maehr, Salili, and Desai (1983) of 30 different cultures found similar results.

In their studies on subjective perceptions of the causes and consequences of success among Americans, Japanese, Greeks, and Indians, Triandis, Kilty, Shanmugam, Tanaka, and Vassiliou (1972) found that the American concept of achievement tends to be more individualistic than that of other cultures. Americans, for example, emphasize the individual's effort, ability, patience, devotion, and planning as the main reasons for success. In two review articles, Yang (1982, 1986) points out that the concept of achievement motivation as defined by McClelland and his colleagues strongly implies an orientation toward the individual or the self.

The nature of achievement motivation for Westerners. McClelland's scoring system for achievement motivation and the results of cross-cultural research show that theories of achievement motivation include the following assumptions: (a) People define achievement goals independently, (b) the degree of incentive value of the achievement goal is a subjective judgment, and (c) people create their own standards of excellence. In this regard, the nature of achievement motivation strongly reflects the cultural values and ethos of the Western middle class (Kornadt, Eckensberger, & Emminghaus, 1980; Maehr, 1974, 1978). We will call this kind of achievement motivation *individual-oriented achievement motivation* (IOAM) (Yang & Yu, 1988; A.-B. Yu, 1990; Yu & Yang, 1987).

Some critical analyses. Many scholars (as represented by McClelland) believe that achievement motivation in different cultures differs only in quantity and not quality. McClelland's (1961, 1963) interpretations of results that show lower levels of achievement motivation in Japan, Brazil, and traditional Chinese societies do not hold up under close scrutiny. It is clear that errors in McClelland's theory resulted mainly from his recognition of only one type of achievement motivation (i.e., IOAM) and as such his work has been criticized by many scholars (e.g., Kornadt et al., 1980; Maehr, 1974, 1978). McClelland failed to examine cultural influences on achievement motivation (Maehr, 1974, 1978; Maehr & Nicholls, 1980). Achievement may exist in many forms, and the value of achievement may also vary for different cultural groups.

THE NATURE OF ACHIEVEMENT
MOTIVATION IN EAST ASIAN SOCIETIES

E. S. Yu (1974, 1980) asserts that McClelland's concept of achievement motivation is based on individualism. Therefore, McClelland's scoring system measures only achievement motivation that is individual oriented. Yu assessed the need for achievement among 401 Chinese junior high school students, using the TAT. In addition, she evaluated the subjects' self-reported statements on achievement. She found a significant negative correlation ($r = -.10$) between scores on these two instruments. The subjects' scores on the TAT did not correlate significantly with the filial piety and familism scales. However, the scores from the self-reported achievement statements correlated significantly with the filial piety ($r = .25$) and familism scales ($r = .55$). Moreover, the scores from the self-reported achievement statements correlated with the scores on the extended familism scale ($r = .32$) more than the scores from the self-reported achievement statements correlated with the scores on the nuclear familism scale ($r = .20$).

E. S. Yu (1974, 1980) points out that Chinese culture strongly emphasizes filial piety and familism. These values carry a collectivist orientation. What is more, the TAT achievement motivation score differed qualitatively from the self-reported statements on achievement. We see then that McClelland's scoring system is unable to measure achievement motivation among the Chinese, and that self-reported measure can compensate for the shortcomings of the TAT. Chinese students perceive achievement not as individual achievement, but rather as their responsibility and obligation to an extensive family and kinship network system. In brief, achievement for Chinese reflects a collectivist orientation.

DeVos and his associates have also criticized McClelland's theory (see Caudill & DeVos, 1956; DeVos, 1973; DeVos & Wagatsuma, 1961). For the Japanese, success and achievement for self-interest or personal benefit are viewed as immoral and egocentric. The Japanese place emphasis not on attaining individual glory, but rather on continuing family tradition.

Wilson and Pusey (1982) and Pusey (1977) found that Chinese parents encourage their children to seek individual and collective achievement simultaneously. They are also trained to identify individual achievement with collective achievement. Chinese culture emphasizes sharing the fruits of individual success with the group. The group accepts and admires an individual if what he or she has achieved benefits the group or if other members of society can share his or her success. Driven by such group or societal values, an individual senses the pressure that characterizes Chinese achievement motivation. Therefore, Chinese often emphasize the driving force of a social group when explaining their achievement motivation (Pusey, 1977; Wilson & Pusey, 1982).

Blumenthal (1976) analyzed the content of children's stories from mainland China and found that Chinese emphasize collective goals rather than individual goals. In comparing achievement motivation between Chinese and Americans, Pusey (1977) also found that Chinese achievement needs reflect a desire to fulfill the expectations of groups such as the family, the clan, or the whole society. Hsu (1953, 1981) also points out that Americans are more individualist oriented when seeking achievement, whereas Chinese seek to achieve because they are not only concerned about their families, but also want to maintain the prosperity of the family or clan.

Chen (1987a, 1987b, 1989) has observed that "glorifying the ancestors," "glorifying established virtues," "heightening family reputation," "glorifying parents," "enlarging the family's estate," "glorifying relatives," and "fulfilling filial piety" motivated many traditional Chinese businessmen to switch from trade to scholarship. He has shown that the ultimate concerns of traditional Chinese rested on the continuation of a clan; being in trade or pursuing scholarship were only strategies to attain this goal. The honor of a clan was (and, in fact, still is) the ultimate concern of traditional Chinese, and success in civil examinations was the primary avenue to this goal. From Chen's analysis, we can further understand why the highest achievement goals for Chinese were—and in many families still are—honoring the clan and glorifying the ancestors. Success or failure in achieving these goals was the basis for evaluating an individual's achievement. This further illustrates the collectivist nature of achievement goals and the meaning of achievement in Chinese society. In modern Chinese society this goal can also be achieved through other methods, such as business. It is clear that in Chinese society, other people—the family, the clan, or other groups—determine the standards the individual and others use to evaluate the individual's achievement. Furthermore, these groups encourage and praise the individual after he or she reaches his or her achievement goals.

Thus empirical research on Chinese and Japanese cultures shows that society prescribes the content and form of achievement goals for the individual. Individual goals must conform with the values of an in-group, and only by achieving the goals of the in-group can the individual realize him- or herself. The in-group also determines the standards of excellence for the individual. We term achievement motivation with these characteristics *social-oriented achievement motivation* (SOAM) (Yang & Yu, 1988; A.-B. Yu, 1990; Yu & Yang, 1987).

CONSTRUCTION
OF SOAM AND IOAM SCALES

Achievement motivation is related closely to social or cultural characteristics. Conceptually, we now understand that IOAM and SOAM are contrasting types of achievement motivation. We would also like to be able to measure the varying degrees of SOAM and IOAM, which are present in all individuals regardless of whether they belong to collectivist or individualist societies. Consequently, we have developed two scales to measure SOAM and IOAM.

Scale Development

We wrote and selected 150 items for the preliminary scales, basing our choices on (a) our conceptual analysis of the contrasting characteristics of SOAM and IOAM; (b) Western scales of achievement motivation and/or need for achievement, including EPPS (Edwards, 1959) and CPI (Gough, 1960); and (c) questionnaires designed by Guo (1972) and Chang (1981). About half of the items constituted the SOAM scale, and the other half were for the IOAM scale.

All items were checked thoroughly, and those that were improper or ambiguous were deleted. Examples of SOAM scale items include "The major goal in my life is to work hard to achieve something which will make my parents feel proud of me" and "When I am working, I'll make a greater effort to meet my parents' expectations." The preliminary SOAM scale contained 44 items. The preliminary IOAM scale also contained 44 items, including the following: "I prefer to follow my own will to do the right thing rather than take my parents' opinions into account" and "No matter how many times I fail, I'll keep on trying even without others' encouragement." In addition, the second author selected and translated into Chinese 12 items from the Marlowe and Crowne (1964) social desirability scale in order to measure social desirability (Hwang & Yang, 1972).

A sample of 400 adults (aged 18 to 50; 182 males and 218 females) living in the greater Taipei metropolitan area completed the questionnaire in their homes or workplaces. Education levels of the sample were as follows: 30.7% had completed senior high school, 47.3% had graduated from college, and 15.7% had completed postgraduate study. We adopted a 6-point Likert-type scale.

RESULTS AND DISCUSSION

Deleting five items from the SOAM scale because their item-total correlation was lower than .25 left 39 items in that scale. We also deleted 2 items from the IOAM scale, retaining 42 items. To control for social desirability, we then deleted items that correlated positively or negatively .35 or greater with social desirability. As a result, we retained 38 items for the SOAM scale and 42 for the IOAM scale. Finally, we deleted items with low face validity, leaving 29 items on the SOAM scale and 28 on the IOAM scale.

The Cronbach's alpha coefficients for the final versions of the SOAM and IOAM scales were both .89. In addition, a second sample of 152 elementary school teachers (135 males, 17 females) was used to check internal consistency and test-retest reliability. The Cronbach's alpha for SOAM was .91 and the test-retest reliability coefficient (three-week interval) was .73. The Cronbach's alpha for the IOAM scale was .91, and the test-retest reliability coefficient was .68. These reliability indices show that the two achievement motivation scales have high internal consistency and moderate stability. Some descriptive statistics and reliability indices of the SOAM and IOAM scales are presented in Table 16.1.

We conducted principal-component analyses to examine the preliminary SOAM and IOAM scales. After an orthogonal rotation, the 29 items in the final SOAM scale loaded on the first factor (.30 or greater) and the 28 items in the final IOAM scale loaded on the second factor showed similar results. These two factors explained 24% of the total variance. Results from factor analysis indicated that SOAM and IOAM are independent psychological constructs.

Yang and Cheng (1987) developed two simplified versions of the final SOAM and IOAM scales as tools for exploring the relationships among an individual's achievement motivation, work preference, and organizational behavior. They found that people with higher SOAM score consider family benefits and welfare when choosing jobs. These people want simple, stress-free jobs near their homes so that they can spend more time taking care of their families. They also hope for higher salaries and bonuses to give their families. Jobs that strongly correlate with IOAM are those that can help people improve and develop their personal potentials and specialties. People with higher scores on IOAM prefer these kinds of jobs because they can work in harmonious environments with "teamwork" climates that emphasize consideration, equality, and respect. They also like meaningful, challenging, and responsible jobs that can help them learn more. Although SOAM was not related to organizational commitment or work effectiveness, IOAM correlated strongly and positively with these two variables.

In another study, we adopted SOAM and IOAM scales for Chinese high school and college students (Yu & Yang, 1987). The reliability was high: Cronbach's alpha of .91 for SOAM and .87 for IOAM. The test-retest reliability of these two scales ranged from .79 to .86. The correlation coefficient between SOAM and IOAM was .02.

From the above-reported results, we conclude that the SOAM and IOAM scales have high internal consistency and stable test-retest reliability. The factor analysis and correlational analysis indicate that these two scales are not only independent, but also represent two different psychological constructs. In addition, both the SOAM and IOAM scales have discriminant validity and predictive validity.

Table 16.1 Descriptive Statistics and Reliability Indices for the SOAM and IOAM Scales

Scale	Total Items	Sample	Mean	SD	Range of Item-Total Correlation	Cronbach's Alpha	Test-Retest Correlation
SOAM	29	adults[a]	98.43	20.57	.25-.63	.89	
		teachers[a]	109.44	19.32	.23-.69	.91	.73
IOAM	28	adults	136.20	16.53	.31-.58	.89	
		teachers	137.93	15.98	.22-.71	.91	.68

NOTE: a. Adult sample, $N = 400$; teacher sample, $N = 152$.

Our review of cultural factors in modernization has been presented to highlight their role in the success of developed and developing economies in East Asia (Berger & Hsiao, 1988; Kahn, 1979; Sit, 1984). Although this economic development has taken place only during the past 20 years, numerous scholars have concluded that cultural values serve as a foundation for achievement motivation. These cultural factors play an important, even fundamental, role (Berger, 1983; Hwang, 1988).

The above discussion demonstrates that the strong achievement orientation of East Asian peoples is best characterized as social-oriented achievement motivation. McClelland and his colleagues have described an individual-oriented achievement motivation that reflects the individualist characteristics found in North American and European societies but is incapable of adequately explaining what motivates East Asians.

NOTE

1. The *Three Character Classic* is a book that most children in traditional China had to read and memorize. It gives guidelines for such things as parenting, increasing self-discipline, honoring ancestors, and filial piety. It occasionally appears in the classrooms and homes of students.

17

SIGNIFICANCE OF PATERNALISM AND COMMUNALISM IN THE OCCUPATIONAL WELFARE SYSTEM OF KOREAN FIRMS
A National Survey

UIMYONG M. KIM

The study presented in this chapter was designed to explore the nature of communalism and paternalism in Korean organizations. Communalism reflects an orientation in which the needs and goals of individuals are sacrificed for the attainment of collective interests. The value of solidarity has its roots in Korean traditional communalism. It specifies that collective needs always supersede individual interests. An individual is perceived as merely an adjunct of the family system, and the identity of an individual is neither independent nor important; group cohesion and conformity dominate the family structure.

Family-oriented communalism has been transformed into corporate-oriented communalism in the Korean business sector. Applied to the organizational setting, communal attachment of individuals has been the generalized orientation, with particular emphasis placed upon the importance of communal obligations and integration. This "communal particularism" appears to permeate the "diffused, shared" systems of occupational welfare in Japan. When communalism is coupled with paternalism, the long arms of the company's concern reach the employee and family through a variety of welfare schemes designed to cultivate company solidarity. This aspect is particularly apparent in Japan, and enterprise unionism appears to be a perfect example (Okochi et al., 1973, p. 235).

Titmuss (1974) laments the growth of sectional solidarities that tend to obstruct the development of society as a whole. According to Reisman (1977), occupational welfare reinforces the power of corporations in society in the same way communion and confession reinforced the power of the medieval Catholic church. This concept of communalism is important in explaining the social control function of production (efficiency motive of occupational welfare). In Korea, employees are forced to conform to a company's policies in order to maximize company solidarity, and organizational commitment is the dominant factor that enhances production and efficiency in Korean industries.

Contrary to Titmuss's (1974) expectation, sectional solidarity is largely reinforced and accentuated by the Korean traditional familism so important to the conduct and thought of Korean people. Park (1969) argues that the Korean family forms a close-knit unit with a strong sense of family solidarity, but it tends to exclude the external world. This strengthened familism, in turn, hampers the process of forming society as a whole. As a result of the emphasis on the family unit, as opposed to the individual or society, neither national unity nor modern individualism can fully develop in Korea, only family-centered egoism. In the corporate sphere, this egoism is transformed into corporate-oriented solidarity, which, in turn, jeopardizes social integration. In this sense, sectional solidarity, which is largely nurtured by the Korean cultural heritage, is further consolidated within the exclusive nature of occupational welfare in Korean industry.

Evidence provided in the following sections convincingly points toward the fact that management in Korean industry is in full pursuit of sectional solidarity at the corporate level. Moreover, evidence indicates that such efforts of individual forms appear to be supported wholeheartedly by the Korean government. As an illustration, former President Chun stated that "especially through promoting the company as the secondary family movement, the employer should endeavor to improve the well-being of the employee" (quoted in the *Korea Daily Times,* March 21, 1983).

PATERNALISM

Paternalism was a fundamental value held by the founding fathers of welfare capitalism. Paternalism suggests a relationship between the agents in any economic organization in which the employers act toward their employees in a manner similar to how parents behave toward their children (Bennet & Iwao, 1963; Dore, 1958).

Bennet and Iwao (1963), in their analysis of paternalism from an international perspective, suggest two salient features of paternalism. One is a degree of hierarchy that is greater than the minimal amount any employer-employee relationship should display in an organizational setting. The other is the concern shown by employers for aspects of their employees' lives that have nothing to do with the actual work performed (see also Dore, 1958). Thus, for the worker, employment in a given firm constitutes a career and promotes a sense of loyalty and belonging. In return, the company shows interest in the worker through concern for the health, education, and personal problems of the employee and the employee's family.

The paternalistic aspect of occupational welfare in Western industrial nations, particularly in the United States, has gradually lost significance because of the adamant opposition of trade unions. The collective bargaining system is perhaps the single most important factor in the demise of paternalism in occupational welfare. However, paternalism is still a predominant concept in Japanese industry. Nishio (1982) states that Japanese communal corporatism is based on "neopaternalism." In Korea, the ideas of occupational welfare are primarily based upon traditional paternalism, which grew out of Confucianism, the dominant social value system since the time of the Yi dynasty (1392-1910). The most fundamental base of Korean paternalism and Confucianism is the traditional value of familism.

Up until the beginning of the twentieth century, the Korean family structure was characterized mainly by patriarchal, patrilocal, and patrilineal familism (Yim, 1969). Familism in Korea was extended to a village-centered clan organization and constituted the basic unit of society, superior to any other social institution in its importance. The most outstanding characteristic of Korean familism is the hierarchical nature of the relations among family members. The ethical relation between father and son has been understood chiefly as the one-sided duty of filial piety. Filial duty consists of respectful obedience and a great deal of personal sacrifice. In the patriarchal family system, the authority of the father is absolute (Yim, 1969).

Paternalistic relationships are extended to outside the family boundary, so that hierarchical and authoritative relationships based on seniority and gender influence human relations both at work and in private life; hence the paternal nature of occupational welfare in Korea may be interpreted as an expression of corporate paternalism or, according to Nishio (1982), neopaternalism. Authoritative paternalism is characterized by heavy emphasis on duty and a downplaying of sincere warmth and generous concern on the part of the superior. On the other hand, benevolent paternalism places the opposite emphasis, featuring the subordinate's loyalty and the superior's genuine and generous concern for that subordinate. Paternalism in Korean industry can be seen as more akin to authoritative paternalism than to the benevolent type. An employee's obedience and wholehearted loyalty appear to be required by management by virtue of management's higher status, without the need to display concern for or generosity to employees in return.

The significance of paternal-oriented management in the Korean business community is further reinforced by the recent influx of rural workers; the ratio of urban to rural population has tripled in the past 20 years. The economically active population in rural areas went from 7,891,000 to 5,743,000, a decline of 27%, between 1980 and 1987, whereas the economically active population in urban areas rose from 16,572,000 to 23,212,000, an increase of 40%, during the same period (Ministry of Labor, Korea, 1988). Thus the majority of Korean industrial workers are from rural areas and are accustomed to the values of the rural, patriarchal, extended family system. Weak labor unions in Korea are also likely to solidify and perpetuate paternalism in the Korean business sector.

Occupational welfare as an expression of paternalism is best seen as part of a transformation process. The popularity of livelihood protection assistance schemes is testimony to this. Like father figures who attend to their families' material and social needs, employers attend to their employees' basic needs, such as food, clothing, and shelter. In addition, like many fathers, many employers express a certain degree of interest in the education of their subordinates.

SOCIAL OBLIGATION

A substantial portion of occupational benefits can be interpreted as the expression of employers' sense of responsibility for their employees. Generally, paternalism coupled with humanitarianism constitutes the value base of social obligation. However, because of traditional Korean culture, an employer's expression of social obligation toward employees is paternalistic and, to a much lesser extent, humanitarian in form.

ENHANCEMENT
AND PRODUCTION EFFICIENCY

On a general level, there are multiple reasons for offering occupational welfare benefits. Experts generally agree that in the West, enhancement of production and efficiency is the most cited reason for providing occupational welfare. Shamir and David (1982) claim that goals that promote employee welfare or community welfare are clearly secondary to other goals, particularly the enhancement of production and efficiency.

Occupational welfare in Korea is expected to enhance production and efficiency by cultivating organizational commitment to the enterprise. *Organizational commitment* may be defined as the relative strength of an individual's identification with and involvement in a particular organization (Steers, 1977). Most views of organizational commitment include three dimensions: a strong belief in and acceptance of organizational goals and values, a willingness to extend considerable effort on behalf of the organization, and a strong desire to maintain membership in the organization (Porter et al., 1974).

Shamir and David (1982) propose that occupational welfare increases organizational commitment by drawing employees' attention to the organization's concern with individual goals and values, and so increases identification with the organization (see also Porter et al., 1974). Occupational welfare may attract prospective employees as well as reduce turnover through increasing commitment to an organization. Organizational commitment may in turn contribute to increased productivity by positively affecting labor mobility. This effect of occupational welfare appears to be well understood by managers.

SOCIAL CONTROL

The term *social control* is widely used in conjunction with social policy, but there have been few attempts to define it or to explore its various meanings and connotations (Higgins, 1980). It has become commonplace to argue that occupational welfare is "a means of social control" and that managers are "agents of social control." To be more specific, exertion of social control through the granting of occupational welfare benefits can be interpreted as an inclination to conformity rather than conflict. In this thesis, the practice of social control is defined as disciplining workers to make them conform to management policy, thereby diffusing discontent and so maintaining order in the workplace and a stable industrial environment.

In the United States, fringe benefits often take the form of cash or the equivalent. Cash benefits, various types of insurance, payment for time not worked, and profit-sharing plans are among the voluntary (nonstatutory) schemes that constitute the main fabric of the American occupational welfare system. But benefits in-kind, such as employee meals and service awards, play a very small part in terms of number and cost (about 10% of the total employee benefit cost) in the United States (U.S. Chamber of Commerce, 1985).

The heavy use of in-kind benefits in Korean industry might be explained by the advantages of in-kind benefits to employers. Alva Myrdal (1968; cited in Gilbert, 1983) suggests that in-kind benefits are less expensive than cash payments because large-scale activities can save money on the purchase or production of certain items of consumption. For instance, supplying standardized meals to all employees in a firm is naturally more cost-effective than providing meal allowances. The same holds true for work uniforms, company housing, and so on.

Myrdal suggests that assistance in-kind is also more effective than cash subsidies for the following reasons (see Gilbert, 1983). The effectiveness of social provisions can be measured according to different criteria, but the major criterion is undoubtedly the degree to which the benefit has the intended effect on the true beneficiary. Company schools in Korean industry present a good illustration. The company in reality benefits the most because the school provides a dedicated, highly skilled, and stable workforce for a definite period. Students in postsecondary institutions are devoted and grateful to the company. The students are also skilled, because a large proportion (approximately one-third) of their school curriculum is allocated to teaching the knowledge and skills necessary to perform in the company. The students provide a stable workforce for at least three years because they seldom leave the firm during the period of school enrollment. In an interview, the personnel manager of Hanil Textile Co. Ltd., one of Korea's leading textile manufacturers, stated, "We spend a big chunk of money, approximately $1.7 million a year, to run our affiliated school, but the return for the investment is too astronomical to figure out" (personal communication, October 28, 1987). The predominance of in-kind benefits over cash reflects the two main objectives commonly held by business leaders, because in-kind benefits satisfy both the economic objective by being cost-effective and the social objective of enhancing employee loyalty and obedience through the social control function.

The second form of social control applicable to the occupational welfare system is integration. Titmuss (1968, 1974) argues that as rapid industrial change has given rise to disparities in the patterns of work and family, it is the proper responsibility of the state to provide services that will enhance the physical and mental well-being of workers and ensure their integration into industrialized society. Similarly, employers have a responsibility to ensure that their employees are integrated into the industrialized society through occupational welfare. T. H. Marshall also emphasizes that social services can create and maintain solidarity in modern society (cited in Higgins, 1981). In Korea, an overwhelming majority of employees are wholly dedicated to the collectivist approach and its objective of promoting company solidarity and loyalty.

In Western countries, the general attitude of employers toward their employees' families is that they are the concern and responsibility of the employees only. Conversely, Japanese companies take primary responsibility for employees' families. Accordingly, benefits for employees in Japan generally also cover whole families. In addition, employee paychecks normally include family allowances of varying sizes, according to the number of dependents. To enhance employee commitment and dedication, firms encourage the policy of *kazoku gurumi* (family members are all included). For example, limited remuneration for a retired worker who settles with his adult son's family is normally included in the son's paycheck (Nishio, 1982).

Similarly, occupational welfare in Korea includes a variety of benefits oriented toward employees and their families, including housing, family allowances, family medical clinics, congratulatory and condolence allowances, and education funds for the children. All these provisions mean that employees become more dependent on their employers. Westerners are usually surprised when they see that this dependency is not resented, but usually appreciated by employees. This willingness to welcome dependency, however, is more explicable to Westerners if they understand Korean familism and paternalism.

METHODOLOGY

The following sections present the results of a survey conducted to examine Korean communalism and paternalism. Questionnaires were hand delivered and administered, over a period of two months in the summer of 1986, to all mining and manufacturing firms in Korea with more than 100 employees. A total of 1,097 companies were identified and surveys distributed, and 985 questionnaires were returned, for a response rate of 90%. The survey asked factual questions about the provision of occupational welfare services and benefits and also asked for respondents' opinions on occupational welfare and, to a lesser extent, public welfare. The questionnaires were completed by firms' personnel managers or general managers.

RESULTS AND DISCUSSION

Communalism

Empirical evidence suggests that the majority of managers in Korean industry share the view that a company's responsibility extends to include

Table 17.1 Occupational Welfare Provisions and Family Inclusiveness

Services and Facility	Employee Only	Coverage Employees' Family Inclusive	Total Provisions
Company hospital			
no.	50	42	92
%	54	46	100
Sports facilities			
no.	343	123	466
%	75	26	100
Cultural and recreational facilities			
no.	273	100	373
%	73	27	100
Average			
no.	312	129	
%	70	30	

SOURCE: U. M. Kim (1986).

employees' family members. A large majority (90%) of the sample believes that the company is responsible for the well-being of employees and their families; a mere 8% hold the opposite view.

The vast majority (82%) of the managers who responded are of the opinion that when the claims of the family on an employee and the claims of the firm are in conflict, the latter should take precedence, whereas only 18% observed otherwise. The data support the notion that corporate-oriented solidarity is a value shared by the majority of managers in Korean industry.

More often than not, there is a gap between ideals and practice. Although 9 of every 10 managers support the view that the company is responsible for the well-being of employees and their families, only an average of 3 of 10 firms furnish services and facilities to family members of employees (see Table 17.1).

Similarly, although there are grounds for believing that corporate-oriented solidarity is generally promoted through a variety of welfare schemes, complementary action has not materialized in the Korean business community. The gap between attitude and actual performance is revealed in that firms with communalist orientation provide an average of 17 welfare services, whereas those with noncommunalist orientation provide 16 welfare services. The *t* test indicates that the relationship between a belief in corporate-oriented solidarity and the provision of occupational welfare is statistically insignificant.

In summary, management's strong desire to build enterprise solidarity has not really been substantiated by a high degree of occupational welfare provision. Of course, it is possible that company solidarity is still only an idea for management or that managers still resort to traditional social control mechanisms to promote this solidarity and do not recognize the potential usefulness of occupational welfare schemes for enhancing company solidarity.

Paternalism and the Occupational Welfare System

Two questionnaire items were designed to examine the concept of paternalism; they were derived from Bennet and Iwao's (1963) definitions of paternalism. The first implied a relationship between the agents in any economic organization in which employers act toward employees as parents behave toward their children (Dore, 1958). The empirical data show that 81% agree with the view that the relationship between an employer and employee is similar to that between parent and child, whereas only 18% oppose the view. Bennet and Iwao also define paternalism as "the concern shown by the employer for aspects of his employee's lives which have nothing to do with the actual work performance." A total of 82% of the respondents reported that an employer's relationship with an employee goes beyond merely that of boss-worker. The results indicate that the boss is perceived as a "father figure" who can give guidance on and guidance to an employee's private life. Overall, results strongly support the hypothesis that traditional paternalism has been internalized in the form of corporate paternalism in Korean industry.

Social Obligation

More than 93% of the sample believe that occupational welfare schemes are used by employers to improve workers' morale and to promote a sense of belonging and loyalty to the company. The data collected reveal that 32% of 902 companies provide tuition fees for employees to attend night school. Moreover, the company-affiliated school, established and run by the firm, usually has a curriculum similar to that of the regular high schools, so that graduates of the company school are awarded a high school graduation diploma upon completion. By 1987, 49 firms had established affiliated schools (44,147 students), a total of 16% of all Korean firms with more than 1,000 workers (Ministry of Labor, Korea, 1988).

Another expression of paternalism is the employer's concern for employees' family members. For example, 46% of the sample companies report paying tuition fees for their employees' children at the high school level, and 33% pay for university education for employees' children. About 71% of the firms pay more than half of the education costs for high school and 51% pay for half of university.

Perhaps the best indication of a company's paternalistic concern for its employees and their families is the found in the congratulatory and condolence gifts given on various occasions. An employee's family members are commonly considered peripheral members of the company family, and they receive gifts at certain times from the employer, a practice based on the principle that the joys and sorrows of the company family members are the joys and sorrows of the employer. Several generalizations may be drawn from the empirical data shown in Table 17.2. First, congratulation and condolence donations are widely used, and the company's gift gesture ranges from 90% for employees' own marriages to 15% for school admission of employees' children. Second, the list of who receives gifts and for what is extensive. Third, the degree of the company's commitment to offering a gift declines in proportion to the degree of kinship distance. For instance, companies who give condolence gifts to an employee and spouse on the occasion of the death of a parent average 78%, compared with 39% for the death of an employee's parent-in-law. Similarly, 89% of firms furnish gifts for the employee's marriage, whereas only 38% supply gifts upon the marriages of the employee's siblings. Fourth, discriminatory treatment against in-laws is shown by the data. As illustrated in Table 17.2, 85% of firms provide condolence gifts upon the death of an employee's parent, but company gift offerings drop drastically, to 40%, upon the death of an in-law. Such discrimination reflects the Korean traditional family structure, which is based on patriarchal familism, and the fact that most industrial workers are male. A daughter's marriage generally symbolizes her break from her parents and her joining with her husband's family.

The paternalism of the occupational welfare system in Korea is also evident in company activities that promote company solidarity and fellowship among employees and their families. A total of 61% of firms have fellowship and hobby clubs, 70% report annual sports days, and 89% hold annual picnics. More than 8 of every 10 employers pays the entire cost for the sports days and picnics. The survey also revealed that 16% of firms furnish company-owned resort facilities, a practice that implicitly encourages employees to spend their vacations within the company circle.

In summary, paternalism is so prominent in the Korean occupational welfare system that service facilities and amenities are mainly designed to express employers' paternalistic attitude through taking care of the basic needs of employees and their families. Paternalism is also expressed and encouraged through the promotion of fellowship among employees

Table 17.2 Extent of Coverage of Congratulatory and Condolence Gifts

Coverage Beneficiary	Occasion	Support Absolute Frequency	Relative Frequency (%)
Self	marriage	757	89
	death	648	76
Spouse	death	674	80
Children	marriage	672	79
	birth	624	74
	school admission	130	15
	death	640	76
Parents	birthdays	619	73
	death	719	84
Parents-in-law	birthday	263	31
	death	331	40
Sibling	marriage	324	38
	death	304	36
Grandparents	death	399	47
Average		503	60

and, thereby, the creation of company solidarity. In a sense, the collectivist approach taken by the majority of Korean managers, such as providing comprehensive coverage under various schemes, can be taken as a paternalistic infringement on individual responsibility or as a means of ensuring workers' loyalty.

Enhancement of Production and Efficiency

The responses of the vast majority of the companies in the present survey show that organizational commitment is considered the most important factor in improving workers' production and efficiency, according to managers. The vast majority of the respondents agreed with the statement "The occupational welfare system is mainly dictated by the need to attract productive workers as well as to reduce the rate of turnover." A total of 14% of the sample strongly agreed with the statement, and 73% agreed; only 12% disagreed with the statement, and 1% strongly disagreed.

Thus organizational commitment was singled out by managers as the most significant factor contributing to improved job performance, of the three factors proposed: job satisfaction, increased motivation, and organizational commitment. Organizational commitment is encouraged not only through occupational welfare schemes but also through paternalistic infringement. The development of individuals' identification with and involvement in a particular firm appears to rely not so much on the provision of occupational welfare benefits as on the family-oriented cultural imperative that explicitly demands employees' loyalty and obedience to the enterprise.

Social Control

A total of 76% of the sample saw occupational welfare schemes as part of management's need to enhance conformity and diffuse discontent in the workplace; 24% took the opposite view. Analysis of the social control function involves three different forms and mechanisms of social control. The first consists of social control as paternalism. Paternalism can be seen as involving a loss of liberty, because benefits tend to be in-kind rather than in the form of cash. An investigation of the occupational welfare system in Korea reveals the dominance of in-kind benefits (see Table 17.3). The managers surveyed were in favor of providing in-kind benefits over wages because this enables them to exercise control over employees. Only a few schemes, such as housing loans, transportation allowances, and group insurance, involve cash or the equivalent. Of the 28 services, facilities, or benefits listed in the survey, only 6, or 15%, are directly related to cash benefits, and total welfare costs for these schemes are negligible compared with the costs of benefits in-kind.

Social control in occupational welfare is evident in the quality of occupational welfare in Korea. Services and facilities such as medical offices, company hospitals, sports facilities and activities, fellowship gatherings, picnics, cooperative societies, and company resorts are basically designed and distributed so that the full effects, particularly company solidarity and loyalty, are centered on the company's need to enhance the collective entity, the "enterprise family." The notion of control as integration is further reinforced by corporate familism, in which the company's paternal protection encompasses both employees and their dependents.

Benevolent Versus Authoritarian Paternalism

An inquiry into the nature of paternalism in Korean industry presumes close links between benevolent paternalistic orientation and the provision of occupational welfare services. In other words, the more benevolently paternalistic the management, the more the company should provide occupational welfare, whereas authoritative paternalism should not generate

Table 17.3 Nature of Occupational Welfare Services in Korea

Welfare Services	Absolute Frequency (N = 902)	Relative Frequency (%)
In-kind		
dining hall	838	93
work uniform	845	94
commuting bus	573	64
shower	758	84
change room	824	91
library	395	44
recreation room	562	62
sports facilities	714	78
picnic	804	89
athletic meet	629	70
cultural and		
recreational programs	482	53
Cash		
housing loan	95	10
transportation allowance	242	27
group insurance	447	50
medical assistance	280	31

SOURCE: U. M. Kim (1986).

an increase in occupational welfare provisions because of its unilateral emphasis on the subordinate's loyalty over the superior's generosity.

The empirical data show nearly unanimous support (98%) among managers for the notion that an important function of occupational welfare is to improve labor-management relationships through promoting company solidarity and allegiance. However, firms with paternalistic orientations provide an average of 18 services, whereas firms with nonpaternalistic attitudes also provide an average of 18 services. This result may not be sufficient to determine the nature of the paternalism prevalent among managers in Korean industry, because both arguments, that paternalistic orientation does not necessarily result in more welfare provision and that a substantial number of managers are not aware of the possible links between paternalistic attitudes and providing employee benefits, are plausible. Nevertheless, even considering the limits and ambiguities involved in this issue, it is still reasonable to speculate that the paternalistic attitudes prevalent among the majority of managers in Korean industry more closely resemble authoritative paternalism than benevolent paternalism. Therefore, a plausible albeit unconfirmed conclusion can be drawn: The social control function of occupational welfare does not influence the quantity of occupational welfare services offered by Korean industry. In spite of logical expectations that firms that agree with the social control function are more likely to supply occupational welfare benefits than are firms that disagree with the function, the data show no difference between the two groups.

In summary, the evidence indicates that communalism and paternalism profoundly influence and play a pivotal role in the functions of occupational welfare, not only in the employer's sense of social obligation toward employees but also in the enhancement of production and efficiency as well as social control. Therefore, it can be concluded at this stage that the cultural legacy of paternalism and communalism seems to be dominant over the economic imperative, at least at the cognitive level of Korean business managers.

A similar trend also prevails between the kind of value and the magnitude of the welfare provision. The number of welfare provisions remains nearly constant regardless of value orientation, whether it is paternalism (mean frequency of 17.8), communalism (mean = 17.3), reward principle (mean = 17.4), or inequality (mean = 17.1). This result reveals that an ideological background sympathetic to occupational welfare has failed to make actual welfare provisions materialize in Korean industry. Perhaps some other currently unknown factor or factors may account for this extremely low correlation, or the full potential of the occupational welfare system is either not fully understood or not fully embraced by the management or owners of Korean industry. Whatever the reasons, present occupational welfare programs do not seem to derive their existence from the values that might be thought to encourage the proliferation of occupational welfare schemes in Korean industry.

GENERAL DISCUSSION

The predominance of cultural legacy over economic realities in Korean industry seems most pertinent. Specifically, family-oriented paternalism and communalism are highly valued by management. Paternalism, particularly, appears to be deeply ingrained, not only in employers' sense of obligation toward employees, but also in employers' desire for production efficiency and social control.

What essential values are at stake here? Has traditional Korean familism been transformed into corporate familism? Nishio's (1982) notion of neopaternalism seems to provide valuable insight here. Traditional Korean paternalism may have been partially subsumed into the neopaternalism of the modern industrial system. Numerous aspects of the Korean occupational welfare system suggest the imprint of traditional values. Employer programs that respond to employees' basic needs appear to be either the result of benevolent paternalism in return for worker loyalty or a response to the low wages paid the average Korean industrial worker, or both. In fact, a vast majority of management personnel seem to see their role in industry as akin to that of a father in the traditional Korean family.

Then again, other evidence contradicts this claim. Traditional Korean familism is more like nepotism, engendering an attachment to lineage so tenacious that it often takes precedence over that to society or nation (Yi, 1983). Thus Korean corporate familism may not be a transformation of traditional familism, because the latter is too strong to be absorbed into Korean industrial organization. Unlike in Japan, traditional familism in Korea has tended to remain in its pure form, given that family groups own and manage most Korean enterprises (S. Kim, 1987). Loyalty to ownership or management in a family-based company is likely to supersede that of the company per se, often resulting in undue concern for the "safety and well-being of an owner upon bankruptcy of his company" (S. Kim, 1987, p. 240). S. Kim (1987) claims that employees who perceive their employers as father figures or guardians are actually few in number, and familial ties are generally considered more important than business relationships. He further notes that because the hierarchical nature of kinship takes precedence over the functional nature of work-related relationships in Korean industries, neither traditional familism nor paternalism has been transformed into industrial familism or neopaternalism in the Korean business community.

So two possible arguments exist, one borne out by an analysis of the empirical data found in this research, and one based on the more general assertions of a number of Korean critics. But the two apparently contradictory arguments do not necessarily negate each other; both are valid in their own right and merely describe two sides of the same coin. The transformation of values from the traditional family structure to the modern corporate organization is one aspect of a process that must also include the transformation of values into performance.

Titmuss (1968) emphasizes the importance of values in his definition of social policy, noting that social policy is all about social purposes and the choices among them. But, although values themselves are abstract and metaphysical, in the realm of applied science such as social work they reach their fullest potential in the form of action or practice.

The gap between belief and performance in the Korean business sector is too wide to be ignored. Actually, there is not much to indicate that the belief system of Korean management personnel is accompanied by performance. Empirical evidence suggests that the value orientation of the management is largely cognitive rather than behavioral; value differences have very little significant impact on the occupational welfare system in Korea. As shown in the case of paternalism and communalism, no correlation exists between the degree of commitment to a certain value and the magnitude of a welfare provision.

To conclude, the degree of transformation (whatever the process) is much less significant in the Korean business community than it is, say, in the case of Japan. Occupational welfare in Korea is still in its initial stages, a fact that, in turn, suggests that perhaps the next stage of transition is now taking place. Firm conclusions seem premature. A complete conceptual picture should include employee attitudes toward paternalism in the workplace. Therefore, it may be appropriate to speculate that traditional familism has been partially transformed into industrial familism in Korean society.

18

SOCIAL SUPPORT AS A MODERATOR OF THE RELATIONSHIP BETWEEN ALLOCENTRISM AND PSYCHOLOGICAL WELL-BEING

JAI B. P. SINHA
JYOTI VERMA

Triandis, Leung, Villareal, and Clark (1985) have proposed a parallel dimension of idiocentrism/allocentrism to take into account individual-level variations in individualism/collectivism. Although the two levels need to be examined separately, it is likely that a majority of people in collectivist cultures will be allocentrics and a majority in individualist cultures will be idiocentrics.

In earlier work, we showed that a sample of Indian adults perceived themselves to be allocentrics and believed that Indian people behave collectively (Sinha & Verma, 1987). Marriot (1976) has observed that Indians are so embedded in their predominantly primordial groups that they may be called "dividuals" rather than individuals. Within the group, the self-other boundary is blurred, allowing ideas and feelings to flow freely. Relationship is characterized by "an intense emotional connectedness and interdependence with a constant flow of affect and responsiveness between persons; by a strong mutual caring and dependence, with an intensely heightened asking and giving in an emotional atmosphere usually of affection and warmth, with full expectations for reciprocity" (Roland, 1988, p. 220). Not all Indians are allocentrics; however, those who score high

AUTHORS' NOTE: We would like to thank Professor Harry C. Triandis for commenting on an earlier draft of this chapter, Mr. S. Ahmad for computer analysis, Mr. J. Pandey for typing the manuscript, and A.N.S. Institute of Social Studies for providing facilities for research.

on allocentrism are likely to define themselves with reference to their in-groups. They prefer to be with others, depend on others, and seek out their in-groups' suggestions and help in making decisions. They attach greater importance to others' opinions, desires, and suggestions than to their own. When left alone, allocentrics are likely to feel lonely and sad, with little confidence in their own capacity to handle difficult problems. They have a fear of being separated from loved ones and a consequent preference to maintain relationships even at the cost of their own interests (Kakar, 1978). Roland (1988) observed a symbiotic mode of thinking in Indians (p. 196), who maintain radarlike sensitivity to each other (p. 155) and a disposition to live in emotionally and responsibly interdependent relationships (p. 60).

Allocentrics in the United States are reported to be low on anomie, alienation, and loneliness (Triandis, Bontempo, Villareal, Asai, & Lucca, 1988). They perceive receiving more social support of a better quality than do idiocentrics, and value cooperation, equality, and honesty. The relationship between allocentrism and mental health is probably mediated by the extent and quality of social support. Social support for an individual means that he or she believes that there are people who are willing and available to take pains in order to listen, support, and help him or her through difficulties. Social support acts as a buffer of life stresses (Cohen & Syme, 1985). Because one of the core attributes of allocentrics is the concern to maintain relationship (Sinha & Verma, 1987), allocentrics are likely to extend as well as expect social support.

The Indian conceptualization of mental health (*swath*) adds an emphasis on stability and balance (J. B. P. Sinha, 1982, 1985). A mentally healthy person is not carried away by too much joy or sorrow, too much optimism or pessimism, or euphoria or depression. He or she maintains a sense of detachment and focuses on doing his or her duties rather than being concerned about the outcomes. Such a person has a great deal of control over his or her feelings, ideas, and emotions. There is evidence that detached persons experience less stress as well as cope more effectively with whatever stress they experience (see, e.g., Naidu, 1991; Pandey, 1990). Kakar (1978) reports that an Indian believes that the world is a benign place and someone will always turn up to help should an exigency arise. Kakar (1982) has further observed that "Indian society is organized around the primacy of the therapeutic in the sense that Indians seem to emphasize protection and caring in their social (and political) relations" (p. 272).

In sum, Indian culture is postulated to be collectivist, with a majority of Indians being allocentrics. There exists a normative pressure to extend social support. Allocentrics in India, just as in the United States (Triandis et al., 1988), are expected to give and receive more social support than idiocentrics. However, it is unlikely that all allocentrics would receive high social support. Those who do are likely to have a sense of psychological well-being. Those who fail to receive social support will feel much more miserable than idiocentrics, who are less sensitive to social support. Thus the study reported on below aimed to test the following hypotheses:

1. Allocentrism and collectivism will be positively related.
2. Allocentrism will be positively correlated to the extent and quality of social support
3. In a condition of high social support, allocentrism and psychological well-being will be positively correlated.
4. Allocentrism and psychological well-being will be negatively correlated in a condition of low social support.

METHOD

The subjects for this study were 110 master of arts-level students, ages 20 to 23 years, from a university located in a city in the western part of India. Only 10 subjects were females.

Measures

Subjects responded to a questionnaire containing a number of measures for allocentrism, collectivism, social support, and psychological well-being. A multimethod approach was adopted for measuring allocentrism. It was reasoned that the facets of allocentrism may be differentially amenable to different methods. Four measures of allocentrism were used: embedded self, allocentric attitudes, a forced-choice preference measure, and a graphic scale.

The embedded self. Subjects were asked to write 20 sentences about themselves that were supposed to reflect the way allocentrics and idiocentrics define themselves. The details of this method and scoring are provided by Chan in Chapter 13 of this volume. The correlation between our ratings of the self-embedded scores and the proportion of group-related response was 72%.

Allocentric attitude. The respondents also rated themselves on 10 items drawn from a pool of items for cross-cultural studies (Triandis et al., 1986) and found suitable in the Indian setting (Sinha & Verma, 1987). The items measured subjects' emotional closeness with and dependence upon their families and friends on a 5-point scale, from *quite false* (1) to *quite true* (5). Of the 10 items, 7 were keyed toward allocentrism and the remaining 3 toward idiocentrism. The alpha coefficient for the scale was found to be .77.

Forced-choice preference measure. Subjects were asked to choose one of two alternatives on three items that asked: What does the subject prefer to do (a) during leisure hours—doing things alone or with friends? (b) while making a decision—making own decision or going by the opinion of friends? (c) when unannounced friends drop in while he or she is busy with some work—doing one's work or entertaining friends? Preference for friends was scored as 3 and for oneself as 1; if the subject failed to choose, the score of 2 was assigned. The alpha coefficient was .56.

Graphic scale of importance given to own versus others' desires, opinions, and behavior. Six items required subjects to indicate on a 5-inch graphic scale the importance they attached to their own and others' desires, opinions, and behavior. "Others" were defined as either friends or relatives. Thus the distance in inches from own to friends' or relatives' desires/opinions/ behavior provided six scores of importance attached to others reflecting subjects' cognition of the extent to which they tended to yield to the in-group members. The Cronbach's alpha coefficient was .63.

Social support. The measure of social support was derived from Sarason, Levine, Basham, and Sarason (1983). Subjects were provided with three situations: (a) having a difficult problem, (b) having a need to express one's inner thoughts to someone, and (c) being in serious trouble. They were asked to give, for each situation, (a) the initials of those they could approach for support, (b) the supporters' relationships with the subjects, and (c) the extent to which each of the supporters was available to listen with understanding and to help without caring for his or her own inconvenience or costs. The extent of help and support was obtained on a 5-point scale and constituted the *quality* of social support. The number of persons available provided a measure of the *degree* of social support. The support persons were categorized as (a) mother, (b) father, (c) spouse, (d) siblings, (e) members of the joint family (e.g., uncles, aunts, grandfather, grandmother), (f) relatives outside the family, and (g) friends.

Psychological well-being. Tellegen (1979) has developed a scale to measure psychological well-being that includes 24 items that are rated as true or false. A panel of five judges having master's degrees or Ph.D.s in psychology identified (with 80% agreement) 12 items that clearly measured cheerfulness (three items, with one negatively keyed), optimism (four items), and playfulness (five items). We then developed 15 items to measure self-control (four positive and four negative items), a sense of detachment (two positive and two negative items), and freedom from frustration, anxiety, and loneliness (three negatively worded items). We derived a composite score of psychological well-being by adding the scores of five dimensions (after reversing the score of negative items). The items were rated on a 5-point scale ranging from *quite false* (1) to *quite true* (5). The Cronbach's alpha for all subscales combined was .69.

Collectivism. We drew 11 items from the cultural collectivism scale we had used in earlier research (Sinha & Verma, 1987). The scale measured the extent to which subjects perceived *people in general* (not themselves) as behaving in collectivist fashion. Each item describes a normative behavior or practice of people in general, for example: "Old people live with their grown-up children." Subjects rated whether the behaviors and practices were prevalent on a 5-point scale. The range of scores was 11 to 55. The alpha coefficient was .81.

RESULTS

As there were only 10 female students in the sample, we did not analyze gender differences. A striking finding was the low level of allocentrism manifested by the subjects. On measures of allocentrism, the mean scores were lower than the midpoint, except for the embeddedness of self ($M = 2.00$, $SD = .35$): allocentric attitudes, $M = 1.28$, $SD = .45$; cultural collectivism, $M = 40.34$, $SD = 4.63$; preferences during leisure, $M = 1.38$, $SD = .49$; decision making, $M = 1.22$, $SD = .49$; preference for friends and relatives over work, $M = 1.14$, $SD = .34$; and importance given to friend's desires, $M = 1.40$, $SD = .90$; friend's opinions, $M = 1.65$, $SD = 1.20$; friend's behavior, $M = 1.74$, $SD = 1.16$; relative's desire, $M = 1.48$, $SD = 1.16$; relative's opinion, $M = 1.52$, $SD = 1.05$; and relative's behavior, $M = 1.64$, $SD = 1.11$. Both college students as well as adult males perceived people in general as behaving in collectivist fashion. However, the former rated themselves toward idiocentrism, whereas they rated the latter toward allocentrism.

The embeddedness of self was mildly correlated with allocentric attitude ($r = .20$), cultural collectivism ($r = .23$), and preference for spending leisure with friends ($r = .20$).

Allocentric attitude was correlated with the decision to follow friend's opinions ($r = .20$) and importance given to friend's opinions ($r = .20$), but not with cultural collectivism. Thus Hypothesis 2 was not confirmed. Preference of spending leisure with friends was correlated with seeking friend's opinions in decision making ($r = .22$), entertaining friends even at the cost of studying ($r = .23$), and yielding to friend's opinions ($r = .23$). Preference given to friends and relatives over work was correlated with importance given to friend's desires ($r = .23$), opinions ($r = .44$), and behavior ($r = .26$). Similarly, graphic ratings of the importance of friends' and relatives' desires, opinions, and behaviors over one's own were positively intercorrelated.

Statements made in response to the "who am I" test frequently referred to the immediate context and concerns, such as "I am a psychology student" and "I live in a hostel" (75.5%). Immediate concerns were reflected in statements such as "I want to be self-reliant" (65.5%), "I want a job" (59.1%), "I am dedicated to my education" (59.1%), and "I like art, culture, music, and sports" (46.4%). The most frequently occurring responses (83.6%) pertained to either having or desiring to have a sense of psychological well-being. The need for self-reliance seemed to spring from concern for the family (e.g., "I do not want to be a burden on the family," 41.8%).

The extent of social support and the number of persons extending social support was highly correlated ($r = .84$). Among the 77 coefficients of correlations between the 7 sources of social support and 11 indicators of allocentrism, only 3 reached even a weak level of statistical significance. Similarly, the number of persons from whom subjects received support did not correlate with their allocentric attitudes. Thus Hypothesis 2 was not confirmed.

In order to test the remaining two hypotheses, we divided subjects by median split into those receiving high social support ($N = 53$) and those receiving low social support ($N = 57$). The indicators of allocentrism and the indices of psychological well-being were correlated separately for the high support and low support conditions.

Subjects receiving low support did not see any significant association between allocentrism and psychological well-being. Embeddedness of self was correlated with optimism ($r = .29$), preference during leisure was correlated with playfulness ($r = .26$), and preference for friends and relatives over work was negatively correlated with playfulness ($r = -.38$) and with psychological well-being ($r = -.32$). Importance given to relative's opinions correlated with freedom from frustration ($r = .28$) and relative's behavior was correlated with optimism ($r = -.30$).

Allocentrics receiving high social support recorded higher level of psychological well-being on the indices of (a) freedom from frustration, loneliness, and anxiety, (b) cheerfulness, (c) optimism, and (d) playfulness (see Table 18.1). Self-control and a sense of detachment were unrelated to allocentrism (except three mildly significant coefficients).

DISCUSSION

The subjects in the present study were master's-level college students who were in their early 20s. They share with the adults we have sampled in earlier studies (Sinha & Verma, 1987; Verma, 1988) the view that Indians in general behave in a collectivist fashion. They differ, however, with respect to their own orientations. The adults reported themselves as inclined toward allocentrism, whereas the students perceived themselves as idiocentrics. Master's-level students in India are educated through Western literature and are exposed to mass media that present a glamorous picture of individualist lifestyles. Furthermore, master's-level students often are worried about their final examinations and job prospects. Both Western influences and immediate life concerns probably led the student subjects to express more idiocentric than allocentric orientation.

Allocentrism, however, was not altogether missing. The student subjects wanted to be self-reliant so that they would stop being a burden on their families. Indian parents support even their grown children until the sons get jobs and settle down and the daughters get married. The findings indicate that these subjects attach greater importance to their own desires, opinions, and behaviors than to those of their friends and relatives.

In our earlier work, family was shown to be the most important in-group in India (Sinha & Verma, 1987). The present study also shows that subjects received more social support from immediate family members (mother, father, and siblings) than from distant relatives. Their friends, however, were perceived to extend even more social support than family members ($F = 16.36$, $df = 6/554$, $p < .01$). It is interesting to note that the subjects did not yield to their friends' opinions, desires, and behavior, and yet perceived receiving a great deal of social support from their friends. Probably the peer group at this stage of life serves as the most salient in-group for social support but not necessarily for subordinating the individual's needs and goals.

Social support seems to be a part of the normative system of Indian society. People are expected to give and receive social support, irrespective of their allocentrism/idiocentrism. The findings in this study indeed show that the extent of social support is unrelated to allocentrism/idiocentrism. Under the condition of high social support, allocentrism was highly correlated with the overall sense of psychological well-being. Under the

Table 18.1 Coefficients of Correlations Between Allocentrism and Psychological Well-Being Under High Support Condition (N = 53)

Variables	Self-Control	Detachment	Freedom From Frustration, etc.	Cheerfulness	Optimism	Playfulness	Psychological Well-Being[a]
Embeddedness of self	.09	.21	.73**	.51**	.76**	.74**	.73**
Allocentric attitude	.14	.16	.49**	.44**	.60**	.55**	.57**
Preference during leisure: being alone (1) /with others (3)	.20	.04	.56**	.33**	.53**	.60**	.56**
Decision: own (1) /according to friends (3)	.26	.16	.54**	.46**	.59**	.56**	.60**
Preference for friends and relatives (3) over work (1)	.30*	.33*	.47**	.57**	.65**	.69**	.71**
Importance of							
friend's desires	-.01	.00	.34**	.27*	.31*	.27*	.28*
friend's opinions	.12	.12	.32*	.29*	.32*	.31*	.35**
friend's behavior	.20	.07	.26*	.34**	.32*	.32*	.36**
relative's desires	.08	.16	.42**	.34**	.34**	.36**	.39**
relative's opinions	-.07	.08	.48**	-.00	.17	.28*	.23*
relative's behavior	-.03	.15	.54**	.35**	.34**	.34**	.38**
Mean	3.28	2.34	6.89	5.55	13.38	17.34	48.87
SD	3.82	3.08	3.12	2.71	4.87	6.38	17.70

NOTE: a. Composite score.
*p < .01; **p < .05.

condition of low social support, there was virtually no relationship between allocentrism and psychological well-being.

The two measures of psychological well-being noted above, a sense of detachment and self-control, were found in this study to be unrelated to allocentrism. They probably constitute a different facet of psychological well-being. Two post hoc interpretations may be advanced to account for this finding. First, these two measures are parts of a psychospiritual conceptualization of an inner transformation of the self through which an Indian aspires to rise on the scale of spiritual merit. The transformation consists of (a) developing self-control over impulses and emotions and (b) cultivating a sense of detachment in performing social roles and duties. Both of these are parts of the private self of an Indian, whereas allocentrism pertains to the collective or public self. The private self of an Indian is guarded quite strictly, and may not be readily accessible even to a therapist (Roland, 1988). It is probable that subjects did not see the relevance of self-control and detachment to their allocentrism.

Second, inner transformation has been found to be related to the stages of life (J. B. P. Sinha, 1990b). In one study, the spiritual orientation of Indians was found to become more salient after the age of 50 (J. B. P. Sinha, 1989). The subjects in the present study were in their early 20s, and hence were not particularly sensitive to their need to cultivate a sense of self-control and detachment.

It may be concluded that allocentrics experience a sense of psychological well-being under conditions of high social support, especially with respect to those aspects of psychological well-being that pertain to the public or collective self.

19

COLLECTIVISM AND INDIVIDUALISM AS DIMENSIONS OF SOCIAL CHANGE

JANUSZ REYKOWSKI

One of the most significant historical events of recent years has been the sudden breakdown of the sociopolitical system in Eastern and Central Europe. The most dramatic changes took place in 1989, but they were the result of processes that matured over a long time. The changes can be described on different dimensions: economic, political, social, and even moral ones. There is also a psychological dimension; changes in sociopolitical systems have psychological antecedents and concomitants.

Looking at the changes in Eastern and Central Europe from a psychological perspective, one notices that the most salient characteristic is the move away from collectivist forms of societal organization and mentality toward individualist forms. Although this transformation is probably true of all of the socialist countries in the former Soviet Bloc, it is certainly true in Poland. Formerly, in Poland, the officially advocated concept of society was based on the assumption that the "socialist state" is the highest form of organization and the highest social value. Society was ideally depicted as one harmonious whole; everyone was expected to care for the state as a moral imperative. The state, in return, was obliged to care for everyone. The state's role and responsibilities were to ensure that all legitimate needs of its citizens were duly satisfied (i.e., full employment, free education, free health care, cheap housing, cheap or free vacations, and even guidance for the moral posture and ideological rectitude of all members of society).

The state's ability to meet all the needs of its citizens was, in fact, limited. Over the past 15 years, the Polish state's ability to provide services gradually deteriorated. At the same time, there was growing desire among the populace for emancipation; the idea of individual responsibility for one's own lot gained in popularity. Attempts at economic reform weakened the central planning and distribution of goods and services; the "command economy" was in retreat, and belief in the feasibility of market regulation grew. The state's role shrank and capitalist principles were on the ascent.

Once the socialist state had collapsed, the implementation of capitalist principles and ideals intensified. Capitalist ideology became very popular, and the concept of privatization gained growing acceptance. For example, in 1987, in a survey of 2,299 workers from state enterprises employing more than 500 workers, 36.6% of workers approved of allowing private capital to have access to medium-sized factories and 23.0% approved of access to large factories; 22.3% approved of private capital having access to banks in Poland (Centrum Badnia Opinii Spolecznej, 1989). In a 1989 survey, the respective figures rose to 68.6%, 40.6%, and 60.4%. At present, there is a very strong trend toward privatization of factories, stores, education, health care, mass media, and cultural institutions. Nevertheless, the transition has turned out to be extremely difficult.

What conclusions can we draw from these observations? Should we assume that the processes described above mean that the collectivist ideology and the collectivist mentality are decaying in Poland? Do they indicate the belated process of liquidation of the old and traditional forms of social life based on communal (collectivist) principles, a historical process that took place much earlier in the most advanced Western industrialized nations? Is it just one more proof that a collectivist society is not a viable entity? Looking for answers to such questions, we should first look more closely at the nature of individualist and collectivist mentalities.

INDIVIDUALISM AND COLLECTIVISM
AS PSYCHOLOGICAL CONCEPTS

In defining the concepts of individualism and collectivism, some authors tend to focus on the manifest level of psychological functioning, such as specific opinions, attitudes, and behavioral tendencies that cover such phenomena as "togetherness" versus isolation, dependency versus self-sufficiency, and cooperativeness versus competitiveness. Others consider deep-level processes—so-called implicit knowledge. They refer to assumptions that people make in their relations with their social worlds.

These assumptions have been well articulated by Hui and Triandis (1986), who postulate that the main difference between collectivism and individualism concerns the "basic unit of survival": For individualists, the basic unit is the self; for collectivists, it is a group or collectivity. In other

SOCIAL AND APPLIED ISSUES

words, from the individualist perspective the well-being of the self is the main criterion of adaptation; from the collectivist viewpoint it is the well-being of the group. All cognitive, attitudinal, and behavioral differences between collectivism and individualism stem from this fundamental difference in implicit assumptions about the social world. (For further discussion of this point, see, in this volume, Kim, Chapter 2; Triandis, Chapter 3; Kagitçibasi, Chapter 4; Schwartz, Chapter 7.)

The main implication of this difference concerns the relationship between an individual and a group and the interpretation of group norms. The norms of the group based on collectivist principles differ from individualist norms with respect to issues that are crucial for the existence of a group (e.g., distribution of power, resources, rights, and responsibilities). Legitimate power in individualist groups is based upon the principle of common agreement among independent individuals. In collectivist groups, the conviction that power is executed for the sake of group interests lends legitimacy to power holders. Access to resources in individualist groups is, in principle, regulated by the norm of equity. The distribution of resources is considered fair if each person's share depends on his or her output as defined by its market value. In collectivist groups, fair allocation implies that the needs of all the members of the group are taken into consideration; hence equality or need is, often, regarded as the major criterion of distributive justice (see Triandis, 1989).

The dispensation of human and political rights in individualist groups is based on the principle of individual freedom, whereas the principle of supremacy of rights of a group over the rights of an individual is valued by collectivist groups. The allotment of responsibilities in individualist groups is based on the assumption of self-directed and self-reliant individuals. In collectivist groups, there is a common responsibility of the group for the well-being and moral posture of each member, and each member feels responsible for his or her group (Triandis, 1989).

These differences have a common feature: Basic social relations in collectivist groups are founded on the normative principle that the well-being of the group should take priority over the well-being of an individual. Groups based on individualist principles do not espouse this normative principle; rather, they assume that each individual cares for his or her own well-being and cooperates with the group as long as it meets his or her own interests. Thus a collectivist orientation is associated with a lower need for autonomy, a higher need for affiliation (see Hui & Villareal, 1989), and a higher level of interdependence (Markus & Kitayama, 1991), whereas an individualist orientation is associated with a higher need for self-reliance (Triandis et al., 1986).

COGNITIVE MECHANISMS
OF INDIVIDUALIST AND COLLECTIVIST
ORIENTATIONS: THE ROLE
OF SELF-IDENTITY

There is a close link between individualist and collectivist orientations and assumptions on one hand and self-identity on the other (Reykowski, 1988). The process of self-identity formation involves the establishment of a conceptual relationship between an individual and his or her social surroundings. The formation of personal identity is based on two principal mechanisms: individuation and identification (Maslach, Stapp, & Santee, 1985). The development of a self-concept involves both a cognitive separation between self and not-self (separation from other social and physical beings) and identification with various parts of the outside (social) world (i.e., the recognition of one's essential sameness or close similarity with them). The processes of cognitive separation and recognition of similarity between the self and others are interconnected with analogous processes concerning perception of the social world.

Individuation and identification are the two opposing processes. *Individuation* leads to the development of an image of a (social) world as consisting of a number of separate objects (individuals). If applied to oneself, it contributes to the growing differentiation of "I/they." The process of *identification,* on the other hand, blurs the boundaries between "I" and "they" and fosters a conception of the self as similar or identical to others. Individuation leads to cognitive separation of a person from his or her environment and lays the groundwork for acquisition of the individualist orientation. Identification leads to the opposite outcome; it is a precondition for the development of the collectivist orientation. Because both processes are involved in the formation of a self-identity, self-identity contains two facets: personal identity (the effect of individuation) and social identity (the effect of identification). The concept of these two facets of identity has been elaborated within the theory of social identity theory (Tajfel, 1982).

It should be acknowledged that the two facets of self-identity develop unequally in different social settings. Some cultures foster individuation, whereas others foster identification. For example, according to Clifford Geertz, culture in Bali minimizes individuality: It "acts to strengthen the standardization . . . and generalization implicit in the relation between individuals" (quoted in Smith, 1978, p. 1056). Contemporary industrial and Western societies put great emphasis on differentiation and individuation (Hogan, 1975).

There can also be major differences within a single society. These are apparently associated with class-related differences in living conditions and job requirements. The job requirements of blue-collar workers, for example, tend to foster conformity, whereas those of professionals foster self-directedness (Kohn, 1969; Kohn & Slomczynski, 1990). There is an apparent similarity of these two value orientations to individualism and collectivism.

This line of reasoning has important implications. First, we may say that because in each person's mind both facets of identity (personal and social) are present, all people have the potential for both individualist and collectivist orientations. This proposition can be buttressed by the fact that individualism and collectivism are orthogonal factors (Triandis et al., 1986). The second implication consists of the proposition that factors that activate one particular facet of identity (personal or social) tend to evoke a particular orientation. A social identity is activated by conditions that make salient a subject's participation in a referent group. There are a number of such factors (see Breckler & Greenwald, 1986; Brown & Turner, 1981; Tajfel, 1978). It has also been shown that the salience of group membership influences the processing efficiency of group-related information (Gurin & Markus, 1988).

On the other side, according to McGuire's (1984) "distinctiveness postulate," factors that accentuate differences between an individual and his or her surroundings are likely to activate individuation. Triandis (1989) has similarly posited that different aspects of the self (i.e., private, public, and collective self) could be sampled with different probabilities in different contexts. Trafimow, Triandis, and Goto (1991) found that introduction of collective prompts in a stimulus situation increased the importance of the collective self.

The fact that both individualist and collectivist assumptions can coexist in a human mind does not deny that individuals and cultures differ widely in this respect. The differences among people can be explained as a result of unequal availability of the two facets of self-identity. People tend to behave, predominantly, in individualist ways if availability of the personal identity is high, and vice versa. It is postulated that the availability of personal versus social identity is related to the degree of individuation. As far as differences among cultures are concerned, Triandis (1989) concludes that "aspects of the self . . . are differentially sampled in different cultures" (p. 517).

Because people's normative beliefs and psychological functioning depend on the kind of self-identity they engage (or sample) in a given situation, there is no one-to-one correspondence between the manifest, attitudinal level and the level of implicit assumptions about the social world. In other words, such assumptions do not exert exclusive control over attitudes, opinions, and behavioral acts. There are other factors (such as modeling, social pressure, and concern about feasibility) that can play important roles. This means that in many instances there might be large discrepancies between deep and manifest levels of functioning.

As an implication of the postulate concerning the links between self-identity and I/C, I posit that three different kinds of change are theoretically possible. The first consists of a temporary shift in attitudes and opinions influenced by a number of situational factors. Some of them may have direct impacts on attitudes (e.g., contacts with attractive people who espouse particular opinions); others could act indirectly as self-identity-related cues (e.g., the conditions that make salient a personal identity tend to evoke individualist opinions and attitudes). As the level of individuation remains the same, such a shift can be rather superficial, and people may make inconsistent evaluations of social phenomena. Another kind of change, one that might endure, may result from an increase in individuation. This type of change could appear in a society on a massive scale if there are major changes in socialization practices associated with changes in education, types of work, or organization of social life. An increase in individuation should foster an individualist outlook. The third kind of change becomes possible as a result of a qualitative reorganization of cognitive structures.

Drawing on Piaget's (see Flavell, 1963) and Kohlberg's (1981) works, it is postulated that the structural reorganization in cognition may lead to formation of a higher-order cognitive organization, representing a network of social relations; an individuated self-concept may be included in such an organization as a part of it. This appears to be a precondition for coordination of perspectives and interests of different social objects. For example, a person can develop a concept of justice that engenders attitudes of greater subjective importance than the ones originating from the self. In other words, individuation is not the final stage of development of self-identity. Taking the framework described above as the point of departure of the analysis, I will now examine the meaning of the social changes developing in Poland.

INDIVIDUALISM AND COLLECTIVISM IN POLISH SOCIETY

As far as opinions and attitudes are concerned, in the 1980s there was a major shift from collectivism to individualism in Poland. There were a number of indications of this shift. One was the attitude toward the principle of income limitation, which received diminishing approval. Approval of limits on income makes sense if one looks at society as a collective whole rather than as an aggregation of independent individuals struggling for their own benefits. In 1980, 71% of the Polish population expressed the opinion that the highest incomes should be limited. In 1984 only 30% expressed such an opinion, and in 1988 the figure had declined to 27%. Another indication was the reduction of support for the principle of full employment (compatible with the collectivist assumption that society is responsible for the fate of individuals); it was supported by 51% in 1980, and only 25% in 1984 and 1988. The same can be said about public opinion that expenditures for support of the poor should be reduced (apparently an individualist claim—let everyone care for him- or herself): This notion was supported by 15% of respondents in 1984, but by 24% in 1988 (Kolarska, 1989). These data seem to indicate that in the 1980s the collectivist concept of society was diminishing in popularity in Poland.

This conclusion, however, appears less certain if we take into consideration some deeply rooted normative beliefs. To describe them, I will refer to a study my colleagues and I conducted in the late spring of 1988. It was based on a representative sample of 2,000 Polish adults. The subjects were individually interviewed by means of a closed-ended questionnaire. The main findings I will discuss here are based on factor analyses of 15 empirically derived scales. The scales assessed subjects' normative beliefs about distribution of resources, rights, obligations, and power in different social settings (such as family, state, and workplace). In addition, there were also scales that tapped into parental values.

A three-factor solution was identified through quartimax rotation. Factor 1 (accounting for 16% of the variance) contained the belief that an individual should play an active role in society: He or she should take an enterprising attitude in life and strive to be independent and self-directed in family relationships, in the workplace, and in society at large. Factor 2 (explaining 14% of the variance) was composed of the beliefs that an individual should work hard, take a positive attitude toward other people, have modest aspirations, and emphasize harmony in social groups. Factor 3 (explaining 11% of the variance) contained normative beliefs of two kinds: that individuals should strive to maximize their own advantage, trying to get for themselves as much as possible, and that authorities in the family and in the state are obliged to take care of each individual. The scales that loaded on these factors and their factor loadings are listed in Table 19.1.

The three factors differed with respect to their association with political values and opinions. Factor 1 was associated with democratic values ($r = .49$) and rejection of the existing "monocentric" political system. Both Factors

Table 19.1 Description of the Three-Factor Solution

Constructs	Factor 1	Factor 2	Factor 3
1. Parental values: industry	.68		
2. Agency in sociopolitical domains	.65		
3. Industry in workplace	.62		
4. Agency in local affairs	.55		
5. Agency in family circle	.45		
6. Parental values: prosocial attitudes	.40	.64	
7. Parental values: minimalist attitudes		.60	.46
8. Values of hard work		.57	
9. Normative individualism		−.51	
10. Agency in local affairs		−.45	
11. Criteria for job selection: light work			.74
12. Parental values: material competitiveness			.69
13. Demanding attitude toward state			.50
14. Expectation of help from parents			.42

NOTE: Examples of scale items follow. *Item 1:* "Would you like that your child, when grown up, is full of initiative and industry?" *Item 2:* "Which of these two opinions is closer to your own: (a) The political system that exists in our country should be determined by all of its citizens (by representatives), or (b) The political system should be determined by the experienced political leaders." *Item 4:* "People living in a given region should have the right to prevent construction of an object that is unsafe for the environment" versus "It is the prerogative of local authorities to decide what objects are necessary for the economical advancement of the region." *Item 5:* "When there is a difference of opinion in the family it is better that every member stays with his or her own" versus "It is better that members accept the majority opinion." *Item 6:* "I would like that my child, when grown up, is able to get involved in other people's problems and help them." *Item 7:* "I would that my child, when grown up, is able to accept what he or she has" (do not expect too much). *Item 8:* "Whose income should be much higher than others? Those who work hard (mostly in the physical sense)." *Item 9:* "Society would function better if everybody took care of his or her own business" versus "Society would function better if everyone cared for other people's well-being." *Item 11:* "What would you regard as important criteria for job selection? It is easy and does not require too much work." *Item 12:* "I would like that my child, when grown up, is able to get for him- or herself more than others." *Item 13:* "The well-organized state should guarantee for every family housing conditions according to its needs." The response format for items 1, 6, 7, 8, 9, 11, 12, and 13 is from *definitely yes* to *definitely no*; for 2, 3, and 4, *I fully agree with the first opinion* to *I fully agree with the second opinion*. All are based on 5-point scales.

2 and 3 had almost no correlation with the scale of democratic values ($r = .06$ and $.08$, respectively). Factor 2 was associated with approval for the existing system. Factor 3 was correlated with criticism of it, but not with total rejection of the existing system.

Factor 1 is labeled Individualist Orientation (IO). The remaining two factors have collectivist overtones. Factor 2 suggests a normative orientation consisting of modest aspirations and preoccupation with good relations within society, labeled Social Harmony Orientation (SHO). Factor 3, labeled Receptive Collectivist Orientation (RCO), represents a mixture of assertion of selfishness with a belief that one is entitled to protection and care by the authorities of one's own social groups (small and large).

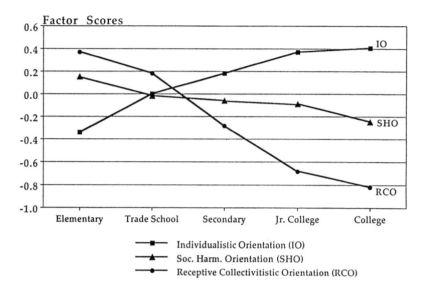

Figure 19.1. Educational Level and Orientations: Means of Factor Scores

Although Factor 3 is based on collectivist assumptions, it is a specific kind of collectivism; it is focuses on responsibilities of the collective toward the individual.

Because the three factors are orthogonal, they can coexist in a single mind. They are, however, unequally distributed in the various strata of Polish society (see Figure 19.1 and Table 19.2). Results presented in Table 19.2 show a strong association between IO and levels of education: the higher the level of education, the higher the IO. There is an opposite trend in the case of RCO: The lower the education level, the more probable is this orientation. No clear relationship was found between SHO and education. Table 19.2 also shows a consistent relationship between IO and occupation. IO is more likely among self-employed craftsmen, professionals, managers, and other white-collar workers, but quite unlikely among unskilled workers, peasants, and people with low-skilled white-collar jobs.

The Social Harmony Orientation was more likely among individuals holding jobs strongly connected with the regime (high-level managers, military officers), but also among some less-educated strata of the society. The Receptive Collectivist Orientation was high among peasants and unskilled workers. It was most commonly rejected among the well educated.

The most significant result is the relationship between education and the normative orientations. Other studies have similarly shown a system-

Table 19.2 Sociopolitical Orientations of People Belonging to Different Social
Categories: Means of Factor Scores

Orientations	Factor 1 Democratic (IO)	Factor 2 Social Harmony (SHO)	Factor 3 Receptive Collectivism (RCO)
Education:			
elementary	−.33	.14	.37
trade school	.00	−.02	.17
secondary	.19	−.06	−.28
junior college	.38	−.08	−.68
college	.41	−.24	−.82
Profession:			
manager	.28	.25	−1.12
professional	.43	−.10	−.78
white-collar			
worker	.24	−.10	−.22
skilled worker	.06	−.07	.06
unskilled worker	−.36	.16	.23
peasant	−.21	.06	.38
craftsman	.61	−.50	−.24
military officer	.20	.21	−1.00
Sex:			
male	.08	.00	−.11
female	−.08	.00	.10

atic relationship between education and value orientations; higher levels
of education tend to be associated with higher acceptance of self-direction
(Alwin, 1989). This result has important bearing on the explanation of the
social change in Poland. In the past 40 years, the educational level of the
Polish population has undergone major change. In 1945, there were about
80,000 people in Poland with a college education and 300,000-400,000
with a high school education. In the early 1980s, the respective figures were
1.5 million and 5.5 million. The country's population increased about
150% over this time period, and the educated class grew more than 1,500%.
Noting the relationship between education and normative orientations,
one may anticipate an increase in aspirations, attitudes, and normative
beliefs connected with the individualist orientation.

Should we conclude that the apparent increase in the degree of individualism of the Polish people is a consequence of increased educational
levels? This seems to be true. But we should note that the level of individualism is different when social attitudes and normative beliefs are taken
into consideration. On the one hand, data indicate that a large proportion
of Polish society tends to express individualist attitudes in relation to many

social issues (in fact, on some of them a majority). On the other, as far as normative beliefs are concerned, many people seem to adhere to collectivist views—the individualist orientation is expressed by a minority of the population (i.e., the better-educated strata of the society).

Moreover, the dynamics of changes in attitudes and opinions do not parallel the dynamics of changes in social structure. For example, although the changes in the social structure developed over the entire 45-year postwar period, a rapid increase in individualist attitudes appeared during the 1980s. There seem to be other factors at work here. First, we should take into account that attitudes and opinions, like all other elements of individuals' psychological makeup, are modified by social influences. According to social impact theory (Latané, 1981; Nowak, Szamrej, & Latané, 1990), changes in opinions and attitudes will expand at an accelerated pace as the number and importance of the sources of impact increase. In other words, we may expect that the greater the number of people espousing an individualist orientation and the higher their social position, the faster will be the dissemination of individualist beliefs. Thus, as the educated class (the bearer of the individualist beliefs) increases in size and importance, the attitudes that it engenders have a greater chance to be conveyed to other groups.

There is another factor that could contribute to the fast increase in popularity of individualist attitudes and opinions, namely bankruptcy of the so-called command economy based on central planning and central distribution of major goods. In the protracted crisis, many people lost their faith in the feasibility of a collectivist organization of society; more and more of them looked for another form that would, supposedly, better suit their social needs. Many of them came to the conclusion that free enterprise and free competition are the proper remedies for the Polish economy. This type of thinking paved the way for the adoption of an individualist perspective.

It was not only disillusionment with the collectivist state that fostered the individualist orientation. The objective situation had changed: The protective state was falling down and the market economy was on the rise. People faced a completely different reality: They had to learn that they must take care of themselves, because there was no longer a viable larger collective that could care for them. We may conclude that the reorientation toward individualism that can be observed in Poland seems to be the result of changes in educational structure, social impact, and citizens' experience of the collectivist state's failures. The effect of the reorientation has different meanings for different people. In some people it is a result of more enduring changes of their self-identity, but in others it seems to have only superficial sources.

DISCREPANCIES AMONG
DIFFERENT LEVELS OF FUNCTIONING

The above analysis suggests that there is a discrepancy between the manifest level of popular attitudes and the deep level of implicit normative assumptions. In other words, the data seem to indicate that individualist opinions and attitudes can be "superimposed" on collectivist normative beliefs. Additional data from a Polish-German longitudinal study of the social development of youth seem to support this line of thinking.

The Polish-German study (originated by R. Silbereisen) was conducted in collaboration with the Technische Universität in Berlin (former West Berlin). A sample of Polish adolescents from Warsaw and German adolescents from former West Berlin, from ages 11 to 18 years, participated in the study between 1986 and 1989. The data that are of particular relevance for the present topic come from the program dealing with the values of adolescents carried out by Smolenska and her colleagues (Smolenska & Fraczek, 1987; Smolenska & Wieczorkowska, 1990).

One of their measures concerned evaluative standards: Subjects were asked to indicate what criteria they might consider when making important decisions, such as choice of profession. Smolenska and her colleagues found that in younger groups there were striking differences between the two countries. From the list of 13 criteria of choice, the German adolescents tended to adopt these that were related to their own individual interests, but the Polish adolescents declared that they would also consider the interests of other people. The German adolescents manifested, rather clearly, an individualist orientation ("My fate is my business only"), but the Polish adolescents had collectivist inclinations ("In deciding my fate I must take into account other people's well-being").

Between the ages of 14 and 17, the responses of the German sample did not alter much. In the Polish adolescents (especially among boys), however, there was a substantial increase in importance of egocentric (individualist) criteria (see Figures 19.2 and 19.3). Smolenska and her colleagues also found in the Polish sample that there was a marked increase in the importance of such values as freedom, achievement, and money, similar to the level that was found for Germans adolescents. By the age of 17, both groups manifested similar patterns of values. These results indicate that the socializing conditions in Poland in the late 1980s fostered an individualist orientation. In the Polish sample, this individualist orientation was more pronounced in older groups (i.e., it increased with age). In the German sample, the indices of an individualist orientation appeared at earlier ages.

Additional data, however, contradict the thesis about the increase in individualism of Polish adolescents. Schonpflug and Jansen (in press),

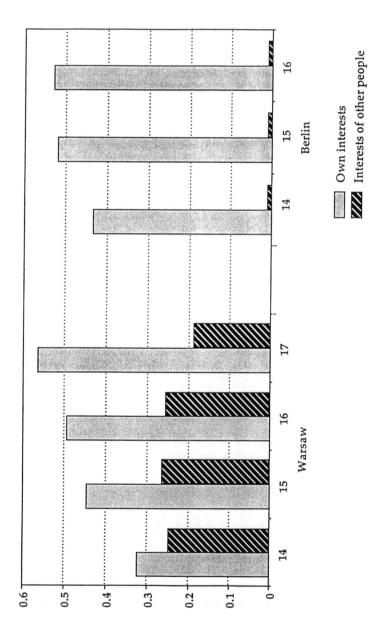

Figure 19.2. Evaluative Standards: Warsaw and Berlin, Boys Ages 14–16

SOURCE: Smolenska and Wieczorkowska (1990).

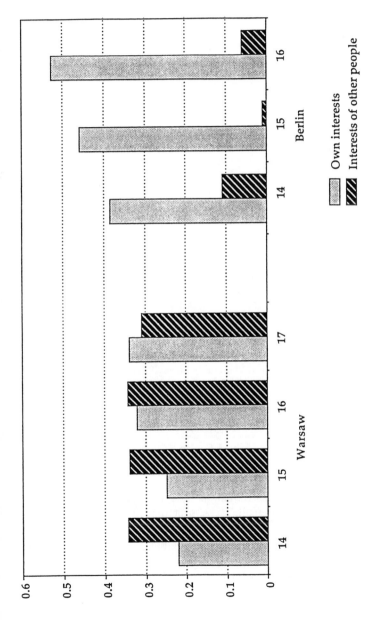

Figure 19.3. Evaluative Standards: Warsaw and Berlin, Girls Ages 14-16

SOURCE: Smolenska and Wieczorkowska (1990).

analyzing another part of the data from the German-Polish longitudinal study, found important differences in coping strategies between the two samples. When German youngsters encountered problems (such as finding a partner, getting the approval of peers, or making a choice of specialization at school), they adopted active coping strategies and relied on themselves. In contrast, the Polish adolescents stated that they would rely on their parents for help, much more than did the German adolescents. Incidentally, Turkish adolescents living in Germany used coping strategies that were in between those used by the Polish and German samples.

Let me stress this point: As far as values and criteria of choice (standards of evaluation) were concerned (i.e., in the measures that were close to attitudinal level), the Polish adolescents showed an increase in individualist orientation with age. When they encountered minor difficulties, however, they turned to their families as the main source of support instead of relying on themselves. This lack of self-reliance reveals deep-seated beliefs about the responsibility of one's group for one's fate, a reaction that is in apparent contradiction with the individualist posture demonstrated in other contexts. It appears that the individualist orientation of these Polish adolescents is not well consolidated (as reflected in their ambivalent attitudes). This ambivalence cannot be dismissed as a mere developmental phenomenon that will disappear with age, because it was not observed among the German subjects.

The above-reported results reflect confusion that exists in the society at large, where both individualist and collectivist tendencies seem to be present. Should we conclude that this confusion is simply a reflection of the transition period, and that the next inevitable stage of Polish society is simply a "triumph" of individualism? Although such an outcome is quite possible, there are still some unresolved issues that warrant caution in drawing such a conclusion.

UNCERTAINTIES CONCERNING FUTURE DEVELOPMENT

In 1989, the Solidarity movement took over the government in Poland and initiated a series of dramatic transformations in the entire system (in political, economic, and social institutions). The enormous difficulties of this task were fairly obvious from the beginning. Much less obvious was the fact that the Solidarity movement itself was heterogeneous with respect to ideas about how society should be organized. There were at least two major factions. The first, composed primarily of the intelligentsia and skilled workers, was oriented toward a free, open society with a heavy emphasis on democratic values. Individualist beliefs seem to prevail within this group: Free markets, free enterprise, self-reliance, and fast, unlimited privatization were regarded as the preconditions of prosperity for all. The second faction of the movement, comprising less-educated workers and peasants, was deeply disappointed with the economic performance of the crisis-ridden old regime. These people felt that their legitimate needs had not been satisfied and hoped for new opportunities. They tended to prefer a form of collectivist society that would provide them with protection. As a matter of fact, the ideology of the Solidarity movement from its very inception had strong collectivist overtones: The solidarity of the people was one of its top values.

The heterogeneity of the Solidarity movement was not apparent during its struggle against a common enemy, the communist regime. It surfaced after the enemy was defeated. It became a source of a serious conflict within the movement and, in fact, in the political system as a whole.

What could be a possible outcome of this conflict? In responding to this question, I leave aside its political and economic concomitants to focus instead on the issue of collectivism and individualism. We might consider three different paths of further transformation in Polish society. One possible direction of change is an expansion of individualism and the development of social institutions based on individualist assumptions. After the long dominance of the collectivist ideology, there is a profound shift toward the individualist direction. The probable growth of a middle class, resulting from reinforcement of a market economy, should contribute to this process.

Another possibility is a partial revival of collectivist sentiments. As indicated above, large social groups in Poland harbor collectivist beliefs and are not fully converted to the idea of a society composed of free, independent, and self-sufficient individuals. The hardship of everyday life and the vivid social consequences of a transition to "efficient capitalism" might induce a wave of reaction against the idea of an individualist society. In fact, many people seem to be having second thoughts about the feasibility of freedom without protection. This possibility should be regarded as real, but it does not necessarily mean that a "collectivist reaction" has much chance of succeeding in the long run.

There is still another possibility that we might consider: the emergence of an orientation that is neither collectivist nor individualist in a strict sense. It can develop as a result of individuation and, at the same time, formation of a concept of interdependence among people,[1] or, as it is described by Staub (1990), formation of relational self. Such an orientation can be conducive to prosocial attitudes and motives. There are some data available that support this contention. Jarymowicz and her colleagues found that individuation and well-defined boundaries between self and others are not a hindrance to prosocial involvement; in fact, people with high and low levels of individuation do not differ with respect to the strength of the involvement, they differ in motivation: Low-individuated people tend to be motivated, first of all, by normative considerations (e.g., they help because they have internalized the group norms related to helping), whereas high-individuated people are likely to be motivated by genuine concern for others (Jarymowicz, 1988, 1989). I might add that individuation is not a sufficient condition of genuine concern for others (Reykowski, 1982).

The thesis that individualism can take a form that fosters prosocial orientation should not be confused with "ensembled individualism" as described by Sampson (1988); this concept refers to lack of boundaries between self and nonself. I propose, instead, that individuation can be an important precondition in the development of a specific form of bonds between an individual and his or her social surroundings. People who develop clear boundaries between the "self" and "we" are able to identify with larger social wholes; they are not limited by the close boundaries of their in-group.

The idea that there may exist an orientation that can transcend the opposition between individualism and collectivism has been formulated by other authors. Oyama (1990), for example, has recently pointed out that the opposition of individualism and collectivism misses an important category of human values. She proposes a threefold classification: In addition to individualist and collectivist orientations, she introduces the universalist orientation, which she describes as "the relative priority that a person gives to general human happiness."

The likelihood that a universalist orientation will develop among a large part of society is very remote. The more probable course of events is a protracted conflict between individualism and collectivism. Such conflict can, under certain conditions, be conducive to the discovery of integrative solutions, new orientations that might transcend both individualism and collectivism. What are the necessary conditions? Seeking an answer to this question could be a challenging task for social scientists.

NOTE

1. Tomaszewski (personal communication) has suggested the concept of "interdependent individualism." The concept of interdependence is also discussed by Markus and Kitayama (1991).

REFERENCES

Adamopoulos, J., & Bontempo, R. (1986). Diachronic universals in interpersonal structures. *Journal of Cross-Cultural Psychology, 17,* 169-189.

Adelman, I., & Morris, C. T. (1967). *Society, politics and economic development: A quantitative approach.* Baltimore: Johns Hopkins University Press.

Adler, P. S. (1975). The transitional experience: An alternative view of culture shock. *Journal of Humanistic Psychology, 15,* 13-23.

Agarwal, R., & Misra, G. (1986). A factor analytic study of achievement goals and means: An Indian view. *International Journal of Psychology, 21,* 717-731.

Alcock, J. (1975). Motivation in an asymmetric bargaining situation: A cross-cultural study. *International Journal of Psychology, 10,* 69-81.

Allport, F. H. (1924). *Social psychology.* Boston: Houghton Mifflin.

Allport, G. W. (1943). The ego in contemporary psychology. *Psychological Review, 50,* 451-478.

Allport, G. W. (1968). The historical background of modern social psychology. In G. Lindzey & E. Aronson (Eds.), *Handbook of social psychology* (2nd ed., Vol. 1, pp. 1-80). Reading, MA: Addison-Wesley.

Alwin, D (1989). Social stratification, conditions of work, and parental socialization values. In N. Eisenberg, J. Reykowski, & E. Staub (Eds.), *Social and moral values.* Hillsdale, NJ: Lawrence Erlbaum.

Amir, Y., & Sharon, I. (1987). Are social psychological laws cross-culturally valid? *Journal of Cross-Cultural Psychology, 18,* 383-470.

Angyal, A. (1951). A theoretical model for personality studies. *Journal of Personality, 20,* 131-142.

Araki, H. (1973). *Nihonjin no koudou youshiki* [Behavioral style of the Japanese]. Tokyo: Kodansha. (in Japanese)

Azuma, H. (1986). Why study child development in Japan? In H. Stevenson, H. Azuma, & K. Hakuta (Eds.), *Child development and education in Japan* (pp. 3-12). New York: W. H. Freeman.

Bakan, D. (1966). *The duality of human existence.* Chicago: Rand McNally.

Bakan, D. (1968). *Disease, pain, and sacrifice.* Chicago: University of Chicago Press.

Bandura, A. (1982). Self efficacy mechanism in human agency. *American Psychologist, 37,* 122-147.

Barry, H., Child, I. L., & Bacon, M. K. (1959). Relations of child training to subsistence economy. *American Anthropologist, 61,* 51-63.

Basham, A. L. (1971). *The wonder that was India.* Calcutta: Rupa.

Baumeister, R. (1986). *Public self and private self.* New York: Springer.

Befu, H. (1986). The social and cultural background of child development in Japan and the United States. In H. Stevenson, H. Azuma, & K. Hakuta (Eds.), *Child development and education in Japan* (pp. 13-27). New York: W. H. Freeman.

Bellah, R. N., Madsen, R., Sullivan, W. M., Swidler, A., & Tipton, S. M. (1985). *Habits of the heart: Individualism and commitment in American life.* Berkeley: University of California Press.

Bendix, R. (1967). Tradition and modernity reconsidered. *Comparative Studies in Society and History, 9,* 292-346.

Benjamin, L. T., Jr., & Lawman, K. D. (Eds.). (1981). *Activities handbook for the teaching of psychology.* Washington, DC: American Psychological Association.

Bennet, R. W., & Iwao, M. (1963). *Paternalism in the Japanese economy.* Minneapolis: University of Minnesota Press.

Berger, P. L. (1983). *Secularity: West and East—cultural identity and modernization in Asian countries.* Paper presented at Kokugakuin University Centennial Symposium.

Berger, P. L., & Hsiao, M. H. H. (Eds.). (1988). *In search of an East Asian development model.* New Brunswick, NJ: Transaction.

Berlin, I. (1967). Two concepts of liberty. In A. Quinton (Ed.), *Political philosophy.* Oxford: Oxford University Press.

Berman, J. J., Murphy-Berman, V., & Singh, P. (1985). Cross-cultural similarities and differences in perceptions of fairness. *Journal of Cross-Cultural Psychology, 16,* 55-67.

Berry, J. W. (1966). Temne and Eskimo perceptual skills. *International Journal of Psychology, 1,* 207-229.

Berry, J. W. (1967). Independence and conformity in subsistence-level societies. *Journal of Personality and Social Psychology, 7,* 415-418.

Berry, J. W. (1975). An ecological approach to cross-cultural psychology. *Nederlands Tijdschrift voor de Psychologie, 30,* 51-84.

Berry, J. W. (1976). *Human ecology and cognitive style: Comparative studies in cultural and psychological adaptation.* New York: Halsted.

Berry, J. W. (1979). A cultural ecology of social behavior. In L. Berkowitz (Ed.), *Advances in experimental social psychology* (Vol. 12, pp. 177-207). New York: Academic Press.

Berry, J. W. (1980). Social and cultural change. In H. C. Triandis & R. W. Brislin (Eds.), *Handbook of cross-cultural psychology: Vol. 5. Social psychology* (pp. 211-280). Boston: Allyn & Bacon.

Berry, J. W. (1991). Understanding and managing multiculturalism: Some possible implications of research in Canada. *Psychology and Developing Societies, 3,* 17-49.

Berry, J. W., & Annis, R. C. (1974). Acculturative stress: The role of ecology, culture and differentiation. *Journal of Cross-Cultural Psychology, 5,* 382-406.

Berry, J. W., Bennett, J. A., & Denny, J. P. (1990). *Ecology, culture and cognitive processing.* Unpublished manuscript, Queen's University, Ontario, Canada.

Berry, J. W., Kim, U., Minde, T., & Mok, D. (1987). Comparative studies of acculturative stress. *International Migration Review, 31,* 491-511.

Berry, J. W., Poortinga, Y. H., Segall, M. H., & Dasen, P. R. (1992). *Cross-cultural psychology: Research and applications.* New York: Cambridge University Press.

Berry, J. W., Van de Koppel, J. M. H., Senechal, C., Annis, R. C., Bahuchet, S., Cavalli-Sforza, L. L., & Witkin, H. A. (1986). *On the edge of the forest: Cultural adaptation and cognitive development in Central Africa.* Lisse, Netherlands: Swets & Zeitlinger.

Béteille, A. (Ed.). (1977). *Inequality among men.* Oxford: Basil Blackwell.

Billings, D. K., & Majors, F. (1989). Individualism and group orientation: Contrasting personalities in Melanesian cultures. In D. Keats & L. Mann (Eds.), *Heterogeneity in cross-cultural psychology*. Lisse, Netherlands: Swets & Zeitlinger.

Blumenthal, E. P. (1976). *Models in Chinese moral education: Perspectives from children's books*. (University Microfilms No. 77-7876)

Bochner, S. (Ed.). (1981). *The mediating person: Bridges between cultures*. Cambridge, MA: Shenkman.

Boldt, E. D., & Roberts, L. (1979). Structural tightness and social conformity: A methodological note with theoretical implications. *Journal of Cross-Cultural Psychology, 10,* 221-230.

Bond, M. H. (Ed.). (1986). *The psychology of the Chinese people*. Hong Kong: Oxford University Press.

Bond, M. H. (1988). Finding universal dimensions of individual variation in multicultural studies of value: The Rokeach and Chinese Value Surveys. *Journal of Personality and Social Psychology, 55,* 1009-1015.

Bond, M. H. (1991). Chinese values and health: A cultural-level examination. *Psychology and Health, 5,* 137-152.

Bond, M. H. (1992). The process of enhancing cross-cultural competence in Hong Kong organizations. *International Journal of Intercultural Relations, 16,* 395-412.

Bond, M. H., & Forgas, J. P. (1984). Linking person perception to behavior intention across cultures: The role of cultural collectivism. *Journal of Cross-Cultural Psychology, 15,* 337-352.

Bond, M. H., Hewstone, M., Wan, K. C., & Chiu, C. K. (1984). Group-serving attributions across intergroup contexts: Cultural differences in the explanation of sex-typed behaviours. *European Journal of Social Psychology, 15,* 435-451.

Bond, M. H., Leung, K., & Schwartz, S. (1992). Explaining choices in procedural and distributive justice across cultures. *International Journal of Psychology, 27,* 211-225.

Bond, M. H., Leung, K., & Wan, K. C. (1982). How does cultural collectivism operate? The impact of task and maintenance contributions on reward distribution. *Journal of Cross-Cultural Psychology, 13,* 186-200.

Bond, M. H., Leung, K., Wan, K. C., & Giacalone, R. A. (1985). How are responses to verbal insult related to cultural collectivism and power distance? *Journal of Cross-Cultural Psychology, 16,* 111-127.

Bond, M. H., Nakazato, H., & Shiraishi, D. (1975). Universality and distinctiveness in dimensions of Japanese person perception. *Journal of Cross-Cultural Psychology, 6,* 346-357.

Bond, M. H., & Pang, M. K. (1991). Trusting to the Tao: Chinese values and the re-centering of psychology. *Bulletin of the Hong Kong Psychological Society, 26/27,* 5-27.

Bontempo, R. N., & Rivero, J. C. (1990). *Cultural variation in cognition: The role of self-concept and the attitude-behavior link*. Unpublished manuscript.

Bosland, N. (1985). *The cross-cultural equivalence of the power distance-, uncertainty avoidance-, individualism-, and masculinity-measurement scales* (Working paper 85-2). Maastricht, Netherlands: Institute for Research on Intercultural Cooperation.

Breckler, S. J., & Greenwald, A. G. (1986). Motivational facets of the self. In R. M. Sorrentino & E. T. Higgins (Eds.), *Handbook of motivation and cognition*. New York: Guilford.

Brinberg, D., & McGrath, J. E. (1985). *Validity and the research process*. Beverly Hills, CA: Sage.

Brislin, R. W. (Ed.). (1990). *Applied cross-cultural psychology*. Newbury Park, CA: Sage.

Brislin, R. W., Lonner, W. J., & Thorndike, R. M. (1973). *Cross-cultural research methods*. New York: John Wiley.

Brodbeck, M. (1976). Methodological individualism: Definition and reduction. In J. O'Neill (Ed.), *Modes of individualism and collectivism.* London: Heinemann.

Brown, H. P. (1990). The counter revolution of our time. *Industrial Relations, 29,* 1-15.

Brown, R. (1986). *Social psychology* (2nd ed.). New York: Free Press.

Brown, R. J., & Turner, J. C. (1981). Interpersonal and intergroup behaviour. In J. C. Turner & H. Giles (Eds.), *Intergroup behaviour* (pp. 33-65). Oxford: Basil Blackwell.

Buss, D. M., et al. (1990). International preferences in selecting mates: A study of 37 cultures. *Journal of Cross-Cultural Psychology, 21,* 5-47.

Campbell, D. T. (1986). Science's social system of validity-enhancing collective belief change and the problems of social sciences. In D. W. Fiske & R. A. Shweder (Eds.), *Metatheory in social science.* Chicago: University of Chicago Press.

Campbell, D. T., & Fiske, D. W. (1959). Convergent and discriminant validation by the multitrait-multimethod matrix. *Psychological Bulletin, 56,* 81-105.

Carment, D. W. (1974). Indian and Canadian choice behaviour in a maximizing difference game and in a game of chicken. *International Journal of Psychology, 9,* 213-221.

Carstairs, G. M. (1957). *The twice-born: A study of the community of high caste Hindu.* London: Hogarth.

Caudill, W., & DeVos, G. A. (1956). Achievement, culture and personality: The case of the Japanese Americans. *American Anthropologist, 58,* 1102-1126.

Centrum Badnia Opinii Spolecznej. (1989). *Propozycje przeksztalcen stosunkow wlasnosci w opinii robotnikow i kadry kierowniczej przedsiebiorstw.* Warsaw: Komunikat z badan.

Cha, J.-H. (1979). Old and new values of children in Korea. *Korea Journal, 19,* 19-31.

Cha, J.-H. (1980). The personality and consciousness of the Korean people. In S. B. Han et al. (Eds.), *Studies on the continuity and change of a culture* (pp. 6-58). Seoul: Korean Social Science Research Council. (in Korean)

Cha, J.-H. (1986). Value changes. In Korean Social Science Research Council (Ed.), *The changes in Korean society and its problems: Forty years after liberation* (pp. 397-437). Seoul: Bom'munsa. (in Korean)

Cha, J.-H. (1990). *Changes in Koreans' values.* Seoul: Kangwon National University Student Guidance Center. (in Korean)

Cha, J.-H. (1994). Changes in value, belief, attitude, and behavior of the Koreans over the past 100 years. *Korean Journal of Psychology: Social, 8,* 40-58.

Cha, J.-H., & Cheong, J. W. (1993). Collectivism in modern Korean society. *Korean Journal of Psychology: Social, 7,* 150-163.

Cha, J.-H., & Park, J. H. (1991). An analysis of the use of the expression "woori" (we) from a collectivism research perspective. In Korean Psychological Association (Ed.), *Abstracts of papers read at the KPA Annual Convention '91* (pp. 351-357). Seoul: Korean Psychological Association. (in Korean)

Chan, D. K.-S. (1991). *Effects of concession pattern, relationship between negotiators, and culture on negotiation.* Unpublished master's thesis, University of Illinois, Urbana-Champaign, Department of Psychology.

Chang, G. H. (1981). *The achievement motive, femininity, occupational choice, and attributional characteristics of college students in Taiwan.* Unpublished master's thesis, National Taiwan University. (in Chinese)

Chaudhuri, N. C. (1966). *The continent of Circe.* Bombay: Jaico.

Chen, C. N. (1987a). Confucian culture and occupational ethics of the traditional merchants. *Contemporary, 10,* 54-61. (in Chinese)

Chen, C. N. (1987b). Reanalyzing Confucian culture and occupational ethics of the traditional merchants: Confucianism and occupational ideas of the merchants in the Hui state during the Ming and Ch'ing dynasties. *Contemporary, 11,* 72-85. (in Chinese)

Chen, C. N. (1989). Family ideology and economic ethics of enterprise. *Contemporary, 34,* 57-65. (in Chinese)

Chinese Culture Connection. (1987). Chinese values and the search for culture-free dimensions of culture. *Journal of Cross-Cultural Psychology, 18,* 143-164.

Chiu, C.-Y. (1990). Normative expectations of social behavior and concern for members of the collective in Chinese society. *Journal of Psychology, 124,* 103-111.

Choi, S.-C., Kim, U., & Choi, S.-H. (1993). Indigenous analysis of collective representations: A Korean perspective. In U. Kim & J. W. Berry (Eds.), *Indigenous psychologies: Research and experience in cultural context* (pp. 193-210). Newbury Park, CA: Sage.

Choi, S.-H. (1992). Communicative socialization processes: Korea and Canada. In S. Iwawaki, Y. Kashima, & K. Leung (Eds.), *Innovations in cross-cultural psychology* (pp. 103-121). Lisse, Netherlands: Swets & Zeitlinger.

Cialdini, R. B., Reno, R. R., & Kallgren, C. A. (1990). A focus of normative conduct: Recycling the concept of norms to reduce littering in public places. *Journal of Personality and Social Psychology, 58,* 1015-1026.

Clark, L. A. (1987). Mutual relevance of mainstream and cross-cultural psychology. *Journal of Consulting and Clinical Psychology, 55,* 461-470.

Cohen, S., & Syme, S. L. (1985). *Social support and health.* New York: Academic Press.

Cole, M., & Scribner, S. (1974). *Culture and thought: A psychological introduction.* New York: John Wiley.

Cook, T. D., & Campbell, D. T. (1979). *Design and analysis of quasi-experimental designs for research.* Chicago: Rand McNally.

Cooley, C. H., Angell, R. C., & Carr, L. J. (1933). *Introductory sociology.* New York: Charles Scribner's Sons.

Crocker, J., & Luhtanen, R. (1990). Collective self-esteem and ingroup bias. *Journal of Personality and Social Psychology, 58,* 60-67.

Dasen, P. R. (1974). The influence of ecology, culture and European contact on cognitive development in Australian Aborigines. In J. W. Berry & P. R. Dasen (Eds.), *Culture and cognition* (pp. 213-256). London: Methuen.

Davison, M. (1983). *Multidimensional scaling.* New York: John Wiley.

Dawson, J. L. M. (1963). Traditional values and work efficiency in West African mine labour force. *Occupational Psychology, 37,* 209-218.

Dawson, J. L. M. (1967). Tradition versus Western attitudes in West Africa: The construction, validation and application of a measuring device. *British Journal of Social and Clinical Psychology, 6,* 81-96.

Denny, P. J. (1988). Contextualization and differentiation in cross-cultural cognition. In J. W. Berry, S. H. Irvine, & E. B. Hunt (Eds.), *Indigenous cognition* (pp. 213-256). Dordrecht, Netherlands: Martinus Nijhoff.

Deutsch, M. (1990). Forms of social organization: Psychological consequences. In H. T. Himmelweit & G. Gaskell (Eds.), *Societal psychology* (pp. 157-176). Newbury Park, CA: Sage.

Devine, P. G. (1989). Automatic and controlled processes in prejudice: The role of stereotypes and personal beliefs. In A. R. Pratkanis, S. J. Breckler, & A. G. Greenwald (Eds.), *Attitude structure and function* (pp. 181-212). Hillsdale, NJ: Lawrence Erlbaum.

DeVos, G. A. (1973). *Socialization for achievement: Essays on the cultural psychology of the Japanese.* Berkeley: University of California Press.

DeVos, G. A., & Wagatsuma, H. (1961). Value attitudes toward role behavior of women in two Japanese villages. *American Anthropologist, 63,* 1204-1230.

Dion, K. K., Pak, A. W., & Dion, K. L. (1990). Stereotyping physical attractiveness: A sociocultural perspective. *Journal of Cross-Cultural Psychology, 21,* 378-398.

Doi, T. (1981). *The anatomy of dependence.* Tokyo: Kodansha International.

Doi, T. (1986). *The anatomy of self.* Tokyo: Kodansha International.

Doob, L. W. (1960). *Becoming more civilized.* New Haven, CT: Yale University Press.

Dore, R. P. (1958). *City life in Japan.* Berkeley: University of California Press.

Druckman, D., Benton, A. A., Ali, F., & Berger, J. S. (1974). Cultural differences in bargaining behavior: India, Argentina, and the United States. *Journal of Conflict Resolution, 20,* 413-452.

Dumont, L. (1970). *Homo hierarchicus: The caste system and its implications.* Chicago: University of Chicago Press.

Durkheim, E. (1930). *The division of labor in society* (G. Simpson, Trans.). Glencoe, IL: Free Press.

Dworkin, R. (1977). *Taking rights seriously.* Cambridge, MA: Harvard University Press.

Earley, P. C. (1989). Social loafing and collectivism: A comparison of the U.S. and the Peoples Republic of China. *Administrative Science Quarterly, 34,* 565-581.

Edwards, A. L. (1959). *Manual for the Personal Preference Schedule.* New York: Psychological Corporation.

Elliott, D. (1989, January 23). With change comes a generation gap: China's young people discard their legacy. *Newsweek,* pp. 32-33.

Enriquez, V. G. (1988). The structure of Philippine social values: Towards integrating indigenous values and appropriate technology. In D. Sinha & H. S. R. Kao (Eds.), *Social values and development: Asian perspectives* (pp. 124-148). New Delhi: Sage.

Enriquez, V. G. (1993). Developing a Filipino psychology. In U. Kim & J. W. Berry (Eds.), *Indigenous psychologies: Research and experience in cultural context* (pp. 152-169). Newbury Park, CA: Sage.

Eysenck, S. B. G., & Chan, J. (1982). A comparative study of personality in adults and children: Hong Kong vs. England. *Personality and Individual Differences, 3,* 153-160.

Fawcett, J. H. (Ed.). (1972). *The satisfactions and costs of children: Theories, concepts, and methods.* Honolulu: East-West Center.

Feather, N. T. (1979). Values, expectancy, and action. *Australian Psychologist, 14,* 243-260.

Feldman, S. S., & Rosenthal, D. A. (1991). Age expectations of behavioural autonomy in Hong Kong, Australian and American youth: The influence of family variables and adolescents' values. *International Journal of Psychology, 26,* 1-23.

Fenigstein, A., Scheier, M. F., & Buss, A. H. (1975). Public and private self-consciousness: Assessment and theory. *Journal of Consulting and Clinical Psychology, 43,* 522-527.

Fishbein, M., & Ajzen, I. (1975). *Belief, attitude, intentions, and behavior: An introduction to theory and research.* Reading, MA: Addison-Wesley.

Fiske, A. (1990). *Structures of social life.* New York: Free Press.

Fiske, D. W. (1986). Specificity of method and knowledge in social science. In D. W. Fiske & R. A. Shweder (Eds.), *Metatheory in social science.* Chicago: University of Chicago Press.

Flavell, J. (1963). *The developmental psychology of Jean Piaget.* Princeton, NJ: Van Nostrand.

Forgas, J. P., & Bond, M. H. (1985). Cultural influences on the perception of interaction episodes. *Personality and Social Psychology Bulletin, 11,* 75-88.

Freud, S. (1964). An outline of psychoanalysis. In J. Strachey (Ed.), *The standard edition of the complete psychological works of Sigmund Freud* (Vol. 23). London: Hogarth. (Original work published 1940)

Fyans, L. J., Jr., Maehr, M. L., Salili, F., & Desai, K. A. (1983). A cross-cultural exploration into the meaning of achievement. *Journal of Personality and Social Psychology, 44,* 1000-1013.

Gabrenya, W. K., Jr. (1988). Social science and social psychology: The cross-cultural link. In M. H. Bond (Ed.), *The cross-cultural challenge to social psychology* (pp. 48-66). Newbury Park, CA: Sage.

Gabrenya, W. K., Jr., Wang, Y. E., & Latané, B. (1985). Social loafing on an optimizing task: Cross-cultural differences among Chinese and Americans. *Journal of Cross-Cultural Psychology, 16,* 223-242.

Geertz, C. (1984). From the native's point of view. In R. A. Shweder & R. A. Levine (Eds.), *Culture theory: Essays on mind, self and emotion.* Cambridge: Cambridge University Press.

Georgas, J. (1986). *Social psychology.* Athens: University of Athens Press. (in Greek)

Gergen, K. J. (1973). Social psychology as history. *Journal of Personality and Social Psychology, 26,* 309-320.

Gibney, F. (1991, June 10). How to beat the system. *Newsweek,* pp. 34-35.

Giddens, A. (1984). *The constitution of society: Outline of the theory of structuration.* Cambridge: Polity.

Gilbert, N. (1983). *Capitalism and the welfare state.* New Haven, CT: Yale University Press.

Gillespie, J. M., & Allport, G. W. (1955). *Youth's outlook on the future: A cross national study.* Garden City, NY: Doubleday.

Gilligan, C. (1982). *In a different voice: Psychological theory and women's development.* Cambridge, MA: Harvard University Press.

Gough, H. G. (1960). *Manual for the California Psychological Inventory* (rev. ed.). Palo Alto, CA: Consulting Psychologists Press.

Greenberg, J. (1981). The justice of distributing scarce and abundant resources. In M. J. Lerner & S. C. Lerner (Eds.), *The justice motive.* New York: Plenum.

Greenwald, A. G. (1982). Ego task analysis: An integration of research on ego-involvement and self-awareness. In A. Hastorf & A. M. Isen (Eds.), *Cognitive social psychology* (pp. 109-147). New York: Elsevier North Holland.

Greenwald, A. G., & Breckler, S. J. (1984). To whom is the self presented? In B. R. Schlenker (Ed.), *The self and social life* (pp. 126-145). New York: McGraw-Hill.

Greenwald, A. G., & Pratkanis, A. R. (1984). The self. In R. S. Wyer, Jr., & T. K. Srull (Eds.), *Handbook of social cognition* (Vol. 3, pp. 129-178). Hillsdale, NJ: Lawrence Erlbaum.

Gudykunst, W., Yoon, Y. C., & Nishida, T. (1987). The influence of individualism-collectivism on perceptions of communication in ingroup and outgroup relationships. *Communication Monographs, 54,* 295-306.

Guo, S. Y. (1972). *A study of psychological traits of low achieving students in Taiwan.* Unpublished master's thesis, National Taiwan Normal University. (in Chinese)

Gurin, P., & Markus, H. (1988). Group identity: The psychological mechanisms of durable salience. *Revue International de Psychologie Sociale, 1,* 257-274.

Gusfield, J. R. (1967). Tradition and modernity: Misplaced polarities in the study of social change. *American Journal of Sociology, 73,* 351-362.

Guttman, L. (1968). A general nonmetric technique for finding the smallest coordinate space for a configuration of points. *Psychometrica, 33,* 469-506.

Hamaguchi, E. (1977). *"Nihonrashisa" no saihakken.* [Rediscovery of "Japaneseness"]. Tokyo: Nihon Keizai Shinbunsha. (in Japanese)

Hamaguchi, E. (1982). Nihonteki shudan shugi towa nanika [What is Japanese collectivism?]. In E. Hamaguchi & S. Kumon (Eds.), *Nihonteki shudan shugi* [Collectivism in Japanese style] (pp. 1-26). Tokyo: Yuhikau. (in Japanese)

Hamaguchi, E., & Kumon, S. (Eds.). (1982). *Nihonteki shudan shugi* [Collectivism in Japanese style]. Tokyo: Yuhikau. (in Japanese)

Han, S. (1990). *Individualism and collectivism: Its implications for cross-cultural advertising.* Unpublished doctoral dissertation, University of Illinois, Department of Advertising.

Harré, R. (1984). Some reflections on the concept of "social representation." *Social Research, 51,* 927-938.

Herskovits, M. J. (1955). *Cultural anthropology.* New York: Knopf.

Hicks, G. L., & Redding, S. G. (1983). The story of the East Asian "economic miracle": Part one. Economic theory be damned! *Euro-Asia Business Review, 2*(3), 24-32.

Higgins, J. (1980). Social control theories of social policy. *Journal of Social Policy, 9*(1).

Higgins, J. (1981). *States of welfare.* Oxford: Basil Blackwell.

Ho, D. Y.-F. (1973). Changing interpersonal relationships in Chinese families. In H. E. White (Ed.), *An anthology of seminar papers: The changing family, East and West* (pp. 103-118). Hong Kong: Hong Kong Baptist College.

Ho, D. Y.-F. (1986). Chinese patterns of socialization: A critical review. In M. H. Bond (Ed.), *The psychology of the Chinese people* (pp. 1-37). Hong Kong: Oxford University Press.

Ho, D. Y.-F., Hong, Y. Y., & Chiu, C.-Y. (1989, May). *Filial piety and family-matrimonial traditionalism in Chinese society.* Paper presented at the International Conference on Moral Values and Moral Reasoning in Chinese Societies, Academia Sinica Conference Center, Taipei.

Hofheinz, R., Jr., & Calder, K. E. (1982). *The Eastasia edge.* New York: Basic Books.

Hofstede, G. (1980). *Culture's consequences: International differences in work-related values.* Beverly Hills, CA: Sage.

Hofstede, G. (1983a). Dimensions of national cultures in fifty countries and three regions. In J. B. Deregowski, S. Dziurawiec, & R. C. Annis (Eds.), *Expiscations in cross-cultural psychology* (pp. 335-355). Lisse, Netherlands: Swets & Zeitlinger.

Hofstede, G. (1983b). National cultures revisited. *Behavior Science Research, 18,* 285-305.

Hofstede, G. (1991). *Cultures and organizations: Software of the mind.* London: McGraw-Hill.

Hofstede, G., & Bond, M. H. (1984). Hofstede's culture dimensions: An independent validation using Rokeach's value survey. *Journal of Cross-Cultural Psychology, 15,* 417-433.

Hofstede, G., & Bond, M. H. (1988). The Confucius connection: From cultural roots to economic growth. *Organizational Dynamics, 16,* 4-21.

Hogan, R. T. (1975). Theoretical egocentrism and the problem of compliance. *American Psychologist, 30,* 533-540.

Holten, G. (1973). *Thematic origins of scientific thought: From Kepler to Einstein.* Cambridge, MA: Harvard University Press.

Hong, D. S. (1989). Yongo jui wa jiyok gamjong [Yongoism and regional antagonism]. In *Regionalism and Regional Antagonism.* Symposium conducted at the meeting of the Korean Sociological Association. (in Korean)

Hoppe, M. H. (1990). *A comparative study of country elites: International differences in work-related values and learning and their implications for management training and development.* Unpublished doctoral dissertation, University of North Carolina, Chapel Hill.

Hsu, F. L. K. (1953). *Americans and Chinese: Two ways of life* (1st ed.). New York: Abelard-Schuman.

Hsu, F. L. K. (1971). Psychosocial homeostasis and jen: Conceptual tools for advancing psychological anthropology. *American Anthropologist, 73,* 23-44.

Hsu, F. L. K. (1972). *Psychological anthropology* (2nd ed.). Cambridge, MA: Schenkman.

Hsu, F. L. K. (1981). *Americans and Chinese: Passage to difference* (3rd ed.). Honolulu: University of Hawaii Press.

Hsu, F. L. K. (1983). *Rugged individualism reconsidered.* Knoxville: University of Tennessee Press.

Huang, C. H. (1987, December 19). Myth or fact? Confucian ethics and economic development. *China Times* (Taipei). (in Chinese)

Hui, C. H. (1988). Measurement of individualism-collectivism. *Journal of Research in
Personality, 22,* 17-36.

Hui, C. H., & Triandis, H. C. (1986). Individualism-collectivism: A study of cross-cultural
researchers. *Journal of Cross-Cultural Psychology, 17,* 225-248.

Hui, C. H., & Triandis, H. C. (1989). Effects of culture and response format on extreme
response style. *Journal of Cross-Cultural Psychology, 20,* 296-309.

Hui, C. H., & Villareal, M. J. (1989). Individualism-collectivism and psychological needs:
Their relationships in two cultures. *Journal of Cross-Cultural Psychology, 20,* 310-323.

Humana, C. (1986). *World human rights guide.* London: Pan.

Hwang, K. K. (1988). *Confucianism and East Asian modernization.* Taipei: Chu-Liu. (in
Chinese)

Hwang, K. K. (1991). *Dao* and the transformative power of Confucianism: A theory of East
Asian modernization. In W. M. Tu (Ed.), *The triadic cord: Confucian ethics, industrial
East Asia and Max Weber* (pp. 229-278). Singapore: The Institute of East Asian Philosophies.

Hwang, K. K., & Yang, K.-S. (1972). Chinese individual modernity and social orientation.
Bulletin of the Institute of Ethnology, Academia Sinica, 32, 245-278. (in Chinese)

Inglehardt, R. (1977). *The silent revolution: Changing values and political styles among
Western publics.* Princeton, NJ: Princeton University Press.

Inkeles, A. (1969). Making men modern: On the causes and consequences of individual
change in the developing countries. *American Journal of Sociology, 75,* 208-225.

Inkeles, A. (1983, November/December). The American character. *Center Magazine,* pp. 25-39.

Inkeles, A., & Smith, D. H. (1974). *Becoming modern: Individual change in six developing
countries.* Cambridge, MA: Harvard University Press.

Iwawaki, S. (1986). Achievement motivation and socialization. In S. E. Newstead, S. H.
Irvine, & P. L. Dann (Eds.), *Human assessment: Cognition and motivation.* Boston:
Martinus Nijhoff.

James, W. (1890). *The principles of psychology* (Vols. 1-2). New York: Dover.

Jarymowicz, M. (1988). *Studia nad spostrzeganiem relacji ja-inni: Tozsamosc, indiwiduacja,
przynaleznosc.* Wroclaw: Ossolineum. (in Polish)

Jarymowicz, M. (1989). Spostrzeganie samego siebie. *Studia Psychologiczne, 27,* 7-13.

Jha, H., Sinha, J. B. P., Gopal, S., & Tiwary, K. M. (1985). *Social structures and alignments:
A study of rural Bihar.* New Delhi: Usha.

Jung, C. G. (1978). *Psychology and the East.* Princeton, NJ: Princeton University Press.

Kagitçibasi, Ç. (1970). Social norms and authoritarianism: A Turkish-American comparison.
Journal of Cross-Cultural Psychology, 4, 157-174.

Kagitçibasi, Ç. (1973). Psychological aspects of modernization in Turkey. *Journal of Cross-
Cultural Psychology, 45,* 157-174.

Kagitçibasi, Ç. (1987). Individual and group loyalties: Are they compatible? In Ç. Kagitçibasi
(Ed.), *Growth and progress in cross-cultural psychology* (pp. 94-104). Lisse, Netherlands: Swets & Zeitlinger.

Kagitçibasi, Ç. (1990). Family and socialization in cross-cultural perspective: A model of
change. In J. Berman (Ed.), *Nebraska Symposium on Motivation, 1989* (pp. 135-200).
Lincoln: University of Nebraska Press.

Kagitçibasi, Ç. (1992). Linking the indigenous and universalist orientations. In S. Iwawaki,
Y. Kashima, & K. Leung (Eds.), *Innovations in cross-cultural psychology.* Lisse, Netherlands: Swets & Zeitlinger.

Kagitçibasi, Ç., & Berry, J. W. (1989). Cross-cultural psychology: Current research and
trends. *Annual Review of Psychology, 40,* 493-531.

Kagitçibasi, Ç., Sunar, D., & Bekman, S. (1988). *Comprehensive Preschool Education Project final report*. Ottawa: IDRC.

Kahl, J. A. (1968). *The measurement of modernism: A study of values in Brazil and Mexico*. Austin: University of Texas Press.

Kahn, H. (1979). *World economic development: 1979 and beyond*. Boulder, CO: Westview.

Kahn, H., & Pepper, T. (1979). *The Japanese challenge: The success and failure of economic success*. New York: Thomas Y. Crowell.

Kakar, S. (1978). *The inner world: A psycho-analytic study of childhood and society in India*. New Delhi: Oxford University Press.

Kakar, S. (1982). *Shamans, mystics, and doctors*. New Delhi: Oxford University Press.

Kanbara, M., Higuchi, K., & Chimizu, N. (1982). Locus of control shakudo no sakusei to shinraisei datousei no kentou [New locus of control scale: Its reliability and validity]. *Japanese Journal of Educational Psychology*, pp. 302-307.

Kapp, W. K. (1963). *Hindu culture, economic development and economic planning in India*. Bombay: Asian Publishing House.

Kashima, E. (1989). *Determinants of perceived group heterogeneity*. Unpublished doctoral dissertation. Urbana-Champaign, IL. University of Illinois Department of Psychology.

Kashima, Y., & Triandis, H. C. (1986). The self-serving bias in attributions as a coping strategy: A cross-cultural study. *Journal of Cross-Cultural Psychology, 17*, 83-98.

Katju, P. (1986). *Certain factors related to member integration in a multinational organization*. Unpublished doctoral dissertation, Allahabad University..ulture and achievement motivation. *American Psychologist, 29*, 887-896.

Kim, J. E. (1981). *The psychology of Korean families*. Seoul: Chang-Ji-Sa. (in Korean)

Kim, S. (1987). *Hyundae sahoe wa sahoe junkchaek* [Modern society and social policy]. Seoul: Seoul National University Press. (in Korean)

Kim, U., & Berry, J. W. (Eds.). (1993). *Indigenous psychologies: Research and experience in cultural context*. Newbury Park, CA: Sage.

Kim, U., & Choi, S. C. (in press). Individualism, collectivism, and child development: A Korean perspective. In P. M. Greenfield & R. Cocking (Eds.), *Cross-cultural roots of minority child development*. Hillsdale, NJ: Lawrence Erlbaum.

Kim, U. M. (1986). *A critical examination of occupational welfare and its implications for Korea* (Publication Series No. 16). Toronto: University of Toronto, Faculty of Social Work.

King, A. Y. C., & Bond, M. H. (1985). The Confucian paradigm of man: A sociological view. In W. T. Tseng & D. Wu (Eds.), *Chinese culture and mental health*. New York: Academic Press.

Kleinman, A. (1980). *Patients and healers in context of culture*. Berkeley: University of California Press.

Kluckhohn, C. (1951). Values and value orientations in the theory of action: An exploration in definition and classification. In T. Parsons & E. Shils (Eds.), *Toward a general theory of action*. Cambridge, MA: Harvard University Press.

Kluckhohn, F. R., & Strodtbeck, F. L. (1961). *Variations in value orientations*. Evanston, IL: Row Peterson.

Koestler, A. (1960). *The lotus and the robot*. New York: Harper & Row.

Kohlberg, L. (1969). Stage and sequence: The cognitive-developmental approach to socialization. In D. A. Goslin (Ed.), *Handbook of socialization theory and research*. Chicago: Rand McNally.

Kohlberg, L. (1981). *Essays on moral development*. San Francisco: Harper.

Kohn, M. L. (1969). *Class and conformity: A study in values*. Homewood, IL: Dorsey.

Kohn, M. L., & Schooler, C. (1983). *Work and personality*. Norwood, NJ: Ablex.

Kohn, M. L., & Slomczynski, K. M. (1990). *Social structure and self-direction.* Oxford: Basil Blackwell.

Kolarska, L. (1989). Egalitaryzm i rynkowy lad gospodarczy—zmiana preferencji spolecznych. In W. Adamski (Ed.), *Dynamika konfliktu spolecznego Polacy '80-'88* (Syzyfus Vol. 8). Warsaw: IFiS, PAN. (in Polish)

Kornadt, H. J., Eckensberger, L. H., & Emminghaus, W. B. (1980). Cross-cultural research on motivation and its contribution to a general theory of motivation. In H. C. Triandis & W. J. Lonner (Eds.), *Handbook of cross-cultural psychology* (Vol. 3, pp. 223-321). Boston: Allyn & Bacon.

Kuhn, M. H., & McPartland, T. (1954). An empirical investigation of self-attitudes. *American Sociological Review, 19,* 68-76.

Lapierre, D. (1986). *The city of joy.* London: Arrow.

L'Armand, K., & Pepitone, A. (1975). Helping to reward another person: A cross-cultural analysis. *Journal of Personality and Social Psychology, 31,* 189-198.

La Rosa, J., & Diaz-Loving, R. (1988). Diferencial semantico del autoconcepto en estudiantes. *Revista de Psicologia Social y Personalidad, 4,* 39-57. (in Spanish)

Latané, B. (1981). The psychology of social impact. *American Psychologist, 36,* 343-355.

Lawler, J. (1980). Collectivity and individuality in Soviet educational theory. *Contemporary Educational Psychology, 5,* 163-174.

Lebra, T. S. (1976). *Japanese patterns of behavior.* Honolulu: University of Hawaii Press.

Lee, E. S. (1988). Chosun huki dangjengsa yongu. [Historical research on political parties in the Yi Dynasty.] Seoul: Ilchogak. (in Korean)

Lee, S. J., & Kim, J. O. (1979). The value of children: Korea. *Economic Development, 186,* 324. (in Korean)

Lee, Y., & Ottati, V. (1990). *Determinants of ingroup and outgroup perceptions of heterogeneity: An investigation of Sino-American stereotypes.* Unpublished manuscript.

Leung, K. (1987). Some determinants of reactions to procedural models for conflict resolution: A cross-national study. *Journal of Personality and Social Psychology, 53,* 898-908.

Leung, K. (1988a). Some determinants of conflict avoidance. *Journal of Cross-Cultural Psychology, 19,* 125-136.

Leung, K. (1988b). Theoretical advances in justice behavior: Some cross-cultural inputs. In M. H. Bond (Ed.), *The cross-cultural challenge to social psychology* (pp. 218-229). Newbury Park, CA: Sage.

Leung, K. (1989). Cross-cultural differences: Individual-level vs cultural-level analysis. *International Journal of Psychology, 24,* 703-719.

Leung, K., & Bond, M. H. (1984). The impact of cultural collectivism on reward allocation. *Journal of Personality and Social Psychology, 47,* 793-804.

Leung, K., & Bond, M. H. (1989). On the empirical identification of dimensions for cross-cultural comparisons. *Journal of Cross-Cultural Psychology, 20,* 133-151.

Leung, K., Bond, M. H., Carment, D. W., Krishnan, L., & Liebrand, W. B. C. (1990). Effects of cultural femininity on preference for methods of conflict resolution: A cross-cultural study. *Journal of Experimental Social Psychology, 26,* 373-388. (See also correction in *Journal of Experimental Social Psychology,* 1991, *27,* 201-202.)

Leung, K., Bond, M. H., & Schwartz, S. H. (1993). *Explanatory mechanisms for cross-cultural differences: Values, valences, and expectancies.* Manuscript submitted for publication.

Leung, K., & Iwawaki, S. (1988). Cultural collectivism and distributive behavior. *Journal of Cross-Cultural Psychology, 19,* 35-49.

Levy, S. (1985). Lawful roles of facets in social theories. In D. Canter (Ed.), *The facet approach to social research* (pp. 59-96). New York: Springer-Verlag.

Lin, C. Y. C., & Fu, V. R. (1990). A comparison of child rearing practices among Chinese, immigrant Chinese, and Caucasian-American parents. *Child Development, 61,* 429-433.

Lingoes, J. C. (1977). *Geometric representations of relational data.* Ann Arbor, MI: Mathesis.

Lingoes, J. C. (1981). Testing regional hypotheses in multidimensional scaling. In I. Borg (Ed.), *Multidimensional data representations: When and why* (pp. 280-310). Ann Arbor, MI: Mathesis.

Lomax, A., & Berkowitz, N. (1972). The evolutionary taxonomy of culture. *Science, 177,* 228-239.

Loomis, C. P. (1957). Introduction. In F. Tönnies, *Community and society* (C. P. Loomis, Ed. and Trans.). New York: Harper & Row. (Original work published 1887)

Lukes, S. (1973). *Individualism.* Oxford: Basil Blackwell.

Maday, B. C., & Szalay, L. B. (1976). Psychological correlates of family socialization in the United States and Korea. In T. Williams (Ed.), *Psychological anthropology.* The Hague: Mouton.

Maehr, M. L. (1974). Culture and achievement motivation. *American Psychologist, 29,* 887-896.

Maehr, M. L. (1978). Sociocultural origins of achievement motivation. In D. Bar-Tal & L. Saxe (Eds.), *Social psychology of education: Theory and research* (pp. 205-227). Washington, DC: Hemisphere.

Maehr, M. L., & Nicholls, J. G. (1980). Culture and achievement motivation: A second look. In N. Warren (Ed.), *Studies in cross-cultural psychology* (Vol. 3, pp. 221-267). New York: Academic Press.

Marin, G. (1985). Validez transcultural del principio de equidad: El colectivisimo-individualisimo como una variable moderatora [Transcultural validity of the principle of equity: Collectivism-individualism as a moderating variable]. *Revista Interamericana de Psicologia Occupational, 4,* 7-20. (in Spanish)

Marin, G., & Triandis, H. C. (1985). Allocentrism as an important characteristic of the behavior of Latin Americans and Hispanics. In R. Diaz-Guerrero (Ed.), *Cross-cultural and national studies in social psychology* (pp. 85-104). Amsterdam: North Holland.

Marks, G., & Miller, N. (1987). Ten years of research on the false-consensus effect: An empirical and theoretical review. *Psychological Bulletin, 102,* 72-90.

Markus, H., & Kitayama, S. (1991). Culture and self: Implications for cognition, emotion, and motivation. *Psychological Review, 98,* 224-253.

Marlowe, D., & Crowne, D. P. (1964). *The approval motive: Studies in evaluative dependence.* New York: John Wiley.

Marriot, M. (1976). Hindu transactions: Diversity without dualism. In B. Kapferer (Ed.), *Transaction and meaning* (pp. 109-142). Philadelphia: Institute for the Study of Human Issues.

Maslach, C., Stapp, J., & Santee, R. T. (1985). Individuation: Conceptual analysis and assessment. *Journal of Personality and Social Psychology, 49,* 729-739.

Massimini, F., & Calegari, P. (1979). *Il contesto normativo sociale.* Milan: Angeli. (in Italian)

Mazrui, A. (1968). From social Darwinism to current theories of modernization. *World Politics, 21,* 69-83.

McAdams, D. (1982). Intimacy motivation. In A. Stewart (Ed.), *Motivation and society* (pp. 133-171). San Francisco: Jossey-Bass.

McArthur, L. Z., & Baron, R. M. (1983). Toward an ecological theory of social perception. *Psychological Review, 90,* 215-238.

McClelland, D. C. (1961). *The achieving society.* Princeton, NJ: Van Nostrand.

McClelland, D. C. (1963). Motivational patterns in Southeast Asia with special reference to the Chinese case. *Journal of Social Issues, 19,* 6-19.

McClelland, D. C. (1980). Motive dispositions: The merits of operant and respondent measures. In L. Wheeler (Ed.), *Review of personality and social psychology.* Beverly Hills, CA: Sage.

McClelland, D. C., Atkinson, J. W., Clark, R. W., & Lowell, E. L. (1953). *The achievement motive.* New York: Appleton-Century-Crofts.

McClelland, D. C., Atkinson, J. W., Russel, A. C., & Lowell, E. L. (1958). A scoring manual for the achievement motive. In J. W. Atkinson (Ed.), *Motives in fantasy, action, and society* (pp. 179-204). Princeton, NJ: Van Nostrand.

McCrae, R. R., & John, O. P. (1992). An introduction to the five factor model and its applications. *Journal of Personality, 60,* 175-215.

McGuire, W. (1984). Search for self: Going beyond self-esteem and the reactive self. In R. A. Zucker, J. Aronoff, & A. I. Rabin (Eds.), *Personality and the prediction of behavior* New York: Academic Press.

Mehrabian, A., & Ksionsky, S. (1974). *A theory of affiliation.* Lexington, MA: Lexington.

Mehta, V. (1962). *Portrait of India.* New York: Penguin.

Messick, D. M. (1988). On the limitations of cross-cultural research in social psychology. In M. H. Bond (Ed.), *The cross-cultural challenge to social psychology* (pp. 41-47). Newbury Park, CA: Sage.

Miller, J. G. (1984). Culture and the development of everyday social explanation. *Journal of Personality and Social Psychology, 46,* 961-978.

Miller, J. G., Bersoff, D. M., & Harwood, R. L. (1990). Perceptions of social responsibilities in India and the United States: Moral imperatives or personal decisions? *Journal of Personality and Social Psychology, 58,* 33-47.

Minami, H. (1971). *Psychology of the Japanese people.* Tokyo: University of Tokyo Press.

Ministry of Labor, Korea. (1988). *Yearbook of labor statistics.* Seoul: Author.

Minturn, L., & Hitchcock, J. T. (1966). *The Rajputs of Khalapur, India.* New York: John Wiley.

Mishra, R. C., & Tiwari, B. B. (1980). *Dialogues on development.* New Delhi: Sage.

Misumi, J. (1985). *The behavioral science of leadership.* Ann Arbor: University of Michigan Press.

Misumi, J. (1988). *Small group activities in Japanese industrial organizations and behavioral science.* Paper presented at the Twenty-fourth International Congress of Psychology, Sydney, Australia.

Mitchell, T. R., & Silver, W. S. (1990). Individual and group goals when workers are interdependent: Effects on task strategies and performance. *Journal of Applied Psychology, 75,* 185-193.

Morris, C. W. (1956). *Varieties of human value.* Chicago: University of Chicago Press.

Mullen, B., Atkins, J. L., Champion, D. C., Edwards, C., Hardy, D., Story, J. E., & Vanderklok, M. (1985). The false consensus effect: A meta-analysis of 115 hypothesis tests. *Journal of Experimental Social Psychology, 21,* 262-283.

Mullen, B., & Rosenthal, R. (1985). *Basic meta-analysis: Procedures and programs.* Hillsdale, NJ: Lawrence Erlbaum.

Murdock, G. P. (1967). *Ethnographic atlas.* Pittsburgh: University of Pittsburgh Press.

Murphy, G. (1969). Psychology in the year 2000. *American Psychologist, 24,* 523-530.

Murray, H. A. (1938). *Explorations in personality.* New York: Oxford University Press.

Murray, H. A. (1943). *Thematic Apperception Test manual.* Cambridge, MA: Harvard College.

Myrdal, A. (1968). *Nation and family.* Cambridge: MIT Press.

Na, G. C. (1988). *Jigup gyechung ganui sahoejog gurigam yongu* [Research on the social distance among various occupations]. Unpublished doctoral dissertation, Korea University, Seoul, Department of Sociology. (in Korean)

Naidu, R. K. (1991, October). *Indigenization as I see it.* Paper presented at the second convention of the National Academy of Psychology, Bhubaneswar.

Nakamura, H. (1964). *Ways of thinking of Eastern peoples.* Honolulu: University of Hawaii Press.

Naroll, R. (1956). A preliminary index of social development. *American Anthropologist, 58,* 687-715.

Newcomb, T. M. (1953). An approach to the study of communicative acts. *Psychological Review, 60,* 393-404.

Nishio, H. (1982, August). *Is Japan a welfare state?* Paper presented at the Tenth World Congress of Sociology, Mexico City.

Nowak, A., Szamrej, J., & Latané, B. (1990). From private to public opinion: A dynamic theory of social impact. *Psychological Review, 97,* 362-376.

Okochi, K. B., et al. (Eds.). (1973). *Workers and employers in Japan.* Tokyo: Tokyo University Press.

O'Neill, J. (1976). Scientism, historicism and the problem of rationality. In J. O'Neill (Ed.), *Modes of individualism and collectivism.* London: Heinemann.

Oyama, N. (1990). *Some recent trends in Japanese values: Beyond individual-collective dimension.* Paper presented at the International Congress of Sociology, Barcelona.

Pandey, N. (1990). *Detachment as a moderator of stress-strain relationship.* Unpublished doctoral dissertation, Allahabad University.

Park, H. K. (1969). The Korean social structure and its implications for education. In C. I. Kim (Ed.), *Aspects of social change in Korea.* Kalamazoo, MI: Korea Research.

Parsons, T., & Shils, E. A. (1951). Values, motives, and systems of action. In T. Parsons & E. A. Shils (Eds.), *Toward a general theory of action.* Cambridge, MA: Harvard University Press.

Pelto, P. (1968, April). The difference between "tight" and "loose" societies. *Transaction,* pp. 37-40.

Pepitone, A. (1976). Toward a normative and comparative bicultural social psychology. *Journal of Personality and Social Psychology, 34,* 142-148.

Pepitone, A. (1981). Lessons from the history of social psychology. *American Psychologist, 36,* 972-985.

Phalet, K., & Claeys, W. (1993). A comparative study of Turkish and Belgian youth. *Journal of Cross-Cultural Psychology, 24,* 319-343.

Poortinga, Y. H., & Malpass, R. S. (1986). Making inferences from cross-cultural data. In W. J. Lonner & J. W. Berry (Eds.), *Field methods in cross-cultural research* (pp. 17-46). Newbury Park, CA: Sage.

Popper, K. R. (1976). The poverty of historicism. In J. O'Neill (Ed.), *Modes of individualism and collectivism.* London: Heinemann.

Porter, L. W., et al. (1974). Organizational commitment, job satisfaction and turnover among psychiatric technicians. *Journal of Social Psychology, 59,* 603-609.

Pusey, A. W. (1977). *A comparative study on achievement motivation between Chinese and Americans.* Unpublished master's thesis, Bucknell University.

Quattrone, G. (1986). On the perception of group variability. In S. Worchel & W. Austin (Eds.), *Psychology of intergroup relations* (pp. 25-40). Chicago: Nelson-Hall.

Radford, M. H. B., Mann, L., Ohta, Y., & Nakane, Y. (1991). Differences between Australian and Japanese students in reported use of decision processes. *International Journal of Psychology, 26,* 35-52.

Ramanujan, A. K. (1990). Is there an India way of thinking? An informal essay. In M. Marriot (Ed.), *India thought through Hindu categories* (pp. 41-58). New Delhi: Sage.

Rank, O. (1945). *Will therapy and truth and reality.* New York: Knopf.

Redding, S. G. (1984). *Operationalizing the post-Confucian hypothesis: The overseas Chinese case.* Paper presented at the seminar "Chinese style of enterprise management," Faculty of Business Administration, Chinese University of Hong Kong.

Redding, S. G. (1990). *The spirit of Chinese capitalism.* Berlin: Walter de Gruyter.

Redding, S. G., & Wong, G. Y. Y. (1986). The psychology of Chinese organizational behavior. In M. H. Bond (Ed.), *The psychology of the Chinese people* (pp. 267-295). New York: Oxford University Press.

Reishauer, E. O. (1978). *The Japanese.* Cambridge, MA: Belknap.

Reisman, D. A. (1977). *Richard Titmuss.* London: Heinemann.

Reykowski, J. (1982). Social motivation. *Annual Review of Psychology, 33,* 123-154.

Reykowski, J. (1988). *On the mechanisms of socio-political judgments.* Paper presented at the Twenty-fourth International Congress of Psychology, Sydney, Australia.

Riesman, D. (1961). *The lonely crowd: A study of changing American character.* New Haven, CT: Yale University Press.

Roberts, L. W., Boldt, E. D., & Guest, A. (1990). Structural tightness and social conformity: Varying the source of external influence. *Great Plains Sociologist, 3,* 67-83.

Rohner, R. P. (1984). Toward a conception of culture for cross-cultural psychology. *Journal of Cross-Cultural Psychology, 15,* 111-138.

Rokeach, M. (1968). *Beliefs, attitudes, and values: A theory of organization and change.* San Francisco: Jossey-Bass.

Rokeach, M. (1973). *The nature of human values.* New York: Free Press.

Roland, A. (1984). The self in India and America: Toward a psychoanalysis of social and cultural contexts. In V. Kovolis (Ed.), *Designs of selfhood* (pp. 123-130). Cranbury, NJ: Associated University Presses.

Roland, A. (1988). *In search of self in India and Japan: Toward a cross-cultural psychology.* Princeton, NJ: Princeton University Press.

Rosenberg, M. (1965). *Society and the adolescent self-image.* Princeton, NJ: Princeton University Press.

Ross, L., Greene, D., & House, P. (1977). The "false-consensus effect": An egocentric bias in social perception and attribution process. *Journal of Experimental Social Psychology, 13,* 279-301.

Rotter, J. B. (1966). Generalized expectations for internal vs. external locus of reinforcement. *Psychological Monographs, 80* (1, Whole No. 609).

Roy, R., & Srivastava, R. K. (1986). *Dialogues on development.* New Delhi: Sage.

Rubin, J. Z., & Brown, B. (1975). *The social psychology of bargaining and negotiation.* New York: Academic Press.

Salili, F., & Maehr, M. L. (1975). *A cross-cultural analysis of achievement-related concepts.* Unpublished manuscript, University of Illinois, Urbana-Champaign.

Sampson, E. E. (1977). Psychology and the American ideal. *Journal of Personality and Social Psychology, 35,* 767-782.

Sampson, E. E. (1981). Cognitive psychology as ideology. *American Psychologist, 36,* 730-743.

Sampson, E. E. (1987). Individuation and domination: Undermining the social bond. In Ç. Kagitçibasi (Ed.), *Growth and progress in cross-cultural psychology.* Lisse, Netherlands: Swets & Zeitlinger.

Sampson, E. E. (1988). The debate on individualism: Indigenous psychologies of the individual and their role in personal and societal functioning. *American Psychologist, 43,* 15-22.

Sampson, E. E. (1989). The challenge of social change for psychology: Globalization and psychology's theory of the person. *American Psychologist, 44,* 914-921.

Sarason, I. G., Levine, H. M., Basham, R. B., & Sarason, B. R. (1983). Assessing social support: The social support questionnaire. *Journal of Personality and Social Psychology, 44,* 127-139.

Scanlon, T. (1978). Rights, goals, and fairness. In S. Hampshire (Ed.), *Public and private morality.* Cambridge: Cambridge University Press.

Schmitt, M. J., Schwartz, S. H., Steyer, R., & Schmitt, T. (1993). Measurement models for the Schwartz Values Inventory. *European Journal of Psychological Assessment, 9,* 107-121.

Schonpflug, U., & Jansen, X. (in press). Self-concept and coping with developmental demands in German and Polish adolescents. *International Journal of Behavioral Development.*

Schulberg, L. (1968). *Historic India.* Nederland, NV: Time-Life International.

Schwartz, S. H. (1990). Individualism-collectivism: Critique and proposed refinements. *Journal of Cross-Cultural Psychology, 21,* 139-157.

Schwartz, S. H. (1992). Universals in the content and structure of values: Theoretical advances and empirical tests in 20 countries. In M. Zanna (Ed.), *Advances in experimental social psychology* (Vol. 25). Orlando, FL: Academic Press.

Schwartz, S. H., Antonovsky, A., & Sagiv, L. (1991). *The stability and social desirability of value priorities.* Unpublished manuscript, Hebrew University of Jerusalem.

Schwartz, S. H., & Bilsky, W. (1987). Toward a psychological structure of human values. *Journal of Personality and Social Psychology, 53,* 550-562.

Schwartz, S. H., & Bilsky, W. (1990). Toward a theory of the universal content and structure of values: Extensions and cross-cultural replications. *Journal of Personality and Social Psychology, 58,* 878-891.

Schwartz, S. H., & Ros, M. (1994). Value priorities in West European nations: A cross-cultural perspective. In G. Ben Shakhar & A. Lieblich (Eds.), *Studies in psychology: A volume in honor of Sonny Kugelmas. Scripta Hierosoly Mitana, 36.* Jerusalem: Magnes.

Schwartz, S. H., & Sagiv, L. (in press). *Identifying culture specifics in the content and structure of values.* Journal of Cross-Cultural Psychology.

Segall, M. H. (1983). On the search for the independent variable in cross-cultural psychology. In S. H. Irvine & J. W. Berry (Eds.), *Human assessment and cultural factors.* London: NATO.

Segall, M. H., Dasen, P. R., Berry, J. W., & Poortinga, Y. H. (1990). *Human behavior in global perspective: An introduction to cross-cultural psychology.* New York: Pergamon.

Shamir, B., & David, B. (1982). Occupational welfare and organizational effectiveness: Some theoretical notes. *Administration in Social Work, 22,* 45-46.

Shweder, R. A. (1973). The between and within of cross-cultural research. *Ethos, 1,* 531-545.

Shweder, R. A., & Bourne, E. J. (1982). Does the concept of the person vary cross-culturally? In A. J. Marsella & G. M. White (Eds.), *Cultural conceptions of mental health and therapy* (pp. 97-137). New York: Reidel.

Shweder, R. A., & Sullivan, M. A. (1993). Cultural psychology: Who needs it? *Annual Review of Psychology, 44,* 497-523.

Shye, S. (1985). Nonmetric multivariate models for behavioral action systems. In D. Canter (Ed.), *The facet approach to social research* (pp. 97-148). New York: Springer-Verlag.

Singer, M. (1972). *When a great tradition modernizes.* New York: Praeger.

Sinha, D. (1962). Cultural factors in the emergence of anxiety. *Eastern Anthropologist, 15*(1), 21-37.

Sinha, D. (1969). *Indian villages in transition: A motivational analysis.* New Delhi: Associated.

Sinha, D. (1979). The young and old: Ambiguity of role models and values among Indian youth. In S. Kakar (Ed.), *Identity and adulthood.* New Delhi: Oxford University Press.

Sinha, D. (1987, January). *Ahimsa as conflict resolution technique and instrument of peace: A psychological appraisal.* Paper presented at the seminar "Peace and conflict resolution in the world community," Nehru Memorial Museum Library, New Delhi.

Sinha, D. (1988a). Basic Indian values and behaviour disposition in the context of national development: An appraisal. In D. Sinha & H. S. R. Kao (Eds.), *Social values and development: Asian perspectives.* New Delhi: Sage.

Sinha, D. (1988b). Family scenario in a developing country and its implication for mental health: The case of India. In P. R. Dasen, J. W. Berry, & N. Sartorius (Eds.), *Health and cross-cultural psychology: Toward applications.* Newbury Park, CA: Sage.

Sinha, D. (1990). Concept of psychological well-being: Western and Indian perspective. *NIMHAS Journal, 8*(10), 1-11.

Sinha, D., & Sinha, M. (1990). Dissonance in work culture in India. In A. D. Moddie (Ed.), *The concept of work in Indian society.* Shimla: Indian Institute of Advanced Study.

Sinha, D., & Tripathi, R. C. (1990, July). *Individualism in a collective culture: A case of coexistence of dichotomies.* Paper presented at the International Conference on Individualism and Collectivism: Psychocultural Perspectives From East and West, Seoul.

Sinha, J. B. P. (1980). *Nurturant task leader.* New Delhi: Concept.

Sinha, J. B. P. (1982). The Hindu (Indian) identity. *Dynamic Psychiatry, 3/4,* 148-160.

Sinha, J. B. P. (1985). Concepts of health and healing in India. *Dynamic Psychiatry, 18,* 30-39.

Sinha, J. B. P. (1989, April). *Spiritualism in Indian managers.* Paper presented at the 7th Congress of the World Association for Dynamic Psychiatry, Berlin.

Sinha, J. B. P. (1990a, October). *Inner transformation of Hindu Identity.* Paper presented at the 8th Congress of the World Association for Dynamic Psychiatry, Berlin.

Sinha, J. B. P. (1990b). The salient Indian values and their socio-ecological roots. *Indian Journal of Social Science, 3,* 477-488.

Sinha, J. B. P., & Verma, J. (1987). Structure of collectivism. In Ç. Kagitçibasi (Ed.), *Growth and progress in cross-cultural psychology.* Lisse, Netherlands: Swets & Zeitlinger.

Sit, V. F. S. (1984). *The urban horizon of Asia: A reassessment.* Paper presented at the Conference on Urban Growth and Economic Development in the Pacific Region. Institute of Economics, Academia Sinica, Taipei.

Smith, D. H., & Inkeles, A. (1966). The OM Scale: A comparative socio-psychological measure of individual modernity. *Sociometry, 29,* 353-377.

Smith, F. J., & Crano, W. D. (1977). Cultural dimensions reconsidered: Global and regional analyses of the ethnographic atlas. *American Anthropologist, 79,* 364-387.

Smith, M. B. (1978). Perspectives on selfhood. *American Psychologist, 33,* 1053-1064.

Smith, M. B. (1993, August). *Selfhood at risk: Post-modern perils and the perils of post-modernism.* Murray Award Address, presented at the annual meeting of the American Psychological Association, Toronto.

Smith, P. B., Misumi, J., Tayeb, M., Peterson, M., & Bond, M. H. (1989). On the generality of leadership style measures. *Journal of Occupational Psychology, 62,* 97-109.

Smolenska, M. Z., & Fraczek, A. (1987). Life goals and evaluative standards among adolescents: A cross-national perspective. In J. L. Hasekamp, W. Meeus, & Y. T. Poel (Eds.), *European contribution to youth research.* Amsterdam: Free University Press.

Smolenska, M. Z., & Wieczorkowska, G. (1990). *Changes in evaluative processes across adolescence: A cross-cultural perspective.* Unpublished manuscript, Polish Academy of Science, Warsaw.

Snyder, C. R., & Fromkin, H. L. (1977). Abnormality as a positive characteristics: The development and validation of a scale measuring need for uniqueness. *Journal of Abnormal Psychology, 86,* 518-527.

Snyder, M. (1974). Self-monitoring of expressive behavior. *Journal of Personality and Social Psychology, 30,* 526-537.

Sorokin, P. A. (1948). *The reconstruction of humanity.* Boston: Beacon.

Spence, J. (1985). Achievement American style: The rewards and costs of individualism. *American Psychologist, 40,* 1285-1295.

Spencer, H. (1990). *First principles.* Akron, OH: Werner.

Staub, E. (1990). *Individual and group selves, motivation and morality.* Unpublished manuscript.

Steers, R. M. (1977). Antecedents and outcomes of organizational commitment. *Administrative Science Quarterly, 22,* 45-46.

Stevenson, H., Azuma, H., & Hakuta, K. (Eds.). (1986). *Child development and education in Japan.* New York: W. H. Freeman.

Swap, W. C., & Rubin, J. Z. (1983). Measurement of interpersonal orientation. *Journal of Personality and Social Psychology, 44,* 208-219.

Tajfel, H. (1978). *Differentiation between social groups: Studies in social psychology of intergroup behavior.* New York: Academic Press.

Tajfel, H. (1982). *Social identity and intergroup relations.* London: Cambridge University Press.

Taylor, C. (1985). *Philosophy and the human sciences: Philosophical papers* (Vol. 2). Cambridge: Cambridge University Press.

Taylor, C. (1989). *Sources of the self: The making of modern identity.* Cambridge, MA: Harvard University Press.

Taylor, W. S. (1948). Basic personality in orthodox Hindu culture patterns. *Journal of Abnormal and Social Psychology, 43,* 3-12.

Tellegen, A. (1979). *Well-being subscale.* Minneapolis: University of Minnesota Press.

Titmuss, R. M. (1968). *Commitment to welfare.* London: Allen & Unwin.

Titmuss, R. M. (1974). *Social policy.* London: Allen & Unwin.

Tönnies, F. (1957). *Community and society* (C. P. Loomis, Ed. and Trans.). New York: Harper & Row. (Original work published 1887)

Torgerson, W. S. (1958). *Theory and methods of scaling.* New York: John Wiley.

Trafimow, D., Triandis, H. C., & Goto, S. G. (1991). Some tests of the distinction between the private and the collective self. *Journal of Personality and Social Psychology, 60,* 649-655.

Triandis, H. C. (Ed.). (1972). *The analysis of subjective culture.* New York: John Wiley.

Triandis, H. C. (1978). Some universals of social behavior. *Personality and Social Psychology Bulletin, 4,* 1-16.

Triandis, H. C. (1980a). Introduction. In H. C. Triandis & W. W. Lambert (Eds.), *Handbook of cross-cultural psychology* (Vol. 1). Boston: Allyn & Bacon.

Triandis, H. C. (1980b). Values, attitudes and interpersonal behavior. In H. Howe & M. Page (Eds.), *Nebraska Symposium on Motivation, 1979* (pp. 196-260). Lincoln: University of Nebraska Press.

Triandis, H. C. (1984). Toward a psychological theory of economic growth. *International Journal of Psychology, 19,* 79-95.

Triandis, H. C. (1987). Individualism and social psychological theory. In Ç. Kagitçibasi (Ed.), *Growth and progress in cross-cultural psychology* (pp. 78-83). Lisse, Netherlands: Swets & Zeitlinger.

Triandis, H. C. (1988a). Collectivism and development. In D. Sinha & H. S. R. Kao (Eds.), *Social values and development: Asian perspectives.* New Delhi: Sage.

Triandis, H. C. (1988b). Collectivism and individualism: A reconceptualization of a basic concept in cross-cultural psychology. In G. K. Verma & C. Bagley (Eds.), *Personality, attitudes, and cognitions* (pp. 60-95). London: Macmillan.

Triandis, H. C. (1989). Self and social behavior in differing cultural contexts. *Psychological Review, 96,* 269-289.

Triandis, H. C. (1990). Cross-cultural studies of individualism and collectivism. In J. Berman (Ed.), *Nebraska Symposium on Motivation, 1989* (pp. 41-133). Lincoln: University of Nebraska Press.

Triandis, H. C., Bontempo, R., Betancourt, H., Bond, M., Leung, K., Brenes, A., Georgas, J., Hui, C. H., Marin, G., Setiadi, B., Sinha, J. P. B., Verma, J., Spangenberg, J., Touzard, H., & de Montmollin, G. (1986). The measurement of etic aspects of individualism and collectivism across cultures. *Australian Journal of Psychology, 38,* 257-267.

Triandis, H. C., Bontempo, R., Leung, K., & Hui, C. H. (1990). A method for determining cultural, societal, and personal constructs. *Journal of Cross-Cultural Psychology, 21,* 302-318.

Triandis, H. C., Bontempo, R., Villareal, M. J., Asai, M., & Lucca, N. (1988). Individualism and collectivism: Cross-cultural perspectives on self-ingroup relationships. *Journal of Personality and Social Psychology, 54,* 323-338.

Triandis, H. C., Chan, D. K.-S., Bhawuk, D., Iwao, S., & Sinha, J. B. P. (1993). *Multimethod probes of allocentrism and individualism.* Manuscript submitted for publication.

Triandis, H. C., Kilty, K. M., Shanmugam, A. V., Tanaka, Y., & Vassiliou, V. (1972). Cognitive structures and the analysis of values. In H. C. Triandis (Ed.), *The analysis of subjective culture* (pp. 181-261). New York: John Wiley.

Triandis, H. C., Leung, K., Villareal, M. V., & Clark, F. L. (1985). Allocentric versus idiocentric tendencies: Convergent and discriminant validation. *Journal of Research in Personality, 19,* 395-415.

Triandis, H. C., McCusker, C., Betancourt, H., Iwao, S., Leung, K., Salazar, J. M., Setiadi, B., Sinha, J. B., Touzard, H., & Zaleski, Z. (1993). An etic-emic analysis of individualism and collectivism. *Journal of Cross-Cultural Psychology, 24,* 366-383.

Triandis, H. C., McCusker, C., & Hui, C. H. (1990). Multimethod probes of individualism and collectivism. *Journal of Personality and Social Psychology, 59,* 1006-1020.

Tripathi, R. C. (1988). Aligning development to values in India. In D. Sinha & H. S. R. Kao (Eds.), *Social values and development: Asian perspectives.* New Delhi: Sage.

Tripathi, R. C. (1990). Interplay of values in the functioning of Indian organizations. *International Journal of Psychology, 25,* 715-734.

Turner, J. C. (1982). Towards a cognitive redefinition of the social group. In H. Tajfel (Ed.), *Social identity and intergroup relations* (pp. 15-40). Cambridge: Cambridge University Press.

U.S. Chamber of Commerce. (1985). *Employee benefits.* Washington, DC: U.S. Department of Commerce.

Verma, J. (1988). Allocentrism, collectivism, ingroup influence and some background variables. *Psychological Studies, 33,* 20-23.

Vogel, E. F. (1963). *Japan's new middle class.* Berkeley: University of California Press.

Vogel, E. F. (1979). *Japan as number one: Lessons for America.* Cambridge, MA: Harvard University Press.

Vogel, E. F., & Vogel, S. H. (1961). Family security, personal immaturity, and emotional health in a Japanese sample. *Marriage and Family Planning, 23,* 161-166.

Waterman, A. S. (1981). Individualism and interdependence. *American Psychologist, 36,* 762-773.

Waterman, A. S. (1984). *The psychology of individualism.* New York: Praeger.

Westen, D. (1985). *Self and society.* Cambridge: Cambridge University Press.

Wheeler, L., Reis, H. T., & Bond, M. H. (1989). Collectivism-individualism in everyday social life: The Middle Kingdom and the melting pot. *Journal of Personality and Social Psychology, 57,* 79-86.

White, M. I., & LeVine, R. A. (1986). What is a *li ko* (good child)? In H. Stevenson, H. Azuma, & K. Hakuta (Eds.), *Child development and education in Japan* (pp. 55-62). New York: W. H. Freeman.

Whiting, B. B. (1976). The problem of the packaged variable. In K. F. Riegel & J. A. Meacham (Eds.), *The developing individual in a changing world.* Hawthorne, NY: Aldine.

Whiting, B. B., & Whiting, J. W. M. (1975). *Children of six cultures: A psycho-cultural analysis.* Cambridge, MA: Harvard University Press.

Whiting, J. W. M. (1974). *A model for psycho-cultural research* (Annual Report 1973). Washington, DC: American Anthropological Association.

Williams, J. E., & Best, D. L. (1982). *Measuring sex stereotypes: A thirty-nation study.* Beverly Hills, CA: Sage.

Wilson, R. W., & Pusey, A. W. (1982). Achievement motivation and small-business relationship patterns in Chinese society. In S. L. Greenblatt, R. W. Wilson, & A. A. Wilson (Eds.), *Social interaction in Chinese society* (pp. 195-208). New York: Praeger.

Witkin, H. A., & Berry, J. W. (1975). Psychological differentiation in cross-cultural perspective. *Journal of Cross-Cultural Psychology, 6,* 4-87.

Witkin, H. A., et al. (1962). *Psychological differentiation.* New York: John Wiley.

Yamaguchi, S. (1990a). Collectivism and age. Unpublished raw data.

Yamaguchi, S. (1990b). *Personal and impersonal comparison: Accurate self-evaluation and maintenance of self-esteem.* Paper presented at the meeting of the Japanese Group Dynamics Association, Osaka.

Yamaguchi, S. (1990c). *Personality and cognitive correlates of collectivism among the Japanese: Validation of Collectivism Scale.* Paper presented at the Twenty-second International Congress of Applied Psychology, Kyoto, Japan.

Yang, K.-S. (1981). Social orientation and individual modernity among Chinese students in Taiwan: Further empirical evidence. *Journal of Social Psychology, 113,* 159-170.

Yang, K.-S. (1982). The Sinicization of psychological research in Chinese society: Directions and issues. In K.-S. Yang & C. I. Wen (Eds.), *The Sinicization of social and behavioral science research in China* (pp. 153-187). Taipei: Institute of Ethnology, Academia Sinica. (in Chinese)

Yang, K.-S. (1986). Chinese personality and its change. In M. H. Bond (Ed.), *The psychology of the Chinese people* (pp. 106-170). Hong Kong: Oxford University Press.

Yang, K.-S. (1988). Will societal modernization eventually eliminate cross-cultural psychological differences? In M. H. Bond (Ed.), *The cross-cultural challenge to social psychology* (pp. 67-85). Newbury Park, CA: Sage.

Yang, K.-S., & Bond, M. H. (1990). Exploring implicit personality theories with indigenous or imported constructs: The Chinese case. *Journal of Personality and Social Psychology, 58,* 1087-1095.

Yang, K.-S., & Cheng, P. S. (1987). Confucianized values, individual modernity, and organizational behavior: An empirical test of a post-Confucian hypothesis. *Bulletin of the Institute of Ethnology, Academia Sinica, 64,* 1-49. (in Chinese)

Yang, K.-S., & Lee, P. H. (1971). Likability, meaningfulness, and familiarity of 557 Chinese adjectives for personality trait description. *Acta Psychologica Taiwanica, 13,* 36-57. (in Chinese)

Yang, K.-S., & Liang, W. H. (1973). Some correlates of achievement motivation among Chinese high school boys. *Acta Psychologica Taiwanica, 15,* 59-67. (in Chinese)

Yang, K.-S., & Yu, A.-B. (1988). Social-oriented and individual-oriented achievement motivation: Conceptualization and measurement. In *Chinese personality and social psychology*. Symposium conducted at the Twenty-fourth International Congress of Psychology, Sydney, Australia.

Yi, Y. (1983, October). Chulsae hyundae uime. *Kwang Jang, 125.* (in Korean)

Yim, S. (1969). Changing patterns in Korean family structure. In C. I. Kim (Ed.), *Aspects of social change in Korea.* Seoul: Korea Research and Publication.

Yu, A.-B. (1990). *The construct validity of achievement motivation.* Unpublished doctoral dissertation, National Taiwan University, Taiwan. (in Chinese)

Yu, A.-B., & Yang, K.-S. (1987). Social-oriented and individual-oriented achievement motivation: A conceptual and empirical analysis. *Bulletin of the Institute of Ethnology, Academia Sinica, 64,* 51-98. (in Chinese)

Yu, A. C. (1984). *Child-rearing practices in the traditional Korean society.* Seoul: Jung-Min-Sa. (in Korean)

Yu, E. S. (1974). *Achievement motive, familism, and hsiao: A replication of McClelland-Winterbottom's studies.* Unpublished doctoral dissertation, University of Notre Dame, Indiana.

Yu, E. S. (1980). Chinese collective orientation and need for achievement. *International Journal of Social Psychiatry, 26,* 184-189.

Zhang, J. X., & Bond, M. H. (1993). Target-based interpersonal trust: Cross-cultural comparison and its cognitive model. *Acta Psychologica Sinica,* 164-172. (in Chinese)

Zola, E. (1983). *Socio-medical inquiries.* Philadelphia: Temple University Press.

AUTHOR INDEX

Lapierre, D., 125
L'Armand, K., 132
La Rosa, J., 50
Latané, B., 86, 286
Lawler, J., 55
Lebra, T. S., 25
Lee, E. S., 214
Lee, P. H., 70
Lee, Y., 48
Leung, K., 2, 4, 11, 29, 33, 42, 48, 53, 55,
    68, 69, 71, 72, 73, 74, 80, 86, 92, 95,
    177, 186, 189, 200, 204, 207, 208,
    223, 267
Levine, R. A., 39
Levy, S., 100
Liang, W. H., 70
Liebrand, W.B.C., 69
Lin, C.Y.C., 64
Lingoes, J. C., 100
Lomax, A., 81
Lonner, W. J., 67
Loomis, C. P., 22
Lowell, E. L., 242, 243
Lucca, N., 29, 49, 52, 69, 200, 268
Luhtanen, R., 176, 177
Lukes, S., 41, 138

Maday, B. C., 11, 29
Madsen, R., 11, 29, 41
Maehr, M. L., 243, 244
Majors, F., 60, 82
Malpass, R. S., 94
Mann, L., 42
Marin, G., 49, 53
Marks, G., 185
Markus, H., 2, 10, 28, 29, 30, 33, 34, 38,
    39, 46, 49, 62, 65, 95, 176, 278, 280
Marlowe, D., 247
Marriot, M., 125, 267
Marshall, T. H., 256
Marx, K., 22
Maslach, C., 279
Massimini, F., 41, 73
Mazrui, A., 58
McAdams, D., 223
McArthur, L. Z., 71
McClelland, D. C., 15, 54, 206, 242, 243,
    244, 245, 250
McCrae, R. R., 71

McCusker, C., 11, 49, 51, 118, 200, 201, 202
McGrath, J. E., 200
McGuire, W., 280
McPartland, T., 176, 202
Mehrabian, A., 180
Messick, D. M., 74
Metha, V., 125
Miller, J. G., 26, 29, 41, 95, 101
Miller, N., 185
Minami, H., 70
Minde, T., 79
Minturn, L., 128
Mishra, R. C., 5, 14, 15, 36
Misra, G., 64
Misumi, J., 25, 70, 72
Mitchell, T. R., 49
Mok, D., 79
Morris, C. T., 41
Morris, C. W., 92
Mullen, B., 183, 185
Murdock, G. P., 81
Murphy, G., 76
Murphy-Berman, V., 53
Murray, H. A., 242, 243
Myrdal, A., 256

Na, G. C., 217
Naidu, R. K., 268
Nakamura, H., 70
Nakane, Y., 42
Nakazato, H., 67
Naroll, R., 59-60
Newcomb, T. M., 174
Nicholls, J. B., 243, 244
Nishida, T., 50, 177
Nishio, H., 253, 257, 264
Nowak, A., 286

Ohta, Y., 42
Okochi, K., 251
O'Neill, J., 3
Ottati, V., 48
Oyama, N., 291

Pak, A. W., 49
Pandey, N., 268
Pang, M. K., 70

SUBJECT INDEX

Abstract principle, 29
Acculturation, 23, 78, 79, 195, 197
Achievement, 15, 25, 45, 47, 54, 57, 87,
　　88, 89, 96, 133, 135, 140, 146, 147,
　　148, 152, 154, 239-250, 287
Actions, 132, 142, 146, 163
Active, 123
Activism, 57
Activity, 213, 215, 220
Adaptation, 78, 79
Adolescent, 16, 99, 287, 289
Advice, 198, 209
Affection, 34
Affective autonomy, 12, 202-103, 105,
　　106, 109, 112, 116
Affiliation, 140, 146, 183, 223, 278
Affiliative Tendency Scale, 180, 181, 182,
　　183
Affluence, x, 43, 44, 50, 59
Africa, 1, 24, 41
Age, 166, 184, 187, 215, 217, 219, 220,
　　226, 227, 228, 229, 231, 235, 237
Agency, 71
Aggression, 117
Agriculture, 21, 43, 79, 80-81, 83, 227
Affluence, 184, 225
Allocentrism, 2, 42, 44, 45, 46, 47-48, 55,
　　73, 80, 190, 201, 267-275
Altruism, xi, 59, 138, 142, 146, 147, 152,
　　55, 236
Amae, 34, 35, 37-38, 39
Ambiguity, 86, 130

America, 30, 31, 42, 44, 48, 53, 55, 64, 66,
　　67, 71, 154, 158, 172, 186, 201, 203,
　　204, 205, 207, 208, 239, 243
Ancestor, 162, 163, 164, 165, 166, 240, 246
Anonymity, 209
Anthropology, vii, ix, xiv, 2, 10, 56, 59,
　　67, 80, 82
Anxiety, 271, 272
Architecture, 126
Argentina, 133
Asia, 1, 24, 41, 50, 67, 72, 175, 191
Asian-American, 176
Association, 45
Atmosphere, 267
Attachment, 104, 157, 179
Attitude, 4, 5, 11, 13, 14, 22, 34, 42, 44,
　　47, 50, 57, 74, 85, 117, 118, 126,
　　138, 154, 157, 158, 162, 167, 168,
　　170, 173, 180, 185, 189, 190, 194,
　　202, 206, 208, 215, 219, 220, 221,
　　222, 223, 224, 238, 257, 258, 260,
　　263, 269, 271, 272, 274, 277, 278,
　　281, 286, 282, 283, 285, 287, 291
Attitude-behavior model, 49
Attraction, 180
Attribution, 12
Australia, xv, 41, 42, 71, 112, 114, 115
Authoritarianism, 128
Authority, 57, 241, 283
Authority ranking, 45
Autonomy, 2, 13, 47, 63, 93, 95, 96, 98,
　　103, 108, 110, 111, 117, 139, 146,
　　147, 148, 171, 278

Subject Index

ABOUT THE AUTHORS

John W. Berry is Professor of Psychology at Queen's University in Ontario, Canada. He received his Ph.D. from the University of Edinburgh in 1966. He has been a lecturer at the University of Sydney, a Fellow of Netherlands Institute for Advanced Study, a Visiting Professor at the Université de Nice and the Université de Genève, and is a Past President of the International Association for Cross-Cultural Psychology. He is the author or editor of 20 books in the areas of cross-cultural, social, and cognitive psychology.

Günter Bierbrauer is Professor of Psychology at the Universität Osnabruck, Germany. He received his diploma from the Universität München, Germany, and his Ph.D. from Stanford University. His research interests include the areas of social, cross-cultural, and legal psychology. He is currently cooperating in a cross-cultural study on procedural preferences that examines how values, beliefs, and procedural preferences interact in everyday and organizational disputes. In addition, he is working on projects related to cultural identity, acculturation, and peace and conflict research.

Michael Harris Bond is Professor of Psychology at the Chinese University of Hong Kong. He is Canadian by birth, was educated in the United States, and held his first teaching position in Japan. His research interests include social perception, values, and cultural differences in organizational behavior. He consults for multinational corporations in Hong Kong and recently cowrote *Social Psychology Across Cultures* (1994).

Jae-Ho Cha is Professor of Psychology at Seoul National University, Korea. He received bachelor's and master's degrees at Seoul National University, a master's degree at the University of Arizona, and a doctoral degree in social psychology from the University of California, Los Angeles (1971), where he studied with Professor Harold H. Kelley. He is the Director of the Institute of Psychological Science, Seoul National University, and Past President of the Korean Psychological Association. He is the author of *Laboratory Manual for Social Psychology Experiments, Son Preference in Korea,* and *Psychology of Culture Design.*

Darius Kwan-Shing Chan is Lecturer in Psychology at the Chinese University of Hong Kong. He received his master's and doctoral degrees from the University of Illinois at Urbana-Champaign. His cross-cultural research has focused on comparing negotiation behavior across cultures, developing a theory of tight versus loose cultures, and designing instruments to measure individualism and collectivism. His current research interests include attitude theories and their applications, negotiation, social dilemmas, and cross-cultural social psychology.

Chi-Yue Chiu is a Ph.D. candidate in personality and social psychology at Columbia University. He obtained his master's degrees at the University of Hong Kong and at Columbia University. His primary research interests are in the areas of moral reasoning, interpersonal judgments, and cross-cultural psychology.

Sug-Man Choe is Associate Professor in the Department of Sociology in Chonnam National University at Kwangju, Korea. He received his Ph.D from Pennsylvania State University. His research areas include social movements, political sociology, and comparative sociology, with primary interest in Southeast Asian countries. He once served as a Guest Lecturer at the University of Iowa.

Sang-Chin Choi is Professor of Psychology at Chung-Ang University. He received his Ph.D. from the University of Hawaii. His recent research has focused on the cultural psychology of Koreans. He has published a number of papers on folk concepts and themes associated with Korean psychology.

Gyuseog Han is Associate Professor in the Department of Psychology in Chonnam National University at Kwangju, Korea. He received his Ph.D. from Ohio University at Athens, in the United States. His areas of research interest include individualism and collectivism, social conflict, communication acts, and cultural specificity of social psychological principles.

David Yau-Fai Ho received his doctoral training in psychology and logic in the United States. In 1968, he returned to his birthplace, Hong Kong, and devoted his time to the introduction and development of clinical psychology in that society. Currently, he is Professor of Counseling at California State University at Fullerton. His research interests have focused on personality development, psychopathology, and social behavior in Chinese culture, and he is the author of numerous contributions in psychology, psychiatry, sociology, linguistics, and education. He is committed to the enrichment of mainstream psychology derived from conceptions indigenous to Asian cultures. He has had multicultural experiences in North America, Hawaii, and the Far East, and has served as President of the International Council of Psychologists (1988-1989).

Geert Hofstede is Emeritus Professor of Organizational Anthropology and International Management of the University of Limburg at Maastricht, the Netherlands. He was the founding director of the Institute for Research on Intercultural Cooperation at this university. He has conducted extensive research in the area of national and organizational cultures. His best-known book is *Culture's Consequences: International Differences in Work-Related Values* (1980). A more recent book, *Cultures and Organizations: Software of the Mind* (1991) has been or is being translated into 12 languages, including Chinese, Korean, and Japanese.

Çigdem Kagitçibasi is a cross-cultural psychologist affiliated with the Psychology Department of Bogazici University, Bebek, Istanbul, Turkey. She received her Ph.D. from the University of California, Berkeley. She is an Executive Board Member of the International Union of Psychological Science and Past President of the International Association for Cross-Cultural Psychology. She is the recipient of the APA 1993 Distinguished Contributions to the International Advancement of Psychology Award. She is one of the founding members of the recently established Turkish Academy of Sciences, and she holds several other awards and honors as well, including Fellow of the Netherlands Institute for Advanced Study (1993-94). She is a past Associate Editor of the *Journal of Cross-Cultural Psychology* and the author of 15 books and some 100 articles and chapters in English and Turkish.

Uichol Kim was born in Korea, emigrated to Canada in 1968, and moved to Hawaii in 1988. He received his B.Sc. from the University of Toronto, majoring in psychology and Korean studies, and graduate degrees (M.A. and Ph.D.) from Queen's University. His cross-cultural research has focused on cultures of East Asia, particularly Korean people living in Korea and abroad. His research interests include topics such as indigenous psychologies, culture and self, socialization, group dynamics, health care systems, acculturation, and ethnic relations. He recently coedited (with John W. Berry) another book in Sage's Cross-Cultural Research and Methodology Series, *Indigenous Psychologies: Research and Experience in Cultural Context.* Currently, he is an Assistant Professor in the Department of Psychology, University of Hawaii at Manoa.

Uimyong M. Kim is Associate Professor in the Department of Industrial Welfare, Taegu University, Korea. He was born in Korea and emigrated to Canada in 1968. He received his B.A. and Ph.D. from the University of Toronto, majoring in social welfare and policy administration. His current research interests are in the areas of occupational welfare, social welfare policy, and the Korean model of the welfare state.

Ramesh C. Mishra is Professor of Psychology at Benaras Hindu University.

Janusz Reykowski is Professor of Psychology and Head of the Institute of Psychology, Polish Academy of Science (Warsaw, Poland), and a member of the Polish Academy of Science and the European Academy. In the academic year 1990/1991 he was a Fellow at the Center for Advanced Study in the Behavioral Sciences in Stanford, California. He has written several books in the field of personality and motivation and has conducted extensive research on prosocial behavior. In recent years his research has focused on the formation and change of sociopolitical mentality (values and belief systems). In 1984 he wrote *Logic of Fight: On the Psychological Aspects of the Social Conflict in Poland*; he has also written a number of articles related to this issue. He is involved in extensive research on the transformation of the sociopolitical mentality in Poland.

Shalom H. Schwartz is Leon and Clara Sznajderman Professor of Psychology at the Hebrew University of Jerusalem. Before he moved to Israel, he received his Ph.D. at the University of Michigan and taught at the University of Wisconsin—Madison. His research focuses on two theories he has developed regarding the content and structure of human values, one applying to individual persons and the other to cultural groups. He is currently studying antecedents, correlates, and consequences of differences in value priorities among individuals (e.g., socialization, religiosity, political behavior, well-being) and among nations (e.g., family size, economic development, heterogeneity, public policy).

Durganand Sinha has been a National Fellow of the UGC (University Grants Commission and the ICSSR Indian Council for Social Science Research); Director of A.N.S. Institute of Social Studies, Patna, India; and

Professor and Head of the Department of Psychology, Allahabad University. He has also for short periods been Nehru Professor in the Department of Human Development and Family Studies, M.S. University of Baroda, and Visiting Professor in the Department of Psychology, University of Hong Kong. He has been Past President and a Fellow of the IACCP, and a member of the Executive Committee of the International Union of Psychological Science. His current areas of interest include cross-cultural psychology, psychology and national development, and indigenization in psychology. He is the author of many books, including *Indian Villages in Transition: A Motivational Analysis*; *Motivation and Rural Development*; and *Psychology in a Third World Country: The Indian Experience.* He is coeditor (with Henry Kao) of *Social Values and Development: Asian Perspectives.*

Jai B. P. Sinha is Professor of Social Psychology at A.N.S. Institute of Social Studies, Patna, India. He received his early education from Bihar University and a Ph.D. from Ohio State University in Columbus, Ohio. He has been a Visiting Professor at Hunter College of the City University of New York; a National Lecturer of the University Grants Commission, New Delhi; a Senior Fulbright Fellow at the University of Illinois at Urbana-Champaign; and a National Fellow of the Indian Council of Social Science Research. He is currently a Vice President of the World Association For Dynamic Psychiatry. He has published more than 100 research papers and five books. His research interests include leadership, power, work culture, values, social change, and national development.

Harry C. Triandis has been Professor of Psychology at the University of Illinois in Urbana-Champaign since 1966. He was named University of Illinois Scholar in 1987. His books include *The Analysis of Subjective Culture* (1972), *Variations of Black and White Perceptions of the Social Environment* (Illinois University Press, 1976), *Interpersonal Behavior* (1977), and *Culture and Social Behavior* (1994). He also served as general editor of the six-volume *Handbook of Cross-Cultural Psychology* (1980-1981). He has been a Guggenheim Fellow (1973), a Fellow of the American Association for the Advancement of Science (1984), a Distinguished Fulbright Professor to India (1983), and President of the Society for the Psychological Study of Social Issues (Division 9 of APA), the Society for Personality and Social Psychology (Division 8 of APA), the International Association of Cross-Cultural Psychology (Honorary Fellow since 1982), the Interamerican Society of Psychology (whose Award for Major Contributions to the Science and Profession of Psychology he received in 1983), and the Society for Cross-Cultural Research. He is currently President of the International Association of Applied Psychology (1990-1994). In 1987, he received an honorary doctorate from the University of Athens, Greece.

Rama Charan Tripathi is Professor and Head of the Department of Psychology and Centre for Advanced Study in Psychology at the University of Allahabad. He was educated at Sagar and Kharagpur in India and received his doctoral degree from the University of Michigan. Among his publications are *Environment and Structure of Organizations* and *Deprivation: Its Social Roots and Consequences* (with D. Sinha and G. Mishra), and *Norm Violation and Intergroup Relations* (with R. De Ridder). He currently serves as Editor of *Psychology and Developing Societies: A Journal*. His research interests include the areas of social change, intergroup relations, and organizational socialization.

Jyoti Verma is a Reader in Psychology in Patna University, Patna, India. She received her graduate degree and a gold medal from Benaras Hindu University, Varanasi, and her master's and Ph.D. degrees from Patna University. She has been awarded a postdoctoral Fulbright fellowship from the U.S. Educational Foundation in India and a Young Scientist Award from the Indian Science Congress Association. She has published a large number of papers in national and international journals. Her research interests include organizational behavior, social values, and psychophilosophy as contained in the ancient texts of India.

Susumu Yamaguchi is Associate Professor in the Department of Social Psychology, University of Tokyo. He received his B.Sc., M.A., and Ph.D. from the University of Tokyo. He has conducted experimental research on Japanese social behavior, and his publications include works on social psychology in Japanese. In addition to cross-cultural research on individualism and collectivism, he has been interested in social comparison processes, sense of justice, and Japanese group behavior. Currently, he is involved in a cross-cultural study on the generality of "sweet dependence" (*amae*), which has been thought to be unique to Japanese culture.

Kuo-Shu Yang is Professor in the Department of Psychology, National Taiwan University, and Research Fellow at the Institute of Ethnology, Academia Sinica, Taipei, Taiwan. He received his Ph.D. degree from the University of Illinois, Urbana-Champaign. His areas of research interest include Chinese traditionalism and modernism, Chinese personality and its change, Chinese socialization, and Chinese historical psychology in indigenous perspective.

Gene Yoon received his B.A. and M.A. degrees from Seoul National University and the Ph.D. in social psychology from St. Louis University in the United States. Before returning to Korea after earning his doctorate, he taught at the University of Wisconsin—Manitowoc and worked as a postgraduate fellow at the Andrus Gerontology Center at the University of Southern California. His major research interests are in life-span developmental psychology, social psychology, and adjustment. He has published more than 40 articles and four books, including *Psychology of Adulthood and Aging* and *Psychology: Understanding Human Behavior* (both in Korean), and has translated three books into Korean: E. Aronson's *The Social Animal* (5th ed.), M. Seligman's *Helplessness,* and E. Erikson's *Childhood and Society.* In 1990, he served as cochair of the KPA's Organizing Committee for the International Conference on Individualism and Collectivism. He has also served as Secretary General (1987-1988) of the Korean Psychology Association and as President of the Division of Social Psychology (1989-1990) and of the Division of Developmental Psychology (1992-1994). Since 1982, he has been Professor of Psychology at Yonsei University in Seoul.

An-Bang Yu is Associate Research Fellow of the Institute of Ethnology, Academia Sinica, Taipei, Taiwan. He received his M.S. and Ph.D. degrees from National Taiwan University, where he majored in social and personality psychology. His areas of research interest include value, self, and achievement motivation. His indigenous psychological research has focused on Chinese family psychology, the Chinese concept of the person, and the Chinese concept of achievement.